AUTHORS DIGEST

THE WORLD'S GREAT STORIES IN BRIEF, PREPARED
BY A STAFF OF LITERARY EXPERTS, WITH
THE ASSISTANCE OF MANY
LIVING NOVELISTS

ROSSITER JOHNSON, Ph.D., LL.D.

EDITOR-IN-CHIEF

ISSUED UNDER THE AUSPICES OF THE

AUTHORS PRESS

AUTHORS DIGEST

VOLUME XIX

A DICTIONARY OF BIOGRAPHIES
OF THE AUTHORS
REPRESENTED IN THIS SERIES

Issued under the auspices of the
AUTHORS PRESS

SPECIAL CONTRIBUTORS TO
THIS VOLUME

————

Oscar Fay Adams

Arvède Barine

Arthur Elmore Bostwick

Frederick Russell Burton

John Denison Champlin

Henry Fielding Dickens

Nathan Haskell Dole

Émile Faguet

Francesco Flamini

Rossiter Johnson

Andrew Lang

Eugène Lintilhac

Léopold Mabilleau

Marion Mills Miller

Maurice Paléologue

Dora Knowlton Ranous

Edouard Rod

Albert Sorel

Frederick Cæsar de Sumichrast

Alfred Trumble

Katharine Prescott Wormeley

BIOGRAPHIES OF AUTHORS

In this volume the titles of novels that are treated in the first seventeen volumes of the series are in italic.

About, Edmond François Valentin (Dieuze, France, Feb. 14, 1828; Paris, Jan. 16, 1885). This writer displayed great talent during his schooldays, and in 1848, when he entered the École Normale, he took the second place among the candidates for admission, Taine holding the first. Sarcey, Prévost-Paradol, and Taine were among his college contemporaries, and, according to Sarcey, About was the most brilliant of them all. On leaving college he spent some time in Greece, and his La Grèce Contemporaine (1855), which handled Greek politicians with some sharpness, was successful. His novel Tolla appeared in the Revue des Deux Mondes soon after, and subjected him to accusations of plagiarism; in fact, he admitted among his intimates that the story was borrowed. He was an indefatigable writer and produced in rapid succession novels, short stories, plays, art criticisms, newspaper articles and popular manuals of political economy. He was a friend of the Empire and ardently supported the Franco-Prussian war; but with the fall of the Empire he became a Republican and for several years wielded in his paper, La Siècle XIXe, a powerful influence in behalf of the republic, although Republicans in general never fully forgave the lateness of his conversion to their views. He was elected to the French Academy in 1884, but died before taking his seat. During his lifetime his popularity in his own country was very great and even extended to England and America, so far as his lighter novels were concerned. Such serious fictions of his as Madelon (1863), L'Infame (1867), the trilogy that constitute La Vielle Roche and Le Roman d'un Brave Homme (1880) contain striking passages, but they are often stagey and overweighted by tiresome dissertation. His journalistic work was purely ephemeral in character, merely serving a useful purpose at the moment of writing. His fame will rest upon his farcical tales, in which his wit and fancy and vivacity are afforded free scope. These are The Notary's Nose (Le Nez du Notaire, 1861); *The Man with a Broken Ear* (*l'Homme à l'oreille cassée*, 1862); Le Cas de M. Guérin (1863); *The King of the Mountains* (*Le Roi des Montagnes*); and Le Capitaine Bitterlin.

Achard, Louis Amédée Eugène (Marseilles, France, April 19, 1814; Paris, March 25, 1875). Achard was a merchant in Algiers in early manhood, but soon took up journalism in his native city, and in 1838 was a contributor to several Paris journals. He accompanied the Duc de Montpensier to Spain in 1846 as a reporter, and after the revolution of 1848 he was prominent as a royalist political writer. His early literary reputation was founded upon his Lettres Parisiennes, issued in 1838 under the pseudonym of "Grimm"; and from 1848 to 1872 he published a novel almost annually in the Revue des Deux Mondes. He was likewise the author of several plays, none of which possesses enduring excellence, and among his miscellaneous works the Histoire de Mes Amis (1874) is the best known; but it is as a novelist that he will be longest remembered. His fictions are mainly concerned with quarrels and differences both in family life and general society, and their number is large. Among them may be named Nelly (1842); *Belle-Rose* (1847); La Chasse Royale (1849); Les Châteaux en Espagne (1854); La Robe de Nessus (1855); Histoire d'un Homme (1863); Les Chaines de Fer (1867); Marcelle (1868); Olympe de Mezières (1874). In 1847 Achard was decorated with the cross of the Legion of Honor, and became an officer of the Legion in 1866. In 1858 he fought a duel with Fiorentino, the editor of Le Corsair, and was very severely wounded.

Aguilar, Grace (Hackney, England, June 2, 1816; Frankfort, Germany, Sept. 16, 1847). Miss Aguilar was of Jewish parentage and her earliest writings were concerned with Jewish themes, The Spirit of Judaism (American edition, 1842) and The Jewish Faith (1846) giving her established rank as an author. She presently turned to fiction and became famous as a novelist, though *Home Influence* (1847), which passed through more than thirty editions, was the only one of her novels issued in her lifetime. It still remains her most popular book, although The Days of Bruce (1852) almost equaled it in the general estimation. Her other works include *The Mother's Recompense* (1850); The Vale of Cedars (1850); Woman's Friendship (1851); and Home Scenes and Heart Studies (1853). These were edited by her mother. Her stories are strongly sentimental in cast and are concerned with the usual happenings of domestic existence. All her works reveal the intensely religious nature of their author, but bigotry and sectarian bias are conspicuously absent from her pages. In the early summer of 1847 her health gave way and she went to Frankfort, where a brother was then living, the Jewish ladies of London presenting her on the eve of her departure with a testimonial and an address "as the first woman who had stood forth as the public advocate of the faith of Israel." Shortly after her arrival in Frankfort her illness became serious, and upon its fatal termination she was buried in the Jewish cemetery of Frankfort. She possessed singular sweetness of character, and many stories are told of her charities to her literary contemporaries. Her literary fame was not confined to her own country, for not only did her stories secure a wide reading in the United States, but two of them, *The Mother's Recompense* and The Vale of Cedars, were translated into German. In her day and generation Miss Aguilar attained a position and influence not very dissimilar, in many respects, to that held forty years later in America by Miss Emma Lazarus, who was equally loyal to the Jewish faith in which she was born, and which she, as did Grace Aguilar, accounted a glorious heritage.

Aïdé, Charles Hamilton (Paris, France, 1829; Paris, Dec. 13, 1906). He was the son of a Greek diplomatist who came to England during the Regency, where his talents gave him general acceptance in society and where he married in 1824 the daughter of Admiral Collier. The son was but three months old when the father was killed in a duel in Paris, and the lad was then educated among his English kindred till at sixteen he went to the University of Bonn. Receiving a commission in the English army, he entered the 85th Regiment, serving until 1853. He then turned his attention to literature and was for many years conspicuous in London literary society as novelist, song-writer, and dramatist, as well as an amateur artist of distinction. He was a thorough musician with a highly individual method, and set many of his poems to music. His songs have been widely popular both in England and America, among the best known being The Danube River, The Maid of the Mill, Oh, Let Me Dream, and The Spanish Boat Song. The pathetic poem, The Pilgrim, has had a much-prized setting by Blumenthal. His novels are never especially strong in conception, but they are always carefully written and in the best of English. He visited the United States about 1888, and one result of his trip was the novel of American society entitled *A Voyage of Discovery* (1892), in which appreciative discernment of national characteristics is continually manifest. Earlier novels by him include Confidences (1859); Carr of Carlyon (1862); *Rita* (1864); Mr. and Mrs. Falconbridge (1864); and A Nine Days' Wonder (1874), dramatized as a comedy and presented at the Court Theater simultaneously with its issue in book form. In 1872 his Philip, a drama in four acts, was produced at the Lyceum in London, the title-rôle being assumed by Henry Irving, while A Nine Days' Wonder was not only successful in the metropolis with Mr. and Mrs. Kendal in the chief rôles, but met with popular favor when brought out in a tour of the larger English cities and towns.

Ainsworth, William Harrison (Manchester, England, Feb. 4, 1805; Reigate, Jan. 3, 1882). He was the son of a prosperous solicitor and was educated at the Manchester grammar-school. At sixteen he was articled to a prominent Manchester solicitor, a profession not much to his taste, but he gave a large portion of his time to literary pursuits and had published several works before he was twenty. In 1826 his novel, Sir George Chiverton, was published, now considered the joint production of Ainsworth and John Partington Aston, a story which brought him to the notice of Walter Scott. He had a short experience as a publisher, and presently achieved a reputation as a historical novelist by the publication of Rookwood (1834). In 1840 he followed Charles Dickens as editor of Bentley's Miscellany. His *Jack Sheppard* had appeared in that periodical in 1839, a work of much power, but criticized as creating a romantic hero out of a vulgar thief and murderer. He established Ainsworth's Magazine in 1842, and on its discontinuance in 1853 acquired the New Monthly Magazine, which he edited for many years. He was now one of the most popular authors of his day, and at his home at Kensal Manor House he exercised an extensive hospitality— Thackeray, Dickens, Jerrold, Landseer, Talfourd, and many more celebrities being his frequent guests. In the mean time he was writing fiction with tireless energy, more than forty historical romances coming from his pen, the latest being Stanley Brereton (1881). The history of his native Lancashire attracted him strongly, and one critic has noted that a group of his novels including Lancashire Witches (1848), Guy Fawkes (1841), The Leaguer of Lathom (1876), Beatrice Tyldesley (1878), Preston Fight (1875), The Manchester Rebels (1873), and Mervyn Clitheroe (1857) forms almost a novelist's history of Lancashire. Boscobel (1872), Old St. Paul's (1841), and *The Tower of London* (1840) are others that created a great sensation in their day.

One does not go to Ainsworth's fictions for especial charm of style, keen analysis of motives, or subtle description, but as a narrator he exhibits both force and directness and holds the reader's interest. He began to write when the hold of the society novel was loosening, and his spirited narrative found a ready audience. A banquet was given him in Manchester in 1881, on his 77th birthday, on which occasion the mayor stated that in the public libraries of that city there were 250 volumes of Ainsworth's works, and during the twelve months previous these had been read 7,660 times. This meant that in Manchester alone twenty volumes of his writings were being read every day of the year. Ainsworth outlived most of his literary associates and was buried in Kensal Green cemetery, his wife, and three daughters by an earlier marriage, surviving him. He prohibited the publication of his own letters, and no complete biography of him has been issued. The Early Life of William Harrison Ainsworth, by John Evans, was reprinted from the Manchester Quarterly in 1882. His portrait was painted by the artists Pickersgill and Maclise.

Alarcón y Ariza, Pedro Antonio de (Guadix, Spain, March 10, 1833; Madrid July 20, 1891). He was educated at the University of Grenada and was originally intended for the priesthood. He turned, however, to literature, beginning as a journalist on the editorial staff of the Cadiz El Eco de Occidente. He then settled at Grenada as a Radical editor, and in this capacity displayed so much ability that he was appointed in 1854 the editor of El Látigo in Madrid. The violence of his Radical utterances soon brought about a duel between him and the poet José Heriberto García Quevado. In 1855 his earliest novel appeared, *Brunhilde: or, The Last Act of Norma* (*El Final de Norma*), a work which discovers its author to be a master of polished prose. His drama, El Hijo pródigo, was hissed from the stage in 1857, which so chagrined Alarcón that he enlisted as a volunteer under O'Donnell for the war in Morocco. The Diario de un testigo de la Guerra (1859) brilliantly summarizes the incidents of that expedition, and the first edition of 50,000 copies was disposed of in a fortnight. Alarcón at once became famous, and on his return from Africa he aided the cause of Liberalism as editor of La Politica, though his marriage, in 1866, to the devout Paulina Contrera y Reyes, helped to modify his views. When the monarchy was overthrown, in 1868, he supported the claims of the Duc de Montpensier, and on the restoration of royalty in 1874 he announced himself a Conservative. These alternations of political faith lost him his former allies and did not gain him the confidence of the Royalists; but as a writer he was more successful than ever. His short story in the Revista Europa (1874) entitled El Sombrero de tres picos—a masterpiece of picaresque literature—gave him a wide fame beyond Spanish frontiers, and he followed up this success by other works in the same vein. His long novel, El Escándalo (1875), revealed him in the light of a defender of the Jesuits, but here again his changes of faith caused him to be misunderstood, for while Radicals called him an apostate, Catholics themselves professed to believe that El Escándalo was penetrated with Jansenism. He was consequently the target for attacks on all sides. He was elected a member of the Spanish Academy in 1875.

Alcott, Louisa May (Philadelphia, Pa., Nov. 29, 1832; Boston, Mass., March 6, 1888). This popular American writer was a daughter of the noted Concord philosopher, Amos Bronson Alcott, and was educated at home, Thoreau being her teacher for a time after the Alcotts removed to Concord, Mass., in 1840. While in Concord the Alcotts occupied the house afterward owned by Nathaniel Hawthorne and called by him "Wayside." Louisa Alcott was at this time a playmate of the children of Ralph Waldo Emerson, and for their amusement, and that of her sisters, she wrote at sixteen the stories which constituted her first book, Flower Fables (1855). For about seven years she was a teacher or governess, and in 1862 she served for some months as a nurse in the army hospitals at Washington. Here she contracted an illness which nearly proved fatal. Her hospital experiences were printed in the form of letters to the Boston Commonwealth in 1862, and their issue in book form, as Hospital Sketches, made her widely known. Her earliest novel, *Moods*, appeared in 1864, and in 1868 she published *Little Women*, a book for girls, which was immediately popular and has since passed through almost countless editions. An Old-Fashioned Girl followed in 1869, a continuation of Little Women in 1870, and Little Men, a book for boys, in 1871. Later works of hers were Aunt Jo's Scrap-Bag (1872); Work (1873); Eight Cousins (1875); A Rose in Bloom (1870); Under the Lilacs (1878). Her style was not polished and the literary worth of her writing as a whole was not great, but she wrote with so much force and ease, and displayed so much humor, such keen observation and such intuitive knowledge of what interests young persons, especially girls, that she soon came to be esteemed one of the most popular authors of the United States and won an extensive fame in England as well. Nothing quite like her stories for the young had appeared before, and her fame in her lifetime was unrivaled. She introduced into her stories much of her own family history, thus making them in some sense autobiographical. The plots of her stories are simple and life-like and the tales themselves possess some dramatic power. She would have preferred to win success as a novelist rather than as a writer of juvenile fiction, but it must be said that her novels are somewhat ineffective as compared with the children's books so intimately associated with her name, with the possible exception of A Modern Mephistopheles, issued in the No Name Series. From the point of view of pure literature, her meditative poem, Thoreau's Flute, is her finest piece of writing. Her life was spent mainly in Boston and Concord, and her death succeeded that of her aged father with an interval of but two days.

Aldrich, Thomas Bailey (Portsmouth, N. H., Nov. 11, 1836; Boston, Mass., March 19, 1907). Until he was thirteen years old, Aldrich passed a part of each year in New Orleans, and subsequently lived with his grandfather in Portsmouth, a town which figures as Rivermouth in his slightly veiled juvenile autobiography, *The Story of a Bad Boy* (1869), and also as the scene of his novel, Prudence Palfrey. In 1853 he entered his uncle's banking house in New York, and began a literary career almost at the same time. His poem, Baby Bell, published when its author was but nineteen, brought him fame immediately, and thenceforward he made literature the aim of his life. He was on the editorial staff of the New York Home Journal 1856–'59, and from 1865 to 1874 was editor of the eclectic Every Saturday, of Boston. Already a frequent contributor to the Atlantic Monthly, he succeeded William Dean Howells as its editor in 1881 and retired from that office in 1892. Aldrich was not a great poet, but he was as nearly perfect a poetic craftsman as it is ever given humanity to be. Quick to take advantage of unfavorable criticism, he revised and re-revised his lines till they satisfied his own exacting requirements. A competent critic has declared that his *technique* as a writer of short stories remains unexcelled by that of any American, not even excepting Poe, and whoever reads his most famous short story, Marjorie Daw, will hardly be inclined to dispute this judgment. It is probable that by his short stories and the briefer of his poems he will be held longest in grateful remembrance. His three novels, Prudence Palfrey (1874), The Queen of Sheba (1877), and *The Stillwater Tragedy*, are most carefully worked out and possess great charm in characterization and descriptive details, but it will probably be admitted that the novel was not for him the readiest vehicle for his thought, however he might excel in what might be termed the miniature treatment of the short story. Personally Aldrich was one of the most delightful of men, reverently regardful of the fame of older authors and most hospitable in his attitude toward younger ones whose promise was greater than their performance. He was married in 1865 to Miss Lilian Woodman of New York, but only one of their two sons survived him. Among published volumes of his not already named are, in verse, The Sisters' Tragedy, Wyndham Towers, Mercedes and Later Lyrics, and Unguarded Gates; and in prose, Two Bites at a Cherry, with Other Tales, and Ponkapog Papers, a collection of essays marked by the greatest charm of style and the utmost delicacy in the handling of its various themes.

Aleman, Matteo: born in Seville, Spain, about the middle of the sixteenth century; the time and place of his death are unknown. He obtained his bachelor's degree at the Seville University in 1565. In 1568 he was appointed Royal Treasurer, and his fame depends in no small degree on the fact that he resigned the office twenty years later as poor as when he assumed it. It is supposed that he went to America, and that he died in Mexico during the reign of Philip III. He wrote a poetical biography of St. Anthony of Padua (1604), and Ortografia Castellana, which was published in Mexico in 1608. His greatest work, *Guzman d'Alfarache* (1599), went through twenty-six editions, about 50,000 copies, in six years, without counting French and Italian translations. Its first English version appeared in 1623.

Alexander, Annie (Mrs. Hector) **French** (Dublin, Ireland, 1825; London, England, July 10, 1902). At a very early age she attempted literary composition, but with such poor success that on her marriage in 1858 to Alexander Hector, a Scotsman, she temporarily gave up further effort of the kind. The death of Mr. Hector, nearly fifteen years later, forced her to find some employment for her support, and she resumed her writing. She wrote *The Wooing o't* (1873), which was first issued serially in Temple Bar and was immediately successful. It then passed through many editions in book form and gave her almost world-wide fame. She had feared failure for herself, and chose as a disguise the pen-name of "Mrs. Alexander." This novel was followed in 1876 by Her Dearest Foe, which was equally successful, and she continued to use the same pseudonym for the remainder of her career. For almost a generation she was one of the most industrious novelists of her time, and although her popularity waned somewhat with the passage of years, she retained to the end an audience of no mean extent which awaited her successive fictions with unabated admiration. She laid no claim to originality of conception, but she wrote with singular ease and fluency, and the tone of all her work is genuinely wholesome. Though a prolific novelist, she wrote leisurely and her stories frequently suggested themselves to her by some character trait she had somewhere observed. Her *dramatis personæ* were rarely actual portraits, but rather mosaics in their makeup. Character was all-important in her view, and if she could interpret for her readers its actual development the accompanying incidents were of lesser importance to her. To one inquirer she said: "I like to live with my characters, to get thoroughly acquainted with them; and I am always sorry to part with the companions who have brought me many a pleasant hour of oblivion from the cares outside my study door." *The Wooing o't* still ranks as one of her best books, but among others of more than average merit should be named Ralph Wilton's Weird (1875); Maid, Wife or Widow: an Episode of the '66 War in Germany (1879); The Admiral's Ward (1883), which contains much genuine play of humor; and The Freres (1882). The last-mentioned book was written

Mr. Punch's Pocket Ibsen (1893); Lyre and Lancet (1896); Baboo Hurry Bungsho Jabberjee, B.A. (1897). Anstey has had an extensive following in the United States as well as in England, and the greater number of his books have been immediately reprinted here after appearing in England.

Arthur, Timothy Shay (Newburg, N. Y., June 6, 1809; Philadelphia, Pa., March 6, 1885). At eight years of age he removed with his parents to Baltimore, where his early youth was passed and where he received a small amount of schooling, which he supplemented by careful reading in his leisure hours. He mastered a trade, but his sight failed for a time and he was forced to abandon it. In 1834 he became editor of the Baltimore Athenæum, and in 1839 he edited the Baltimore Literary Monument also. Removing to Philadelphia in 1841, the city which continued to be his home for the rest of his life, he there edited the Ladies' Magazine from 1844, and in 1850 he edited The Sons of Temperance Offering. By this time he had written many stories, nearly all upon temperance themes, and in 1852 he founded Arthur's Home Magazine and was its editor till his death. In conjunction with W. H. Carpenter he prepared a series of State histories, but it was by his moral tales that he was best known. He was one of the most voluminous of American authors and published more than one hundred volumes of tales which enjoyed an extended popularity, the greater number of them being republished in England. Mainly of a moral and domestic character, and frequently more or less directed against the evil of intemperance, they are to be esteemed solely in the light of their excellent intention. There can be no doubt that for more than a generation their author was one of the leading moral forces of his day, exerting an influence over a wide circle of distinctly unliterary persons through his magazine and his published books, an influence which at this day is as hard to understand as it was difficult to over-estimate at the period of its height. The best known of his temperance stories are: *Ten Nights in a Bar-room* (1850); Six Nights with the Washingtonians; and Three Years in a Man-Trap, of which last 25,000 copies were sold in the year of issue. It was afterward successfully dramatized. The *Ten Nights in a Bar-room* is the one book by which Arthur is now remembered. To the present generation his name is but a name, and perhaps not even that, but an earlier one recalls the extraordinary vogue once enjoyed by this volume with its sensational title, and is grateful to the author who, however crudely, threw all the weight of his great influence upon the right side, as he saw it. Timothy Shay Arthur was neither a great man nor a great author, but he held to one unswerving purpose throughout a long career, to leave the world, if possible, better than he found it.

Astor, John Jacob (Rhinebeck-on-Hudson, N. Y., July 13, 1864). He is the only son of William Astor (1829–1892), and after preparing for college at St. Paul's School, Concord, N. H., he entered Harvard University, where he completed a course of scientific study in 1888. He inherited a taste for travel, and after leaving Harvard journeyed extensively both in Europe and Asia as well as in South America. On his return he entered the office of the Astor Estates, and in addition became a director in many noted financial concerns. At the opening of the Spanish-American war in 1898 he placed his great steam-yacht, *Nourmahal*, at the service of the Navy Department, and at his own expense equipped a battery of artillery. Receiving a commission as lieutenant-colonel of volunteers, he served on General Shafter's staff as inspector-general. In 1893 he published a novel, *A Journey in Other Worlds: a Romance of the Future*, which attracted widespread attention, not only having a large sale in the United States but being republished in London and translated into French. In memory of his father he presented to Trinity Church, New York City, in 1895, six magnificent bronze doors designed by Karl Bitter. He took out patents for several useful inventions and devoted much time to scientific research. In 1891 he married Miss Ava Willing, a member of an old Philadelphia family.

Astor, William Waldorf (New York, N. Y., March 31, 1848). He was the son of John Jacob Astor (3d) and was educated mainly by private tutors, at twenty-three years of age being taken into the office of the Astor Estates. Discovering the need of legal training in the management of the property, he studied at the Columbia Law School and was admitted to the bar in 1875, where he soon became known as an expert in real-estate law. Two years later he was elected to the New York State Legislature, and in 1879 became a State Senator from the Tenth District. He labored extensively in the direction of municipal reform, and his course in this particular was much commended. He was defeated in 1881 in his efforts to enter Congress, and was appointed Minister to Italy in 1882, succeeding the Hon. George P. Marsh, and was a popular diplomatist. He held this post till 1885, his great wealth allowing him to entertain on a lavish scale, and he was a social favorite in Rome. With strong tastes for archeology and literature, he devoted much time to the study of Italian history and art, the immediate outcome of which was his novel Valentino, a tale of medieval Italy. Much careful attention to details is manifest in this romance, and the same may be said of his novel *Sforza, a Story of Milan* (1889), in which the conquest of Italy by the French King, Charles VIII, is described. He succeeded to the headship of the Astor family on the death of his father in 1890, and in the same year he removed to London, where he purchased the costly mansion at No. 18 Carlton House Terrace; and in 1893 he bought the famous estate of Cliveden-on-Thames from the Duke of Westminster. The magnificent New York hotels the New Netherlands, the Waldorf-Astoria, and the Hotel Astor were erected by him, and in London he entered a career in journalism by the purchase in 1893 of the Pall Mall Gazette, and the establishing, a little later, of the Pall Mall Magazine. His inherited fortune was estimated as about $200,000,000, and this has been much increased by his income from railroad and other interests. Within a few years he has become an English subject.

Auerbach, Berthold (Nordstetten, Württemberg, Germany, Feb. 28, 1812; Cannes, France, Feb. 8, 1882). Auerbach was of Jewish parentage, and he attended the Talmudical In-

stitute at Hechingen at twelve, completing his college preparation at Carlsruhe and Stuttgart. He then entered the University of Tübingen, and as he took an active part in the
student disturbances of 1836, he was imprisoned some months
in the fortress of Hohenasperg, and in the same year published his book, Das Judenthum und die neueste Literatur.
He followed this by a series of romances based on Jewish
history entitled Das Ghetto, Spinoza (1837), Dichter und
Kaufmann (1839), a translation of Spinoza's writings, pref-
aced by a critical life of that philosopher (1841), and other
works of a philosophic cast. All this while he was publishing
in periodicals tales illustrative of peasant life, and when these
were collected and republished with the title Schwarzwälder
Dorfgeschichten (1843) they were most enthusiastically received by the public. A second series appeared in 1853-'54
which were re-issued in New York as Black Forest Village
Stories (1858). Many editions of these have since been
issued and they have been translated into nearly every tongue
in Europe. They exhibit a most genial humor as well as
genuine purity of sentiment. In 1846 Auerbach was married, but his wife died two years later, and in consequence of
her death he lived in retirement in the midst of great political
unrest, although when the banks of the Oder were claimed
by the Panslavists as Polish territory he opposed the claim
successfully in several public addresses. His dramas Andreas
Hofer (1850) and Der Wahrspruch (1856) were not especially
successful, but other works were greeted with enthusiasm.
Among these were Neues Leben (1851), Barfüssle (1856),
which was translated into many languages, Mrs. Eliza Lee's
translation, entitled Little Barefoot, being everywhere popular in America. Joseph im Schnee (1860), Edelweiss (1861),
an English translation of which, by Miss Ellen Frothingham,
appeared in New York (1870), and Auf der Höhe (1871).
This was his most noted work and is well known to the English-speaking public as On the Heights. The romance is an
exposition of Spinoza's philosophy and contrasts most effec-
tively the restless ambitions of court life with the simplicity
of peasant life. A collected edition of his writings in 22
volumes was issued in Stuttgart in 1863-'64, and after this

time he wrote The Villa on the Rhine (1869), Waldfried
(1874), and various other romances, most of which, if not
all, appeared in English as well as in German, Der Forst-
meister (1879), translated as The Foresters (1881), and Bri-
gitta being as important as any. Auerbach lived in various
German cities, but mainly in Berlin after 1859, and his death
occurred while he was visiting Cannes in the hope of restor-
ing his broken health. He was buried in his native village.

Austen, Jane (Steventon, Hampshire, England, Dec. 16,
1775; Winchester, July 18, 1817). She was the second
daughter of the Rev. George Austen, and in the rectory at
Steventon the greater part of the first twenty-five years of
her life was passed. To some extent the description of Catherine Morland's home in *Northanger Abbey* is that of the
novelist's early home likewise. In the spring of 1801 the
Austens removed to Bath, Mr. Austen's son James succeeding him as rector of Steventon, and this remained their home
four years, Jane's father dying in 1805. Mrs. Austen and
her daughters lived at Southampton for the next few years
till in 1809 her son Edward, who had taken for property considerations the name of Knight, offered them Chawton Cottage, near Chawton House, Hampshire, as a residence. This
was accepted and continued their home thenceforward. Save
for numerous visits at the houses of her extensive kindred,
Miss Austen's life was passed in uneventful fashion in Steventon, Bath, Southampton, and Chawton, but she saw much of
fashionable watering-place life while dwelling in Bath, and
visits to her brother Henry in London gave her views of life
there as well. Her knowledge of the world, therefore, was
not extensive, but she was an acute observer of whatever was
before her, and never wrote of a life that was not familiar to her
in its essentials. All critical judgments of Jane Austen agree
in ascribing to her absolute fidelity to the truth of things as
she saw them. In this particular consists her superiority to
all the fiction-writers of her day. A fine sense of proportion
withheld her from exaggerating any one detail at the expense
of another. Recognizing the limitations of her art, she was
careful not to overstep them. She never overweighted a

novel with a moral.   The moral is there, but it is construc-
tively there, not as an adjunct.   She never was melodramatic,
and simplicity with her did not become sentimentality.   In
her lifetime her fame was circumscribed and her actual personality never was made public, although it was known in-
formally to many persons.   Her novels continued the delight
of a small circle of discerning readers for fifty years after her
death, but not until the last quarter of the nineteenth century
did she become popular.   In the seventh decade of that century a memoir of Jane Austen was published by her nephew,
Mr. Austen-Leigh, which revealed a very charming personality little known before; and from this event may be dated
the great and increasing popularity of her novels both in England and America.   She is now everywhere acknowledged a
mistress of English style, and editions of her works grow
more numerous with the passing of every year.   She may be
called the founder of realism in English fiction, and Trollope
and Howells may in this respect at least be classed as her
lineal successors.   Although a contemporary of Jane Porter,
Mrs. Inchbald, Mrs. Radcliffe, and Fanny Burney, her novels
are as modern in their spirit as if written to-day, a statement
which could not possibly be declared of those of the four
clever women whose fame so far outstripped hers a century
ago.   *Pride and Prejudice, Sense and Sensibility,* and *Northanger Abbey* were written at Steventon before she was twenty-
three, and *Mansfield Park, Emma,* and *Persuasion* date from
the Chawton period of her career.   In the last year of her
life she was engaged upon a seventh novel which was left uncompleted and is still in manuscript.   Lady Susan (1870)
was published by Mr. Austen-Leigh and has always been
supposed to be an early production, while a fragmentary tale,
to which he gave the title of The Watsons, was included by
her nephew in his Memoir, with the suggestion that its composition might be referred to the period of Miss Austen's life
in Bath.

Austin, Jane Goodwin (Worcester, Mass., Feb. 25, 1831;
Roxbury, Mass., March 30, 1894).   She was the daughter of
Isaac Goodwin, a lawyer of Worcester, and was educated in

private schools. Both parents were descended from the Pilgrims of the Mayflower, a circumstance that had its influence in determining her literary likings. Almost in childhood she began writing stories of the Pilgrims, and a literary career was already prophesied for her when at seventeen she married Loring Austin of Cambridge, a college classmate of Edward Everett Hale. After the lapse of thirteen years she took up her pen again and was for years a valued contributor to the best magazines. Her first novel was Cypher (1869), a tale which did not fulfil the excellent promise of its earlier chapters, but Mrs. Beauchamp Brown (1880) and The Desmond Hundred (1882) won deserved popularity. It is not, however, by these stories that she is remembered, but by a series of tales dealing with the Plymouth Pilgrims. No other writer has done so much as Mrs. Austin to impress upon the perceptions of readers of to-day the character and customs of the Pilgrim colonists. Not only was she a careful student of Pilgrim history, but she wrote with enthusiasm. Although an extreme High Churchwoman, her literary sense was too keen to allow any religious prejudice to affect her work, and, staunch Anglican as she was, she wrote of the Pilgrims with entire sympathy. The first of these tales was *A Nameless Nobleman* (1881), and in 1889 appeared Standish of Standish, which was received with enthusiasm, its success stimulating her to fresh effort. After it came Doctor Le Baron and His Daughters (1890); Betty Alden (1891); and David Alden's Daughter (1894). In the lapse of time since her death the popularity of her Pilgrim tales has continued unabated, and visitors to Plymouth consult her picturesque pages with the same confidence with which one turns to a faithful guidebook that never yet has been caught tripping.

Azeglio, Massimo Taparelli, Marchese d' (Turin, Italy, Oct. 4, 1798; Milan, Jan. 15, 1866). He came of a distinguished Piedmontese family, and, going to Rome at the age of eighteen, devoted his attention to painting and music and soon achieved distinction as a painter of landscape. On his father's death, in 1830, he removed to Milan, where he married the daughter of the famous novelist, Manzoni, and thus entered the literary circle of the time although he had as yet written nothing of moment. In 1833, however, he published a patriotic romance entitled *Ettore Fieramosca*, which was warmly received, and this was followed by Niccolò de' Lapi (1841), a novel which proved a strong stimulus to the growth of an Italian national spirit. He subsequently wrote the first chapters of a third romance, La Lega Lombarda, but soon abandoned the work and thereafter devoted himself almost exclusively to national political affairs. In his attack on the Papal Government—Degli ultimi casi di Romagna—he urged the necessity of a definite national policy upon the Italian princes, and after the election of Pope Pius IX D'Azeglio went to Rome, where certain reforms with which the new Pope began his reign were commonly ascribed to his influence. He was actively engaged in the campaign of 1848 against Austria, and was severely wounded at the battle of Vicenza, where he fought at the head of the papal army. When the Sardinian Parliament was opened D'Azeglio was a member of the Chamber of Deputies, and after the battle of Novara, in 1849, he was assigned by Victor Emmanuel II the task of forming a ministry. His policy was marked by ability and shrewdness, but in 1852 he resigned his office of president of the cabinet to his political opponent, Count Cavour. After the peace of Villafranca, in 1859, he was appointed Commissioner Extraordinary to England, and was subsequently Governor of Milan. He withdrew from public life in his latest years and spent much time in Florence, engaged in the preparation of his Memoirs, which he left uncompleted. He was a patriot of the most exalted character, and among his latest words were " Non posso far niente per l'Italia !" ("I can do no more for Italy!"). Among his posthumous publications are: L'Italie de 1847 à 1865 (1866); Scritti politici e letterari (1872); I miei Ricordi, an autobiography (1873).

Bacheller, Irving (Pierpont, N. Y., Sept. 26, 1859). He was graduated at St. Lawrence University, at Canton, N. Y., in 1882, and entering journalism at once was successively employed on the staff of the Daily Hotel Reporter of

Balzac died five months from his marriage-day. They buried him in Père-Lachaise, where, in his glowing youth, he roamed and thought: "the noblest epitaphs are the single names, La Fontaine, Molière!—names that tell all and make the passer dream."

Victor Hugo was present at his burial and thus describes the scene: "The priest said a last prayer, and I a few words. While I was speaking the sun went down. All Paris lay before me afar off in the splendid mists of the sinking light, the glow of which fell into the grave at my feet as the dull sound of the earth upon the coffin interrupted my last words.—No! it is not the Unknown to him. No, I have said it before, and I shall never weary of saying it—no, it is not darkness to him, it is Light! It is not the end, but the beginning; not nothingness, but eternity! Is not this true, ye who listen to me? Such coffins proclaim immortality. In presence of certain illustrious dead we feel the divine destiny of that intellect which has traversed earth to suffer and be purified. Do we not say to ourselves here, to-day, that it is impossible that a great genius in this life can be other than a great spirit after death?"

Banim, John (Kilkenny, Ireland, April 2, 1798; Kilkenny, Aug. 13, 1842). His father, a farmer and a trader in outfits for sportsmen and anglers, was able to give him and his elder brother Michael (born in 1796) a good education. John was sent to Kilkenny College, where he developed so much talent for drawing and composition that he determined to be an artist. In 1813 he became a pupil in the drawing academy of the Royal Society in Dublin and won the highest prize for drawing in the first exhibition held after his entrance. Becoming a teacher of drawing in Kilkenny, he had a romantic love-affair which ended in the death of the lady and inspired one of the best of his early poems; but it also caused him much unhappiness and several unprofitable years. In 1820 he removed to Dublin and gave up art for literature.

After considerable ephemeral work, he produced a long poem entitled The Celts' Paradise, which was followed by an unsuccessful tragedy, Turgesius. But in his twenty-fourth year he won a brilliant success with a second tragedy, Damon and Pythias, which was produced at Covent Garden Theater in 1821, with Macready and Kemble in the two leading rôles. In the following year he and his brother Michael conceived the idea of writing a series of novels illustrative of Irish life, which should be for Ireland what the Waverley novels were for Scotland. John was then married and living in London, where he wrote the tragedy of The Prodigal, which was accepted by Drury Lane Theater but never acted. A series of essays, entitled Revelations of the Dead Alive, met in 1824 with considerable favor.

In 1825 appeared the first of the projected series of novels, under the collective title of Tales by the O'Hara Family, and was followed in 1826 by a second series. John's contributions to the series were: The Fetches, John Doe, or the Peep o' Day, *Boyne Water*, The Smuggler, The Disowned, Peter of the Castle, The Denounced, and The Nowlans. Michael claimed the authorship of Crohoore of the Billhook, The Croppy, The Ghost-Hunter, The Mayor of Windgap, The Bit o' Writin', Father Connell, and The Town of the Cascades; but the brothers wrote some in collaboration. *Boyne Water* was a political novel of the time of William of Orange and James II. Banim wrote also much for periodicals and in 1826 the tragedy of Sylla, founded on the play of the French dramatist, M. Victor Jouy.

In 1829 he went abroad, became pecuniarily embarrassed, and suffered much from ill-health, losing the use of his lower limbs. In 1835 he was brought home to Kilkenny, where he was received with enthusiasm. The Government gave him in 1836 a pension of £150, to which a further allowance of £40 was made to enable him to educate his daughter.

John Banim has been called the Scott of Ireland, and none has excelled him in the delineation of the manners and national characteristics of the Irish peasantry. The English critics say that he united the truth and circumstantiality of Crabbe with the gloomy power of Godwin; while in the knowledge of Irish character, habits, customs, and feelings, he was superior to Miss Edgeworth or Lady Morgan. His strength lay in the depicture of the peasantry.

Baring-Gould, Sabine (Exeter, Devonshire, England, Jan. 28, 1834; Port Elizabeth, Cape Colony, South Africa, June 4, 1906). He was educated privately and at Clare College, Cambridge, where he received his degree of B.A. in 1857, and M.A. in 1860. In 1864 he was ordained curate of Horbury, Yorkshire, and in 1867 incumbent of Dalton in the same county. He became rector of East Mersea, Essex, and in 1881 rector of Lew-Trenchard, a position which he held until shortly before his death.

The Goulds are an ancient family, originally of Seaborough, Somerset, but removed in 1518 into Devonshire. In 1626 they came into possession of the Manor of Lew-Trenchard, named from a family which once owned it, and have held it ever since. In the eighteenth century the heiress of the Goulds married Charles Baring, and their son, by royal license, took the name Baring-Gould. On the death of his father, Edward Baring-Gould, in 1872, Sabine, the eldest son, came into possession of the Manor of Lew-Trenchard, and in 1881 he presented himself to the rectory on the decease of his uncle. The manor house of Lew-Trenchard is honored by the attendance of a White Lady, said to be the spirit of a former Madam Gould. She haunts the avenue of the old house, appearing always in white, with long hair, and sparkling as if covered with water drops.

Sabine Baring-Gould visited Iceland in 1861, and afterward traveled extensively in Europe. In 1868 he married Grace, daughter of Joseph Taylor, Esq., of Horbury, Yorkshire. His literary work represents a great number of titles, of which only the more important can be given. On his return from Iceland, he published (1862) Iceland, its Scenes and Sagas, which was followed by: Post-Mediæval Preachers (1865); Book of Were-Wolves (1865); Curious Myths of the Middle Ages (1866–'68); Origin and Development of Religious Belief (1869–'70); Legendary Lives of Old Testament Characters (1871); and Lives of the Saints (1872–'77).

Prominent among his many novels are: Mehalah, a Story of the Salt Marshes (1880); *Grettir the Outlaw* (1890); The Broom Squire (1896); Guavas the Tinner (1897); and The Crock of Gold (1899).

Barr, Amelia Edith (Ulverston, Lancashire, England, March 29, 1831). She was the daughter of the Rev. William Henry Huddleston, and in 1850 she married Robert Barr, a merchant, of Glasgow, son of the Rev. John Barr, of the Scottish Free Kirk, and emigrated with him to the United States, settling first in Austin, Texas, but eventually in Galveston. There, in 1867, she lost her husband and three sons by yellow fever, and two years later she removed, with her three daughters, to New York.

After teaching for two years she began to write for newspapers and magazines, with encouragement from Henry Ward Beecher and Robert Bonner. She contributed much to their periodicals, The Christian Union and the New York Ledger, both weeklies, and also to daily newspapers, and when fifty years old she began to write novels. She has published, in the United States and England, thirty or more novels, besides translations from the French and German. Among her works are: Cluny McPherson (1883); Jan Vedder's Wife (1885); A Daughter of Fife (1886); *A Bow of Orange Ribbon* (1886); Friend Olivia (1891); A Sister to Esau (1892); Birds of a Feather (1893); Remember the Alamo (1897); Prisoners of Conscience (1897); Trinity Bells (1898); The Maid of Maiden Lane (1900); and Thyra Varrick (1904).

Barrie, James Matthew (Kirriemuir, Forfarshire, Scotland, May 9, 1860). He was educated in Dumfries and at Edinburgh University, from which he was graduated in 1882, and became a journalist, at first in Nottingham and in 1885 in London, where he was connected with the St. James's Gazette, The Speaker, and The National Observer.

In 1887 he published his first tale, entitled Better Dead, a satire on London life. This was followed by Auld Licht Idylls, and When a Man's Single (1888); *A Window in Thrums* (1889); An Edinburgh Eleven, and My Lady Nicotine (1890), the latter a humorous essay on smoking; *The Little Minister* (1891); Sentimental Tommy, and Margaret Ogilvie (1896), the latter a biographical sketch of his mother; Tommy and Grizel (1900); The Little White Bird (1902).

Barrie has written also several dramas, either original or

adaptations from his novels, some of which have been very successful, both in England and in the United States. In 1882 his comedy entitled Walker was produced at Toole's Theater, London, with great success, and was followed in 1893 by Jane Annie. The Professor's Love Story was produced in 1895, and The Little Minister in 1897, the latter having a great run in England and in this country, equaled only by the success of his fanciful fairy play entitled Peter Pan. Other successful plays are The Wedding Guest (1900); Quality Street (1900); The Admirable Crichton (1900).

While Barrie has considerable narrative power and a strong sense of humor, which bubbles up without apparent effort and on the least provocation, he is a pure sentimentalist. The emotions which most men have lived down by the time they are out of their teens are still fresh and fragrant with him, and he discusses bread-and-butter themes as if they were the only subjects in life—themes no other writer could treat without becoming somewhat absurd. There is a bond of sympathy between him and all simple and unspoiled natures, and he has a certain pathos adapted to the comprehension of children, including children of older growth. But this strong sentimentality, incurable as it is, is relieved by his whimsical sense of humor and his subtle power of contrast which at once amuses and entrances the reader.

Barrili, Antonio Giulio (Savona, Gulf of Genoa, Italy, Dec. 14, 1836). In 1859 he took part in the campaign against the Austrians, and served under Garibaldi in the Tyrol in 1866 and at Rome in 1867. He engaged early in journalism, for which he abandoned the profession of law, and became the editor of Il Movimento, and in 1872 of Il Caffaro, a principal journal of Genoa. In 1876-'79 he was a member of the Chamber of Deputies, and in 1889 became professor of Italian literature in the University of Genoa.

Barrili is one of the most prolific of Italian writers and has published since 1865 more than sixty volumes of romances, plays, poems, addresses, essays, and historical and critical studies.

Among his novels are: Capitan Dodero (1865); Santa

Cecilia (1866); Semiramide (1873); Castel Gavone (1875); The White Blackbird (Il merlo bianco, 1878); *The Eleventh Commandment* (*L'undecimo comandamento*, 1881); and Men and Beasts (Uomini e Bestie, 1886).

Bates, Arlo (East Machias, Maine, Dec. 16, 1850). He is the son of Dr. Hiram and Susan (Thaxter) Bates, and a descendant of Clement Bates, who settled in 1635 in Scituate, Mass. He was graduated in 1876 at Bowdoin College, where he edited the college periodical, The Orient. After leaving Bowdoin he engaged in newspaper work, and from 1880 to 1893 was editor of the Boston Sunday Courier. In the latter year he was appointed Professor of English Literature in the Massachusetts Institute of Technology, a chair which he still holds.

Besides many short stories and poems, Mr. Bates has published novels, collections of verse, and professional works, in the following order: Patty's Perversities (1881); Mr. Jacobs, a parody on Marion Crawford's Mr. Isaacs (1884); The Pagans (1884); *A Wheel of Fire* (1885); Love in a Cloud (1900); The Diary of a Saint (1902); and Talks on Teaching Literature (1906).

Baylor, Frances Courtenay (Fayetteville, Arkansas, Jan. 20, 1848). Her parents were Virginians, and, soon after her birth they returned to their home in Winchester, where she lived until her marriage, in 1896, to George Sherman Barnum. She removed then to Savannah, Ga., and later to Montreal. Her education, conducted at home, was supplemented by extensive foreign travel. Her place in literature was established by the publication in one volume of two related short stories, On One Side, and On the Other, under the general title *On Both Sides* (1884). Her other novels: Behind the Blue Ridge; Claudia Hyde (1894); Juan and Juanita (1897); The Ladder of Fortune (1899); A Georgian Bungalow; Nina Barrow; Featherlings of Ferneyhaugh.

Bazin, René (Angers, Maine-et-Loire, France, Dec. 6, 1853). He was educated for the law and has held for many years the chair of law in the Catholic University of

Angers. He has been also connected with journalism, having been a correspondent of the Journal des Débats; but he is best known by his novels, romances, and travel impressions in France, Spain, and Italy. This earlier work was written under the pseudonym Bernard Seigny.

M. Bazin is a small, swarthy man, wearing no beard but a moustache, with quiet and elegant manners and perfect courteousness, and a poise and distinction not easily ruffled. His conversation is not fluent, but is precise and judicial, alert and grave, and full of charm. Believing that the novel of fashion, with its men of the world and its great ladies, its wonderful boudoirs and gilded salons, has been overdone, he has devoted himself to the depiction of the lives of the lowly, of the men and women who run their course in the shadows of the small village, who make no noise in the world, but whose careers are often full of pathos and of true humanity. Bazin is thus the novelist and poet of provincial people, and his work has given him a reputation which he values highly, preferring to be loved than admired. His style is original, simple, refined, and captivating, and his stories, while written in excellent French, are ultra-modest in sentiment, such as every girl may read and every guardian of youth may keep in his library.

Several of Bazin's stories have been crowned by the Academy, and on April 2, 1903, he took a place among the forty "Immortals" as the successor of Legouve. M. Brunetière, in his speech of welcome, criticized his work in some detail, characterizing it as that of one who thoroughly understands the class of which he writes, and has a human interest as well as an artistic value.

Bazin's best known works are: Ma Tante Giron (1886); Victor Pavie (1887); *The Ink-Stain*, 1888 (*Une tache d'encre*, 1888); Les Noellet (1889); La Sarcelle bleue (The Blue Teal, 1892); Madame Corentine (1893); Les Italiens d'aujourd'hui (The Italians of the Present, 1894); Terre d'Espagne (The Land of Spain, 1895); En province (1896); De toute son âme (With all his Soul, 1897), published in English under the title Redemption (1908); L'isolée (in English as The Nun, 1908); Le Blé qui leve (in English as Growing Grain, 1908).

Beckford, William (Wiltshire, England, Sept. 29, 1759; near Bath, May 2, 1844). He was descended from a family long settled in Gloucestershire, where the parish of Beckford still marks the site of the ancient manor, which in the Domesday Book is called *terra regis* in the time of the Confessor. About the middle of the seventeenth century Peter Beckford, a descendant of Sir William Beckford who fell at Bosworth, emigrated to Jamaica, where the family became opulent and important, some of its members holding high official places. In 1736 the immense estates came into the possession of William Beckford, the father of the subject of this sketch, who expanded his operations as a merchant in London. He bought a palatial country seat in Wiltshire, became a member of Parliament in 1746 for Shaftesbury and afterward for the city of London, of which he was successively alderman, sheriff, and twice Lord Mayor. He died in 1770, and his son William, a boy of nine years, came into possession of a fortune of more than £100,000 a year.

William's mother, Maria, daughter of the Honorable George Hamilton, son of James, sixth Earl of Abercorn, was prejudiced against universities and had him educated privately, the great Earl of Chatham, his father's friend, being his sponsor and the promoter of his education. His private tutor was the Rev. Dr. Lettice, and his musical education was entrusted to Mozart. After spending a year and a half in Geneva, he went in 1778 to Paris, where he made the acquaintance of Voltaire, and from 1780–'82 traveled extensively, especially in Italy and the Low Countries. In 1783 he married Lady Margaret Gordon, a daughter of the Earl of Aboyne, and lived with her in Switzerland until her death in 1786. She bore him two daughters, the eldest of whom married Colonel (afterward Lieutenant-General) James Orde, without her father's consent, and never was forgiven, while the other became Duchess of Hamilton.

After his wife's death Beckford spent many years in travel, visiting Portugal in 1787, and then Spain and France. He witnessed the destruction of the Bastile in 1789, was in Paris in 1791–'92, then went to Lausanne, where he bought Gibbon's library; in 1794 he went again to Portugal, where he

ing.   Rice was also the business manager and attended to the commercial side of the partnership.

The two produced many excellent novels in collaboration, beginning with *Ready-Money Mortiboy* (1872) and ending with The Seamy Side (1881).

Among the most noteworthy novels written by Besant alone is *All Sorts and Conditions of Men* (1882), dealing with social conditions in the East Side of London, which led to the establishment of the People's Palace in the East End of London.   It aided materially the cause of social reform and gave him standing as a reformer.   In 1884 he founded the Society of Authors, was its first chairman in 1884-'85, and again its chairman from 1887 to 1892.   He was also editor of The Author, the official publication of the society.   He was knighted in 1895.

Among other novels by Besant are: All in a Garden Fair (1883); Children of Gibeon (1886); The World Went very Well Then (1887); *Herr Paulus* (1888); The Bell of St. Paul's (1889); Armorel of Lyonnesse (1890); St. Catherine's by the Tower (1891); The Story of King Alfred (1901); No Other Way (1902), his last complete work.

Besides these, Sir Walter did much other literary work, including topographical and descriptive works on London, in the latest of which, East London (1901), he gave a graphic account of the conglomeration of villages spreading over what once was a manor belonging to the Bishop of London, but is now compacted into a dense city, with a population of more than two million souls.   It is a vast manufacturing district, fringed with wharves and docks, a city of the poor, with row on row of houses all alike, with here and there an old church, but with no hotel, no fashionable quarter, no restaurants but coffee-houses and drinking saloons of the poor.   It was here that he lived to see erected, on Mile End Road, a continuation of Whitechapel Road, the People's Palace, intended for the recreation and amusement and the intellectual and material advancement of the vast population of the region, the idea and general style of which were suggested by the Palace of Delight in his novel *All Sorts and Conditions of Men*.

In 1903 a site for a memorial to Besant was assigned in

the crypt of St. Paul's Cathedral, the work to be done by George Frampton, with an inscription to be prepared by Anthony Hope and Austin Dobson.

Bird, Robert Montgomery (Newcastle, Delaware, Dec. 16, 1803; Philadelphia, Jan. 22, 1854). After the usual school training he studied medicine in Philadelphia, and practised about a year, when he began to contribute articles to the Monthly Magazine, published in that city. Among these were three tales, The Ice Island, the Spirit of the Reeds, and The Phantom Players.

About 1830 he turned his attention to writing for the stage, and produced The Gladiator, a tragedy founded on the story of the servile insurrection against the Romans (B.C. 73–71), under the leadership of the Thracian gladiator Spartacus. It is a very effective drama and was produced with great success by Edwin Forrest.

In 1834 Bird published a novel entitled Calavar: or, The Knight of the Conquest, a Romance of Mexico, an interesting historical picture of the expedition of Cortez; and in 1835 The Infidel: or, The Fall of Mexico, a story of the same period.

Bird's best story was published in the following year (1837), entitled *Nick of the Woods: or, The Jibbenainosay*, a tale of Kentucky in the time soon after the Revolution.

In 1838 appeared Peter Pilgrim, or a Rambler's Recollections, a collection of magazine papers, in one of which is given the first attempt at a minute description of the Mammoth Cave of Kentucky, of which he was one of the early explorers. In 1839 he published his last novel, The Adventures of Robin Day.

Björnson, Björnstjerne (Kvikne, Österdalen, Norway, Dec. 8, 1832). The son of a clergyman, he studied at the University of Christiania, and early connected himself with the press, to which he contributed articles, stories, and dramatic criticisms. In 1857–'59 he was manager of a theater in Bergen, during which time he published two novels, Synnöve Solbakken (1857) and Arne (1858), pastoral tales, and

Halte Hulda (Lame Hulda, 1858), a tragedy. In 1859 he edited the Aftenbladet, a political journal in Christiania, but his democratic tendencies created so much opposition that he left Norway and spent several years in Copenhagen, where he edited a periodical. He returned in 1862 to Christiania, and in 1863 the Storthing voted him a yearly stipend. After this he was connected with the Christiania Theater as director, and at the same time (1865–'67) edited the journal Norski Folkeblad.

Björnson has passed much of his life abroad, but has always exercised great political influence at home as the champion of the people and of popular representation, and is regarded as the leader of the Norwegian republicans. To his influence and teachings is largely due the political revolution which severed the relations between Norway and Sweden and gave the former an independent flag and sovereignty. He is recognized at home not only as the greatest living Norwegian writer but also as a patriot deserving everything of his country.

During 1880–81 he traveled and lectured in the United States, and he has since lived on his estate Olested, in the Gausdal, north of Christiania. His tales descriptive of Norwegian popular life, his dramas, and his poetry have given him a wide reputation, most of his principal works having been translated into English, German, and other foreign languages. Among his dramas the themes of which are derived from the sagas, from history, and from modern life, are: Kong Sverre (King Sverre, 1861); Sigurd Slembe (a trilogy, 1862); Maria Stuart i Skotland (Mary Stuart in Scotland, 1863); De Nygifte (The Newly Wedded, 1865); Sigurd Jorsalfar (Sigurd the Crusader, 1873); Redaktören (The Editor, 1874); En Fallit (A Bankruptcy, 1875); Kongen (The King, 1877); Leonardo, and Det Nye System (The New System, 1879) and En Handske (A Glove, 1883).

Besides his earlier stories of peasant and pastoral life, he has written En Glad Gut (A Happy Boy, 1860); *The Fisher Maiden* (*Fiskerjenten*, 1868); and many shorter tales. Among his more ambitious novels, including stories of tendency, are: Brude Slaatten (The Bridal March, 1873); *Arne* (a tale of middle-class life in Norway, 1877); and Captain Mansana (an Italian story, 1879).

Björnson's earlier works contain a number of lyrics, and in 1870 he published a collection of verse entitled Poems and Songs, and an epic poem entitled Arnljot Gilline. His poetical works are widely read, but it is in his prose that he has gained so powerful a hold on his countrymen, and he is universally recognized as having done for literature with his novels what Ibsen has done with his dramas.

Black, William (Glasgow, Scotland, Nov. 13, 1841; Brighton, England, Dec. 10, 1898). He studied art with the view of devoting himself to architecture, but drifted into newspaper work, at first on the staff of the Glasgow Weekly Citizen. In 1864 he went to London and was engaged that year and the next on the staff of the Morning Star, for which he acted, in 1866, as special correspondent in the Austro-Prussian war. After this he was for a short time assistant editor of the London Daily News. In 1868 he published a novel entitled Love or Marriage, which had but a moderate success; but in the following year his story In Silk Attire gained him a large circle of readers, and from that time he devoted himself to this branch of literature and became one of the most popular of novelists, his works having a wide circulation both in England and the United States.

Black lived in London in rooms in a building in Buckingham Street, Strand, overlooking the Thames Embankment, which had been occupied in times past by prominent men, among them Peter the Great, if one may trust a tablet on the front. In later days the apartment was for a time the home of Charles Dickens when a gallery reporter, and is described in David Copperfield as the place where David got somewhat confused before going to the theater with Steerforth. Black had also a residence at Brighton, Paston House, where he spent most of his later years and where he died, and a summer home at Oban, in Argyleshire, the scene of his yachting experiences, for he was a skilful sailor and loved his "white wings."

In 1884 he was the guest of Andrew Carnegie in a coach-

ing-trip through southern England, together with Matthew
Arnold and his family, Samuel Storey, M.P. for Sunderland,
Edwin A. Abbey the painter, John Denison Champlin, and
others. Although familiar with the country, he evinced the
interest of a stranger in the storied landscape and pointed
out each historic site, especially those famous through literary
associations, with the enthusiasm of a schoolboy. He afterward used the incidents of this trip as material for an article
in Harper's Magazine, and Mr. Champlin enlarged on them
in his volume entitled Chronicle of the Coach (1886). Black
derived the idea of the Strange Adventures of a Houseboat
on this jaunt, for many of these peripatetic houses were passed
on the Thames on the road to Kingston, and the subject was
freely discussed and commented upon in relation to his previous story of a phaeton.

Mr. Black published in all more than thirty novels, including the following: Love or Marriage (1868); In Silk
Attire (1869); Kilmeny (1870); A Daughter of Heth (1871);
The Monarch of Mincing Lane (1871); *The Strange Adventures of a Phaeton* (1872); *The Princess of Thule* (1873); The
Maid of Killeena, and Other Stories (1874); Three Feathers
(1875); Madcap Violet (1876); Lady Silverdale's Sweet-
heart, and Other Stories (1876); Green Pastures and Picca-
dilly (1877); *Macleod of Dare* (1878); White Wings (1880);
Shandon Bells (1883); Yolande (1883); Judith Shakespeare
(1884); White Heather (1885); In Far Lochaber (1888);
Strange Adventures of a Houseboat (1888); Donald Ross of
Wolfenberg (1892); The Handsome Humes (1893); Highland
Cousins (1894); Briseis (1896); Wild Eelin (1898).

Blackmore, Richard Doddridge (Longworth, Berkshire,
England, June 7, 1825; Teddington, Middlesex, Jan. 20,
1900). The son of the Rev. John Blackmore, he was educated at Blundell's School, Tiverton, and at Exeter College,
Oxford, of which he was Scholar and where he was graduated
in 1847. In 1852 he was called to the bar at the Middle
Temple, London, and became a conveyancer. His health
failing, he was obliged to leave London and established himself as a fruit-grower at Teddington on the Thames.

He soon turned his attention to literature, beginning his career as a poet, publishing in 1853 a collection of verse entitled Poems by Melanter. This was followed by Epullia (1854); The Bugle of the Black Sea (1855); The Fate of Franklin (1860); and a translation of Virgil's Georgics (1862-'71).

In 1864 he produced a novel entitled Clara Vaughn, which was soon followed by others: Cradock Nowell: a Tale of the New Forest (1866); *Lorna Doone: a Romance of Exmoor* (1869); The Maid of Sker (1872); Alice Lorraine: a Tale of the South Downs (1875); Cripps the Carrier (1876); Erema: or, My Father's Sin (1877); Mary Anerley (1880); and Christowell (1882).

Blackmore was at his best in historical novels, like *Lorna Doone* and Alice Lorraine, and of these *Lorna Doone* is the stronger. Exmoor, the scene of the romance, is a wild country of hill and moor, with few good roads, and even now visited chiefly by pedestrians. *Lorna Doone* is rich in picturesque descriptions of the neighborhood, and embodies many local traditions, especially of Jan or John Ridd, the strong man. This is one of the most admired of modern English novels and it has a steady sale year after year.

Boccaccio, Giovanni (Paris, France, 1313; Certaldo, Italy, Dec. 21, 1375). He was the natural son of Boccaccio di Chellino, a merchant of Certaldo in Val d' Elsa, and of a noble Frenchwoman named Jeanne. His father intended him for a commercial life, and about 1330 he resided in Naples. There, amid the charms of nature and the splendors of art, in the light of knowledge shed upon the city from the court of King Robert, his intellect opened to the appreciation of the beautiful. His father had allowed him to leave business for the study of law, but he gave his attention more to literary studies, frequenting the society of the court and the nobility, making love and writing poetry. Maria d' Aquino, a natural daughter of King Robert, who was married to a gentleman of the court, attracted his attention in church, and, like Petrarch, he fell in love; but the lady was not like the haughty Laura; she returned the love of the young poet, encouraged

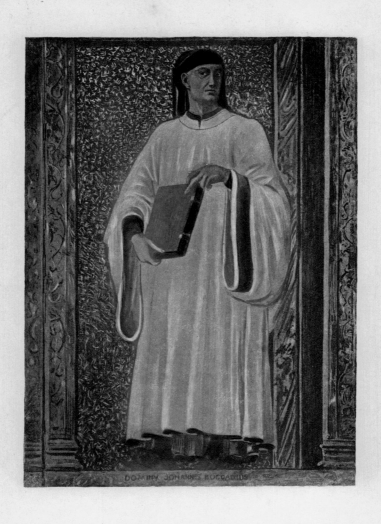

him to write verses and stories, and was for a long time his blond and beautiful lady, his "Fiammetta."

But in 1340-'41, recalled by his father, Boccaccio was obliged to leave the gay court of Naples for towered Florence. In 1346 he was at Ravenna; in the two succeeding years at Forlì, then again at Naples, and once more at Florence, honored by his fellow citizens with offices and embassies. He was sent to the papal court at Avignon in 1354 and 1356, and to Rome in 1367; but the lack of a permanent office involved him in straits from which he made many unsuccessful attempts to free himself. Leaving the capital of the kingdom where he had been invited by the great seneschal, Niccolo Acciaiuoli, a Florentine whom he had known at his first sojourn in that city, he found noble hospitality with Petrarch in Venice. Nevertheless he stayed there only three months, and, jealous of his own dignity and independence, refused the proffers of his friend and of others. In 1373 he obtained at last from the Signoria of Florence an annual allowance of a hundred florins as a public expositor of Dante's Divina Commedia; but in the autumn of the next year he was obliged by illness to retire to the castle of Certaldo, the home of his ancestors.

Boccaccio left many works, in prose and in verse, in Italian and in Latin. In his love poems he gives some reflection of the lyric splendor of Dante, whom he passionately admired, and of whom he wrote an enthusiastic biography, in addition to a commentary on the first seventeen cantos of the Inferno. He followed often in the steps of Petrarch as well, in these poems, though not without some originality. But more original and important are his longer poems—the Filocolo and the Teseide, the Filostrato, the Ameto, the Amorosa Visione, and the Ninfale Fiesolano ("Nymph of Fiesole").

He began writing the Filocolo in 1338 at the instance of Maria d' Aquino; it narrates the love of Floris and Blanchefleur, the material having been drawn, as it seems, from a Franco-Venetian poem now lost except from oral tradition and a remembered song. It is a long romance in prose, a mixture of classic mythology and Christianity in the dress of Chivalry; it abounds in minute descriptions, interminable speeches, tangled threads of historic and mythologic names. But the fantastic story of these two lovers often adumbrates the actual love of the poet, and the smiling natural beauty and the gallant society of Naples are mirrored in more than one passage.

Better is *La Fiammetta*, a romance in prose, in which the leading character (Maria d' Aquino) recounts to the ladies, in a style between the elegiac and the declamatory, the vicissitudes of her passionate love for Panfilo (Boccaccio). The realistic element and the psychologic analysis, the first of that sort of writing, render this little book unique and attractive.

Among the poems of Boccaccio the Teseide takes by its length the first place. It is in *ottava rima*, is divided into twelve books with solemn invocations; is interspersed with pagan divinities, descriptions of battles and festivals, reviews of heroes; it was intended to be for Italy what was for the Romans, if not the Æneid, at least the Thebaïd of Statius, which was in great part the author's model.

But it is surpassed in artistic value by Filostrato, which, written in the same measure, but with truer sentiment and simpler form, tells of the love of Troilus and Cressida, the daughter of Clachas. The title Filostrato, according to the poet, means a man "vanquished and subdued by love"; and so it is with the hero whose passion is represented in alternations of felicity and grief, of despair and intoxication.

Boccaccio certainly had Dante's work in mind when he wrote the Ameto and the Amorosa Visione. The Ameto or "Nymph of Ameto," written in 1341 or 1342, which belongs to the class of compositions with which the poets celebrated the beauties of their time, is the earliest writing of a pastoral nature in Italian verse. Short poems in *terzine* are introduced into the prose story of the loves of Ameto and Lia. The perfecting of man by the instrumentality of the cardinal and theological virtues, personified by seven nymphs, appears to be the subject of the moral allegory, which, despite the license of some of the descriptions and stories, is adumbrated from beginning to end.

Having gained facility in fictitious writing by these works in prose and verse, and inspired more or less directly by his

Brontë, Charlotte (Thornton, Yorkshire, England, April 21, 1816; Haworth, England, March 31, 1855); **Emily Jane Brontë** (Thornton, July 30, 1818; Haworth, Dec. 19, 1848); **Anne Brontë** (Thornton, Jan. 17, 1820; Scarborough, May 28, 1849). The father of these three remarkable girls, Patrick Brontë (the name is said to have been originally Brunty or Prunty.), was a clergyman of Irish lineage, a native of County Down; their mother was Maria Bramwell, a descendant of a Cornish family. On February 25, 1820, the parents, with their six small children, removed from Thornton to Haworth, where a living had been presented to Mr. Brontë. Here, in the gray, grim parsonage, close by the churchyard and backed by a desolate expanse of moorland, Mrs. Brontë died September 15, 1821. The children were left with a moody, eccentric father and a prim maiden aunt, Miss Bramwell, to care for them. Later the faithful servant, "Tabby," managed the strange household, but the children were left much to their own devices. At eight years of age, Charlotte, with three of her delicate sisters, was sent to the Clergymen's Daughters' School at Casterton, where education was provided for fourteen pounds a year. There a very dangerous illness seized upon the two older girls, Maria and Elizabeth, who died shortly after being taken home. Charlotte and Emily returned to the school after the summer holidays, but were soon removed on account of their poor health. By the time Charlotte was thirteen years old the weaving of imaginary tales, principally about her favorite heroes, had become a fixed habit. Nor was she alone in this singular occupation; her two remaining sisters and her only brother, Bramwell, took an active part in the composition of juvenile romances. In 1831 Charlotte attended Miss Wooler's school in Roehead, between Leeds and Huddersfield, where she became an appreciated pupil, a favorite of her instructors, and formed a few lasting friendships with chosen companions. Subsequently she was appointed a teacher by Miss Wooler, but left the place to accept one as governess. But sorrowful experiences came to her in this capacity, and she resolved to quit servitude and devote herself to teaching. The better to qualify themselves, therefore, for joint work, **Charlotte and Emily**

went to Brussels in 1842, and took up their abode in the *Pensionnat Héger*, where Charlotte fell under the influence of the fiery master of the establishment. M. Héger has been identified as the original of two of her best drawn male characters, Paul Emanuel and Mr. Rochester. Within a year the sisters returned to Haworth, but Charlotte afterward became a teacher in the Brussels *pensionnat*. Meanwhile, Anne had taken a place as governess, and the three sisters were separated.

Secretly each sister pursued her favorite amusement of composition, and, following Charlotte's final return home in 1844, because her father was threatened with blindness, they discovered to one another their literary labors. The three sisters now faced a gloomy prospect, for besides the helplessness of their father, their idolized brother, Bramwell, was becoming a victim of detestable vices. School-teaching could hardly afford them sufficient resources, so the sisters determined to try their hands at literature. Correspondence with publishers was opened, and in the spring of 1846 a small volume of poems appeared bearing their assumed names—names which preserved their respective initials—Currer, Ellis, and Acton Bell. It was barely noticed by the reviewers and attracted no especial attention. Thereupon the three "Bells," undaunted, turned their attention to prose. Each prepared a story: Charlotte wrote *The Professor;* Emily, *Wuthering Heights* (1847); and Anne, *Agnes Grey* (1847); the last two were accepted, but Charlotte's novel was everywhere refused. She was not discouraged, but set to work on *Jane Eyre*, which was published in October, 1847. At once it achieved extraordinary success, taking the public by storm. No novel since Waverley had created such a sensation. Many were the conjectures as to the identity of "Currer Bell," but the secret was well kept, and became generally known only with the publication of *Shirley* (1849). During the period of composing this last story Charlotte Brontë had a life of unrelieved gloom. Her father's sight had been restored, true enough, but to offset this death stalked through the cheerless parsonage, taking her brother Bramwell and her beloved sister Emily within a year, and in the following spring (1849) her youngest sister,

Anne, passed away, a short time after her novel, *The Tenant of Wildfell Hall* (1848) had been given to the world. Alone with her aged father, in a dreary home among the graves, Charlotte continued her literary labor. *Villette*, written in spite of bad health and depressed spirits, appeared in 1853. On June 29, 1854, she married her father's curate, the Rev. Arthur Bell Nicholls, but the felicity of married life was taken from her in less than a year. She was ill two months and then died with surely the most pathetic words on her lips in the whole range of literary biography. Turning to her husband, she said: "I am not going to die, am I? He will not separate us, we have been so happy." The manuscript of *The Professor*, her first luckless tale, was published after her death. Of the worth of the work of the three sisters, Anne's is said to possess the least, though it is not at all commonplace. Emily's single, extraordinary novel, *Wuthering Heights*, has often been eulogized. Matthew Arnold declared that in the expression of passion, vehemence, and grief, Emily had had no equal since Byron; while Clement Shorter said that "Wuthering Heights is the greatest book ever written by a woman." The chief characteristic of Charlotte Brontë's work is its realism. The least that can be said of her is that she is distinctly an individual figure in literature. Nowhere else do we find so intimate an association of the personality of the author with the work, so thorough an identification with it of the author's own life, even to the smallest detail. Technically, the work of the sisters is faulty, but Charlotte's is most free of such accusation.

Brooks, Charles William Shirley (London, England, April 29, 1816; London, Feb. 23, 1874). He was the son of William Brooks, an architect, who articled him to the law in 1832, after his preliminary education had been gone through. In November, 1838, he passed the Incorporated Law Society's examination, but there is no record of his ever having become a solicitor. Like that of Dickens and Disraeli, his genius impelled him to follow literature, and he began writing for the press. At first (1842) he signed his articles (which were appearing in Ainsworth's Magazine) Charles W. Brooks; his next literary cognomen was C. Shirley Brooks, but eventually he became simply Shirley Brooks. For five sessions he occupied a seat in the reporters' gallery of the House of Commons, as a writer of the parliamentary summary in the Morning Chronicle. During 1853 he was commissioned by that journal as their representative to inquire into the questions connected with the subject of labor and the poor in Russia, Syria, and Egypt. His letters from these countries were subsequently collected and published in the sixth volume of the Travellers' Library, under the title of The Russians of the South. Meanwhile Brooks had turned his attention to the drama, and in 1847 his play, The Creole: or, Love's Fetters, had been produced at the Lyceum Theatre; then followed Anything for a Change (1848), and Daughter of the Stars (1850). At the age of thirty-eight he began to assert his claim to consideration as a popular novelist, but in the face of success he dallied with his gift as a fiction-writer. From 1851 he contributed to Punch under the signature of Epicurus Rotundus, and in 1870 he succeeded Mark Lemon as its editor. It was he who initiated the articles headed " The Essence of Parliament." Always a hard and industrious worker, the four years during which he acted as editor of Punch were especially full of activity and bore rich fruit. In 1875 appeared Wit and Humor; Poems from Punch, edited by his son. The novels of Shirley Brooks number four: Aspen Court: A Story of Our Own Time (1855); The Gordian Knot (1860); The Silver Cord (1861); and Sooner or Later (1868).

Broughton, Rhoda (Denbighshire, North Wales, Nov. 29, 1840). She began writing at an early age stories which were at that time regarded as unconventional to the point of audacity, but mingling the qualities of freshness, naturalness, humor, and simplicity to an extent that captivated the reading public. Her first novel, Cometh up as a Flower (1867), burst upon the literary firmament more like a rocket than a flower, and from that time she has held her popularity with young and old. The cant phrase "inferior literary quality" has often been flung at her books, but while her craftsmanship is faulty her passionate sincerity grips the heart and rivets the attention of the reader. As one discerning admirer has put it: "She is neither a great artist nor a profound philosopher; but she is a good story-teller, a brave lover, a true woman, and a smart writer." Miss Broughton may be said to have introduced "the new woman" into English fiction. She has led an uneventful life (save for the furor created by her brilliant novels) in quiet Oxford, where most of her heroines have been created in a charming book-lined study in one of the most picturesque old houses there. One visitor has said of her: "The humor which makes Rhoda Broughton's books the most entertaining in modern English fiction is even more apparent in her conversation, and its spontaneity and pungency make her the most delightful company imaginable." Besides her first memorable novels, she has written: Not Wisely but Too Well (1867); Red as a Rose is She (1870); *Good-bye, Sweetheart, Good-bye!* (1872); *Nancy* (1873); Joan (1876); Second Thoughts (1880); Belinda (1883); Doctor Cupid (1886); Mrs. Bligh (1892); A Beginner (1894); Scylla or Charybdis? (1895); The Game and the Candle (1899); Foes at Law (1901); and Lavinia (1902).

Brush, Christine Chaplin (Providence, R. I., May, 1842; Brooklyn, N. Y., Feb. 3, 1892). She was a daughter of the Rev. Jeremiah Chaplin, D.D., a Baptist clergyman, who wrote many religious works, and of Jane Dunbar, a writer of numerous Sunday-school books. For several years before 1867 she taught drawing in the State Normal School at Framingham, Mass., and after that date she devoted herself to water-color painting, choosing wild-flowers chiefly as her subject. Success was hers in this field, and a number of her flower-pictures, including a well-known one of nasturtiums, were reproduced and published by L. Prang and Company. Several of her canvases were exhibited in New York and in Boston. In 1877 she studied painting in Paris, and two years later she married the Rev. Alfred H. Brush. Her first book, *The Colonel's Opera-Cloak* (1879), appeared originally in the famous No Name Series of Boston. It won immediate favor because of its delicate and delicious humor, and its quaint contrasts between Northern and Southern domestic life, and it was later republished under the author's name. This warm reception accorded her maiden effort did not tempt the young author into sudden fructification, and she waited ten years before producing her next story, Inside Our Gate (1889), which was a delightful idyl of every-day life, with a cook for its heroine. A third and last story was called One Summer's Lessons in Perspective. She also wrote two poems: The Inland Country, which was printed in the Atlantic Monthly, and My June Boy, which appeared in Harper's Magazine.

Buchanan, Robert Williams (Caverswall, Staffordshire, England, August 18, 1841; Streathamton, England, June 10, 1901). The Owenite lecturer and journalist, Robert Buchanan, was his father. From Manchester the family removed to Glasgow, where the boy was educated, first at the High School and then at the University. One of his fellow-students was David Gray, the poet, and these two literary aspirants set off together for London in 1860. Buchanan's essay on Gray, originally contributed to the Cornhill Magazine, records their close friendship and that fame-seeking journey to London. After a period of struggle and disappointment, during which he gradually became known as a journalist, Buchanan made his bow as a poet in Undertones (1863). Then followed more poetry: Idylls and Legends of Inverburn (1865); London Poems (1866); and North Coast, and Other Poems (1868), all of which display an unstudied strength, faculty for poetic narrative, and a sympathetic insight into conditions of humble life. Later poetic flights, though more ambitious, like The Book of Orm (1870) and The Wandering Jew (1893), are not up to the standard he originally set for himself. The drama attracted him from the first, and in 1883 he produced Lady Clare, and later his most successful play Sophia (1886), an adaptation of Fielding's novel, Tom Jones. This he followed with A Man's Shadow (1890) and The Charlatan (1894). As a critic he was acute and sincere, though he had several glaring faults of taste, and was accused of being egoistic and offensively aggressive. These defects were notoriously prominent in his article which appeared in the Contemporary Review (Oct., 1871), under the pen-name of Thomas

Maitland. It was an attack on Dante Gabriel Rossetti, and was entitled The Fleshly School of Poetry; in 1872 it was expanded into pamphlet form, but its author subsequently recanted its criticisms. However, it evoked remarkable replies from Rossetti in a letter to the Athenæum (Dec. 16, 1871), and from the poet Swinburne. Again, Buchanan severely arraigned Rudyard Kipling in the Contemporary Review (Dec. 1899), under the heading The Voice of the Hooligan, an essay which provoked controversy. In 1876 appeared The Shadow of the Sword, one of a series of novels from Buchanan's prolific pen; it was followed by *God and the Man* (1881), a striking tale of a family feud; The Martyrdom of Madeline (1882); Foxglove Manor (1885); Effie Hetherington (1896); and Father Anthony (1898).

Bulwer-Lytton, Edward George Earle (London, England, May 25, 1803; Torquay, Jan. 18, 1873). The novelist and poet was the youngest son of William Earle Bulwer of Heydon Hall, Norfolk, and Elizabeth Barbara Lytton of Knebworth, Hertfordshire, whose surname the novelist assumed at her death in 1843. Young Bulwer attended several schools, and then went to Cambridge, where he was graduated B.A. at Trinity Hall in 1826; while a student he was a great reader of history, and was accounted one of the best orators among his companions. As he composed verse at seven years of age, and had published a volume of poems at seventeen, it was quite natural that he should win the Chancellor's medal for a poetic effusion before he left the University. Paris was a lodestone to him during some months of 1825 and 1826, and he was received into the most brilliant houses of the nobility. Social success flattered him, and he returned to London a typical dandy of the day. In 1827 he married a brilliant Irish girl named Rosina Doyle Wheeler. This alliance estranged him from his mother, and Bulwer was forced to face the problem of making a living. Literature beckoned, and he began to write extensively for the periodicals of the time. Novel succeeded novel with wonderful rapidity. But his married life proved unhappy, and a legal separation was granted June 14, 1836. Seven years later his mother died leaving him sole heir to her Knebworth estate.   Meanwhile he had achieved no small reputation in the House of Commons, where he sat as Liberal member for St. Ives from 1831 to 1832, and for Lincoln from 1832 to 1841.   His political career had two distinct phases, and in 1852 he returned to Parliament as a Conservative, and represented Hertfordshire up to 1866, when he was raised to the peerage.   While Bulwer was not a ready debater, he could prepare an effective speech for delivery. As a poet, he published volumes in 1823, 1825, and 1827. Byron's influence is seen in these productions.   His later poems, The New Timon (1846), King Arthur (1848), and Saint Stephens (1860), attracted considerable attention, the first being marked for its fierce attack on Alfred Tennyson, and for that poet's reply in Punch.   Bulwer was especially happy in the heroic couplet.   As a playwright he won popular approval under the guidance of Macready; his first drama, The Duchess of La Vallière (1836), met with scant success, but The Lady of Lyons (1838), Richelieu (1838), and Money (1840) have long kept the stage, despite their mediocrity as literature.   But as a novelist Bulwer won his more lasting laurels, passing from one phase of the art to another, writing widely-different romances: those of contemporary manners, those exploiting the criminal, and those called historical.   In the latter class Bulwer achieved his more lasting fame.   His novels are: *Falkland* (1827); *Pelham* (1828); *The Disowned* (1829); *Devereux* (1829); *Paul Clifford* (1830); *Eugene Aram* (1832); *Godolphin* (1833); *Last Days of Pompeii* (1834); The Pilgrims of the Rhine (1834); *Rienzi* (1835); *Ernest Maltravers* (1837); *Alice* (1838); *Leila: or, The Siege of Granada* (1838); *Night and Morning* (1841); *Zanoni* (1842); *The Last of the Barons* (1843); *Lucretia* (1847); *Harold* (1848); *The Caxtons* (1850); *My Novel* (1853); *What Will He Do with It?* (1859); The Haunted and the Haunters (1859); *A Strange Story* (1862); *The Coming Race* (1871); *Kenelm Chillingly* (1873); *The Parisians* (1873); and *Pausanias the Spartan* (1876).

Burnett, Frances Eliza Hodgson (Manchester, England, Nov. 24, 1849).   In 1865 the Hodgson family, suffering from pecuniary losses, came to the United States and settled in

no other leading subject than his country, nor any episodes unconnected with her glory. The poem abounds in picturesque descriptions of storms and of scenery, and in pathetic allusions to Portugal's influence in extending the area of Christendom. The most remarkable passages are those referring to the tragic end of Inez de Castro, and to Adamastor, the mythological ruler of the sea, who uses his supreme influence for the purpose of stopping the progress of Vasco da Gama.

The Lusiad was first published in Lisbon in 1572, when Camoëns was forty-eight years old, and was at once successful. A second edition was published the same year; and thirty-eight editions had been printed in Lisbon before 1700. It has been translated into nearly every European language. The first English translation was by Sir Richard Fanshawe (1655); others are by Mickle (1775), Musgrave (1826), Quillinan (5 cantos, 1853), and Sir Thomas Mitchell (1854).

The success of his poem seemed only to add to the malice with which Camoëns was regarded at court. King Sebastian granted him a pension of 15,000 reis ($1,875) a year, but this was soon withheld, and when the King went on his fatal expedition to Africa, another poet was chosen to accompany him and sing his triumphs. Camoëns lived, poor and neglected, supported by a Javanese servant, who collected alms for him by night and nursed him by day. When seized with his last illness he was removed to a hospital and died there. After his death he was called the Apollo Portuguez, Camões o Grande, a monument was erected to his memory, and medals were struck in his honor.

Camoëns wrote also many minor works, as sonnets, comedies, odes, eclogues, ballads, and epigrams. His sonnets were chiefly devoted to his love for Catarina, to the celebration of virtue, and to friendship. Of his three comedies, El Rey Seleuco is founded on the story of King Seleucus, who resigns his wife, Stratonice, to the love of his son Antiochus. The others are: Filedemo, and Os Amphitryões, the last his most valuable contribution to the Portuguese stage. But his fame rests on *The Lusiad*, which has taken its place as one of the world's great epics.

Cantù, Cesare (Brivio, near Milan, Dec. 5, 1804; Milan, March 11, 1895). He was educated at Sondrio, where, soon after graduation, he became instructor in belles-lettres. This place he resigned after four years to take a professorship at Como, and eventually he obtained a professorship at Milan. In 1832 he published Lombardy in the Seventeenth Century, a historical commentary on Alessandro Manzoni's great novel, I Promessi Sposi (The Betrothed). On account of the liberal tendencies displayed in this work he was imprisoned for thirteen months. He utilized his enforced leisure by writing *Margherita Pusterla* (1837), a romance of prison life. Cantù was distinctively a historian. His great work was Storia Universale (Universal History) in thirty-five volumes, the publication of which began in 1837. He was the author also of several other important historical works. In 1874 he was appointed director of the archives of Lombardy.

Carcano, Giulio (Milan, Italy, Aug. 7, 1812; Lesa, Lago Maggiore, Aug. 30, 1884). He was educated at the University of Pavia, and wrote while there a narrative poem entitled Ida della Torre (1834). He had previously published in 1830, when only eighteen, a poem entitled Versi alla Madre, but he did not win success until 1839, when he produced Angiola Maria, a domestic romance of Italian life, regarded as the highest type of Italian romance. This was soon followed by Simple Narratives, in the same vein, and by *Damiano: the Story of a Poor Family*, which brought him fame.

Like most of the literary men of the time, Carcano took an active part in politics, and in 1848 suffered exile, an incident afterward credited to his glory. In 1859 he was appointed a professor in the Academy of Fine Arts in Milan, and in 1876 became a senator. He won success in many departments of literature, and was a member of all the principal academies and literary societies of his own country, as well as some foreign ones. He was vice-president of the Shakespeare Society of London, and had translated into Italian the entire works of the poet in twelve volumes: Teatro di Shakespeare completo (1874-'82).

Carcano was the author of several original dramas, including the melodramas Claudia (1852); La Sorrentina (1857); and Il Cantore di Venezia (1866); and the tragedies Sparta-cus (1857); Ardueno (1860); and Valentina Visconti (1870). Besides the romances already mentioned he published Rachele (1845); Una Sympatia (1847); La Nunziata (1849); Selmo e Fiorenza (1853); and Il Sassi di Piana (1854). All these are distinguished for their charming pictures of Italian family life, acclimating in Italy the romance of actual life which little by little had supplanted the historical romance.

As a critic Carcano contributed largely to periodicals, especially to Il Presagio, a literary journal of the first class. He was author also of many biographical treatises, among them Ugo Foscolo, Rinaldo Giulini, Giam Carlo, Passeroni, Gaetana Agnesi and Alessandro Verri, Pietro Verri and Vincenzo Monti, Muratori, Tasso, Tommaso Grossi, Emilio Dandolo and Felice Bellotti, Massimo d'Azeglio, Dante and Shake-speare, etc.

His poetical works were published in two volumes in 1861 and 1870; and his complete works were published after his decease in 1884.

Carleton, William (Prillisk, County Tyrone, Ireland, 1794; London, Jan. 30, 1869). His parents supported a family of fourteen children, of whom William was the youngest, on a farm of fourteen acres. His father was a peasant, but spoke Irish and English with equal fluency and was familiar with the folk-lore of his native country, while his mother was noted for her sweet voice and her singing of Irish songs. William, who showed early evidences of character fitting him for a clerical education, was destined for the Church. He was sent at first to a hedge-school under the tutorship of one Pat Frayne, who appears as Mat Kavanagh in one of Carleton's stories, and was later under Dr. Keenan of Glasslough, where he made considerable progress, especially in the classics. When finally William was transferred as a poor scholar to Munster, he made up his mind that he did not care to become a priest, and a stray copy of Gil Blas that fell in his way in-duced in him a desire to see the world; so after a period of tutoring in a family in County Louth, he set out for Dublin with two shillings and nine pence in his pocket. With no prospects in view, he thought at first of enlisting in the army, and with that aim he wrote the colonel of a regiment a letter in Latin. The colonel, recognizing his capabilities, dissuaded him, and he soon found employment as a tutor in families, where he met the lady whom he afterward married.

Carleton began his literary career by writing articles for the Christian Examiner, a Protestant periodical, which were collected in a volume in 1830 as Traits and Stories of the Irish Peasantry. A second series appeared in 1833, followed in 1834 by Tales of Ireland, and in 1839 by a powerful story entitled Fardorougha the Miser: or, The Convicts of Lisnamona, in which the passion of avarice is strongly depicted, without its victim being wholly dead to natural tenderness and affection. This story was dramatized and played with success in Dublin. In 1841 appeared, in three volumes, The Fawn of Spring Vale, The Clarionet, and Other Tales. One story in this collection, The Misfortunes of Barney Branagan, was a prodigious favorite. Valentine M'Clutchy, the Irish Agent: or, Chronicles of the Castle Cumber Property (1845), deals with the land question; and Rody the Rover: or, The Ribbonman (1846), exposes the machinations of secret societies.

These were followed by: The Black Prophet (1847); The Tithe Proctor (1849); The Red Hall: or, The Baronet's Daughter (1852); The Squanders of Castle Squander (1853); *Willy Reilly and his dear Colleen Bawn* (1855); The Evil Eye: or, The Black Spectre (1860); Redmond, Count O'Hanlon, the Irish Rapparee (1862); and The Fair of Emyvale and The Master and Scholar (1870), published after his decease.

Notwithstanding Carleton's indefatigable industry he fell into pecuniary difficulties, and, on the recommendation of Lord John Russell, was awarded a yearly pension of two hundred pounds. He is regarded as the truest, most powerful, and tenderest delineator of Irish life and characteristics. While he has not the passionate energy of John Banim, he surpasses him in truth of delineation and in the apparent artlessness of his stories. Most of his works have been translated into French, German, and Italian.

Catherwood, Mary Hartwell (Luray, Licking County, Ohio, Dec. 16, 1847; Chicago, Dec. 26, 1902). She was graduated at the Female College, Granville, Ohio, in 1868, and married, Dec. 27, 1887, James Steele Catherwood, of Hoopeston, Illinois. They settled at Newburg-on-the-Hudson, N. Y., and Mrs. Catherwood began her literary career by writing stories for the magazines. These were soon followed by more ambitious works, and led to her writing a series of historical romances, especially illustrative of French Canada and of the Middle West.

Her novels comprise: The Romance of Dollard (1889); The Story of Tonty (1890), introducing La Salle; A Woman in Armor (1891); The Lady of Fort St. John (1891); Old Kaskaskia (1893); The White Islander (1893); The Chase of St. Castine, and Other Tales (1894); The Spirit of an Illinois Town (1897); Little Renault (1897); Spanish Peggy (1899); The Queen of the Swamp and Other Plain Americans (1899); and *Lazarre* (1902), a story of the mysterious person known as the lost Dauphin of France, the unfortunate son of Louis XVI. and Marie Antoinette. In 1898 she published also Heroes of the Middle West, an account of the French occupation from 1673 to 1763.

Cervantes Saavedra, Miguel de (Alcalá de Henares, Spain, Oct. 9, 1547; Madrid, April 23, 1616). His parents were poor but of noble family. It is conjectured that he was educated at Alcalá and the University of Salamanca, but little is known of his youth save that he wrote verses when very young. A pastoral poem, entitled Filena, attracted the attention of Cardinal Acquaviva, who invited him in 1569 to accompany him to Rome. But ecclesiastical life did not please him, and in 1571 he volunteered as a common soldier in the expedition organized by the Pope, and commanded by Don John of Austria, against the Turks. At the battle of Lepanto (Oct. 7, 1571) he was severely wounded and lost the use for life of his left hand and arm. In 1575 he was honorably discharged, but on his way home to Spain was captured by Algerian corsairs and passed five years in slavery in Algiers. He was ransomed by his family in 1580, but, being depressed by want of means and friends, he reënlisted and served in Portugal and the Azores.

In 1584 he had returned to Madrid and was married. He now turned his attention to earning a living by authorship, produced a pastoral romance, Galatea, and wrote plays for the stage, which brought him neither fame nor money. In 1588 he removed to Seville, where he acted as agent of a royal commissioner, of the American fleet, and afterward as a collector of debts. From 1598, when he seems to have left Seville, to 1603, we know little of his movements, but he is said to have spent part of the time in La Mancha, and part in prison, where it is supposed he began Don Quixote. In 1603 he went to Valladolid, where he lived as a sort of general agent and amanuensis, and there he prepared the first part of his great work, which was published in Madrid in 1605.

In this immortal story Cervantes hit the vulnerable point of his age. The common sense of the world had long rebelled at the mummeries of knight-errantry and the foolish romances that still described a chivalry that was wholly a thing of the past. So, when Cervantes gave the institution its finishing stroke by holding it up to ridicule in his descriptions of the crazy exploits of the knight of La Mancha, people recognized the truth of his pictures and welcomed his account with shouts of laughter. One day, when Philip III observed from his balcony a student on the opposite bank of the Manzanares convulsed with laughter over a book, he said: "He is either crazy or he is reading Don Quixote."

Cervantes settled in Madrid, after the publication of the first part of his book, and suffered from pecuniary embarrassment. Moreover, the success of Don Quixote drew upon him the hostility of many who resented its satire; but he worked hard on his Novelas ejemplares (Exemplary or Moral Tales), of which twelve were published in 1613. In the following year he published Viage al Parnasso (Journey to Parnassus), a satirical work giving a picture of the state of Spanish literature and describing himself as the oldest and poorest of Spanish poets. In 1615 he published the second and concluding part of Don Quixote, with a dedication to the Conde de Lemos, who had befriended him.

Cervantes had now gained the object of his ambition. As Lope de Vega had taken priest's orders, there was no one to dispute with him the literary empire, and the sale of *Don Quixote* had relieved his pecuniary wants. But his health began to fail and he felt that his end was near. On the 19th of April, 1616, he dictated to his wife a message to the Conde de Lemos, concluding: "Yesterday I received extreme unction; to-day I resume my pen. The time is short, my sufferings grow more and more painful; my hopes grow fainter and fainter; yet I should be happy to see you before I die." He died four days later, on the same date with Shakespeare, but not the same day, as commonly said, for there was then a difference of ten days between the Spanish and English calendars. After his death (1617) his widow published his last work, Persiles y Sigismunda, a romance modeled after the Theagenes and Chariclea of Bishop Heliodorus.

Cervantes is said to have been of fair complexion with bright blue eyes and auburn hair. His countenance, handsome in youth, was always spirited, and his manners were cheerful. His disposition, like that which he gives to the knight of La Mancha, was magnanimous, forbearing to his enemies and amiable to his friends; but while in Don Quixote the sentiment degenerates into folly, in Cervantes it bloomed into a genial, witty, and humorous philosophy.

Cervantes was buried in the convent of the nuns of Trinity in a place identified in 1870 by the Marques de Molino. In 1834 a small bust of him was placed over the door of the house in Madrid where he died, and in 1835 a bronze statue of him, of heroic size, was erected in the Plaza del Estamento.

Chambers, Robert William (Brooklyn, New York, May 26, 1865). He was educated as an artist, studying at Julian's Academy, Paris, from 1886 to 1893. He exhibited first in the Paris Salon in 1889, and on his return to this country became connected with various periodicals, as Life, Truth, and Vogue, as an illustrator. He began about the same time to write for magazines and other periodicals, and soon discovered that his vocation was literature rather than art. He has since published many works, and has won a reputation as a

novelist which has extended to both hemispheres. His works
include: In the Quarter (1894); The King in Yellow (1895);
The Red Republic (1895); The Maker of Moons (1896);
A King and a Few Dukes (1896); With the Band (1896);
Lorraine (1897); The Mystery of Choice (1898); *Ashes of
Empire* (1899); The Cambric Mask (1899); The Conspirators
(1900); Cardigan (1901); The Maid-at-Arms (1902); The
Maids of Paradise (1903); In Search of the Unknown
(1904); The Reckoning (1905); The Fighting Chance (1906);
Mountain Land (1906); The Tracer of Lost Persons (1906);
The Tree of Heaven (1907); The Younger Set (1907).

He has written also The Witch of Ellengowan, a drama
for Miss Ada Rehan, played at Daly's Theatre, New York,
and has dramatized A King and a Few Dukes.

Chamisso, Adalbert von, or, in full, Charles-Louis-Adé-
laïde de Chamisso de Boncourt (Château de Boncourt, Cham-
pagne, France, Jan. 27, 1781; Berlin, Aug. 21, 1838). He
went to Berlin in 1790, at the period of the emigration,
studied at the French gymnasium, and became a page to the
Queen of Prussia. He entered an infantry regiment, became
an ensign in 1798 and a lieutenant in 1801, and resigned in
1806 to avoid taking arms against France. Returning to
France, he went again to Berlin in 1811 to study natural
history. During 1815–'18 he accompanied Otto von Kotzebue
as naturalist in Count Rumiantzeff's expedition around the
world, and was subsequently employed in the Botanical Garden, Berlin, and became a member of the Academy of Sciences.
Chamisso had written poetry in French, and in 1803 some
German poems, but had done little to make a reputation until
1814, when he published the story of *Peter Schlemihls wun-
derbare Geschichte* (The Wonderful History of Peter Schlemihl),
which made him famous, and which has been translated into
many languages. It is founded on a popular superstition
that a man might lose his shadow, the devil carrying it off
when he could not get the man himself into his power. The
poet has made Peter a symbolical portrait of himself. Schlemihl means an unlucky wight, and Chamisso has attributed to
his hero, says Scherer, the same incapacity to cope with the

the form of a novel the result of his archeological studies under the title À propos d'un cheval (1860), the second edition of which (1864) was entitled Un cheval de Phidias. Two works of a similar character, Le prince Vitale (1864) and Le grand œuvre (1867), embody his views on the origin, transformation, and destiny of the earth. In 1864 he became connected with the Revue des Deux Mondes, in Paris, and won distinction as an art critic and as an observer of public affairs, both under his own name and under the pseudonym of G. Valbert. These articles have been collected and published under various titles, as L'Allemagne politique (1870); Études de littérature et d'art (1873); L'Espagne politique (1874); Hommes et choses d'Allemagne (1877); Profils étrangers (1889); L'art et la nature (1892), etc.

He published also, chiefly in the Revue des Deux Mondes, a long series of novels, including: Le comte Kostia (1863); Paul Méré (1864); Le roman d'une honnête femme (1864); Prosper Randoce (1868); L'Aventure de Ladislas Bolski (1870); La revanche de Joseph Noirel (1872); Meta Holdenis (1873); Le fiancé de Mdlle. Saint-Maur (1876); Samuel Brohl et Cie. (1877); L'idée de Jean Têterol (1878); Amours fragiles (1880); Noirs et rouges (1881); La ferme du Choquart (1883); Olivier Mougant (1885); La vocation du Comte Ghislain (1888); Une gageure (1890); Après fortune faite (1895); Jacquine Vanesse (1898).

Two of these novels, Samuel Brohl et Cie. and L'Aventure de Ladislas Bolski, were dramatized. In 1880 Cherbuliez was naturalized as a Frenchman, and in 1881 he was elected a member of the Academy. Most of his novels have been translated into English.

Cholmondeley, Mary (Hodnet, Shropshire, England, 1859). Her education was superintended by her father, who was rector of the parish. Her mother's lack of health obliged the daughter to take charge of the household duties when only sixteen years old, and she attended at the same time to much parish work. During this busy period she wrote her first three novels in odd hours.

In 1896 her father's health broke down and the family

removed to London. She had already published several stories: The Danvers Jewels, a detective story (1887); Sir Charles Danvers (its sequel, 1889); and Diana Tempest (1893). The last named was the first published under her own name, she having given the earlier ones to the world under the pen-name Pax. In 1897 she published The Devotee, and in 1899 *Red Pottage*, which achieved great success. Love in Extremis, a series of short stories, appeared in 1902, and in the same year a novel entitled Moth and Rust. Prisoners (1906), her latest novel, is a story of infelicity in marriage, where the characters may be said to be prisoners for life.

Miss Cholmondeley's work is distinguished by humor and pathos, and she writes with graceful ease and with a strong hold on her characters. Her female characters are her best, and are often delicately analyzed.

Churchill, Winston (St. Louis, Missouri, Nov. 10, 1871). He is the son of Edward Spalding and Emma Bell (Blaine) Churchill, and his father, originally of Portland, Maine, and a West India merchant, was a descendant of John Churchill, who landed in 1641 in Plymouth, Mass. After a preliminary education at Smith Academy, St. Louis, Winston received, when seventeen years old, an appointment to the United States Naval Academy. He was noted while there for his devotion to athletic sports, and he organized the first eight-oared rowing crew in the Academy. He was graduated in 1891 and was sent to the cruiser *San Francisco;* but after a brief service he resigned, to devote himself to literature.

He was connected several months with the Army and Navy Journal, and in 1895 was for a short time managing editor of the Cosmopolitan Magazine.

Mr. Churchill was married in 1895 to Mabel Harlakenden, daughter of George D. Hall, of St. Louis, and spent the following winter in writing his first book, The Celebrity, which was not published until 1898. In 1899 he published *Richard Carvel*, a Virginia story of the time of the Revolution, in which are introduced Paul Jones and the famous battle between the *Bon Homme Richard* and the *Serapis*. Of this work, one of the ablest pieces of historical fiction from an American writer, more than three hundred thousand copies were sold the first year. It was followed by The Crisis (1901), a tale of the Civil War; Mr. Keegan's Elopement (1903); The Crossing (1904), dealing with the reconstruction period after the Civil War; Coniston (1906), a tale of New Hampshire politics; and Mr. Crewe's Career (1908), a love story in a setting of the political and social interests of a country district.

Mr. Churchill lives on a large farm in Cornish, New Hampshire, opposite Windsor, Vermont. He has taken a prominent part in New Hampshire politics, and represented Cornish in the State Legislature in 1903 and 1905.

Claretie, Jules Arsène Arnaud, commonly called Jules Claretie (Limoges, Haut-Vienne, France, Dec. 3, 1840). He was the son of a manufacturer, and studied at the Lycée Bonaparte, and published a novel while a pupil there. Resolving to devote himself to belles-lettres, he soon became an art and dramatic critic on well-known journals and magazines, and a lecturer, but was in disfavor by reason of his ultra-republican principles; he was fined as early as 1857 on account of a political article, and in 1865 and again in 1868 was subjected to penalites and forbidden to deliver public lectures. In 1870 he appeared, as a friend of Victor Noir, as a witness in the trial, at Tours, in March, 1870, of Prince Pierre Bonaparte for shooting that young journalist. In the early part of the Franco-Prussian war he followed the army as correspondent of the Assemblée Nationale, and after the downfall of the Empire officiated for a time as chief of the communal libraries in the Hôtel de Ville. In 1871 he was defeated as a candidate for the Assemblée Nationale, and in the following year founded Le Corsair newspaper. On the death of M. Perrin he was appointed director of the Théâtre Français, and in 1885 he became administrator of the Comédie Française. He has also been president of the Society of French Authors, and in 1888 was elected a member of the French Academy as the successor of Cuvillier-Fleury.

He has written Voyages d'un Parisien (1865); Mademoiselle Cachemire (1867); Les derniers montagnards (a historical essay, 1867); Paris assiégé—tableaux et souvenirs (1871); Histoire de la guerre de 1870-'71 (1872); Le roman des soldats (1872); Le Train 17 (1877); Le troisième Dessous (1878); Monsieur le Ministre (1881); Le million (1882); Le Prince Zilah (1884); Jean Mormier (1885); Le candidat (1886); Brichanteau, comédien (1886); Puy joli (1890); and L'Accusateur (1900).

Cobb, Sylvanus, Jr. (Waterville, Maine, June 5, 1823; Hyde Park, Mass., July 20, 1887). He was the son of the Rev. Sylvanus Cobb (1799-1866), a Universalist minister prominent in Maine in the anti-slavery and temperance movements, editor for twenty years of the Christian Freeman and publisher of several religious works. The younger Sylvanus had a high-school education and in 1841 he enlisted in the United States Navy and went on a cruise to the Mediterranean in the frigate Brandywine. On his return, in 1843, he worked in his father's printing-office, and in 1845 married Mary Jane Mead, of Waltham, Mass.

In 1846 Mr. Cobb established a temperance publication entitled The Rechabite. He edited also the New England Washingtonian, and later the Waverley Magazine. He became, too, a prolific story-writer, contributing largely to Gleason's Pictorial, the Flag of Our Union, and the New York Ledger.

In 1851 he published a story entitled The King's Talisman, and in 1856 wrote as a serial for the New York Ledger The Gunmaker of Moscow, which proved a great success, being later published in book form and dramatized. Other successful stories were The Patriot Cruiser (1859); and Ben Hamed (1864). He published in 1867 his father's Autobiography with a memoir by himself; and in 1891 a Memoir of Sylvanus Cobb, Junior, was published by Ella Waite Cobb.

Cockton, Henry (London, Dec. 7, 1807; Bury St. Edmunds, Suffolk, June 26, 1853). Nothing is known of his family, parentage, or education. He sprang at once into popularity with a story entitled Valentine Vox the Ventriloquist, which the London Times declared would keep the most melancholy reader shaking with laughter. It was published first in monthly numbers and later in book form (1840), with sixty illustrations by Thomas Onwhyn. Cockton married May 9, 1841, at Bury St. Edmunds, Ann Howes, and published the same year George St. George Julian, the Prince, in which the hero is a prince of ingenious knaves. The book was intended to put the inexperienced on guard, and to expose the defective state of the laws against bigamy. This was followed by Stanley Thorne (1841); England and France (1842), contrasting life in the two countries; Sylvester Sound the Somnambulist (1844); The Love Match (1845); The Steward (1850); The Sisters: or, The Fatal Marriage (1851); Lady Felicia (1852); and Percy Effingham (1852).

Some of his works, which had great vogue in their day, were illustrated by George Cruikshank, Alfred Crowquill, and John Leech.

Collins, William Wilkie (Tavistock Square, London, England, Jan. 8, 1824; London, Sept. 23, 1889). He was the eldest son of the noted landscape and figure painter, William Collins (1788–1847), and was named after his father's intimate friend, Sir David Wilkie. In later life he dropped his first name, and was always known as Wilkie Collins. After a private education at Highbury, he spent two years (1836–'38) with his parents in Italy, and in 1841–'46 was articled to a London firm in the tea trade. While in this place he turned to account his knowledge acquired in Italy by writing a story entitled *Antonina: or, The Fall of Rome*, which so pleased his father that he took him out of the tea house and placed him in Lincoln's Inn to study, whence he was called in 1851 to the bar.

His father died in 1847, and Wilkie began his literary career by the preparation of his memoirs, which were published (1848) in two volumes. In 1850–'51 he published Rambles beyond Railways, the result of a summer at Penzance in Cornwall. In 1851 he met Charles Dickens, which determined him to devote himself to letters. Their intimacy lasted during Dickens's life, and sometimes they worked in collaboration. Collins contributed many stories to Household Words and to All the Year Round, wrote for the Holly Tree Christmas number of 1855, and spent the following winter with Dickens in Paris. He also collaborated with him in No Thoroughfare, which appeared as a Christmas story in 1867.

Wilkie Collins's principal works are: Basil, a Story of Modern Life (1852); Hide and Seek (1854); After Dark (short stories, 1856); The Dead Secret (1857); The Queen of Hearts (1859); *The Woman in White* (1860); *No Name* (1862); My Miscellanies (1863); *Armadale* (1866); *The Moonstone* (1868); *Man and Wife* (1870); Poor Miss Finch (1872); The New Magdalen (1873); The Frozen Deep, and Other Stories (1874); The Law and the Lady (1875); The Two Destinies (1876); The Fallen Leaves (1879); Jezebel's Daughter (1880); The Black Robe (1881); Heart and Science (1883); I Say No (1884); The Evil Genius (1886); The Legacy of Cain (1888).

Mr. Collins wrote three dramas: The Frozen Deep, which was performed at Tavistock House in 1857, The Lighthouse, and Black and White. He dramatized also four of his novels: *Armadale* (1866; again, as Miss Gwilt, 1875); *No Name* (1870); *The Woman in White* (1871); and The New Magdalen (1873).

In 1873-'74 Mr. Collins visited the United States and gave public readings from his works in the principal cities. His last years were spent in seclusion. He was a hard worker and wrote and rewrote his stories, his manuscripts being heavily scored with corrections and additions. In his style, which was simple, clear, and unornamented, he depended rather on intricacy of plot than on graphic description or subtle delineation of character. *The Woman in White* and *The Moonstone* are masterpieces of construction, involving a mystery so profound as to baffle the reader until the very end of the story.

Connor, Ralph, the pseudonym of the Rev. Dr. Charles William Gordon (Indian Lands, Glengarry, Ontario, Canada, 1860). He is the son of the Rev. Daniel and Mary (Robertson) Gordon, his mother having been a graduate of

Mt. Holyoke Seminary, Mass. After a preliminary education in St. Mary's High School, Toronto, he entered Toronto University and was graduated there in 1883. In 1883-'84 he taught in Chatham High School, and in 1887 took his degree as a graduate in theology at Knox College, Toronto, which gave him the degree of D.D. in 1906.

In 1888 he took a course of post-graduate study at New College, Edinburgh, Scotland, and afterward traveled a year on the continent of Europe. In the mean time he had been ordained as a Presbyterian minister, and from 1890-'94 was a missionary at Banff, in the lumber and mining region of the Rocky Mountains. After another winter of study in Edinburgh, he visited the Presbyterian churches of Great Britain and succeeded in arousing an interest in Canadian missions and in obtaining considerable sums of money to aid in their development. On his return home he was chosen pastor of St. Stephen's Church, at Winnipeg, where he has since lived.

Mr. Gordon has written a number of books dealing with the life, manners, and scenery of Western Canada, which are remarkable for vivid description and careful delineation of character. They are all religious stories, and all are marked by deep feeling, strong powers of observation, and often by heart-moving sentiment and pathos. Among his stories are: Black Rock (1898); Beyond the Marshes (1899); Gwen's Canyon (1899); *The Sky Pilot* (1899); Ould Michael (1900); The Man from Glengarry (1901); Glengarry School Days (1902); The Prospector (1904).

The Rev. Dr. Gordon married, in Toronto, Sept. 28, 1899, Miss Helen King, a graduate of Manitoba College, of which her father was principal.

Conway, Hugh, the pseudonym of Frederick John Fargus (Bristol, England, Dec. 26, 1847; Monte Carlo, Monaco, May 15, 1885). He was the eldest of three brothers, sons of Frederick Charles Fargus, a local auctioneer. His mother, Elizabeth Marson, died in the boyhood of her children. Frederick derived from novel-reading a desire to be a sailor, and when thirteen years old was put as a student on the school-frigate *Conway*, then stationed in the Mersey. He was studious, and won in 1862 prizes for general proficiency and for excellence in mathematics and astronomy. He was desirous to enter the Royal Navy, but his father disapproved and sent him to a private school in Bristol. While there he wrote, when seventeen years old, a burlesque in three acts, entitled *Jason, or the Golden Fleece.*

He was next articled to a firm of public accountants, and while a clerk wrote many songs which were set to music and published as "words by Hugh Conway," a pen-name evolved from his experiences on the school-ship. In 1868 he succeeded to his father's business. In 1879 his songs were collected and published as *A Life's Idylls and Other Poems.* He soon began to contribute to magazines, especially to Blackwood's, where he published in 1881 The Secret of the Stradivarius, in 1882 The Bandsman's Story, and in 1883 Fleurette.

In 1883 also he published *Called Back,* the story by which he is best known. By 1887 more than three hundred and fifty thousand copies of this had been sold, and it had been translated into French, German, Italian, Swedish, Spanish, and Dutch. It was dramatized by the author and ran in 1884 nearly two hundred nights at the Prince's Theater in London. Among other books published by him are: Dark Days (1884); The Red Hill Mystery; Paul Vargas; and Chewton Abbott. In 1885 his health broke down, and he died at Monte Carlo while traveling in search of relief.

Cooper, James Fenimore (Burlington, New Jersey, Sept. 15, 1789; Cooperstown, New York, Sept 14, 1851). His father, Judge William Cooper, a man of excellent social position, removed in 1790 to a tract at the outlet of Lake Otsego, New York, where he had founded in 1788 the settlement named from him, Cooperstown, and here the future novelist spent his boyhood. His middle name was derived from his mother, a daughter of Richard Fenimore, of a New Jersey family of Swedish descent. When thirteen years old he was sent to Yale College, but after his third year there he entered the United States Navy, where he served six years, attaining the grade of lieutenant and acquiring an experience useful in his literary career.

In 1811 he married Susan De Lancey, a sister of Bishop William Heathcote De Lancey, and resigning from the navy went to live at Mamaroneck, Westchester County, New York, the home of the De Lancey family. Here he was first attracted to literature by reading some of the popular novels of the day, and declaring his belief that he could improve on them he wrote *Precaution*, a story of country life on the model then in vogue. It was published in 1819, anonymously and at his own expense, and attracted little attention. But in 1821 he published *The Spy: a Tale of the Neutral Ground*, founded on incidents of the Revolution and introducing historical characters; and this at once met with a success then unprecedented in American literature, becoming popular not only in this country but in Europe, where it was translated into the principal languages.

Two years later (1823) appeared *The Pioneers* and *The Pilot*. The former was first in order of publication, but afterward made the fourth chronologically in the series of *Leather-Stocking Tales;* it deals with the exciting incidents of frontier life, recalling the scenes of his boyhood. *The Pilot*, the first of his sea-stories, is said to have been prompted by the inaccuracies which his sea experience had enabled him to discover in Sir Walter Scott's *The Pirate*, which had appeared two years before. *The Pilot* awakened even greater enthusiasm than *The Spy*, and Long Tom Coffin, one of its characters, has been called the "best sailor character ever drawn." *Lionel Lincoln* (1825), another story of the Revolution, was not so successful; but *The Last of the Mohicans* (1826), the second in chronological order of the *Leather-Stocking Tales*, taking the reader again amid scenes of adventure and danger in the forest, became at once a favorite.

In 1827 Mr. Cooper went to Europe, where he remained six years, visiting the principal cities, but keeping up his literary labors, and publishing the same year *The Red Rover*, a second sea-tale, and *The Prairie*, another of the *Leather-Stocking Tales*. In 1828 he published Notions of the Americans, by a Traveling Bachelor, ostensibly a book of travel in the United

States, but intended to correct the false impressions which he found prevailing abroad concerning America and Americans. In 1829 he published *The Wept of Wish-ton-Wish*, a story of King Philip's War, the fantastic title of which was changed in England to The Borderers, and in France to The Puritans of America. In 1830 appeared *The Water Witch: or, The Skimmer of the Seas*, and in the same year, being then in Paris, he replied in a series of letters in the national newspaper to an article in the Révue Britannique, criticizing the Government of the United States and slandering its institutions.

He wrote also at this time several novels on foreign subjects, publishing in rapid succession *The Bravo* (1831), *The Heidenmauer: or, The Bénédictines* (1832), and *The Headsman of Berne* (1833). The first of these, which Cooper considered his masterpiece, is a story of Venice in the days of the Doges, and was dramatized in 1833; the scene of the second is in Germany, in the beginning of the Reformation; and that of the third in Switzerland. Though involving much historical research, and showing considerable skill in description and character delineation, these stories do not compare favorably with his American tales, on which his reputation must chiefly depend.

In 1835 he published *The Monikins* and The American Democrat, in which he satirized what he considered some failings of his own countrymen, which brought upon him severe attacks in home newspapers. He replied to these assaults in *Homeward Bound* and *Home as Found*, two volumes published in 1838, in which he caricatured newspaper editors and further satirized American peculiarities. The newspaper attacks finally degenerated into personal abuse, and resulted in a series of libel suits involving much time and expense, but in all of which he declared he was successful.

Meanwhile he continued his literary work, and published: Sketches of Switzerland (1836), Gleanings in Europe, etc., (1837), and Naval History of the United States (1839); the last inviting new newspaper attacks. Returning again to the field of fiction, he published rapidly: *The Pathfinder* (1840); *Mercedes of Castile* (1840); *The Deerslayer* (1841); *The Two Admirals* (1842); *Wing and Wing* (1842); *Wyan-*

dotte; or, The Hutted Knoll (1843); Ned Myers: or, A Life before the Mast (1843); *Afloat and Ashore,* and its sequel, *Miles Wallingford* (1844); *Satanstoe* (1845); *The Chainbearer* (1845); *The Redskins* (1846); *The Crater: or, Vulcan's Peak* (1847); *Oak Openings: or, The Bee-Hunter* (1848); *Jack Tier: or, The Florida Reefs* (1848); *The Sea Lions: or, The Lost Sealers* (1849); and *The Ways of the Hour* (1850), the last an exposure of the defects of trial by jury.

Cooper published also in 1846 Lives of Distinguished Naval Officers, a companion to his Naval History, and had in press at the time of his death a historical work entitled The Towns of Manhattan. His later novels did not attain the popularity of some of the earlier ones, and he will be known to posterity chiefly as the author of the *Leather-Stocking Tales* and of some remarkable sea-stories. Several of them have been translated into nearly all the languages of Europe and even into some Oriental tongues.

Cooper was a large man of imposing presence, with a countenance marked by manly beauty and intellectual strength. Socially, he was hospitable, kind, and magnanimous, and his home life was a model of peace and happiness. Though he had many enemies in life, it is now conceded that his strictures on his countrymen, which brought on so many bitter attacks, were actuated by lofty principle and a pure patriotism.

Coppée, Francis Edouard Joachim, called François Coppée (Paris, France, January 12, 1842; Paris, February 8, 1908). He was a weak, nervous, sentimental boy, son of an official in the War Department. His mother died in his childhood, his father while he was a youth. After finishing his studies at the Lycée St. Louis, he obtained a government clerkship, but soon began to indulge his literary aspirations, writing poems that were tinged with the sadness and trials of his early days. He first won notice by a one-act play, Le passant (1869), a comedy in verse, in which Sarah Bernhardt played the title-rôle, and from this dates his reputation, though he had previously published several volumes of poems. But **Coppée's** novels are greater than his poems, and his best story, *The Romance of Youth (Toute ma jeunesse)*, crowned in 1890 by the French Academy, will remain to all time the very essence of life's springtime.

Coppée served as a volunteer in the militia in the Franco-Prussian War. In 1878 he became archivist of the Comédie Française, in 1884 was elected to the French Academy, and in 1888 was made an officer of the Legion of Honor.

Among his poetical works are: Le Réliquaire (1860); L'Exiles (1876); Les mois (1877); Le naufrage (1878); Arrière saison (1899); Une mauvaise soirée (1899). Among his dramas are: Le luthier de Crémone (1876); Severo Torelli (1880); Les Jacobites (1885); and Pour la couronne (1895).

Other works in prose are: Une idylle pendant le siège (1875); Contes en prose (1882); Vingt contes nouveaux (1883); Contes en recits en prose (1885); Contes rapides (1888); Le coupable (1896); Mon franc parler (1895–'99); A voix haute (1899); Fille de tristesse; Henriette; Madame Nunn; Le coucher de soleil, etc.

Coppée called Leconte de Lisle his master, but though he may owe something to him in style he is original in choice of subject and in treatment.

Corelli, Marie, the pen-name of Minnie Mackay, of mingled Italian and Scottish parentage, is said to have been born in Italy in 1864. She was adopted in infancy by Charles Mackay, (1814–1889), the well-known Scottish poet, and brought up during childhood in England. Later she was sent to a French convent, where she received a thorough musical training, her adoptive father intending to fit her for a musical career. She began to write, when only fourteen years old, an elaborate opera entitled Ginevra da Siena, and composed some songs. Among her early attempts in literature were three sonnets on Shakespearean themes, entitled Romeo and Juliet, Rosalind, and Desdemona, which were published in The Theatre, London. In 1886 a curious personal experience caused her to write *A Romance of Two Worlds*. It proved an instant popular success, although entirely unnoticed by the press, and from that time she determined to devote herself to literature. But she never has lost her love for music and is an excellent performer on both the pianoforte and the mandolin. She is fond also of the theater, and takes a keen interest in the principal dramatic events of the day.

Perhaps no other living author has been so extensively translated as Marie Corelli. Her *Romance of Two Worlds* may be had in nearly every language of Europe, including Greek and Russian. Her reputation was largely due to her Barabbas: a Dream of the World's Tragedy (1893), the most reviled, the best praised, and the most widely read book of its day. It speedily ran through all the languages of Europe and invaded the East, being translated into Hindustani, Gujerati, and other East Indian dialects. Aside from the daring of founding a romance on events connected with our Saviour's Passion, it possesses many of the elements of a powerful literary success, with passages of extreme beauty and impressive pathos. It has passed through many editions, one of which (1902) is embellished with a rubricated title-page and other adornments, and illustrated with photogravures from original drawings by Ludovico Marchetti.

Her works are: *A Romance of Two Worlds* (1886); Vendetta (1886); Thelma (1887); Ardath: the Story of a Dead Self (1889); Wormwood; The Soul of Lilith (1892); Barabbas: a Dream of the World's Tragedy (1893); The Silence of the Maharajah (1895); The Sorrows of Satan (1895); Cameos (1896); The Mighty Atom (1896); The Murder of Delicia (1896); Ziska: the Problem of a Wicked Soul (1897); Jane (1897); The Master Christian (1900); Boy (1900); Temporal Power: A Study in Supremacy (1902).

Crawford, Francis Marion (Bagni di Lucca, Italy, Aug. 2, 1854), son of Thomas and Louisa (Ward) Crawford. His name, Francis Marion, is derived from General Francis Marion, the heroic partisan ranger of the Revolution. His father (1814–1857) was the noted American sculptor, pupil of Thorwaldsen, long resident in Italy, and sculptor of the statue of Liberty on the dome and the great bronze doors of the Capitol at Washington, the colossal Washington in Richmond, and other well-known works. His mother was sister to Julia Ward Howe. Marion, the youngest of four children, spent his early years in Italy, but when twelve years old was sent to St. Paul's School, Concord, New Hampshire. Later he studied under a private tutor at Hatfield Regis, England, and at Trinity College, Cambridge. From 1874 to 1876 he was at Karlsruhe and Heidelberg, and then spent two years at the University of Rome, where he studied Sanskrit and the Oriental languages.

In 1879 he went to India and edited The Indian Herald, an afternoon daily at Allahabad; but as the duties were arduous he returned in 1880 to Italy, and in 1881 came again to the United States and entered Harvard as a special student in Sanskrit. In 1882, while dining with his uncle, Mr. Samuel Ward, at a New York club, he related the story of a man he had met at Simla, during his Indian experience, whose real name was Jacobs. "That would make a capital magazine story," said his uncle; "I advise you to write it at once." He began it that same night, and in a little more than a month finished *Mr. Isaacs*, which was accepted by the Macmillans and published at once. It met with instant favor, was followed by Dr. Claudius (1883), and *A Roman Singer* (1884), the latter written by request of Thomas Bailey Aldrich, for the Atlantic Monthly. Since then he has produced a long succession of novels and historical works, remarkable for excellence in the depiction of character and for careful selection and handling of historical and other material. His books have been published in cosmopolitan editions in the United States, England, and Germany, and he himself has made French editions of several of his novels. In recognition of his merits he was awarded by the French Academy the Monbrun prize and a gold medal.

Mr. Crawford spent the most of 1884 in Constantinople, and married there in that year Elizabeth Berdan, daughter of General Hiram Berdan, Commander of Sharpshooters in the Civil War. In the following year he made his home at Villa Crawford, Sant' Agnello di Sorrento, Italy, and has since lived there, making occasional visits to the United States.

His works include, besides those already mentioned: An American Politician (1884); Zoroaster (1885); The Tale of a Lonely Parish (1886); Marzio's Crucifix (1887); Saracinesca (1887); Paul Patoff (1887); With the Immortals (1888); Greifenstein (1889); Sant' Ilario (1889); A Cigarette-Maker's Romance (1890); The Witch of Prague (1891); Don Orsino (1892); Marion Darche (1893); Pietro Ghisleri (1893); Katharine Lauderdale (1894); Love in Idleness (1894); The Ralstons (1895); Casa Braccio (1895); A Rose of Yesterday (1897); Corleone (1897); In the Palace of the King (1898); Via Crucis (1899); Marietta, a Maid of Venice (1901); Cecilia: a Story of Modern Rome (1902); The Heart of Rome (1903); Whosoever shall Offend (1904); Arethusa (1907); The Little City of Hope (1907); Fair Margaret (1908); The Prima Donna, sequel to the last (1908).

Mr. Crawford has written also a play, Francesca da Rimini, which was produced in Paris (1902) by Sarah Bernhardt.

Crockett, Samuel Rutherford (Duchrae, Galloway, Scotland, Sept. 24, 1860). He was educated at Edinburgh, Heidelberg, and at New College, Oxford. In 1886 he entered the Free Church of Scotland, and was for several years minister at Penicuik, in the County of Edinburgh, but finally became a writer and journalist. His principal publications are: The Stickit Minister (1893); The Raiders (1894); *The Lilac Sunbonnet* (1894); Mad Sir Uchtred (1894); The Playactress (1894); The Men of the Moss Hags (1895); Sweetheart Travellers (1896); Cleg Kelly (1896); The Gray Man (1896); Lad's Love (1897); Lochinvar (1897); Sir Toady Lion (1897); The Standard Bearer (1898); The Red Axe (1898); The Black Douglas (1899); Flower o' the Corn (1902); and An Adventurer in Spain (1903).

Croly, George (Dublin, Ireland, Aug. 17, 1780; London, Nov. 24, 1860). He was educated at Trinity College, Dublin, was ordained in 1804, and licensed to a curacy in the north of Ireland, but the obscurity of his position becoming distasteful, he went to London about 1810, and devoted himself to literature as a dramatic critic and contributor to magazines. In 1835 he was presented with the rectorship of St. Stephen's, Walbrook, London, where he acquired a reputation for eloquence and attracted an intellectual congregation.

Croly began his literary career in 1817 with a poem in imitation of Childe Harold, entitled Paris in 1815, in which he describes the works of art collected in the Louvre by Napoleon from the galleries of Europe, prior to their restoration after the surrender of Paris. Five years later this was followed by The Angel of the World: an Arabian Tale, and by several satires and lyrics, which were collected in 1830. In 1822 he published a tragedy entitled Catiline, and in 1824 his comedy, Pride shall have a Fall, was played with great success at Covent Garden Theatre; and in 1827 he published *Salathiel: a Story of the Past, the Present, and the Future,* founded on the legend of the Wandering Jew. Dr. Croly calls this mythical personage, who has wandered down the centuries in legend and poetry since the days of Christ, Salathiel Ben Sadi, and he is supposed to have appeared and disappeared at Venice, toward the close of the sixteenth century, in a manner to attract the attention of Europe.

Salathiel was followed by two other works of fiction: Tales of the Great St. Bernard (1829), and Marston (1846). The Modern Orlando (1846) is an inferior Don Juan. Among other works by Dr. Croly are: Personal History of George IV. (1830); Political Life of Burke (1840); and Historical Sketches, Speeches, and Characters (1842). He was the author also of volumes of sermons, religious works, essays, etc., and was a prolific contributor to periodicals.

Cummins, Maria Susanna (Salem, Mass., April 9, 1827; Dorchester, Boston, Oct. 1, 1866). She was the daughter of Judge David Cummins, of Salem, who took a deep interest in her early education and did much to develop her taste for literature. Her education was finished at Mrs. Charles Sedgwick's school at Lenox, Mass. Although she began to contribute to periodicals when quite young, publishing short stories in the Atlantic Monthly and other magazines, she did not become known popularly until 1853, when her first long story, *The Lamplighter,* brought her fame. It attained at once a phenomenal success, forty thousand copies being sold within eight weeks of its publication, and its ultimate sales being exceeded only by those of Uncle Tom's Cabin and Ben Hur.

It met with success also in England, and two translations of it appeared in France, one entitled Gerty, the other L'allumeur de réverbères. A German translation was published in 1856 in Leipzig.

This success was followed in 1857 by Mabel Vaughan, which, though not as popular as her first book, is considered by some as superior to it. In 1860 she published a story of the East, entitled El Fureidis, which contains graphic and truthful pictures of life and scenes in Palestine. As Miss Cummins never had visited the Holy Land, her accurate descriptions were considered very remarkable by those who did not know the source of her inspiration. Her facts were largely supplied by Dr. Elbert H. Champlin (1818–1883), of New York, who had visited the East frequently, was familiar with its scenes and its people, and had studied its history in a scholarly way.

Haunted Hearts, her last work, was published in 1864, two years before her decease at the early age of thirty-nine. Miss Cummins's work is marked not only by the charm of lively narration which breeds interest, but has behind it a strong moral conviction which appeals to the heart of her readers. Her characters are clearly drawn and true to life, and her descriptions of scenery are well-painted and accurate.

Curtis, George William (Providence, Rhode Island, February 24, 1824; New Brighton, Staten Island, N. Y., August 31, 1892.) His parents were of Puritan stock, his mother being a daughter of the Hon. James Burrill, Jr., a Chief Justice of Rhode Island and a Senator of the United States. His mother died while he was yet a child, and his father married again and removed in 1839 with his family to New York City, where he was cashier of one bank and later president of another.

George William's school education, besides teaching at home, was scanty, involving only two years at an academy at Jamaica Plains, near Boston; but he was an omnivorous reader, and, like most men of genius, was largely self-educated. After a year's work as a clerk, he became disgusted with mercantile life, and in 1842 went with an elder brother to live in the famous Brook Farm community in West Roxbury, Mass., where he spent a year and a half in study and in agricultural labor. After another year or two on a farm in Concord, Mr. Curtis went in 1846 to Europe, and, after a prolonged stay in Italy and Berlin, traveled in Egypt and Syria. In 1850 he returned to the United States, and published his first book, Nile Notes of a Howadji (1851), which was followed by The Howadji in Syria (1852).

In 1851 he joined the editorial staff of the New York Tribune, and wrote a series of letters to it from various watering-places, which were afterward published collectively under the title of Lotus Eating. From 1852–1857 he was connected editorially with Putnam's Magazine, and during this time met with great success as a lyceum lecturer and an orator, taking a prominent part as a speaker in behalf of the Republican party in the Presidential election of 1856. He published also some of his contributions to the magazines under the titles of The Potiphar Papers (1853) and Prue and I (1856), the latter being his first novel.

In 1858 he became associated with Harper's Magazine as editor of the Easy Chair, and in 1860 became editor of Harper's Weekly. In 1858–'59 he published serially in this paper a novel entitled *Trumps*, which later (1862) appeared in book form. When Harper's Bazar was begun in 1867 he contributed to it a series of popular articles which was continued weekly until the spring of 1873.

In 1871 Mr. Curtis was appointed by President Grant one of a commission to draw up rules for the regulation of the civil service, but in 1873 he resigned on account of differences with the President. He was a delegate to the Republican National Conventions of 1860 and 1864, and in the latter year was defeated for Congress in the First District of New York. In 1880 he was president of the New York State Civil Service League, and he was president of the National Civil Service Reform League from its foundation until his death. Mr. Curtis married Miss Anna Shaw, a daughter of Francis George Shaw, the Boston philanthropist, and for more than twenty-five years divided his time between his Staten Island home and his summer residence at Ashfield, Mass., where, in conjunction with Charles Eliot Norton, he organized and conducted for many years gatherings of eminent literary and scientific men who spoke on vital questions of the day at an annual banquet given for the benefit of Sanderson Academy, the high school of this typical little New England town, where "plain living and high thinking" made a strong appeal to Mr. Curtis's simple yet scholarly tastes.

Daudet, Alphonse (Nîmes, France, May 13, 1840; Paris, Dec. 17, 1897). His parents were of the *bourgeoisie*, his father being a silk manufacturer, who seemed selected by fate for misfortune and failure. Until 1856 Alphonse, with frequent truancy, attended the Lyons Lycée, but in that year he was forced to face the stern realities of life. He accepted the place of usher at a school in Alais, but soon found it intolerable, and in November, 1857, he sought refuge with his brother Ernest, three years his senior, who was trying to make a livelihood as journalist in Paris. Alphonse, too, took up the pen, wrote poems, and obtained employment on the Figaro, and in its pages appeared many of his earlier efforts, such as Les Gueux de Province. In 1858 he published his first volume, Les Amoureuses, a collection of poems which met with a fair reception. Next he turned his attention to the stage, and produced, either alone or with collaborators, several plays: Le dernière idole (1862); L'Œillet blanc (1865); Le frère aîné (1868); Le sacrifice (1869); Lise Tavernier, and L'Arlésienne (1872). But his theatrical ventures were inconspicuous. Not so his novels. Le petite chose (1868), a child's autobiography, and Lettres de mon moulin (1869), containing many exquisite bits of story-telling, attracted attention. Meanwhile, the Empress Eugénie had been captivated by one of his poems, Les Prunes, and had persuaded the Duc de Morny, the Minister of State, to give its author a sinecure secretaryship, which Daudet held until the death (1865) of that statesman. This appointment enabled Daudet to travel, and he visited Algeria, Corsica, and Sardinia. During these tours he gained health, as well as local color for some of his most famous stories: Contes du lundi (1873), *Le Nabob* (1877), *Numa Roumestan* (1881), and the three Tartarins—Tartarin as the mighty hunter in *Tartarin de Tarascon* (1872), as the intrepid mountaineer in Tartarin sur les Alps (1886), and as the colonist in Port Tarascon (1890). In 1865 Daudet resigned his government office and devoted himself to literature. Under the spell of Gambetta and Mistral he had successfully caught the secrets of Provençal characters, but in 1874 appeared his first novel of Parisian life, *Fromont jeune et Risler aîné*. It took the world by storm, and struck a new vein in French literature, a vein that gained for Daudet the sobriquet of "the French Dickens." From that time his novels grew in power and subtlety until about 1885, when he became an intensely nervous sufferer, sleepless, and addicted to chloral. His late work betrays gradual decline, though his pen never lost its impressionistic power and picturesque facility. "It is style that perfumes a book," he once said, and his own work never lost its unique fragrance. Among his best known novels, besides those already referred to, are: *Jack* (1876); *Kings in Exile* (1879); *The Evangelist* (1883); *Sappho* (1884); *The Immortal* (1888); *Rose and Ninette* (1891); *The Little Parish Church* (1895); and *The Support of the Family* (1898). Most valuable reminiscences are embodied in his Thirty Years in Paris (1888), and Souvenirs of a Parisian (1888).

Davis, Rebecca Harding (Washington, Pa., June 24, 1831). She was a descendant of an old English family, which settled in the south of Ireland during the reign of Queen Elizabeth, and of the Leetes of Virginia. While she was quite young her parents removed to Alabama, and subsequently to Wheeling, then in Virginia. After writing many short stories which appeared in current magazines, she devoted her attention to more sustained work, and the result, Life in the Iron-Mills (1861), and Margaret Howth (1861), which originally appeared as A Story of To-day, attracted wide popularity in the pages of the Atlantic Monthly, where they were used as serials. Her realistic pictures of artisan life were perhaps the first in this country to present the labor problem in fiction. In 1863 she married L. Clarke Davis, a Philadelphia journalist, who afterward edited the Public Ledger. For several years Mrs. Davis was a regular editorial writer on the New York Tribune. Altogether, her work evinces the combined powers of originality and character drawing. Among her novels are: *Waiting for the Verdict* (1867); Dallas Galbraith (1868); Berrytown (1872); A Law unto Herself (1878); John Andoross (1880); Natasqua (1886); Kent Hampden (1892); Dr. Warrick's Daughters (1895); and Frances Waldeaux (1896).

Davis, Richard Harding (Philadelphia, Pa., April 18, 1864). As son of a popular woman novelist and a journalist, it was natural that after his graduation at Lehigh University young Davis should enter the newspaper world to try his skill. Reportorial work in Philadelphia was succeeded by his coming to New York City (1888), where he soon gained distinction for striking stories contributed to the Evening Sun. These were mainly the result of personal experiences among famous crooks and criminals; he described their characters and habits with such fidelity that many careers of crime were forthwith closed. He published these stories in a volume entitled Gallagher and Other Stories (1891). Again, the next year, he adopted a style of popular favor in Van Bibber Sketches, humorous satires on society life in New York. In 1892 he was made managing editor of Harper's Weekly, but two years of that work only served to convince him that his time should be devoted to fiction, so he resigned. Since that time he has written a number of popular novels, books of travel, and narratives of great events, celebrated persons and places. As a war correspondent he has been signally successful, serving in that capacity in Cuba (1898), and in South Africa (1900). Several of his plays have attained public approval, such as his dramatization of his own novel, *Soldiers of Fortune* (1897), and the comedies: The Galloper (1902), The Dictator (1903), and Miss Civilization (1905). Among other works are: Stories for Boys (1891); Van Bibber and Others (1892); The West from a Car Window (1892); Our English Cousins (1894); The Rulers of the Mediterranean (1894); About Paris (1895); The Princess Aline (1896); Three Gringoes in Venezuela and Central America (1896); Cuba in War Time (1898); The Cuban and Porto Rican Campaign (1898); A Year from a Reporter's Note-book (1898); The King's Jackal (1899); The Lion and the Unicorn (1899); With Both Armies in South Africa (1900); In the Fog (1901); Ranson's Folly (1902); and Real Soldiers of Fortune (1907).

De Amicis, Edmondo (Oneglia, Liguria, Italy, October 21, 1846; April 28, 1908).   After receiving some schooling in Cuneo and in Turin, he was sent to the Modena Military Academy, from which he was graduated; later he became a lieutenant in the Third Regiment of the line (in 1865).   The next year he participated in the battle of Custozza.   In 1867 he became editor of the Florentine journal L' Italia militare, for which he wrote a series of naturalistic tales entitled Bozetti della vita militare, published in book form in 1868.   These proved very popular, and after the Roman occupation of 1870, in which he took part, he abandoned both the military and journalistic careers for a literary life, making his headquarters in Turin.   By inclination a traveler, he indulged in wanderings in his new-found leisure which resulted in a series of brilliant pictures of scenery and the external aspects of life as they appeared to him in the various countries visited.   These books, translated into many languages, achieved wide popularity, and were: La Spagna (1873); Ricordi di Londra (1874); L'Olanda (1874); Morocco (1875); Constantinopoli (1877); and Ricordi di Parigi (1879).   All show a keen power of observation, a genial humor and a cosmopolitan spirit; the style, moreover, is vividly colorful, and may stand comparison with that of Théophile Gautier.   Besides travel description De Amicis has written Poesie (1880), a volume composed chiefly of sonnets; Ritratti letterari (1881), personal impressions of well-known authors; Gli amici (1882), a semi-humorous essay on friendship; and Alle parte d'Italia (1888), a series of historical novelettes.   Fiction has found him equally at home and prolific.   Il cuore, which was translated under the title The Heart of a Boy, recording the events of a single school year in a highly sentimental fashion, has been a great literary success, and has sold by the thousands.   Educational and economic problems have concerned him in his latest novels, and he has openly avowed socialistic theories. Such questions are dealt with in: La maestrina degli operai **(1895)**; *The Romance of a Schoolmaster* (*Il romanzo d'un* *maestro*, 1895); La carozza di tutti (1899); Memorie (1899); Speranza e gloria (1900); and Ricordi d' infanzia e di scuola (1901).

De Bernard, Charles (Pierre Marie Charles de Bernard du Grail) (Besançon, Feb. 25, 1804; Sablonville, March 6, 1850). His family is one of the oldest of the Vivarais, dating from the thirteenth century, but has always been more distinguished for nobility than for wealth. After finishing his elementary studies, he went to Dijon to study law, and amused himself while reading Cujacius and the Institutes by flirting with the Muses, sending to the Academy of the Floral Games at Toulouse a piece of verse entitled Une fête de Néron, which was crowned. Notwithstanding this success, he felt that poetry was not his vocation, and in 1830 published at Besançon, in the Gazette de la Franche-Comté, a series of Legitimist articles, in which he strongly opposed centralization.

In 1831, when Balzac published The Magic Skin, Bernard wrote so favorable a review of it in the Gazette that it brought him a letter from and won him the friendship of the author, and on his solicitation Bernard went to Paris, where he made the acquaintance of Hugo, Dumas, Alfred de Musset, Sainte-Beuve, Antony Deschams, and others. In 1833 he published a second poem, Plus de deuil que de joie (More Sorrow that Joy), an elegiac work, but inspiring despite its pronounced skepticism. But its want of success discouraged him, and he returned to Besançon.

Balzac, whose friendship never failed him, sought him the following year. Bernard was then a man of proud and noble appearance, energetic and martial in figure, and full of the romance of chivalry. Balzac, believing that he recognized in him an epic genius, advised him to undertake historical romance, after the fashion of Frederic Soulié in the Vicomte de Béziers and Le Comte de Toulouse. In response to this, Bernard delved for some time in the archives of Franche-Comté, but, happily for him, discovered that this was not his vein. Introduced by Balzac to the Chronique de Paris, he contributed to it La Femme Gardée with but moderate success. This was followed by L'acte de vertu and La Femme de Quarante Ans, the latter a pleasing history of the deceits of a heart settled and well along in years speculating on new amours with youthful sentimentality, placed Bernard at once by the side of Balzac. The pupil even had the advantage of his master, for his types are originals that one meets at every step in life, while those of Balzac are not copied from nature nor taken from real life.

About the same time Bernard tried the drama and produced at the Gymnase Une Position Delicate and Madame de Valdaunaie, plays which show a fine and delicate observation and great strength and truth in dramatic characterization. Between 1838 and 1847 he published successively the works which have given him so distinguished a place in the literature of the period: Une Aventure de magistrat; L'Arbre de science; Le nœud gordien (a collection of five novels, Une femme de quarante ans, La rose jaune, Un acte de vertu, L'anneau d'argent, and La précurseur); Le pied d'argile; La chasse aux amants; Un beau-père; L'innocence d'un forçat; and Le Veau d'or, which he did not finish.

Gerfaut, his chef-d'œuvre, which appeared in 1838, is the history of an egotistical poet who remains cold in the midst of his lyrical effusions, of a chivalric skepticism which ends in a passion half sensual and half mystical, the *dénouement* of which moves by its somber and sinister originality. This character is strongly contrasted with that of the dauber Marilhac, a sincere and comic enthusiast in the new doctrines on the beautiful and the ugly in art.

In 1839 De Bernard published Les ailes d'Icare (The Wings of Icarus), in which are described the melancholy deceptions and disenchantments of a young man from the provinces who endeavors to find love and glory in Paris.

DeFoe, Daniel (London, England, 1661, London, 1731). Little is known of his early life save that he was the son of James Foe (the name was changed to DeFoe about 1703), a butcher, who sent him to the famous Dissenting Academy kept by Mr. Morton of Stoke Newington, where many notable Nonconformists of that day were educated. Though sent there with a view to his entering the ministry, he relinquished that plan for a business enterprise (1685), in which he failed. If tradition may be relied upon, he took up arms in Monmonth's Rebellion, and at the entry of William and Mary (January 26, 1688) into London he is said to have served as a volunteer trooper "gallantly mounted and richly accoutered." At that time he was engaged in foreign trade, but within four years he became bankrupt. About the middle of the reign of William III, however, he was introduced to the "glorious and immortal" King, and in 1695 was appointed accountant to the commissioners of the glass duty, which office he held four years. From this period all the known events of his life are connected with his work as an author whose vigorous and prolific pen dashed off pamphlet after pamphlet on the religious, political, and economic questions of the time. In 1697 appeared The Character of Dr. Annesley, and in January, 1698, was published his Essay on Projects, but in 1701, The True-Born Englishman, a satirical poem, was given to the public, and it made him famous. It was a vigorous defense of King William, and fully eighty thousand copies, the majority of which were pirated, were sold in the streets. The subsequent death of the monarch was a great misfortune to DeFoe, and his enemies took advantage of the first opportunity to attack him. In 1703 a complaint, made in the House of Commons, against his pamphlet, The Shortest Way with Dissenters (1702), led to his apprehension. He was fined two hundred marks, condemned to the pillory, and imprisoned. But the public disgrace won him cheers from the mob. While in the pillory he wrote his splendid Hymn to the Pillory, and before his release in August, 1704, he had begun The Review, which marked an epoch in periodical literature. In 1706 he published The Apparition of One Mrs. Veal, one of his masterpieces, and the same year he was sent by the ministry on a secret mission to Scotland to promote the Union. This resulted in his valuable History of the Union (1709). But though an active political pamphleteer, producing in his life upward of two hundred works, his fame rests upon his fictions, which are replete with wonderful verisimilitude. At the head of this list stands his inimitable

Robinson Crusoe (1719); then follow: Memoirs of a Cavalier (1720), Captain Singleton (1720), Moll Flanders (1722), Journal of the Plague Year (1722), and Colonel Jack (1722).

De Genlis, Stéphanie Félicité du Crest de Saint Aubin, Comtesse (Champcéri, Burgundy, January 21, 1746; Paris, December 31, 1830). Before she learned to write she extemporized romantic narratives, and when she was a young girl her mother took her to Paris, where her beauty and talents won her a warm welcome. At fifteen years of age she received the offer of the heart and rent-roll of the Baron D'Andlau, a veteran spark of sixty, but she declined the honor, and her mother administered reproof by marrying the ancient suitor herself. In 1762, however, the girl married the Comte de Genlis, an officer of noble family, who had admired her epistolary ability. Shortly after her marriage she took up her abode at the Palais Royal, a move she regretted ever after, because that seeming social paradise proved a nest of serpents. As she was a connection of the Orléans family she gained an entrée into the most exclusive circles. About the time she was thirty, however, the Duc de Chartres—known through the Revolution as Philippe Egalité—persuaded her to retire from the world and devote herself to the education of his four children, one of whom was the future King Louis Philippe. For them she prepared several educational books, among which were: Théâtre à l'usage des jeunes personnes (1779); Théâtre de société (1781); Adèle et Théodore (1782); and Veillées du château (1784); this last being known in English under the title, Tales of the Castle. These were the first productions by which she acquired reputation as an author. Then she launched into pseudo-religious exposition in a work that aroused fierce contention. It was mercilessly attacked by theologians and philosophers, and for the latter she conceived a hatred that was uniform and unrelenting though she knew Rousseau and visited Voltaire at Ferney. During the Revolution she lived in Switzerland, in Berlin, and in Hamburg, always writing voluminously. Her political conduct and printed sentiments were severely criticized, and she deemed it necessary to defend her stand. Upon her eventual return to Paris she burned political incense before Napoleon, and sought refuge under his protection. In thirty years she published not less than one hundred volumes of miscellaneous matter, but she excelled in romantic narrative, of which *Louisa de Clermont* (1802) and Madame de La Vallière (1807) were the finest examples.

De Goncourt, Edmond Louis Antoine Huot (Nancy, France, May 26, 1822; Champrosay, July 16, 1896); **De Goncourt, Jules Alfred Huot** (Paris, Dec. 17, 1830; Paris, June 20, 1870). Until the death of the younger writer these inseparable brothers wrote always in collaboration. At first these "masters of impressionistic prose" turned their attention and labors to minute and valuable studies of French life and art in the eighteenth century, making their histories entirely out of documents, autograph letters, scraps of costume, engravings, songs, etc. Coupled with this scrupulous, realistic presentation of facts was a style unique, unconventional, indeed bizarre, though remarkably supple and clear. But the innovators only succeeded in estranging the general public, though many contemporary writers became their debtors. Undaunted, however, the brothers continued their naturalistic methods, and were daring enough to apply them to fiction, which should present nature unadorned—by discarding every artistic artifice—thus they sought to portray the realities of life. They also have the honor of first directing French attention to Japanese art, especially that of the eighteenth century. Unappreciated while living, the brothers bequeathed the larger part of their fortune to endow an academy of the Goncourts, where their ideals should be fostered, and where prizes should be awarded to kindred strugglers. Of the brothers Arthur Symonds says: "To the Goncourts humanity is as pictorial a thing as the world it moves in; they do not search further than the physical basis of life, and they find everything that can be known of that unknown force written visibly upon the sudden faces of little incidents, little expressive moments. . . . Their novels are hardly stories at all, but picture-galleries, hung with pictures of the momentary aspects of the world." Their eighteenth century studies comprise: Histoire de la société française pendant la révolution (1854); Histoire de la société française pendant le Directoire (1855); La révolution dans les mœurs (1854); Portraits intimes du XVIIIième siècle (1856); Marie Antoinette (1858); Les maîtresses de Louis XV (1860–'79); La femme au XVIIIième siècle (1877); Edmond alone added Watteau (1876); Prud'hon (1877); and Les actrices au XVIIIième siècle (1885–'90). Of novels, they wrote in collaboration: Charles Demailly (1860); Sœur Philomène (1861); *Renée Mauperin* (1864); Germinie Lacerteaux (1865); Manette Salomon (1867); and Madame Gervaisais (1869). Edmond, after the death of Jules, produced four novels: La fille Elisa (1878); Les frères Lamganno (1879); La Faustin (1882); and Chérie (1884). Their Journal des Goncourts (1887–'96) is perhaps a truer, more pathetic transcript of life than any of their "realistic" fictions.

Dekker, Eduard Douwes ("Multatuli") (Amsterdam, Holland, March 2, 1820; Nieder-Ingelheim, Germany, February 17, 1887). He was the son of a captain of a sailing-vessel trading with the East Indies, and after receiving a sound elementary education he entered the Dutch Civil Service at the age of nineteen. He was appointed to an office in the East Indian colonies, and was rapidly promoted; in 1851 he had become President, Assistant Magistrate, and Commissioner of the Province of Amboina. Two years later he was entrusted with the administration of the important province of Lebak in Java. Up to this point his career in the colonies had been brilliant, and his future prospects loomed large. But here he entered upon a course of action that clashed with the interests of his government. In other words, he recognized the cruel oppression of the official *régime*, under which the defenseless population suffered, and sought to correct the flagrant abuses. His humanitarian reforms drew down upon him the indignation of his superiors, and he was severely reprimanded for his "indiscreet behavior." Disgusted at this treatment, he applied for his honorable discharge, and in 1856 returned to Holland, where he presented the details of his case, only to meet with perfunctory attention. Being now a poor man, he retired to Antwerp and then to Brussels, where living was cheap, and wrote *Max Havelaar* (1859), under the pen-name of "Multatuli" (who have suffered much), in which he set forth the startling facts of East Indian conditions. This Dutch Uncle Tom's Cabin created a great sensation among the coffee-traders on the Amstel, and it achieved almost instantaneous fame, but failed to arouse the public conscience. His accusations never were refuted, even at the International Congress for the Promotion of Social Service, held at Amsterdam in 1863, where he challenged his critics. At length, thoroughly disgusted with his countrymen, he withdrew in 1866 to Germany, where, self-exiled, he continued to wield a powerful pen, and published books on political, social, and philosophic subjects. He also produced two plays, The Bride (1859) and The School for Princes (1878), the latter being still popular. In fiction, besides *Max Havelaar* (1859), he wrote The Holy Virgin, and the posthumous incomplete Story of Wonterje Pieterse (1888). The latter was brought out by his widow, who also edited his Letters (1892) and a complete collection of his works.

De Kock, Charles Paul (Passy, near Paris, France, May 21, 1794; Paris, Aug. 29, 1871). He was the son of a Dutch banker who was guillotined in 1794, and began his career as a banker's clerk, but soon occupied his leisure with the composition of melodramas and farces. Georgette, his first novel, was issued in 1820, and Gustave, le mauvais sujet (1821) quickly made him noted. Subsequent novels were Frère Jacques (1822); Mon voisin Raymonde (1822); André le Savoyard (1825); Le Barbier de Paris (1826), which was translated into many languages; Monsieur Dupont (1825); La femme, le mari, et l'amant (1829); and La pucelle de Belleville (1834). Although his voluminous fictions enjoyed a wonderful vogue they receive slight mention in works upon French literature. In 1844–'45 a collected edition of fifty-six volumes was published, and an English translation of his novels was begun in 1903. His stories are not immoral, as is often supposed, but are simply broadly conceived, though displaying ingenuity and dash. They are concerned chiefly with the shadier aspects of Parisian lower middle-class life, showing both observation and a keen sense of humor. Among his many imitators may be mentioned his son Henri (1819–1892).

Deland, Margaretta Wade Campbell (Allegheny, Pa., Feb. 23, 1857). She studied both at Pelham, New Rochelle, N. Y., and at the Cooper Institute in New York City. Finishing her course, she taught (1878–'79) industrial design in the Normal College of the metropolis. In 1880 she married Lorin F. Deland, of Boston, and went to Dorchester as a bride to begin housekeeping. Speaking of herself, Mrs. Deland has given the following naive account of her literary bent: "My early ambitions were divided between being a sculptor, an author, or a circus-rider, and the latter was secretly the most alluring. But I feared it would not be approved, and so I was resigned to the labor of authorship." Out of that resignation came the sleepy, delightful Old Chester village in a half-mythical region of Western Pennsylvania, where the inhabitants are a set of old-fashioned, well-bred gentlefolk, who are a hundred years behind the times. Foremost among the unworldly beings is the kind old clergyman, Doctor Lavender, who for forty years has tended his little flock in all their joys and sorrows. He is a real character-contribution to American literature. Mrs. Deland's first book was one of poems: The Old Garden and Other Verses (1886); this was succeeded by a series of novels and short stories, of which the following is a summary: John Ward, Preacher (1888); Florida Days (1889); Sidney (1890); Story of a Child (1892); Mr. Tommy Dove and Other Stories (1893); Philip and His Wife (1895); The Wisdom of Fools (1897); Old Chester Tales (1898); Dr. Lavender's People (1898); The Common Way (1904); *The Awakening of Helena Richie* (1906), and An Encore (1907).

De Massa, Alexandre Philippe Regnier, Marquis (Paris, Dec. 5, 1831). An army career appealed to him as a boy, and after being duly graduated at the military academy of St. Cyr,

he received a commission in the French cavalry. During the
first part of the Italian campaign he served in the Imperial
Guards, and subsequently took part in the Franco-Prussian
War, for which he was promoted, September 10, 1871, Captain
of the Fifth Regiment Chasseurs à Cheval. Before resigning
from active service he was brevetted, February 3, 1880, Lieutenant-Colonel of the territorial army, and was decorated with
the Legion of Honor. De Massa is well known in French
musical circles, as a gifted amateur composer. His operetta,
in two acts, Royale-Cravate, was produced on April 12, 1861,
at the Opéra Comique; and at the Conservatoire was sung
in May, 1865, the fragments of his opera, La Sposa Veneziana,
and also in March, 1868, his incomplete grand opera on
Dante in five acts was performed. A one-act comic opera,
Tout chemin mène à Rome, and other similar pieces, has been
given by society amateurs from time to time. He has written
a number of one-act comedies, among which are: Le Service
en campagne (1882); La cicatrice (1885); Au mont Ida (1887);
Fronsac à la Bastille (1887); Le Cœur de Paris (1887); La
Czarine (1888); Brouillée depuis Magenta (1888); and La
bonne aventure (1889). He also collaborated on a ballet,
Le Roi d'Yvetôt (1866), the music of which was composed
by Charles Labarre. *Zibeline* (1893), a novel crowned by
the French Academy, is a work showing its author's ability
in more serious and sustained guise.

De Maupassant, Henri René Albert Guy (Château de
Miromesnil, Department of the Seine-Inférieure, France,
Aug. 5, 1850; Paris, July 6, 1893). He received his education
at Yvetôt and the Rouen Lycée, and later was employed in
the Admiralty Office in Paris, where he served fifteen years.
He became a friend of Gustave Flaubert and frequented the
literary meetings that were held at Flaubert's house, where
he met Catulle Mendès, Léon Hennique, Émile Zola, Daudet,
Hérédia, Edmond and Jules de Goncourt, and others. He
submitted various literary sketches to Flaubert, who encouraged him and gave him much useful advice.

During seven years he served an apprenticeship to literature under the direction of Flaubert, who was his literary

godfather, but not until he was thirty years old and his master had died did he publish any writings.

In 1880 he issued Des Vers, a volume of poems which, although interesting and revealing a deeply poetic temperament, show that he was still hesitating in the choice of a medium of expression. Even his friends did not expect much from his talent, and when in the Soirées de Medan—a collection of stories by Zola, Hennique, and others—a tale appeared entitled Boule-de-Suif, signed by De Maupassant, it was a revelation. Then they saw the fruits of Flaubert's instruction, and that De Maupassant had become "the supreme master of the short story," as Brunetière characterized him. This first success was soon followed by another in the shape of a volume of short stories entitled La Maison Tellier. Then followed in quick succession a number of little masterpieces, many of which had been written before Flaubert's death. Some were frankly humorous, others psychological and dealing with subjects which in after years contributed to unbalance the author's mind.

After the appearance of Mademoiselle Fifi (1883) he began to write on a larger scale, and produced *Une Vie*, a novel in which he describes the life of a noble daughter, wife, and mother, who is most unfortunate in all these relations, vainly striving to uphold ideals which are ruthlessly shattered by the baseness of the people who surround her. Then appeared Les Contes de Becasse, a collection of stories as daring as they are clever. Au Soleil, a book of travels (1894), attracted less attention than Miss Harriet, Les Sœurs Rondoli, and Yvette, which were issued in the same year when De Maupassant's powers were climbing to their zenith. Contes de Nouvelles, Contes du Jour et de la Nuit, and Monsieur Parent were published in 1885 and showed that the writer's power of observation was as keen as ever. His striking novel *Bel-Ami* made its appearance in the same year and aroused a storm of criticism from its dealing with the worst phase of Parisian life, though treated in masterly fashion.

In Toine (1886) and Petite Louise Roque (1886) De Maupassant left for a while the study of complex characters and returned to the simple-minded folk he pictured with such success. After this he was less productive and went to various places in search of health. He wrote *Mont Oriol* (1887) as the result of his sojourn in Auvergne. It shows no diminution of his faculties, though Le Horla (1887) and Sur l'Eau (1888) reveal that he was subject to amazing hallucinations. The last-named book is a record of a cruise through the Mediterranean on the Yacht *Bel-Ami*, bought with and named after the proceeds of the novel. In it there is a description of one of the author's sleepless nights, due to overwork, which had become his curse. Having regained a semblance of health by this trip he again returned to work and produced Le Rosier de Madame Husson, a short story replete with the frankest humor; then *Pierre et Jean* (1888), Fort Comme la Mort (1889), and Notre Cœur (1890). These stories are splendid monuments to his genius. Although dealing with psychological problems, they appeal to the universal cry of humanity and show us a tenderer, more sympathetic strain than we are accustomed to find in his earlier writings. In Inutile Beauté (1890) this becomes even more marked, and Le Champ d'Oliviers is a masterpiece of emotional writing. La Vie Errante (1890) practically ended De Maupassant's literary career.

In his search for fame De Maupassant sacrificed health to overwork, and in order to counteract the effects he experimented with drugs. Not only did this undermine his constitution, but an inherited nervous derangement and intense suffering from neuralgia brought on a lesion of the brain, and for nearly two years before his death he was treated in a private sanitarium.

De Maupassant participated in the terrible times of 1870. The Franco-Prussian war broke out when he was barely twenty years old; he entered the ranks of the army, and his experiences suggested to him many of his most powerful stories.

During his brief career, in which he produced more than twenty-seven volumes, he amassed sufficient wealth to enable him to live in luxury. He owned a yacht and a small hôtel situated near the Parc Nouveau, which was the rendezvous of the prominent men of his period.

For a time he took a keen interest in religious problems, and the De Imitatione Christi became his handbook, but his pessimism grew worse and soon he began to suffer from delusions and became a paranoiac.   Then he went to Aix-les-Bains, and in the winter visited Cannes with his mother and brother in an effort to regain his health.   All proved useless, however; his derangement grew worse and more marked, necessitating resort to treatment for brain trouble.   He attempted to take his own life on January 6, 1892, and died the following year.   He is buried in the cemetery of Mont Parnasse. Among his papers were found La Paix du Ménage, a brilliant comedy in two acts, and two collections of short stories, Le Père Milon (1898) and Le Colporteur (1899), which were published posthumously.

De Mille, James (St. John, N. B., August 23, 1833; Halifax, N. S., Jan. 28, 1880).   The family of De Mille were probably of Loyalist origin, the first Demill or De Miltz coming from New York State.   James was the third child of his parents, and at an early age his father, a practical, sturdy ship-owner, put him in his counting-house.   Though the elder De Mille discouraged book-learning, James matriculated at Acadia College, in Wolfville, which afterward afforded material for his popular boys' books, the "B. O. W. C." series: The Boys of the Grand Pré School (1870); Lost in the Fog (1870); Fire in the Woods (1872); Picked up Adrift (1872); and The Treasure of the Seas (1873).   From Acadia College he went to Brown University, but his studies were interrupted by a tour in European waters in one of his father's ships.   Eighteen months were spent abroad, but of all the countries visited Italy impressed him the most, and this influence may be traced in almost every one of his tales.   In 1852 he resumed his studies at Brown, and was graduated in July, 1854.   Business reverses struck the family during the next few years, and in 1860 he was made professor of classics in his boyhood's college in Wolfville.   Here he remained for nearly five years, and then accepted the chair of history and rhetoric in Dalhousie College, Halifax, and held it until his death.   During his lifetime he was the widest read and the most prolific of Canadian writers.   Many of his stories are ultra-sensational, but sensational in the manner of Wilkie Collins, Eugène Sue, and

Charles Reade. As early as 1858 he began contributing to magazines in the United States. Very popular was The Dodge Club (1866); stories for boys, containing The Winged Lion, Among the Brigands, and other thrilling tales. *Cord and Creese* (1867) struck fire everywhere. Aside from his fiction, Elements of Rhetoric (1878) won appreciation for its genuine scholarship. Among his novels may be mentioned: Helena's Household (1858); The Martyr of the Catacombs (1858); Andy O'Hara (1860); John Wheeler's Two Uncles (1860); The American Baron (1869); The Lady of the Ice (1870); The Cryptogram (1871); A Comedy of Terrors (1872), Babes in the Wood (1874), The Living Link (1874), and A Strange Manuscript in a Copper Cylinder (1888).

De Musset, Alfred (Paris, France, Dec. 11, 1810; Paris, May 1, 1857). De Musset came of an ancient family, distinguished by the love of letters. A grand-uncle was a minstrel of the thirteenth century, and an uncle was the author of a notable romance. His father, M. de Musset-Pathay, possessed varied gifts, and from him Alfred inherited his talent for verse-making. On his mother's side he was no less fortunate. His maternal grandfather possessed a quick and poetic imagination, and was a skilful rhymer, if not a great poet. While very young Alfred was impressionable, excitable and very impatient. One day his mother did not dress him fast enough to suit him, and he exclaimed: "Be quicker, mamma, or my new red shoes will be old." At seven he devoured the One Thousand and One Nights, and lived in a world of magic thenceforward. He was an externe at the Henri IV School, and at twenty took the second prize in philosophy. He studied law, abandoned it for medicine, but soon decided to be a poet—"a man," he said, "of no kind in particular." The spirit of revolt against the classicism in which he had been trained was stirring within him, and his original mind was soon in conflict with his forerunners and some of his contemporaries. Shakespeare, Byron, Goethe, and Schiller excited his passionate devotion. While a youth he was introduced to Victor Hugo and became the youngest member of the Cénacle Romantique. He defied convention, and his literary productions received every variety of comment, from that of the Figaro, which found it difficult to consider his poems seriously, to that of the Globe, which pronounced him the only great poet in France. His last years were rendered miserable by the consciousness that his early decay was due to the errors of the past; but, by a singular chance, as his literary activity declined his waning popularity revived. During the Second Empire his fame was at its zenith. He was recognized as neither classicist nor romanticist, but as a man of no "school," an independent genius. But nothing could restore force to his will or strength to his body. Heine called him, at thirty, "a man with a splendid past." He died, an old man at the age of forty-seven, of disease of the heart. His works include: Confessions of an Opium-Eater, translated from De Quincey (Confessions d'un Mangeur d'Opium, 1828); A Venetian Night (Une nuit Vénetienne, 1830); Stories of Spain and Italy (Contes d'Espagne et d'Italie, 1832); Andrea del Sarto (André del Sarto, 1833); *Confession of a Child of the Century* (*Confession d'un enfant du siècle*, 1835); A Night in May (Une nuit de Mai, 1835); A Night in December (Une nuit de Décembre, 1835); The Two Mistresses (Les deux maîtresses); Mademoiselle Mimi Pinson; The White Blackbird (Le merle blanc).

De Quincey, Thomas (Greenhay, Manchester, England, August 15, 1785; Edinburgh, Scotland, December 8, 1859). He was the fifth child of a well-to-do-merchant, and his elementary education was received at a Bath grammar school, and later at a Manchester institution. To illustrate his precocious abilities: one of his masters remarked to a visitor that "that boy could harangue an Athenian mob better than you or I could address an English one." After his father's death he importuned his guardians to send him to Oxford, but they saw fit to procrastinate, and therefore, in 1802, young De Quincey escaped from their authority by running away with ten borrowed guineas, and a volume of Euripides in his pocket. North Wales was his goal, and he wandered there in the manner described in his Confessions of an English Opium-Eater, until his money gave out. Then he turned in the direction of London, and arrived there friendless as well as penniless. For sixteen weeks he roamed through the streets a vagrant dependent upon charity. His family at last located the runaway and he was forthwith sent to Worcester College, Oxford, where he led a singularly reserved and uncommunicative life, absorbed in the study of literature, until 1808, the year he quitted the university. During this period he had become acquainted with Charles Lamb (1804), and with Coleridge (1807), and in 1809 he leased the cottage of Grasmere, Westmoreland, where Wordsworth had lived. Here in the midst of the beautiful lake country he lived for nearly twenty years, becoming one of the famous "lake coterie" which included Wordsworth and Southey. Before he left Oxford he had become addicted to the habit of opium, originally used by him in 1804 to alleviate the pains of rheumatism and toothache. In 1813 a severe attack of stomach trouble forced him to increase the doses of the drug, which finally reached the appalling amount of eight thousand drops a day. Prior to his marriage, in 1816, he endeavored to shake off the vice, and his strong will eventually controlled it. In 1821 he began his Confessions of an English Opium-Eater, which appeared in the London Magazine, and the following year they were incorporated in a volume. From that time he busied himself with writing, and contributed to Tait's Magazine and Blackwood's, in the pages of which appeared his most brilliant essays. In 1843 he left Grasmere and removed first to Edinburgh, then to Lasswade, Mid-Lothian, within the environs of that city. De Quincey is in the front rank of essayists—witness Murder Considered as one of the Fine Arts (1827), Suspira de Profundis (1845), Joan of Arc (1847), The Vision of Sudden Death (1849). His historical speculations—Judas Iscariot, The Roman Meals, and On the Knocking at the Gate in Macbeth (1823)—are very original and brilliant conceptions. The biographical essays upon Shakespeare, Milton, Kant, Goldsmith, Wordsworth, and others are among the finest in any language. His striking novel of Russian life, *The Avenger*, had a great vogue in its day.

De Saint-Pierre, Jacques Henri Bernardin (Havre, France, Jan. 19, 1737; Éragny-sur-Oise, Jan. 21, 1814). When twelve years old he went with an uncle, who was captain of a merchant ship, on a voyage to Martinique, and on his return studied with the Jesuits at Caen and afterward at the College of Rouen. He was next a pupil at the School of Roads and Bridges, received the brevet of military engineer, and served for a time in that capacity in Hesse in 1760 and later in Malta. After various vicissitudes he entered the Russian army, and submitted to the Empress Catherine a scheme for establishing on the shores of the Caspian Sea a republic after the model of Plato, which proved a failure like other of his visionary conceptions.

He next joined Radziwill in Poland, where he had a love affair with a princess, and on her desertion went to Dresden, where he had another romantic adventure. On failing to get employment from Frederick the Great, he returned in 1766 to France, and shipped as an engineer for Madagascar. On discovering that the object of the expedition was the slave trade, he left it and remained at the Isle of France (Mauritius) till 1771, when he returned to Paris. These wanderings supplied him with his stock in trade, for, though he lived forty years more, he never again quitted France.

In Paris he was introduced to D'Alembert and his friends, but took little pleasure in the society of any but Rousseau, whose disciple he became and on whom he founded his literary style. His first publication, Voyage à l'Île de France (1773), gained him some reputation, but his Études de la Nature (1783–'84) was an immense success. Poor and unknown the evening before, he became almost in a moment the popular idol. He was then forty-seven years old.

A convinced deist, like his master, Rousseau, he opposed in this work the popular atheism, endeavoring to prove the divine foresight by sentimental and poetical ideas of the grand spectacle of the harmony of the universe. The savants treated him as a visionary poet, and disdained to reply to him. He was much displeased at their attitude, and complained one day to the First Consul of their significant silence.

"Do you understand the differential calculus?" asked Bonaparte.

"No."

"Ah! go and learn it, and you will refute yourself."

In 1788 he published the work which has given him lasting fame, *Paul and Virginia*, a story which has been translated into many languages, and is the subject of plays and operas in French, Italian, Spanish, German, and English. The scene is chiefly in Mauritius.

If we are to believe Aimé Martin, the author's biographer, *Paul et Virginie* received so chilling a reception when it was read one evening at Madame Necker's that St. Pierre went home with the intention of burning the manuscript. But his friend, the painter Vernet, happening in, asked him to read it to him, and showed such enthusiasm at the recital, declaring it to be a *chef-d'œuvre*, that the author decided to publish it. It was at once so successful that, notwithstanding many spurious editions, it soon brought him money enough to buy a house. While French critics have pronounced its style agreeable and charming, and claimed for it a true immortality, some have called it gaudy and unwholesome in tone. Still others have suggested that the exuberant sensibility of the time found in it an equally exuberant expression.

In 1791 St. Pierre published La chaumière indienne (The Indian Cottage), a philosophical and moral story, full of grace and marked by a love of humanity and a delicate and touching sensibility characteristic of his writings. Bonaparte wrote him from Italy: "Your pen is a painter's pencil; everything it depicts, we see. Your works charm and console us." Under the Consulate St. Pierre received a pension and a residence in the Louvre. In 1792-'93 he was director of the Jardin des Plantes, in 1794 professor of morals at the École Normale, and in 1795 became a member of the Institute.

In 1792 St. Pierre married Félicité Didot, a very young girl, and by her had two children, whom he named Paul and Virginia. His wife died early and he married a second time, in 1800, another young girl, Desirée de Pelleport, with whom he is said to have lived very happily. He died at his home at Éragny, where he resided in his later years. His Harmonies de la nature was published the year after his decease. Aimé Martin, who married his widow, published (1818-'20) his complete works, with a biographical sketch.

In 1852 a monumental statue in bronze, by David d'Angers,

was erected to him in Havre. Bernardin, in Directoire costume, is seated, holding in his right hand a pen and in the left a manuscript inscribed *Paul et Virginie*. At his feet two nude children, a boy and a girl, are sleeping under a tropical palm.

De Staël, Germaine Necker, Baronne (Paris, France, April 22, 1766; Paris, July 13, 1817). The family of Madame de Staël was of Irish origin, but her parents were by birth citizens of the republic of Geneva, and she was a true Parisienne, both by birth and temperament. Her precocity was such that at eleven years of age she was one of the attractions of Madame Necker's salon. It was said of her that she was silent in these years for the rest of her life. Never did a child have greater opportunities for development, and never could they have been more effective. At fifteen she prepared an abstract of her father's Compte rendue, and wrote an essay: The Revocation of the Edict of Nantes. Rousseau was her first idol, and "Werther," she said, "made an epoch in my life." That she should make a great marriage was the desire of her parents, and a suitable husband was found in the Baron de Staël-Holstein, Ambassador from Sweden. He was seventeen years older than she, and there was no love on either side. But the Baron was pleased to pay his debts with the dowry of the banker's daughter, and Germaine, although longing for love, longed also for political distinction, and this marriage gratified her ambition. She became Baronne de Staël in 1786. Catherine of Russia wrote "that the daughter of Necker had made a very unfortunate marriage." But although unhappy, Germaine was not melancholy. She opened at the Swedish embassy a salon which at once rivaled her mother's, and became a feature in the history of the France of the Revolution. The events of this period developed her patriotism and opened to her a new career—that of politics. She entered upon this rôle with such intensity that she became *persona non grata* to the Provisional Government, and was requested to leave Paris, which she did in 1795. Twice she returned and attempted to resume her old life, but she found only the débris of her beloved city. Finally, after meeting Bonaparte, who, with his eyes of steel made her feel as if she could not breathe in his presence, and who hated her and feared her influence, she was definitely forbidden to come within forty leagues of Paris. She turned for diversion to the education of her children, and to her pen. The Baron de Staël died in 1802. Benjamin Constant, long an admirer, offered himself in marriage to Madame de Staël, but she declined. In 1804 she experienced the greatest sorrow of her life in the death of her father. She turned to religion for consolation, and sought distraction in travel. In every country which she visited she sought, and was sought by, persons of the highest distinction. In 1810 she married Albert de Rocca, a French officer, twenty-one years younger than herself. She kept the marriage and her child thereby concealed during her lifetime, but M. de Rocca followed her, and his love not only soothed her last days, but gave her, perhaps, the sweetest happiness of her life. She returned to Paris in 1814 and resumed, to a degree, her former gaiety, but she was weakened by trouble, and was stricken with paralysis one evening at a ball. She died as she had wished, in her sleep. Her works are not numerous, the most notable being: Lettres sur Rousseau (1789); Reflections on the Trial of the Queen (1793); Reflections on Internal Peace (1795); On the Influence of the Passions (1796); Literature in its Relations to Social Institutions (1800); *Corinne* (1805); Germany (1810).

De Vigny, Alfred, Comte (Loches, France, March 27, 1797; Paris, Sept. 17, 1863). The family of De Vigny was ancient and noble; his father was an officer in the French army, and his mother the daughter of the Chief of Squadrons of the Royal Marine. He was sent to college at Paris very young, and his experience there was not happy. The college atmosphere, he says, left a tinge of melancholy in his spirit which never was effaced. Napoleon was the idol of all the youths, and the vision of the Emperor, with his twelve Marshals, his guard, and his *grande armée*, filled De Vigny's sleeping and waking dreams. "The drums," he cried, "deafened my ears to the voices of the masters!" After much urging he obtained permission to enter the army, and soon he was brevetted sublieutenant. The unsettled days of 1814 and 1815 disillusioned him. Instead of victorious marches he had to endure camp life, but its monotony turned his attention to literary production. He was a voracious reader, the Old Testament, the ancient philosophers, and Homer being his favorites. He translated Homer from the Greek into English. He became a conspicuous member of the Cénacle Romantique, and a contributor to its Review, La Muse Française. Between himself and Victor Hugo an intimacy sprang up, and Sainte-Beuve lauded him in phrases of almost absurd eulogy. He was ordered to Spain in 1829. There, again, he was doomed to inaction, to relieve which he wrote his fine historical novel, Cinq-Mars, the first appearance, since Chateaubriand and Madame de Staël, of a great prose romance. In 1825 he married a beautiful English girl, Miss Lydia Bunbury, and at that period he gave assiduous attention to the English writers. It became the aim of the Cénacle to produce Shakespeare at the Théâtre Française, and in 1829 De Vigny put Othello on the stage in verse. The habitués of the Rue Richelieu were shocked by the bold realism of pronouncing the word "handkerchief" instead of such delicate synonyms as *fine linen*, or something even more ambiguous. But the blow was struck and a new era dawned on the French stage. De Vigny's hour of greatest triumph came, however, in 1835, at the presentation of his play entitled Chatterton, a drama of the life of the unhappy boy poet. In 1845 he was elected to the French Academy, and a life of literary and social honors seemed before him. But he withdrew from the public, and even his intimate friends never were able to reawaken his interest in the outside world. A profound pessimism dominated his spirit. He lived in a Platonic world of ideas, and became enamored of his own conceptions. "Oh, my Muse!" he wrote, "why must I live apart from thee?" The problems of the universe he met neither with resignation nor with despair, but with silence. "Let us reply only by silence to the cold silence of Divinity," he said. In this seclusion he produced an occasional work of rare beauty. His style was chaste, his spirit sincere, his taste perfect. He elevated the tone of his literary period by proclaiming Truth to be the only worthy object of Art. He justly claimed for himself the distinction of being the first poet to put philosophic thought into epic or dramatic form. He created philosophic poetry in France. His lingering death from cancer he met with heroic patience. Among his works may be mentioned: The Dryad (Symétha); Poems (1822); Eloa: or, The Sister of an Angel (1822); Moses (1826); *Cinq-Mars* (1826); Othello (translation, 1829); Stello (1832); Grandeur et Servitude Militaires (1835); The Journal of a Poet (1867), published after his death.

Dickens, Charles John Huffham, commonly called Charles Dickens (Landport, near Portsmouth, Feb. 7, 1812; June 9, 1870). His life resembles, in one respect, that of many remarkable men. He began at the very bottom of the ladder, his earlier years being passed in the midst of much misery and hardship. Of social advantages he had none. He was, as a boy, sadly neglected, while his education was of the scantiest. But this neglect could not affect the power of his genius or retard his ultimate triumph. His success, when it did come, was startling in its suddenness, striking in its completeness. When the *Pickwick Papers* first appeared he was but twenty-four years of age. Before that time he had written sketches which had attracted considerable attention in the literary world, but upon the publication of the sixth number of *Pickwick* he leaped at once into the front rank of British humorists and secured a popularity that was not only unique in itself but continued with unabated force down to the day of his death —and afterward.

His father, John Dickens, was a clerk in the Navy Pay Office, and at the time of Charles Dickens's birth was employed at Portsmouth. From there he was moved to Chatham, where Charles was fortunate enough in being sent to a small school kept by a Mr. Giles, for whom he had a great affection. But these pleasant school-days were of very short duration. In the year 1821 his father and his family moved from Chatham to Bayham Street, Camden Town, and from that time for some years the child's education was absolutely and entirely neglected. This was a time of misery and wretchedness for the whole family. In 1822 his father was imprisoned in the Marshalsea Debtors' Prison. But the climax of the boy's wretchedness was reached when he was put to the work of a drudge at Warren's Blacking establishment in the Strand, and was there employed to tie up blacking-bottles for a small weekly pittance.

Of this period of his life Dickens speaks feelingly in a short autobiography. "No words can express the secret agony of my soul as I sank into this companionship and felt my early hopes of growing up to be a learned and distinguished man crushed in my breast. I know that I have lounged about the streets insufficiently and unsatisfactorily fed. I know that, but for the mercy of God, I might easily have been, from any care that was taken of me, a little robber, a little vagabond. No advice, no counsel, no encouragement, no consolation, no support from anyone that I can call to mind, so help me God!" So sad and distressing to him was the memory of these days that he never whispered a word concerning them to any of his children, who knew of them for the first time after his death. That they left their mark upon him there can be no doubt or question, and to this is probably due his sympathy with the poor and suffering, the tenderness in his descriptions of struggling or neglected childhood.

In 1824 he attended for a short time a school in the Hampstead Road, and subsequently for a short time a school kept by a Mr. Dawson; but it is undoubtedly true of him to say that he educated himself.

In 1827-'28 he became a clerk in an attorney's office, after which he began the study of shorthand and was a constant attendant at the British Museum, and in 1831 he entered the gallery of the House of Commons as a reporter for the True Sun, where he remained for several years. In 1834 he published his first piece of writing, which he stealthily dropped one evening in a dark letter-box up a dark court in Fleet Street and was subsequently so overjoyed to find it appear in all the glory of print that he turned down into Westminster Hall for half an hour because his eyes were so dimmed with joy and pride that they could not bear the street and were not fit to be seen there.

This was the first of a number of sketches in the Monthly Magazine, which were published in 1834 and 1835 under the title Sketches by Boz, and which met with much success. But it was in the following year that his name first became known to the world.   On March 31, 1836, appeared the first number of the *Pickwick Papers*—the first of many series of small green volumes which were for years looked forward to with interest and even with excitement.   But though the new venture was received with favor it was not until the appearance of Sam Weller in the sixth number that the work really seized upon the fancy of the public.   It had been intended, in the first instance, that the papers should form a vehicle for Seymour's plates; but Seymour died by his own hand quite early in the production, and it only remained for "Phiz," who took his place, to become an admirable illustrator of the youthful genius who literally took the world by storm.   For Part I the binder prepared four hundred copies; for Part XV the number had grown to forty thousand, and its popularity was daily increasing.

Perhaps a son is not the best critic of his father's work. But it may be of interest to attempt to give some kind of idea of the comparative popularity of his various novels.   *Pickwick Papers* has naturally been considered by many as the foremost and most popular work written by Dickens.   So far as its popularity is concerned, this cannot be gainsaid, but from the point of view of the critic it is much to be doubted whether it can be said to be his masterpiece.   John Forster, his biographer, who was a writer of great ability and a critic of profound judgment, did not take this view.   He does not regard it as comparable to many of his later books.   Its popularity depended upon the freshness and the originality of its humor, the novelty of its methods, the breadth of its characterization. The real pathos of his humor was not displayed until a later period—there was none of the dramatic strength which was so marked a characteristic of *Martin Chuzzlewit, Dombey and Son, A Tale of Two Cities,* and *Great Expectations,* while the grim tragedy of life had yet to be portrayed in *Oliver Twist.* And yet *Pickwick* must always stand out as being the book that made him famous, and, after all, it is the one that probably has been more generally read than any work he ever wrote.   At one of the early dinners of the Boz Club—a club formed for the purpose of perpetuating his memory, which meets at an annual dinner on the 7th of February—a discussion took place as to which were the two best of Dickens's books. The company comprised many literary men of note, and the views entertained were curious and conflicting. *Pickwick* was placed *hors concours* as being from its very nature not comparable with the other works. *David Copperfield* was by general accord placed first on the list, not only for its literary merit but also for the great interest attached to it by reason of its personal association with the author's own life. There was much discussion upon the question as to which book was to be placed second in order of merit. Some were for *Dombey and Son, Martin Chuzzlewit* had many advocates, while *Hard Times* was strongly supported; but in the end the choice fell upon *Great Expectations*, and it is interesting to note that this was the view taken by Dickens himself.

In 1836 he wrote a short pamphlet entitled Sunday under Three Heads, under the pseudonym of "Timothy Sparks," of which, curiously enough, no mention is made by his biographer. In the same year he wrote the story and words for the opera The Village Coquette, which was set to music by John Hullah, and a farce called The Strange Gentleman, which was founded upon one of his sketches.

A few days after the publication of the first number of *Pickwick Papers*, namely, April 2, 1836, Charles Dickens married Catherine, eldest daughter of George Hogarth, a well-known musical critic. The young couple began their married life at Furnival's Inn, moving shortly afterward to Doughty Street. In 1837 he edited The Life of Grimaldi, the Clown. On January 8, 1838, he appears to have published anonymously some papers called The Sketches of Young Gentlemen and Sketches of Young Couples, but of these again no mention is made in Forster's Life. The years 1838-'39 found him engaged on *Nicholas Nickleby*, for which he was paid three thousand pounds for five years' use of the copyright, which was to revert to him at the expiration of that period. The first number had a circulation of fifty thousand. Of *Nicholas Nickleby* it may be noted that so ruthless was his attack upon the Yorkshire schools that he was threatened with actions for libel at the suit of various schoolmasters who obligingly fitted on the cap which they assumed had been presented for their acceptance. It is also significant that Dickens is seen, thus early in his career, appealing for the sympathy of his readers in favor of the suffering and oppressed, through the medium of the story of the miserable Smike; a story which, in its tenderness and pathos, surely never was excelled by anything he ever wrote. But meanwhile, and prior to the conclusion of this work, the publication of *Oliver Twist* was begun. While the book had a very wide and extensive sale, attacks were directed against its subject. Its atmosphere was degrading, it was said—its characters were drawn from the dregs of society. A strange commentary to pass upon a novel which everyone at the present day admits was one of the strongest factors in the abolition of the villainous poor-law system which then prevailed, and which was written with the purpose of showing the hideousness of crime and of demonstrating how innocence can conquer in the face of the most terrible temptations.

In 1840 and 1841 *The Old Curiosity Shop* was published, at first in the pages of Master Humphrey's Clock (a periodical that did not enjoy a very long existence) and subsequently in weekly parts. This form of publication proved to be extremely fatiguing, but in spite of this Dickens in one of his letters describes how he fairly reveled in the anticipation of Dick Swiveller. The success of this book was extraordinary, the pathetic vein being far more prominent than in any of the preceding works. The tribute paid to it by Bret Harte in 1870, in the poem entitled "Dickens in Camp," pathetic as it was in itself, demonstrated in a marked degree the effect of Dickens's pathos upon others.

In 1840 he took up his residence in Devonshire Terrace, and from time to time paid periodical visits to his favorite little house on the cliff at Broadstairs in the county of Kent. In 1841 he edited the Pic Nic Papers in which he published The Lamplighter—neither of which calls for more than passing mention.

In the same year *Barnaby Rudge* made its appearance. This indeed was in striking contrast to anything he had previously written. Its plot and its scene were laid in the time of the Lord George Gordon riots. The period of the novel was not of his own time, and in this respect it resembles Dickens's other historical book, *A Tale of Two Cities*, which dealt with the French Revolution and owed its origin largely to the influence exercised upon him by Carlyle's great work. While *The Old Curiosity Shop* may be said to have shown for the first time to its fullest extent his power of pathos, *Barnaby Rudge* probably was the first novel in which he gave full scope to his powers of description.

In January, 1842, he paid his first memorable visit to the United States. His welcome was enthusiastic in the highest degree, and he was publicly entertained in New York by all the prominent people of the day. Dickens was deeply impressed by this reception, but as time went on there was much that he saw that did not meet with his unqualified approval. The first difficulty arose when he boldly and in strong language inveighed against the absence of any international copyright —an absence from which no man probably suffered more than he did himself. He thus brought down upon himself from some quarters a great deal of violent abuse. Another feature which impressed him very strongly was the want of freedom of opinion in the country. "There is no country on the face of the earth," he writes, "where there is less freedom of opinion on any subject in reference to which there is a broad difference of opinion than this." No doubt the point which most painfully impressed him was the utter want of privacy and quiet which he experienced during his stay. But he made many dear friends, including Washington Irving and Longfellow, while there was much that he could praise without reserve. His criticisms, in short, are contained in the pages of *Martin Chuzzlewit* and American Notes; and though at the time some hostility was displayed toward him in the country, this did not affect the warmth of his reception upon the occasion of his second visit, in 1867.

By many Americans it was thought that his criticism, though possibly harsh, was not wholly undeserved; and even those who took a somewhat different view had long before satisfied themselves that it was at least honest; while it is quite within the bounds of probability that the comparative immaturity of Dickens's judgment may have had something to do with the intensity of the impressions left upon his mind. His experiences in the United States on this second occasion filled Dickens with amazement. He was not only touched by the generous cordiality of his welcome, but he could hardly have believed that any country in so short a time as twenty-five years could have made such marvelous strides. In the course of a speech in New York at a public dinner given to him prior to his departure, at which Horace Greeley presided, he gave the fullest possible expression to his feelings of astonishment and admiration, and every edition of *Martin Chuzzlewit* which has since been issued contains a preface to the same effect.

American Notes appeared in 1842, and *Martin Chuzzlewit* followed it in the next year. This has generally been regarded as one of the best of his works, while Dickens himself, writing to Forster, said: "You know as well as I that I think *Chuzzlewit* in a hundred points immeasurably the best of my stories—that I feel my power now more than I ever did." And yet, strange to say, the original circulation was most disappointing. The circulation of *Pickwick Papers* had been forty thousand, *Nicholas Nickleby* fifty thousand, *The Old Curiosity Shop* and *Barnaby Rudge* sixty thousand, and yet that of *Martin Chuzzlewit* reached barely twenty thousand. It is difficult to gauge the reason for this, as since then its sale has not fallen far short of that of either *Pickwick* or *David Copperfield*.

Just before Christmas, 1843, appeared the Christmas Carol, which made a very marked impression among all classes. "Who can listen," wrote Thackeray, "to objections regarding such a book as this? It seems to me a national benefit, and to every man or woman who reads it a personal kindness." To the mind of the present writer it has always presented itself as the most perfect and touching sermon that ever has been written.

In 1844 Dickens went to Italy, staying for many months at Genoa, during which time he wrote the second of his Christmas stories, The Chimes. The writing of this story appears to have affected Dickens very greatly, the subject of it being one very dear to his heart, while the book itself has the added interest of having a material bearing upon a very prominent feature in Dickens's life.   On November 30, 1844, he gave a private reading of The Chimes to a party which included John Forster, Daniel Maclise, R.A., Clarkson Stanfield, R.A., Douglas Jerrold, the well-known humorist, and Thomas Carlyle. This was undoubtedly the origin of those dramatic readings which at a subsequent stage of his life Dickens gave in public and which showed in a remarkable degree his powers as an actor, but the strain of which seriously affected his physical strength and tended sensibly to shorten his life.

At Christmas, 1845, The Cricket on the Hearth was published, its circulation doubling that of both the previous Christmas stories.   The same year witnessed the beginning of his connection with the Daily News, of which for a time he was editor, though this connection did not last for more than a few months.

The Pictures from Italy were written at about this time, and in 1846 Dickens took up his abode at Lausanne, in Switzerland, where he remained for many months.   The year 1846 also saw the beginning of *Dombey and Son*.   There is a curious little story in connection with this novel.   As he was beginning it Dickens one day took hold of a book from a box he was then unpacking and said: "Now, whatever passage my thumb rests on, I shall take as having reference to my work."   The book was Sterne's Tristram Shandy, and it opened at these words: "What a work it is likely to turn out!   Let us begin it!"   This prophecy would appear to have been amply fulfilled, because the book was received with high favor, and Lord Jeffrey, a man of rare refinement and literary instinct, seems to have uttered the popular feeling when he wrote to Dickens: "Oh, my dear, dear Dickens, what a Number Five you have given us!   I have so cried and sobbed over it, and felt my heart purified by these tears, and blessed and loved you for making me shed them, and I never can bless and love you enough."

The Haunted Man was written in 1848, while in 1850 he established Household Words, a weekly periodical which, either under that name or in its altered form of All the Year Round, enjoyed a large circulation to the time of his death. He had surrounded himself with a brilliant band of writers who worked most loyally under the editorship of "The Chief" as they loved to call him; while the subjects touched upon were infinite in their variety and scope of treatment.

The year 1849 was a memorable one, for it was in this year that Dickens wrote his masterpiece, *David Copperfield.* This was written first at Broadstairs and subsequently at Bonchurch, Isle of Wight. His whole heart and soul were thrown into this book. Of this we find interesting evidence in his contemporaneous letters. "I feel a great hope that I shall be remembered by Little Em'ly a good many years to come." Again, "I have been very hard at work and have still Dora to kill." On another occasion he writes: "Oh, my dear Forster, if I were to say half of what Copperfield makes me feel to-night how strangely, even to you, I should be turned inside out! I seem to be sending some part of myself into the Shadowy World."

The popularity which this work attained at the outset increased to a degree not approached by any previous book excepting *Pickwick Papers*, and the sale has, with the same exception, since taken the lead of all his books. In this novel all his powers were brought into full play—humor, pathos, sentiment, strength of characters, and great dramatic power. At a much later period of his life—in October, 1860—Dickens writes: "I read *David Copperfield* again the other day, and was affected by it to a degree you would hardly believe."

In November, 1851, at Tavistock House, he began *Bleak House.* The keynote of this story was undoubtedly the exposure of the abuses and delays in the Court of Chancery; but beyond that the plot was a strong one and the characters were striking in their contrast and in the difference of their types—Lady Dedlock, Guppy, Chadband, Miss Flite, Tulkinghorn, Poor Jo. Of Jo, Dean Ramsay wrote: "To my mind nothing in the field of fiction is to be found in English literature to surpass the death of Jo." This book was completed at Boulogne, where the author spent three or four happy summers in the country villa he loved so well.

The consideration of *Bleak House* opens up a subject which can conveniently be touched upon here. The book contained a scathing and bitter attack upon the hypocrisy of religion and of the cant connected therewith. This was not the first time Dickens had dwelt on this theme. He had harped upon the same string very loudly when drawing the character of Stiggins in *Pickwick*. One would have thought that none of his readers could possibly have misjudged his views or mistaken his intentions, and yet, strange to say, he was regarded by a small portion of the community, who apparently wholly failed to understand his purpose, as a man who was personally devoid of all religious feeling. After the Staplehurst railway accident, from which he barely escaped with his life on June 9, 1865, he received letters to the effect that this was a punishment upon him for his want of faith. Nothing was so unfair, nothing could have been so grotesquely untrue. The following extract from a letter by him to the present writer will suffice to show what the real state of his feelings in religious matters was: "As your brothers have gone away, one by one, I have written to each of them what I am now going to write to you. You know that you have never been hampered with religious forms of restraint, and that with mere unmeaning forms I have no sympathy. But I most strongly and affectionately impress upon you the priceless value of the New Testament and the study of that book as the one unfailing guide in life. Deeply respecting it, and bowing down before the character of Our Saviour as separated from vain constructions and inventions of men, you cannot go very wrong and will always preserve at heart a true spirit of veneration and humility."

Of *Hard Times*, which was published in 1854, Mr. Ruskin wrote: "The essential value and truth of Dickens's writings have been unwisely lost sight of by many thoughtful persons, merely because he presents his truth with some color of caricature. Unwisely, because Dickens's caricature, though often gross, is never mistaken. Allowing for his manner of telling them, the things he tells us are always true. I wish that he could think it right to limit his brilliant exaggeration to works written only for public amusement, and when he takes up a subject of high national importance, such as that which he handled in *Hard Times*, that he would use severer and more accurate analysis. The usefulness of that work (to my mind, in several respects the greatest he has written) is with many persons seriously diminished because Mr. Bounderby is a dramatic monster instead of a characteristic example of a worldly master; and Stephen Blackpool a dramatic perfection, instead of a characteristic example of an honest workman. But let us not lose the use of Dickens's wit and insight because he chooses to speak in a circle of stage fire. He is entirely right in his main drift and purpose in every book he has written, and all of them, but especially *Hard Times*, should be studied with close and honest care by persons interested in social questions."

It was in this year that he returned to London to preside at a dinner given to Thackeray on his going to lecture in the United States, thanking him in his speech, in the name of thousands who never had touched his hand or seen his face, for the treasures which were contained within the yellow-covered numbers of *Pendennis* and *Vanity Fair*. Dickens and Thackeray had been old friends, and the estrangement that took place between them in 1858, arising out of a quarrel between Thackeray and another member of a club, which was referred to the committee of which Dickens was one, never had the effect of weakening their mutual respect, which is touchingly evidenced in an article written by Dickens which appeared in the Cornhill Magazine of February, 1864, just after Thackeray's death. Indeed, it is delightful to remember that they had been reconciled shortly before that time.

In 1853, 1854, and 1856 Dickens was at Boulogne, and the winter of 1855-'56 he spent in Paris. During that time he wrote the short stories of Richard Doubledick and Boots at the Holly Tree Inn.

At Christmas, 1855, the first number of *Little Dorrit* appeared, and its circulation was such that on New Year's Day alone thirty-five thousand copies of the second number were bought by the public. "*Little Dorrit* has beaten even *Bleak House* out of the field," he writes. "It is a most tremendous start, and I am overjoyed at it."

The political element is more pronounced here than in any of his previous works. Dickens was no lover of the House of Commons. He had, in fact, declined to become a member, and in the description of the Circumlocution Office he severely satirizes the political vices of the time. The sale of this book was large, and yet it cannot be regarded as one of his most successful efforts. During the writing of this novel he appears to have suffered from a temporary weakening in his inventive powers, a fact which gave him some uneasiness, for from that time for some years he kept a book of memoranda, in which he jotted down ideas as they occurred to his mind.

In the spring of 1856 he completed the purchase of Gad's Hill, near Rochester, in the county of Kent. Visions of his becoming its owner had suggested themselves to his youthful mind when still quite a small boy, and he seized with avidity the chance which enabled him to secure the object of his ambition. The enjoyment he derived from this little estate was infinite. He simply loved the life which he lived there, and nothing gave him greater pleasure than to share that delight with his friends. He was ever planning fresh improvements. He used laughingly to say to his daughter Katey: "Now, Katey, you see positively the *last* improvement at Gad's Hill." April 29, 1858, he gave his first public reading. There had been for some time previously much discussion as to the advisability of his thus appearing in public, but the dramatic instinct in him was too strong to be resisted, and his mind was made up. The first series extended over the years 1858–'59; the second during the years 1861–'63; the third during 1866–'67 (including his American readings); the last from 1868–'70.

About the time he began his public readings he was separated from his wife. Upon this episode of his life there is no need to dwell; suffice it to say—and this must be said—that his wife left her husband without the slightest reproach or blame, and retained the affection and regard of her children until her death in 1879.

In the year 1859 Household Words came to an end, and All the Year Round was established in its place. Its first number was published on April 30th of that year, and contained the opening chapters of *A Tale of Two Cities*. In the following year the papers entitled The Uncommercial Traveller were published in the same periodical, as was at a later date a short tale called Hunted Down.

Of *A Tale of Two Cities* it may fairly be said that it is one of his greatest dramatic creations, and its interest is so intense and absorbing that one hardly misses the usual touch of humor. Of Sydney Carton, Mr. Richard Grant White, an American critic, wrote: "There is not a grander, lovelier figure than the self-wrecked, self-devoted Sydney Carton in literature or history; and the story itself is so noble in its spirit, so grand and graphic in its style, and filled with a pathos so profound and simple, that it deserves and will surely take a place among the great serious works of imagination."

In December, 1860, the first chapters of *Great Expectations* appeared. This also was published in the columns of All the Year Round. *Great Expectations* was undoubtedly one of Dickens's favorite works. The humor of it appears to have appealed to him strongly. "You will not have to complain of the want of humor, as in the *Tale of Two Cities*," he writes. "I have made the opening, I hope, in its general effect, exceedingly droll." This sense of humor was undoubtedly shared by his public. Joe Gargery, Uncle Pumblechook, Wemmick, Jaggers, and Trabbs's boy were received with acclamation. But there was much in the book beyond its mere humorous side. The central motive was strong. The selfishness of Pip when he came into his "expectations" from an unknown friend; his surprise and horror when he first knew the degraded source from which his riches came; his gradual regeneration and softening through his association with his strange benefactor, the "low" but patient convict, were worked out with the greatest skill and effect, while the treatment of the dramatic scenes was recognized as being in his best vein.

This book was followed by three short stories contained in the Christmas numbers of All the Year Round for the years 1862, 1863, and 1864, entitled Somebody's Luggage, Mrs. Lirriper's Lodgings, and Mrs. Lirriper's Legacy; while in May, 1864, he began the publication of *Our Mutual Friend*, which came out in the old shape of twenty green bound numbers. Here again he did not move as quickly as in former years. "I have grown hard to satisfy, and write very slowly," he wrote. "Yesterday and the day before I could do nothing; seemed for the time to have quite lost the power; and am only by slow degrees getting back into the track to-day." Forster's view of this book was that though it has fancy, descriptive power, and the characters are well designed, it never will rank with his higher efforts. This criticism may be correct, though Mr. Forster would himself have probably admitted that many of its readers set a much higher value on the book than he did himself.

In 1865, 1866, and 1867 he wrote some more short stories in the Christmas numbers of All the Year Round, called Dr. Marigold's Prescriptions, Barbox Brothers, Mugby Junction, and No Thoroughfare (in collaboration with Wilkie Collins).

In November, 1867, he revisited the United States for the purpose of giving a series of public readings there. This he did solely in the interests of his children, but strongly against their expressed desire, having regard to the fatigue the enterprise must necessarily involve. Of his reception, of his appreciation of it, and of his experiences there, mention has already been made. While contracting many new friendships, he was forced to forbid himself the pleasure of much social enjoyment. His success was triumphant. His audiences were crowded and enthusiastic. The financial result speaks for itself. Between the months of November, 1867, and March, 1868, he made the large sum of twenty thousand pounds. But this was at the expense of much fatigue and suffering. He was throughout ill and overwrought, very often quite unfit even to go upon the platform, and constantly on the verge of breaking down, a calamity, indeed, which was averted only by the exercise of great courage and determination on his part. However, his labors came to an end at last, and in the final week of April, 1868, he sailed for home.

While in the United States he wrote two short papers for publication there: George Silverman's Explanations and a juvenile story in four parts, entitled A Holiday Romance, for which he received the large sum of a thousand pounds. In October, 1868, he began his last series of readings in England, but he was without doubt failing rapidly and the strain upon him was too heavy to bear. On one occasion in February, 1869, his doctor forbade his going upon the platform, and though he struggled on during the month of March his symptoms became so alarming in April that his readings had to be abandoned. But in spite of this, in July he was occupied in the working out of the idea for his new book *The Mystery of Edwin Drood*, which was to be published in twenty numbers as before. It is greatly to be regretted, from a literary point of view, that this work was left unfinished and that the mystery remained unsolved at the last, for there was much in it which approached his very best work.

The beginning of the year 1870 found him no better in health. In March he had an interview with her Majesty Queen Victoria, at her request. In the course of this interview she asked him to give her his writings, and in return her Majesty gave him her own book, My Life in the Highlands, with an autograph inscription: "To Charles Dickens," saying at the same time that the humblest of writers would be ashamed to offer it to "one of the greatest," but added that when Mr. Arthur Helps had been asked to give it, he had remarked that it would be valued most from herself. On March 26th, at the Queen's desire, he attended a levée, and a little later he met the Prince of Wales (his present Majesty the King) at dinner. During February and March he struggled through twelve additional readings, the last being on March 15th, when he took farewell of his reading audiences forever. His last appearance in public was at the annual dinner of the Royal Academy, on April 30th, at which he returned thanks for Literature, and took the opportunity of passing a glowing eulogy on his old and valued friend Daniel Maclise, R.A., who had passed away only three days before.

On June 8th he was occupied upon the sixth number of *Edwin Drood*, which he completed in the afternoon. He then wrote some letters, among others one to the writer of this sketch, and went in to dinner. No one was at Gad's Hill at the time except his sister-in-law, Georgina Hogarth, his dear and well-tried friend, and it was not until they sat down to table that she saw by his face that something was very seriously wrong with him. During dinner he was seized with a fit and fell to the ground. His children were hastily summoned, but he never spoke again and died at six o'clock on the evening of June 9th. A fitting end, among the surroundings which he loved so well, at the very zenith of his career.   On June 14th he was quietly laid to rest in Poets' Corner, Westminster Abbey, his funeral being kept strictly private.

Dickens was very regular in his habits of work, but very uncertain in execution.   He could not, as was the case with some of his contemporaries, sit down and write page after page of copy.   On some occasions the facility with which he wrote was great; but on others a page or even less was the most that he could produce.   But though the amount of work in a day, as represented by actual results, was very often small, it may be truly said that his mind was always at work.

After his regular hours, which were usually from ten till two, he was in the habit of taking very long walks into the country.   The present writer has walked with him sometimes for three hours at a stretch without a word passing his lips, during which time his conceptions were gradually developing themselves in his mind.   He had a singular belief in the reality of his own creations.   They were to him living and moving pictures.   This is curiously exemplified in the advice he gave to a young writer in whom he was interested.   "If you do not yourself believe in what you are describing you will never get your readers to do so.   For myself I can as distinctly see before my eyes the scene which I am describing as I can see you now.   So much so has this been the case with me that on one occasion, in which I had laid out a certain path which one of my characters was to pursue, that character took hold of me and persuaded me to make him do exactly the opposite to what I had originally intended; but I was so sure that he must be right and I wrong that I let him have his own way."

Work, and hard work, was of the very essence of his being. He loved it, he lived for it, his fame was greatly due to it.   It may be truly said of him that from the time he wrote *Pickwick Papers* unto the end he was always at work and always devoting the best of what was in him to what he had on hand.

In a letter to the present writer he said: "I should never have made my success in life if I had been shy of taking pains, or if I had not bestowed upon the least thing I have ever undertaken exactly the same attention and care that I have bestowed upon the greatest.   Do everything at your best.   Look at such of my manuscripts as are in the library at Gad's Hill, and think of the patient hours devoted year after year to single lines."

This rage for work sometimes took the form of veritable fever. It was when he was under the influence of this state of mind, when his brain was teeming with fancies, that he used to rush out into the streets of London in the dead of night and wander abroad for hours until his ideas had taken form and color and his mind was at rest. There is no doubt that these constant calls upon the brain affected his powers in later life. He found more difficulty in writing *Edwin Drood* than he had ever previously experienced; and though, in the opinion of many, that work rises to the highest point of excellence, there is no doubt that the writing of it gave him infinitely greater labor than any other book.

There is a charming description of himself when at work in his châlet at Gad's Hill, contained in one of his letters. "My room is up among the branches of the trees; and the birds and the butterflies fly in and out, and the green branches shoot in at the open windows, and the lights and shadows of the clouds come and go with the rest of the company."

His personal attractions were very great: he was of medium height, with a well set-up figure, a keen face, with eyes of remarkable brilliancy and penetration. No man had more friends, or more friends celebrated in every rank and class in life. One prominent feature of his disposition was his amazing vitality, his extraordinary animal spirits; his main characteristic was his intense earnestness and honesty of purpose. He was at his very best when entertaining friends in the character of host. At such times he would literally bubble over with humor. He was irresistible.

His popularity with the public was remarkable. Upon his appearance on the platform or upon any public occasion his reception was always most cordial; in the streets he was saluted by strangers as a personal friend. This was not merely a matter of a year or two. It was the story of a lifetime. He rejoiced in this popularity, but it never spoiled him. Those who knew him best could not fail to be struck by this. He was simple, modest, kind-hearted, and generous to the last.

His grave, which was kept open for three days after his

burial, was filled with flowers, among which were found **many** poor little bunches tied up with pieces of rag. "We have lost our best friend," one working-man was heard to say to another on the day of his death—a fitting tribute, surely, to one who had throughout the whole of his career worked hard for the cause of the poor. In noble language he expressed to John Forster the great aspiration and aim of his life. The occasion was the completion of the Chimes, and Forster describes it thus: "When we met at its close he was fresh from Venice, which had impressed him as the wonder and the new sensation of the world; but well do I remember how high above it all arose the hope that filled his mind. 'Ah!' he said to me, 'when I saw those places how I thought that to leave one's hand upon the time, lastingly upon the time, with one tender touch for the mass of toiling people that nothing could obliterate, would be to lift oneself above the dust of all the Doges in their graves, and stand upon a giant's staircase that Samson couldn't overthrow."

His family consisted of ten children, to some of whom he gave the most fantastic nicknames, as the following will show: *Charles*, born January 6, 1837, nicknamed *Flaster Floby* (a corruption of Master Toby), later *Charley; Mary*, born March 6, 1838, nicknamed *Mild Glo'ster*, later *Mamey; Kate*, born October 29, 1839, nicknamed *Lucifer Box* and *Katey; Walter Landor*, born Feb. 8, 1841, nicknamed *Young Skull* and *Walley;* Francis Jeffrey, born Jan. 15, 1844, nicknamed *Chickenstalker* and *Frank; Alfred Tennyson*, born October 28, 1845; *Sydney Smith Haldimand*, born April 18, 1847, nicknamed *Hoshen Peck* (a corruption of Ocean Spectre); *Henry Fielding*, born Jan. 16, 1849, known as *Harry* or *H.; Dora Annie*, born August 16, 1850, who survived her birth but a few months; *Edward Bulwer-Lytton*, born March 13, 1852, nicknamed *Plornishghenter* or *Plorn.*

Dinarte, Sylvio (Alfred D'Escragnolle Taunay, Rio de Janeiro, Brazil, Feb. 22, 1843). He came of a noble family of French émigrés, who fled from Portugal during the revolutionary days of the early nineteenth century, and settled in Brazil. When fifteen years of age Alfred was made a bachelor of letters, but chose a military career, and served through the two celebrated campaigns of Matto Grosso and Cordillera (1867-'70). Promotion was rapid and ere he retired from the army he was made, in 1885, a major-general. War experiences, especially those during the protracted and sanguinary hostilities between Paraguay and Brazil, afforded him real dramatic material for his poem, La retraite de Laguna, which depicted the sufferings of the soldiers. This was published by the Brazilian Government in 1871, and certain critics thereupon called him "the modern Xenophon." It was translated into many languages. Again, the campaign of Cordillera (1869-'70) engaged his pen; and after his return to Rio de Janeiro he published the Diario de Campanha, which had the character of an official document. Between 1872 and 1875 he was deputy in the Chamber for the Province of Goïaz, and in 1877 was elected president of the Province of Sainte Catherine. Presented in the list of senators, in 1886, he was chosen senator for life by the Emperor. From that time he has been an active, progressive leader of the Conservative party, advocating advanced ideas in such subjects as immigration, general naturalization, and civil marriage. He also allied himself with the abolition movement in Brazil, and urged the end of all slavery. As a man of letters his activity has been phenomenal, producing works of widely varying character. But the man who wrote Histoires brésiliennes (1876), Narrativas militares (1878), Céos e Terras do Brazil (1882), and Mariage civil (1886) is best known as a romancer, under the pseudonym "Sylvio Dinarte," and among his many novels are: Mocidade de Trajano (1872); Le manuscrit d'une femme (1873); and Innocencia (1873), which is considered his finest effort in fiction. He wrote a drama in four acts called Amelia Smith, and also produced two comedies, in 1887. In the musical world he is known under the name of "Flavio Elysio," and is a composer of waltzes, études, and other compositions, after the manner of Chopin.

Disraeli, Benjamin, Earl of Beaconsfield (London, England, Dec. 21, 1805; April 19, 1881). He was educated by private tutors and by his father, who was himself distinguished in literature. His ability as a writer was displayed while he was yet a boy by the publication of a translation from the Eclogues of Theocritus. In 1821 he was articled to a solicitor in Lincoln's Inn, but his bent for letters was so marked that he was permitted to go his own way, and his first novel, *Vivian Grey*, was published anonymously when he was barely twenty-one years old. Its success was immediate, and after the authorship was disclosed the young Disraeli found himself famous. His health was not of the best, and largely for this reason he went abroad for a leisurely tour of Spain, Italy, and the Levant. This journey covered three years, 1828–'31, and on his return to England he withdrew definitely from Lincoln's Inn and so from the profession of law. Meantime he had published a second novel and written a third. He had also decided upon a political career, and in 1832 stood for Parliament in the Marylebone division. At this time he posed as a Radical. The stunning defeat he suffered in that election evidently induced some heart-searching, for when, not very long afterward, he had another opportunity to be a parliamentary candidate, in a bye-election at High Wycombe, he went forward as a Tory. Again he was defeated and he might have passed into political oblivion if his pamphlets had not already established him as a debater who must be taken seriously. The most important of these was his Vindication of the British Constitution. His polemics compelled attention, and after his defeat at High Wycombe his pen was kept busy answering the gibes of his former Radical associates, who accused him of changing his convictions in the vain hope of personal preferment. Disraeli undertook to prove his consistency, and succeeded at least in returning blows as hard as he received and thus in keeping himself before the public eye. Whether or not he justified his turn from Radicalism to Toryism, it is true that in his subsequent career he persisted in advocating under Tory auspices many of the reforms for which he had agitated as a Radical. It was his constant cry that the Tories must heed popular demands; and one commentator has declared that the distinguishing feature of his career was that he popularized Toryism. Continuing to write progressive political articles, he became a candidate of the Maidstone division in 1837, and was elected. His production of fiction then ceased for several years, but he gave his attention to more than mere politics and statecraft in the interval. He found himself compelled to study the art of oral expression, for his first speech in the House of Commons was a disheartening fiasco. It was a carefully prepared, memorized speech, delivered in the grand manner, with abundance of gestures and tricks of vocal inflection. Even at that day the grand manner had become a tradition of the House, the Commoners yielding to unaffected, plain statements rather than to obvious oratory.

Disraeli's effort excited the risibilities of the members, and the House rocked with laughter. The young member, annoyed, embarrassed, was at length obliged to stop with his speech unfinished. He concluded with the memorable words, "I must sit down now, but the time will come when you will hear me!" It was long before he ventured to speak again, but he was sedulous in the observation of his parliamentary duties, and it is known that he undertook to school himself in a style of utterance more in keeping with the prevailing manner of his time. Meantime his political writings won more and more respect for what he had to say, and when next he addressed the House he was listened to respectfully. His resumption of fiction as an avocation was really a feature of his political career, for he was an agitator within his party for measures of which the majority of his colleagues could not approve, and he wrote *Coningsby* and *Sybil* for the purpose of impressing his views on a wider audience than he could command in the House and thus arousing a public sentiment in their support. These "novels with a purpose" were eminently successful both as literary and political efforts. Disraeli soon found himself the actual leader of the younger element in his party, and his influence increased so rapidly that by 1846 he was, in all except the name, the leader of the Opposition. In 1848 he was formally recognized by the party at large, and he held the leadership for a quarter of a century. Disraeli, in 1839, married the widow of a parliamentary colleague.

This lady's wealth enabled him to purchase Hughenden, a fine estate in Beaconsfield, Buckinghamshire. The county made him its member in 1847, and he held the seat continuously until his elevation to the peerage. He was three times Chancellor of the Exchequer before becoming Prime Minister. His first tenure of office was extremely brief. It was in connection with Lord Derby's government in 1852, when the election that followed the accession of the Tories to power failed to sustain them. Lord Derby was again Prime Minister in 1858, and Disraeli was in his cabinet as Chancellor of the Exchequer; but his second budget was rejected in 1859, and the Tories returned to the Opposition benches. For seven years Disraeli had to contend not only with Lord Palmerston, who had become Prime Minister, but with dissensions in his own party. He maintained his hold on the leadership in spite of the hostility of a suspicious minority, and regained his former office in 1866. Two years later he became Prime Minister. His government was thrown out in the general election of 1869, but in 1874 the Conservatives, as the Tories had come to be called, won a safe majority, and there followed several years during which Disraeli shaped the course of the British Empire. His administration worked out several of the local reforms for which he had formerly contended, but its fame, and its strength with the people, depended on its foreign policy, which Disraeli conducted personally. This policy was aggressive and imperialistic. Through it he acquired for England control of the Suez Canal, interfered with Russia's designs in Afghanistan, proclaimed the Queen, in 1877, Empress of India, in connection with the other powers checked the advance of Russia on Constantinople in 1878, depriving her of the fruits of her hard-won victory, annexed Cyprus, and broke the power of the Zulus. His ministry fell in 1880, when he had to yield the power to his long-time adversary, William Ewart Gladstone. Meantime, in 1877, he had been created an Earl. In addition to his novels and political writings, including several volumes of speeches, he published, in 1852, The Life of Lord George Bentinck. His novels are: *Vivian Grey* (1826); *The Young Duke* (1829); *Contarini Fleming* (1832); *The Wondrous Tale of Alroy* (1832); *Henrietta Temple* (1837); *Venetia* (1837); *Coningsby* (1844); *Sybil* (1845); *Tancred* (1847); *Lothair* (1870); *Endymion* (1880).

Dodge, Mary Elizabeth Mapes (New York City, 1838; Onteora Park, N. Y., August 21, 1905). She was the daughter of Professor James J. Mapes, a scientist, and was brought up in a literary atmosphere. Married young to William Dodge, a New York lawyer, she was soon left a widow with two sons to support. Casting about her for a means of livelihood, she determined to try her hand on juvenile stories, which were contributed to the Hearth and Home, a magazine with which she became connected by conducting one of its departments. Her Irvington Stories (1864) for children met with great success, and the editor of The Independent, desirous to obtain a story from the same pen, requested one. She had been telling her boys skating adventures and so determined to write upon that topic; but it expanded in the working beyond original bounds, and was thus too long for The Independent's use. This was the genesis of the immensely popular *Hans Brinker: or, The Silver Skates* (1865), which has been translated into Dutch, German, French, Italian, and Russian, and was crowned by the French Academy. In 1873 the author of the juvenile classic accepted the chair of editor of St. Nicholas, then newly established, and under her able management, which lasted to her death, it became the foremost magazine among those devised for young people. Besides her several books, two of her minor compositions have attained a permanent place in latter-day American literature; one is a poem, The Two Mysteries—Life and Death, which has been highly praised by eminent poets; the other is a humorous Irish dialect skit called Miss Maloney on the Chinese Question, and was a favorite recitation of Charlotte Cushman's. All her stories evince a constructive ability of high order, while her humor is keen, and her ethical sense unimpeachable. Her volumes of verse are: Rhymes and Jingles (1874); Along the Way (1879); When Life is Young (1894): and Poems and Verses (1904). Other books are: Theophilus and Others (1879); Donald and Dorothy (1883); and The Land of Pluck (1894).

Dole, Nathan Haskell (Chelsea, Mass., August 31, 1852). He was graduated at Harvard University in 1874, and acted for several years as an instructor in secondary schools, until he entered the field of journalism. From Philadelphia, where he was literary and musical editor of the Philadelphia Press, he went (in 1887) to New York City to fill the office of literary adviser to the publishing firm of T. Y. Crowell and Company. Meanwhile he had been industrious in his chosen field, and among other books produced The Young Folks' History of Russia (1881), and The Great Masters of Russian Literature in the Nineteenth Century (1886). As a translator he occupied himself with Spanish, Russian, French, and German. Of the work of Valdes, he put into English the admirable Marquise of Peñalta (1886); Maximinia (1888); and Sister Saint Sulpice (1890); of Tolstoi, he translated Anna Karénina, and War and Peace, and in 1899 edited the complete works (20 vols.) of the Russian master. Dole is also known as a translator of Daudet and of Scheffel. But perhaps his most noteworthy work in this direction was done in 1896, when he compiled a multivariorum edition of the Rubáiyát of Omar Khayyám, containing English translations of French, German, Italian, Hungarian, and Danish versions of the Persian quatrains. The Shah of Persia presented him with a medal for this labor. His principal original works are: A Score of Famous Composers (1891); *Not Angels Quite* (1893); On the Point (1895); The Hawthorn Tree and Other Poems (1895); The Mistakes We Make (1898); Omar, the Tent-Maker (1899); Six Italian Essays (1907); and A Teacher of Dante (1908). Among his miscellaneous volumes may be mentioned: Life of Francis William Bird (1897); The Greek Poets (1904); The Latin Poets (1905); an edition of the Poetical Works of Keats and Shelley (1905); and one of Marat's Polish Letters (1905).

Doyle, Sir Arthur Conan (Edinburgh, Scotland, May 22, 1859). John Doyle, the famous Punch caricaturist, was the grandfather of Arthur, who first studied medicine in Germany, and then returned to Edinburgh, where he finished his course at the medical college of the University. Letters had always been a lure, and while he was still a student a short story of his, The Mystery of the Sassassa Valley, appeared in Chambers' Journal. It signified nothing wonderful, and a year later he was sailing the Arctic as physician of the Scotch whaler *Hope*. Upon his return he set himself up as a practising physician, with literature as a side issue. His literary apprenticeship was long and tedious, and for ten years he earned less than fifty pounds a year with his pen. However, he persevered, and in 1887 produced the successful novel, *A Study in Scarlet*, in which he introduced his now world-famous detective, Sherlock Holmes, who subsequently was the central character of The Sign of the Four (1889), The Adventures of Sherlock Holmes (1891), The Memoirs of Sherlock Holmes (1893), and The Hound of the Baskervilles (1902). These stories are replete with the author's great ingenuity, his rare humor, and his power of producing a sense of mystery and of horror, which has been repeatedly compared with that of Edgar Allan Poe. But the creator of the fascinating scientific detective has always regretted that Holmes should have cast into the shade his historical novels, upon which Sir Arthur labored with infinite care. As an example, he read more than two hundred books, and spent two years to produce *The White Company* (1890). Other works requiring similar painstaking execution were: Micah Clarke (1888); The Refugees (1891); The Great Shadow (1892); Rodney Stone (1896); and The Exploits of Brigadier Gérard (1896). During the Boer War Dr. Doyle acted as a medical registrar of the Langman Field Hospital. Returning to England, he published The Great Boer War (1900), and issued an enlarged edition of it in 1902. For this work and for his spirited defense of British policy in South Africa, he was knighted in 1902. He is also author of a play, Halves (1899), and of the one-act play, Waterloo, which Henry Irving produced. As a poet he has published a collection of verses under the title, Songs of Action (1898). Besides the Sherlock Holmes books other volumes of short stories are: Round the Red Lamp (1894); The Stark Munro Letters (1895); and The Green Flag (1900).

Du Boisgobey, Fortuné Hippolyte Auguste (Granville, Normandy, France, 1824; Paris, Feb. 26, 1891). As the son of a mayor and deputy of Granville he received a good education. In 1844 he went to Algiers in an official capacity, and for many years served as paymaster to the French army there. After much travel in Africa and the East, he returned to Paris as a retired military officer in 1868, only to find himself a middle-aged man without any pecuniary resources whatever. Possessing an admirable education, fortified by wide and varied foreign experiences, he determined to try his hand at writing novels. The first one or two attracted little or no attention, but another one had been begun as a *feuilleton* in the Petit Journal, when the horrible murders of Troppmann became the talk of Paris. The director of the Petit Journal thereupon announced that, in order to give complete details of these assassinations, the publication of M. du Boisgobey's story would have to be temporarily discontinued. At once a general protest arose against such an interruption; the popularity of the writer was established, and from that time his work was sought by all the principal journals of the day, while his hold on the reading public never lessened in spite of the enormous work of his pen. One hardly knows which to admire most, the fertility of his imagination, his constructive powers, the dramatic force of his language, or his tremendous capacity for work. His *forte* was sensational detective fiction after the manner of Émile Gaboriau, and in the space of about twenty-two years he wrote between sixty and seventy novels, which, no sooner finished as *feuilletons*, passed into volume form and made a circuit of the civilized world. Personally, Du Boisgobey was a determined Royalist and had the courage of his convictions; he was a marvelous talker, and his conversation retained all the accuracy and vivacity of his written pages. Extraordinary success attended his L'Homme sans Nom (1872); Les Mystères de Nouveau Paris (1876); and *Le Crime de l'Opéra* (1880).

Dumas Davy de la Pailleterie, Alexandre (*père*) (Villers-Cotterets, France, July 4, 1802; Puys, near Dieppe, Dec. 5, 1870). He was the son of General Dumas, a West Indian mulatto, who was distinguished for gallantry in the Napoleonic wars, and of an inn-keeper's daughter. In later years Alexandre assumed the name and arms of his paternal grandfather, the Marquis Davy de la Pailleterie.

Alexandre's parents were very poor, and in 1823 he went to Paris to seek his fortune. Obtaining a clerkship with 1250 francs a year, he eked out his slender income by writing farces, which were well received. He then saw Shakespeare performed by Macready and other English players in Paris, and was stirred to write grand romantic and historical dramas. His second play, Henri III, produced in 1829, met with extraordinary success, bringing its author 50,000 francs. The Revolution of July of that year interrupted his literary labors. He entered into the struggle with enthusiasm, and after it was over returned to writing with an energy that knew no bounds. Beginning with an original play of sensational immorality, he was tempted by its success to produce as many works as possible, and so boldly plagiarized from Schiller and others. Nevertheless, even in adaptation he showed great genius. Inspired by the example of Sir Walter Scott, he began to write historical romances, upon which his fame now chiefly rests. In 1844 he produced *The Count of Monte Cristo*, which created a greater and more universal interest than had Scott's novel, Waverley. This was followed in the same year by *The Three Musketeers*. Both novels were written rapidly in daily instalments for a newspaper, yet they have ever excited the admiration of the finest literary critics. So great was their popularity that Dumas was beset by publishers who desired similar romances. He contracted to produce stories enough for forty men, and, indeed, by hiring hack-writers to work under his direction, he succeeded in putting out forty volumes in the course of that year (1844). Later he would accept almost any manuscript submitted to him, and publish it as his own. This brought him prodigious wealth, which he spent in building a theater for the exclusive production of his works, and a magnificent castle for his residence. He went on a government expedition to Algeria, and coolly appropriated the vessel for his own purposes in visiting interesting places elsewhere. In order to take the junketing trip he had neglected to fill various contracts with newspapers, and these sued him. He theatrically appeared in his own defense, and lost all his cases. His theater, too, failed. He attempted to recoup his fortunes by founding a newspaper, Le Mousquetaire, to every article in which, though rarely written by himself, he signed his name.   Upon its decline he was reduced to selling his name for advertising various businesses, and even to exhibiting himself for hire in shop-windows.   His old age was associated with wild schemes for making money, and with scandalous and ridiculous amours.   He died penniless.

Of the one thousand two hundred volumes that bear his name the most notable of those showing marks of his genius are: *The Count of Monte Cristo* (1844); *The Three Musketeers* (1844), and its sequels, *Twenty Years After* (1845) and *The Vicomte de Bragelonne* (1868); *Marguerite de Valois* (1845), and its sequels, La Dame de Monsoreau (1846) and *The Forty-five Guardsmen* (1848); *Memoirs of a Physician* (1846), the first of five so-called Marie-Antoinette romances; and two Napoleonic novels, The Companions of Jehu (1857) and The Whites and the Blues (1867); *Chicot the Jester* (1845); *The Page of the Duke of Savoy* (1846); *The Corsican Brothers* (1846); *The Two Dianas* (1846); *The Chevalier de Maison-Rouge* (1846); *Joseph Balsamo* (1848); *The Black Tulip* (1850); *Taking the Bastile* (1853); *The Countess de Charny* (1853); and *Andrée de Taverny* (1855).

Dumas, Alexandre (*fils*), illegitimate son of Alexandre Dumas Davy de la Pailleterie (Paris, July 27, 1824; Marly-le-Roi, Nov. 27, 1895).   In character the son was the antipodes of his father, being a realist and a moralist, rather than a romanticist with any other purpose than an ethical one.   In his novel, *The Clémenceau Case* (1867), he has presented a picture of his youth, shadowed by the cloud of illegitimacy.   Nevertheless, his father's recognition of him and companionship with him in early manhood were anything but beneficial.   It involved him heavily in debt, to extricate himself from which he turned to authorship.   His was not a prolific mind, like his father's.   He took his profession seriously and worked hard at it, and as a result reaped enduring rewards.   In 1848 he produced a novel, *The Lady of the Camelias*, which was popular enough to justify its dramatization.   Upon its appearance on the stage in 1852, it achieved a distinguished success.   Thereafter he devoted himself chiefly to the drama.   All his plays are concerned with problems of modern society—"social sermons," they have been called, each enforcing its lesson of warning against what the author calls: "those charming, terrible little creatures for whom we ruin, dishonor, and kill ourselves, and whose sole occupation in the midst of this universal carnage is to dress now like umbrellas and now like bells." Aside from his literary pursuits he lived a quiet life and had few associates.

Du Maurier, George Louis Palmella Busson (Paris, France, March 6, 1834; London, England, Oct. 8, 1896). Of French blood on his father's side, and having an English mother, young Du Maurier passed his boyhood in France, but when he reached the age of seventeen he was sent to the London University College, where he studied chemistry. For a short while he actually set up as an analytical chemist, but on the death of his father, in 1856, he abandoned science for art. Returning to Paris, he became a pupil of Gleyre, and subsequently put himself under De Kaiser and Van Lerius in Antwerp. In 1860 he again settled in London and began drawing for the pages of Once a Week, the Cornhill Magazine, and Punch, and on the staff of the latter he succeeded the deceased John Leech in 1864. For his clever satirical social sketches he frequently composed equally pointed legends and verses. About 1866 he struck out a new line of illustration in Jerrold's Story of a Feather, which he continued in Thackeray's Henry Esmond (1868), and his Ballads (1878); also executing similar drawings for Fox's Book of Martyrs, and for works by Henry James, Thomas Hardy, and George Meredith. He became a contributor to the Royal Academy, and from time to time exhibited water-colors; in 1881 he was elected a member of the Royal Society of Painters. In 1885 the first exhibition of his collected work was given at the Fine Art Society. To Harper's Magazine he contributed a series of drawings, and in its pages appeared his first novel, *Peter Ibbetson* (1891), which was a fanciful romance of dream life, partly based on recollections of his own early life at Passay. Then the same magazine printed as a serial his *Trilby* (1894), which achieved a phenomenal success, both as a novel and a play. His only other romance was The Martian, which also appeared in Harper's Magazine during the winter of 1896–'97. But his claim to lasting fame will rest upon his inimitable black-and-white drawings, mainly contributed to Punch in the thirty-six years he drew for it.   Separate collections of these have been issued, such as The Collections of Mr. Punch (1880); Society Pictures from Punch (1890); A Legend of Camelot (1890); and Social Pictorial Satire (1890).   In 1897 appeared a volume of full-page drawings, entitled English Society, which he had contributed to Harper's Magazine, and which had an appreciative introduction from the pen of William Dean Howells.

Ebers, George Moritz (Berlin, March 1, 1837; Tutzing, Bavaria, August 7, 1898).   He was a posthumous child, and was educated chiefly by his mother before entering Göttingen, where he studied law.   Abandoning it, however, he devoted all enthusiasm to the study of Egyptology under Lepsius, Brugsch, and Böckh in Berlin, and in 1862 he received his degree.   The next three years were spent at work in the chief Egyptological museums of Europe.   At the end of that time he became *docent* in Egyptian language, history, and antiquity at Jena, and in 1868 was made extraordinary professor of the subjects there.   During part of 1869–'70 he traveled extensively in Egypt, Nubia, and Arabia, and upon his return to Europe he accepted a call to Leipzig as associate professor of Egyptology.   In 1872–'73 he again paid a visit to the land of the Pharaohs, and it resulted in him discovering the valuable medical papyrus now known by his name.   This celebrated well-preserved papyrus Ebers dates from about fifteen hundred years before Christ, and is the chief source of information regarding the medical knowledge of the ancient Egyptians. A fac-simile of it, containing one hundred and ten plates, was published in 1875 by its finder.   The original manuscript was given to the library of the University of Leipzig.   Other scientific works written by Ebers are: Disquisitiones de Dynastia XXVI Regum Ægyptorum (1865); Ægyptum und die Bücher Moses (1868); Eine Galerie antiker Portraits (1889), and Die hieroglyphischen Schriftzlichen de Ægyptus (1890).   Though in 1876 Ebers became partially paralyzed, and in 1889 was compelled to retire from his chair at Leipzig, his literary activity remained unabated. One of his most interesting productions, aside from his novels, is Ægypten in Wart und Bild (1878–'79), translated into English as: Egypt, Descriptive, Historical, and Picturesque (1880). He also wrote a biography of his old master: Richard Lepsius, ein Lebensbild (1885), and an autobiography: Die Geschichte meines Lebens (1892). His reputation as a novelist began with Eine ægyptische Königs-tochter (1864), translated as An Egyptian Princess, and was sustained by *Uarda* (1877), *Homo Sum* (1878), Die Schwestern (1879), Der Kaiser (1880), and Serapis (1885), all of which have been published in several languages. This group of novels deals exclusively with periods of Egyptian history. Two romances, Die Frau Bür germeisterin (1881), and Ein Wort (1882), are laid in Holland and South Germany respectively, and another, Eine Frage (1881), deals with ancient Greek life.

Edgeworth, Maria (Black Bourton, Oxfordshire, England, January 1, 1767; Edgeworthstown, Ireland, May 22, 1849). She was the second child of her father's first marriage (he married four times), and in 1775 was sent to school in Derby. After a short stay in London the Edgeworths removed (in 1782) to the family estate in County Longford, where Maria kept her father's accounts and dealt with his tenants. Save for occasional visits to London, Paris, Switzerland, and Scotland—where, in 1823, she met Sir Walter Scott, and their well-known friendship began—her life was spent mainly at home, helping her father manage his property and his large family. Children were numerous, and Maria's first literary ventures in collaboration with her father were didactic and educational: The Parents' Assistant (1796), and Practical Education (1798), which endeavored to embody the result of their experience in bringing up a family. But she soon abandoned this field of literature for more delightful and rich pastures afforded by her daily contact with different phases of Irish life. *Castle Rackrent*, her first novel, appeared anonymously in 1800, and was instantly recognized as a work of exceptional ability. Encouraged by this, she produced Belinda (1801), and the following year the Essay on Irish Bulls, in which her father had a hand. But alone she kept at her fiction—the stories of peasant life which Scott declared inspired him to write his Waverley novels, and thus do for Scotland what Miss Edgeworth had done for Ireland. One after another her popular books came out: Moral Tales (1801); Popular Tales (1804); and Leonora (1806). From 1809 to 1812 was published the Tales of Fashionable Life, of which Ennui (1812) and *The Absentee* (1812) were most successful. She was also particularly happy in her children's stories: Rosamond and Frank (1822), and Harry and Lucy (1825). Among her other praised novels are: Patronage (1814); Harrington and Ormond (1817); Garry Owen (1832); and Helen (1834).

Edwards, Amelia Blandford (London, England, June 7, 1831; Weston-super-Mare, England, April 15, 1892). Her father was an officer who served under the Duke of Wellington in the Peninsular War. Amelia early evinced precocious talent with both pen and pencil, and her mother guided her immature efforts. At the age of seven years she began writing poems and little stories, some of which found a local market. Eventually she became a contributor to Household Words and All the Year Round. Many of the ghost stories which appeared in Dickens's magazine were the product of her ready pen. She also served on the staff of the Saturday Review and the Morning Post. As a novelist she soon attracted popular attention with her eight romances: My Brother's Wife (1855); The Ladder of Life (1857); Hand and Glove (1859); Barbara's History (1864); Half a Million of Money (1865); Debenham's Vow (1870); *In the Days of My Youth* (1872), and Lord Brackenbury (1880). Each of her novels, she used to repeat, cost her two years of arduous labor. But before the completion of her later ones she had become interested in Egyptology, a visit to Egypt during 1873-'74 making a profound and lasting impression upon her. Forsaking fiction altogether, she devoted the last decade of her life to Egyptian subjects. She was a principal in the formation of the Egypt Exploration Fund, which put an end to the wanton destruction of antiquities in the land of the Nile; and at her death she bequeathed her Egyptological library and rare relics to the University College of London. To that institution she also left enough money to found a chair of Egyptology, which was then the only one in England. Her pen was ever ready on her favorite topic, and she contributed several articles bearing on the theme to the ninth edition of the Encyclopædia Britannica. Once, during the season of 1889–'90 she lectured throughout the United States, and her tour was a triumphal one. She embodied these addresses in Pharaohs, Fellahs, and Explorers (1891). Three American universities conferred honorary degrees upon her, and a few months before her decease the English Government granted her a pension. Among her other Egyptological contributions to literature is a translation of Maspero's Egyptian Archæology, and an original work entitled A Thousand Miles Up the Nile (1877).

Eggleston, Edward (Vevay, Indiana, Dec. 10, 1837; Joshua's Rock, Lake George, N. Y., Sept. 3, 1902). He was the son of a Virginia lawyer. Delicate health prevented the ordinary course of education, but by dint of private study he obtained culture, and in 1856 began life as a Methodist circuit-riding preacher. This was followed by an appointment as general agent for the Bible Society in Minnesota, where he also engaged in such pastoral work as his health permitted. In 1866 he went to Evanston, Ill., to become an associate editor on a juvenile paper. The next year he removed to Chicago, where he edited The Sunday-School Teacher, the circulation of which increased under his management from five to thirty-five thousand copies, and here he gained a considerable reputation as a manager and speaker for Sunday-school interests. Meanwhile he had contributed to the New York Independent and in 1870 he joined its staff, becoming first literary editor, then managing editor. He resigned to assume charge of Hearth and Home, which, in turn, was given up when he founded (in 1874) a creedless church—the Church of Christian Endeavor —in Brooklyn, N. Y. Five years later failing health necessitated the abandonment of this project, and he retired to the shores of Lake George, N. Y., where he devoted himself to writing fiction and American history. Already he had gained

a national renown with The Hoosier Schoolmaster (1871);
The End of the World (1872); The Mystery of Metropolisville
(1873); *The Circuit Rider* (1874); and Roxy (1878); and now
he completed a series of juvenile biographies of American Indians: Tecumseh (1878); Pocahontas and Powhatan (1879);
Brant and Red-Jacket (1879); and Montezuma (1880). Then
he returned to the province peculiarly his own—Indiana—
in The Hoosier Schoolboy (1883); The Graysons (1888); The
Faith Doctor (1891); and Duffels (1893). Fiction, however,
he regarded merely as a means of earning money for his greatest
ambition—that of writing American history, a task he performed, with exceptional insight and skill, and his historical
work ranks among the best. He began with a Household
History of the United States (1888), and followed it up with
the minute and valuable Beginners of a Nation (1896), and The
Transit of Civilization (1900). A posthumous work, A New
Century History of Life in the United States (1904), completes
the list of his historical productions.

Eggleston, George Cary (Vevay, Indiana, Nov. 26, 1839).
Unlike his brother, Edward, he was able to attend the Asbury
(Ind.) University, which he left, however, at fifteen years of age.
Returning home to Madison, whither his mother had removed
from Vevay, the sixteen-year-old boy took a small school on
the edge of the town. Pupils ranged from infancy to adult
age, and the ambitious teacher had his hands full for about six
months, when he resigned. Those who have read The Hoosier
Schoolmaster by Edward Eggleston can appreciate the life
George led until he gave up frontier teaching and went east.
He made his way to Virginia and in 1856 matriculated at Richmond College, studied law, and practised it up to the outbreak
of the Civil War. Enlisting in the Confederate Army, he
served throughout that war, and at its cessation lived for a time
in the West, but in 1870 he accepted an engagement on the
staff of the Brooklyn (N. Y.) Union, where he remained a year.
From 1871 to 1874 he was managing editor of Hearth and
Home, and during the next year edited American Homes.
Then he became literary editor of the New York Evening Post,
a place held until 1881, when he served in the same capacity

on the Commercial Advertiser, and subsequently became its editor-in-chief (1886-'89). Finally he went over to the World as one of its editorial writers. From homiletical literature, of which How to Educate Yourself (1872) was a sample, he turned his attention to fiction, to stirring narratives of the war, and to boys' stories. Among his many excellent books may be mentioned: A Man of Honor (1873); A Rebel's Recollections (1874); The Big Brother (1875); Red Eagle (1878); The Wreck of the Red Bird (1882); Southern Soldier Stories (1890); The Last of the Flatboats (1900); A Carolina Cavalier (1901); Dorothy South (1902); The Master of Warlock (1903); A Captain in the Ranks (1904); A Daughter of the South (1905); Blind Alleys (1906); and Long Knives (1907). Another volume, The First of the Hoosiers (1903), contains recollections of his brother, Edward Eggleston.

Eichendorff, Josef Karl Benedikt, Baron von (Lubowitz, Upper Silesia, March 10, 1788; Neisse, Nov. 26, 1857). He was brought up in the Roman Catholic faith, and studied law at Halle and at Heidelberg (1805-'08), supplementing this course with one in Paris. From Paris he went to Vienna, where, having already come under the Romantic influence through early association with Arnim, Brentano, and Görres, he attached himself to Schlegel. When, on February 3, 1813, the King of Prussia made his famous appeal to every German patriot, Eichendorff enlisted as a volunteer, and subsequently rose in the ranks of the Lützow Corps, made immortal by Körner. During the War of Liberation he served as a faithful fighter, and in 1816, after passing a brilliant examination, he was appointed an officer in the civil service of Prussia. At the end of a quarter of a century or more, after fulfilling various offices for the State, he requested his dismissal and retired in 1844 to private life. Public life, however, had not interfered with his relations with literary celebrities, nor had it checked his poetic and prose work. Belonging to the Romantic School, he wrote many characteristic poems, which still hold their place, some of them having been set to music by eminent composers. His first prose tale, Ahnung und Gegenwart, appeared in 1815 at the end of the Napoleon campaign. Various stories, comedies, and tragedies followed, but it was his *Aus dem Leben eines Taugenichts* (1824), translated into English as *Happy-go-Lucky: or, Leaves from the Life of a Good-for-Nothing*, that established his reputation. Much of his later work is tinged with his ecclesiastical notions. Eichendorff, toward the close of his life, wrote literary history and criticism, beginning with Ueber die ethische und religiöse Bedeutung der neueren romantischen Poesie in Deutschland (1847). With Eichendorff the last great poet of the Romantic School in Germany passed away, Heine having died a year before him.

Eliot, George (Mary Ann Evans Cross) (Arbury, Warwickshire, England, Nov. 22, 1819; December 22, 1880). She spent the first twenty years of her life among farm people, such as she describes in *Adam Bede* and *The Mill on the Floss*, and was educated under strong Calvinistic influences. Endowed with a powerful and inquiring mind, she took up the study of philosophy, science and mathematics, as well as of music and literature. She moved to the town of Coventry at the age of twenty-one, and fell under Unitarian influences, which gradually developed into agnosticism. In 1846 she translated the Life of Jesus, by the German rationalist Strauss. In 1857 she began writing for the Westminster Review, and later became its assistant editor. In 1854 she became the life-companion of George Henry Lewes, an English philosopher, marriage with him being precluded by the fact that he had a wife living, and, though separated from her, he was prevented from divorcing her by laws prevailing in England but in few other civilized countries.

By Mr. Lewes she was encouraged to try her hand at fiction. Her Scenes of Clerical Life appeared under her pseudonym, first serially in Blackwood's Magazine in 1857–'58, and afterward in book form. Thackeray, who warmly commended the stories, supposed the author was a man; but Dickens, in writing to "George Eliot" to express his "admiration of their extraordinary merit," said: "I have observed what seemed to me such womanly touches in those moving fictions that the assurance on the title-page is insufficient to satisfy me even now. If they originated with no woman, I believe that no man ever before had the art of making himself mentally so like a woman since the world began." In 1859 she published *Adam Bede*, her first long novel. This, says Sidney Lanier in his book entitled The English Novel, placed her "decisively at the head of English novel-writers, with only Dickens for second, even." And, says Richard Holt Hutton, the critic: "It is always likely to remain George Eliot's most popular work. Everything about it . . . is at once simple and great, and the plot is unfolded with singular simplicity, purity, and power."

In 1860 she published *The Mill on the Floss*, "a masterly fragment of fictitious biography followed by a second-rate novel," according to Hutton. Then in 1861 came a short novel, *Silas Marner*, which Oscar Browning calls "a perfect gem, . . . in which the demands of art have alone to be considered." *Romola* began to make its appearance serially in The Cornhill Magazine for July, 1862. Of this Oscar Browning says: "It is perhaps the best historical novel ever written. Replete with learning, . . . the finish is so rare that the joint between erudition and imagination cannot be discovered." *Felix Holt, the Radical*, a socialistic novel, was published in 1866. It is generally agreed to be her most unsatisfactory work. *Middlemarch* was published in 1871-'72. It has been well characterized by W. C. Brownell as "a half-dozen novels in one, . . . the microcosm of a community, rather than a story concerned with a unified plot and set of characters; . . . perhaps the writer's fullest expression of her philosophy of life." In 1876 George Eliot published *Daniel Deronda*, that one of her novels over which there has been most dispute, the resultant of opinion having been well expressed by Bayard Taylor: "In it she has reached both her clearest height of (intellectual) achievement and the barriers of art which she is unable to scale."

Mr. Lewes died in 1878, and in the spring of 1880 George Eliot married John Walter Cross, an old friend and admirer. As she was beginning to enjoy her "newly reopened life," to quote from one of her letters, she was stricken with illness, and died before the end of the year.

George Eliot was a poet as well as a novelist, but her verse has been rather harshly criticized by the leading critics. Says

George Saintsbury: "She merely put some of the thoughtful commonplaces of her time and school into wooden verse, occasionally grandiose, but never grand, and her purple passages have the purple of plush, not velvet."

Erckmann, Émile (Pfalzburg, May 20, 1822; Paris, March 14, 1899); **Chatrian, Louis Gratien Charles Alexandre** (Soldatenthal, Dec. 18, 1826; Raincy, September 3, 1890). Having completed his studies at the communal college of his native town, Émile Erckmann went to Paris in 1842, with the intention of studying law. Five years later a severe illness compelled him to return home, and during convalescence he occupied himself by weaving romances. It was about this time, or soon after, that he met his future collaborator, Louis Chatrian, who had come from his native town to teach school in Pfalzburg, and to escape becoming a glassblower like his father. Almost at once the two young men began their Siamese-twin collaboration, which has been compared to that of the brothers Goncourt and that of Beaumont and Fletcher. But for a number of years the result of this co-partnership found its way only to obscure newspapers such as the Democrate du Rhin. After publishing numerous *feuilletons* in this fashion, one story, L'illustre Docteur Mathéus, appeared in the Revue Nouvelle in 1859, and attracted wide attention. From that time their many graphic romances of the Napoleonic era—especially those with a realistic Alsatian background—won universal popularity. They wrote different styles of novels—rustic, sentimental, fantastic, and historical—but in the last-named form they were most successful. Their method of composition was so like that of a single mind that it caused much speculation and comment; but it is now understood that Erckmann did all the writing while Chatrian suggested, criticized, and constructed the plots. Hence, when it came to the dramatization of several of their stories, Chatrian was in his element with his keen dramatic instinct. Finally, over some slight difference of opinion, the literary partnership of years' standing was dissolved, and neither of the men afterward produced any independent work of worth. Best known perhaps of their series of novels is the *Histoire d'un Conscrit de 1813* (1864), which has been translated into several languages, and into English under the title *The Story of a Conscript of 1813*. Its sequel, Waterloo (1865), was also well received. Among other noteworthy tales were: Le Fou Yégof (1862); L'Ami Fritz (1864); Le Blocus (1867); and Histoire d'un Paysan (1868). Two plays of particular merit were L'Ami Fritz (1876), adapted from the novel of that name, and Le Juif Polonais (1869) translated by Leopold Lewis as The Bells, in which Sir Henry Irving achieved great success.

Farjeon, Benjamin Leopold (London, England, 1833; London, July 23, 1903). He was a descendant of a notable Spanish-Hebrew family driven into exile in 1492. On his maternal side he was a cousin to Sidney Lee. A spirit of adventure led him to Australia, where he worked in the gold-diggings. From Australia he drifted to New Zealand, and while there assisted in establishing its first daily journal, the Otago Daily Times. In fact, he became editor and proprietor of the newspaper, and his pen was spurred on to constant activity. Grif: A Story of Australian Life (1870) was his first novel to meet with any considerable success. Charles Dickens read it, and, much impressed, wrote its author an encouraging note, at the same time advising him to return to London. Farjeon took the advice, and once in England became a friend of Dickens the man, and an industrious disciple of Dickens the novelist. He developed rare skill in plot construction and was a master of melodramatic situations. Many of his stories have been translated into Spanish, Italian, French, and German. His method of work was singular, inasmuch as he rarely knew anything of a story before he actually began the writing of it, and never made notes or sketches for use in his fiction. Nevertheless, he was a voluminous writer of exciting dramatic tales, among which may be mentioned: *Joshua Marvel* (1871); London's Heart (1873); Blade o' Grass (1874); Bread-and-Cheese and Kisses (1874); Love's Victory (1875); At the Sign of the Silver Flagon (1876); The Nine of Hearts (1886); Toilers of Babylon (1888); The Betrayal of John Fordham (1897). Some of the best of his stories have been dramatized for the English stage, with considerable success.

Fenn, George Manville (Westminster, England, January 3, 1831). After a private-school education, he became a teacher, but tiring of the drudgery he applied himself to the trade of printer, and eventually bought a provincial newspaper. Discovering his facility as a narrator, he began writing stories and sketches for All the Year Round, Chambers' Journal, and similar organs. In 1871 he accepted the place of editor of Cassell's Magazine, and a few years later he became editor and owner of Once a Week, in which appeared a series of his Christmas stories. He has been a most prolific writer, both of novels and tales of adventure for boys. It is estimated that since his literary career opened, he has produced more than one thousand short stories and magazine articles, and upward of two hundred volumes. He has also dramatized several of his novels, either in collaboration or alone. A partial list of his fictions, popular on two continents, contains: Bent, not Broken (1867); The Parson o' Dumford (1879); In the King's Name (1882); Nat the Naturalist (1882); *The Master of the Ceremonies* (1886); Commodore Junk (1888); The Man with a Shadow (1888); and A Double Knot (1890).

Fern, Fanny (Sara Payson Willis Parton; Portland, Maine, July 9, 1811; Brooklyn, N. Y., Oct. 10, 1872). This sister of Nathaniel Parker Willis, the poet, was educated in the schools of Boston, and took a finishing course in the Young Ladies' Seminary of Miss Catherine E. Beecher, where the famous Harriet Beecher Stowe was a teacher. In 1834 she married Charles Eldridge of Boston, Mass., but it was not till twelve years later, when her husband had died, leaving her to support two children, that she thought of adopting literature to earn money. Assuming the pseudonym of "Fanny Fern," she began, in 1851, contributing sparkling essays to periodicals, which when gathered into book form, under the title Fern Leaves (1853), achieved speedy popularity, and gave her a competence. Within a year one hundred and eighty thousand copies of the book were sold in the United States and Great Britain. Then in rapid succession followed Little Ferns (1853), and Fern Leaves, Second Series (1854). During the latter year *Ruth Hall*, a semi-autobiographical novel, appeared and was sold by the thousand. She made the acquaintance of James Parton, the well-known writer, in the office of the Home Journal, a magazine conducted by her brother, N. P. Willis, and in January, 1856, they were married. For upward of eighteen years she contributed a weekly article to the New York Ledger, and these were afterward incorporated in book form. Her other books were: Rose Clark (1857); Fresh Leaves (1857); The Play-Day Book (1857); and Folly as it Flies (1868).

Ferrier, Susan Edmonstone (Edinburgh, Sept. 7, 1782; Edinburgh, Nov. 5, 1854). She was the youngest of ten children of James Ferrier, writer to the Signet, and a man who gained local celebrity as a manager of large estates. While having charge of the Argyle property, Mr. Ferrier grew intimate with John, fifth Duke of Argyle, through whose influence he was made a principal clerk of session. Scott was one of his colleagues, and Ferrier soon came into touch with the leading literary people of Edinburgh. Of course his daughter Susan benefited by living in such a circle, and the good influence was augmented by frequent visits to Inverary Castle, where she caught glimpses of the fashionable world, which she was to depict in fiction. As early as 1810 she undertook her first novel, in conjunction with her particular friend, Miss Clavering, niece of the Duke of Argyle, but this collaboration was abandoned after Miss Clavering had written a few pages of manuscript. Susan Ferrier, however, finished the tale, and in 1818 she was persuaded to publish it. This was the novel Marriage, which translated into French had a great vogue. At long intervals she produced her other two novels, The Inheritance (1824) and Destiny (1831), both of which sustained and added to her high reputation. But Miss Ferrier seemed to prefer the quiet of domestic life to the noise of literary celebrity, and she led a retired existence, keeping house for her father until his death in 1829. John Curran and Sir Walter Scott, however, were her valued friends, and she paid the latter three visits, once at Ashiestiel in 1811, and twice at Abbotsford in 1829 and in 1831. These sojourns were recorded by her, and the account first appeared in the Temple Bar Magazine for 1874. In his Diary, Scott described her as "simple, full of humor, and exceedingly ready at repartee, and all this without the least affectation of the blue-stocking." Miss Ferrier's eyesight failed rapidly, and in 1830 she made a final visit to London to consult an oculist, but she obtained little relief, and the remainder of her life was spent mostly in darkened rooms. As late as 1850 her publisher, Bentley, urged her to write another novel, but she declined. As a novelist Susan Ferrier has been classed with her two sister-contemporaries, Jane Austen and Maria Edgeworth. At least she shared in the movement which sought to develop the interest, humor, and character of every-day living.

Feuillet, Octave (Saint Lô, Manche, France, August 11, 1821; Paris, Dec. 29, 1890). He was the son of a distinguished Norman gentleman who unfortunately suffered from a nervous disorder, which the boy inherited. Octave attended the Collège de Louis-le-Grand in Paris, where he won high honors. Though intended for the diplomatic service, he rebelled against this mandate, and in 1840 told his father that he had determined to adopt a career of letters. Thereupon the elder Feuillet disowned his headstrong son, who, returning to Paris, entered the lists of journalism. He managed to get on, and after collaborating with Bocage and Aubert under the name of Désiré Hazard, he began to write for the stage with some success. After some years his father relented, a reconciliation was effected, and the struggling author received a liberal allowance. For a while he led a care-free existence, working as his fancy dictated; and several of his proverbs, comedies, and romances appeared in the Revue des Deux Mondes. But in 1850 his father's failing health compelled him to take up his abode at the melancholy château at Saint Lô, where he was virtually chained to an invalid's chair. Marriage with his cousin, Mademoiselle Valérie Feuillet, in 1851, served to lighten his lot, and his genius came to full flower under these singular conditions. He wrote one novel after another, and in 1857 was induced to leave his father long enough to direct the staging of his Dalila at the Vaudeville in Paris. This dramatization of the novel was a huge success. In 1858 he

again left his father to see his *Romance of a Poor Young Man*
produced as a drama, but during this temporary absence the
elder Feuillet died. Subsequently Octave and his wife, together with his mother, lived in Paris where they figured in
the brilliant society of the Second Empire. Feuillet became
a court favorite, and his plays were performed at Compiègne
before the public saw them. Empress Eugénie even conde-
scended to enact a rôle in Les Portraits de la Marquise. In
1862 Octave Feuillet was elected to the French Academy, succeeding M. Scribe, and in 1868 he received the sinecure of
librarian of Fontainebleau Palace. But his later life was spent
either in retirement, or in ceaseless wanderings, the result of
his nervous disease. His most noteworthy dramatic efforts
were: Le Village (1856); Dalila (1857); Le cheveu blanc
(1860); Montjoie (1863); Le sphinx (1874); La partie des
dames (1884); and Chanillac (1886). Best among his numerous romances are: La petite Comtesse (1857); *Le Roman
d'un jeune homme pauvre* (1858), translated as *The Romance
of a Poor Young Man;* Histoire de Sibylle (1862); *Monsieur de
Camors* (1867); Julie de Trécœur (1872); Histoire d'une Parisienne (1881); La morte (1886); and L'Honneur d'artiste
(1890).

Fielding, Henry (Glastonbury, England, April 22, 1707;
Lisbon, Portugal, Oct. 8, 1754). He was the son of a soldier,
who had won his place of honor on fields of battle under the
great Marlborough. General Edmund Fielding was a grandson of the Earl of Denbigh, whose loyal life had gone out in
futile defense of the doomed King Charles.

General Edmund Fielding married, at the age of thirty,
Sarah Gould, the daughter of an honest and thrifty knight,
Sir Henry Gould, of Sharpham Park, near Glastonbury, in
Somerset. Sir Henry was one of the judges of the King's
Bench; he had a handsome fortune and kept up a good es-
tate. When the young soldier married into his family he came
to live in it in the intervals of his campaigns, and it was in
the house of his grandfather that the novelist, Henry Fielding,
saluted the great world in which he was to play his heroic part.
At East Stour the Fieldings resided until April, 1718, when

Mrs. Fielding died, leaving her elder son a boy not quite eleven years of age. How much longer the family remained there is unrecorded; but it is clear that a great part of Henry Fielding's childhood must have been spent by the pleasant banks of sweetly-winding Stour, which passes through it, and to which he subsequently refers in *Tom Jones*.

Fielding's early education was confided to a certain Mr. Oliver, whom Lawrence designates the family chaplain. Keightley supposes that he was the curate of East Stour; but Hutchins, a better authority than either, says that he was the clergyman of Motcombe, a neighboring village. Of this gentleman, according to Murphy, Parson Trulliber in *Joseph Andrews* is a very humorous and striking portrait. It is certainly more humorous than complimentary. From Mr. Oliver's care the boy was sent to Eton, though there are few records of his career there. He appears to have been an apt student and a forward boy. Murphy extols his accomplishments in Greek and Latin, but he himself depreciates them, and in one of his own verses to Walpole some years later, Fielding says:

> " Tuscan and French are in my head;
> Latin I write, and Greek I—read."

However this may have been, it is certain that, as Austin Dobson assures us, "during his stay at Eton, Fielding had been rapidly developing from a boy into a young man. When he left school it is impossible to say; but he was probably seventeen or eighteen years of age." The next we know of young Henry Fielding is that he was shipped off to Leyden to learn civil law, until a not unusual accident happened to him. His remittances failed, his debts oppressed, and his duns bothered him. His father, never a rich man, had married again. His second wife was a widow named Eleanor Rasa, and by this time he was fast acquiring a second family. Under the pressure of his growing cares he found himself, however willing, unable to maintain his eldest son or to discharge his expenses at Leyden. So Henry took his departure from the University. At the end of 1727, or the beginning of 1728, he set foot in London, there to begin as black and bitter a battle as genius ever fought with the selfish world.

His father made him a nominal allowance of two hundred a year; but this, as Fielding himself explained, "anybody might pay that would." The consequence was that not long after the arrival of the youth in the metropolis he had given up all idea of pursuing the law, to which his mother's legal connections had perhaps first attracted him, and had determined to adopt the more seductive occupation of living by his wits. At this date he was in the prime of youth. He possessed every physical characteristic calculated to attract temptation. He had the constitution of an ox, the beauty of a young god, and the heart of a good fellow.

Some resources, as Sir Walter Scott puts it, were necessary for a man of pleasure, and Fielding found them in his pen, having, as he used to say himself, no alternative but to be a hackney coachman. He at first employed himself in writing for the theater, then in high reputation, having recently engaged the talents of Wycherly, of Congreve, Vanbrugh, and Farquhar. Fielding's comedies and farces were brought on the stage in hasty succession; and play after play, to the number of eighteen, sunk or swam on the theatrical sea between the years 1727 and 1736. None of these are now known or read, excepting the mock tragedy of Tom Thumb, the translated play of The Miser, and the farces of The Mock Doctor, and The Intriguing Chambermaid.

During this period Fielding lived the life of a man of wit and pleasure about town. He stretched out his meager and precarious earnings from the stage by private levies on more prosperous friends, and sought and found his amusements in the manifold scenes of gaiety and dissipation provided by the gay and dissipated town. He even became, for a time, the manager of a theatrical company, and no doubt got his fill of this responsible involvement. In 1735 he opened the little theater in the Haymarket.

Then he sought and found at least passing relief in matrimony. He had for some years been acquainted with a good and beautiful girl at Salisbury, who possessed the additional attraction of a small fortune, about fifteen hundred pounds. Her name was Charlotte Cradock, and he made her Mrs. Fielding in 1736. As if fortune never came by halves, he also at the same time fell into a small estate of two hundred pounds a year, part of his mother's property at Stour.

There is a touch of genuine comedy about this portion of Fielding's life. He retired to his little estate at Stour with his wife, and on the income of two hundred pounds, and her poor dowry of one thousand five hundred pounds, set up the state of a great lord for their honeymoon. As Murphy says: "He began immediately to vie in splendor with the neighboring country squires, encumbered himself with a large retinue of servants, all clad in costly yellow liveries. For their master's honor, these people could not descend so low as to be careful of their apparel, and in a month or two were unfit to be seen; the Squire's dignity required that they should be new-equipped; and, his chief pleasure consisting in society and convivial mirth, hospitality made him throw open his doors. Entertainments and hounds and horses entirely devoured a little patrimony which, had it been managed with economy, might have secured to him a state of independence for the rest of his life." And so after a while Henry Fielding was on the town again, this time with a wife upon his shiftless hands, that could not provide for himself alone. It is to the pressure of this necessity that the world owes Fielding, the immortal novelist, where, under temporarily happier circumstances, Henry Fielding, the playwright, might have otherwise been forgotten.

Fielding devoted himself thenceforth with remarkable assiduity to serious work. His old irregularity of life, it is alleged, occasionally asserted itself, though without checking the energy of his application. He applied himself to the study of his profession with all the vigor of a man who has to make up for lost time, so that, when June 20, 1740, the day came for his being called he was very fairly equipped with legal knowledge. It is certain that he made a host of lawyer friends during this period, and that he made a good magistrate, when, in later years, he went upon the bench.

It is also tolerably certain that, whatever his private means may have been—and they were probably nothing at all—Fielding's ready pen contrived to support himself and his family, to which he was fondly attached, until, says Scott, amid this anxious career of precarious expedient and constant labor, he had the misfortune to lose his wife; and his grief at this domestic calamity was so extreme that his friends became alarmed for the consequences to his reason. The violence of the emotion, however, was transient, though his regret was lasting; and the necessity of subsistence compelled him again to resume his literary labors. At length, in the year 1741 or 1742, circumstances induced him to engage in a mode of composition which he retrieved from the disgrace in which he found it and rendered a classical department of British literature.

This inestimable boon English literature owes to a writer who was the antithesis of the manly and thoroughly honest and sincere Henry Fielding. It was the burning spirit of satire in Fielding, and the incredible affectation and literary prudery of Samuel Richardson, that laid the foundation for the English novel of all time, in the satirization of Richardson's *Pamela* by Fielding's *Joseph Andrews*.

No better summary can be made of this historical cornerstone to the future fiction of the English language than is given by Sir Walter Scott in his sketch of the author's life. Scott, writing of the book, and discussing its origin and its character, says: "The novel of *Pamela*, published in 1740, had carried the fame of Richardson to the highest pitch; and Fielding, whether he was tired of hearing it overpraised (for the book, several passages of which would now be thought highly indelicate, was in those days even recommended from the pulpit), or whether, as a writer for daily subsistence, he caught at whatever interested the public for the time; or whether, in fine, he was seduced by that wicked spirit of wit, which cannot forbear turning into ridicule the idol of the day, he resolved to caricature the style, principles, and personages of this favorite performance. As Gay's desire to satirize Phillips gave rise to The Shepherd's Week, so Fielding's purpose to ridicule *Pamela* produced *The History of Joseph Andrews;* and in both cases, but especially in the latter, a work was executed infinitely better than could have been expected to arise out of such a motive, and the reader received a degree of pleasure far superior to what the author himself appears to have proposed. There is, indeed, a fine vein of irony in Fielding's novel, as will appear from comparing it with the pages of *Pamela*. But *Pamela,* to which that irony was applied, is now in a manner forgotten, and *Joseph Andrews* continues to be read for the admirable pictures of manners which it presents; and above all for the inimitable character of Mr. Abraham Adams, which alone is sufficient to stamp the superiority of Fielding over all writers of his class."

The History of the Adventures of Joseph Andrews and of his friend Mr. Abraham Adams was published by Andrew Millar in February, 1742. Fielding was careful to disclaim any personal portraiture in *Joseph Andrews*. In the opening chapter to Book III he declares that he "describes not men, but manners; not an individual, but a species," though he admits that his characters are "taken from life."

Fielding made one more appearance as a dramatist after the success of *Joseph Andrews*, and it proved a failure. No particular interest attaches to Fielding's last dramatic essay, except that of curiosity. He got no gain from it, and its paucity of profit no doubt spurred him to the production of *Jonathan Wild, the Great*.

Jonathan Wild is one of the severest satires ever written. It was, for its time, the most trenchant known to English literature, and it may be questioned whether it has had a successor. The closest approach to it is Thackeray's *Barry Lyndon*, which was obviously suggested by and modeled after it. With the gravity of a historian treating of grave and reverend men, the author traced the career of an unmitigated scoundrel. Every vice and iniquity of his hero, and every vice and iniquity of the society of the time, were glorified in a negative sense. To those who have any knowledge of the manners and methods of Fielding's time, *Jonathan Wild* will have a positive interest and value. To those who have not, it will, except in certain passages, prove dull reading enough. But it is illumined, even for the unilluminated, with superb passages and splendid sketches of character, in every one of which the invariable repetition of human types, from the time when humanity began, will be recognized and prized.

The measure of success of *Jonathan Wild* was only moderate. It was, perhaps, one more of curiosity, following, as it did, after *Joseph Andrews*, than of genuine appreciation. Still, the author got some money by it, which was very much to his purpose at the time. Thenceforward his activity as a producer of fiction subsided for half a dozen years. During this time he produced no work of signal importance. He battled with the gout and with necessity. He edited the Jacobite Journal and other transient publications of a political character, and with proper and characteristic improvidence married a second time. On November 27, 1747, he took to wife one Mary Daniel, with whom he went to housekeeping in two rooms in Back Lane, Twickenham. A year or so later came another eventful turn in his career.

Smollett had begun to exercise his interest for Fielding to secure him an appointment. The Jacobite Journal ceased to appear in November, 1748. In the early part of the December following, by Lord Lyttleton's interest, Fielding was appointed a Justice of the Peace for Westminster.

On the 28th of February, 1749, Andrew Millar published *The History of Tom Jones, a Foundling*, by Henry Fielding, Esq. It appeared in six volumes at sixteen shillings a set, and took the town by storm. *Tom Jones* was dedicated to Lord Lyttleton. The price paid for it by Millar was six hundred pounds, and Horace Walpole, writing to George Montagu in May, 1749, says: "Millar the bookseller has done very generously by him (Fielding): finding *Tom Jones*, for which he had given him six hundred pounds, sell so greatly, he has since given him another hundred."

By all appearances, *Tom Jones* had been begun by the author about the time of his second marriage, and probably under pressure of the necessity that act involved. Its publication carried the author's fame to its height, but besides the money paid him for the copyright it was attended by no appreciable consequences to his fortunes.

No portion of Fielding's career presents stranger contrasts than that upon which he had now entered. As a magistrate he brought little personal dignity to the bench, where he sat in dirty ruffles and tarnished, threadbare garb, with red eyes and jaundiced face. But he did invest his office with a great deal of common sense, and speedily won recognition for the work he did in it. And what with the duties of his post, the useful and satirical pamphleteering that grew out of it, and the social exactions to which he subjected himself, he had his hands so full that he could have been excused for complete inactivity in the field of fiction.

But Fielding was no sluggard, and moreover his needs pressed him. He was by no means a rich man, and, as a Westminster justice he kept his table open to those who had been his friends when young and had impaired their fortunes. Cannot one imagine this ragged regiment feeding upon him, and the incessant pressure for money its voracity produced?

One of the most notable of Fielding's legal papers dates from this period. It is his charge to the Westminster Grand Jury, which he delivered in June, 1749, and in which among other evils he attacked his old love, the stage, for its license of personal abuse, with great severity. The charge for years has been recognized as a model delivery of its kind, dignified, forcible, eloquent, and picturesque. Its compilation is said by one of Fielding's contemporaries to have cost him two gallons of Burgundy and a fit of the gout.

At this time, pinched by poverty and gout, and racked by fever and trouble, Fielding was finding a spare hour now and then to devote to the last of the fictions which have won him immortality. Like *Tom Jones*, it came upon the world with but little preliminary advertisement. In Sylvanus Urban's list of publications for December, 1751, No. 17 is noticed as *Amelia*, in four books, by Henry Fielding, Esq.

"Fielding," wrote Walpole, "hath written a new book, and they tell me put himself in it, though whether as rogue or hero I have not yet read. But what we wonder at is where and how he finds time to write at all."

Amelia was published by Fielding's regular publisher, Andrew Millar. According to a writer in the General Advertiser, its day of issue was December 19, 1751, but it is dated 1752. Dr. Johnson was thoroughly captivated with the book. Notwithstanding that on another occasion he paradoxically asserted that the author was "a blockhead—a barren rascal," he read it through without stopping, and pronounced Mrs. Booth to be "the most pleasing heroine of all the romances." The completion of *Amelia* found its author in a very bad way physically. His gout had become chronic and aggravated. There were forebodings of dropsy. Time and again his physicians commanded him to absolute inactivity and freedom from care. The satire of this prescription is exquisite in its perfection. In order to cure himself, Fielding would have had to starve himself to death. He did nothing of the kind, though. Like a sentinel at his post, he remained in harness in defiance of anguish and flashes and glooms of hopefulness and despair that would have distracted and overturned a feebler mind. "'Tis not the labor that tires me," he writes to a friend at this period, "nor the trouble of thinking. Ideas grow with growth and expand with their execution. If I were a score of years younger, what could I not accomplish?" Alas! it was the old story of powers that mature while men decay. A black and bitter life's lesson was bearing splendid fruits at a day too late for the gardener to enjoy them. Fielding still seems to have cherished hopes for another work of fiction after *Amelia*. He hints at it obscurely in the few letters he found time to write, and several times alluded to it in casual conversation. But it appears never to have got beyond the germ of the idea, and never to have even skeletonized the plan for its performance. In the profound depths of his deep and daring brain, this last infant of his proud originality died stillborn.

But he wrote all the same. He established the Covent Garden Journal, as a sort of critical and censorious review of the Great Britain in which he was so great a figure. The Covent Garden Journal was a bi-weekly paper, in which Fielding, under the style and title of "Sir Alexander Drawcansir," assumed the office of censor of Great Britain. The first number of this new venture was issued on January 4, 1752, and the price was threepence. In plan and general appearance it resembled the Jacobite's Journal, consisting mainly of an introductory essay, paragraphs of current news, often accompanied by pointed editorial comment, miscellaneous articles and advertisements.

Fielding went to Lisbon in search of health and died there, in his forty-eighth year. He was buried in the English cemetery there, and some sort of tomb was set up to him. His first tomb, which Wraxall found, in 1772, almost concealed by weeds

and nettles, was erected by the English factory, in consequence
mainly, as it seems, of a proposal made by an enthusiastic
Chevalier de Meyrionnet, to provide one (with an epitaph) at
his own expense. That now existing was substituted in 1830
by the exertions of the Rev. Christopher Neville, British chaplain at Lisbon. It is a heavy sarcophagus, resting upon a large
base, and surmounted by just such another urn and flame as
that on Hogarth's tomb at Chiswick. On the front is a long
Latin inscription; on the back the better-known words:

Luget Britannia Gremio non dari
Fovere natum.

It is to this last memorial that George Borrow referred in
his well-known book, The Bible in Spain: "Let travelers
devote one entire morning to inspecting the *Acros* and the *Mai
das agoas*, after which they may repair to the English church
and cemetery, Père-la-Chaise in miniature, where, if they be
of England, they may well be excused if they kiss the cold
tomb, as I did, of the author of *Amelia*, the most singular genius
which their island ever produced, whose works it has long been
the fashion to abuse in public and to read in secret."

Fielding left two posthumous works, The Journal of a
Voyage to Lisbon, and a comedy, The Fathers: or, The Good-
Natured Man. The journal was published in 1755. It
proved a commercial failure. The play was acted first in 1778,
by Garrick, at Drury Lane.

The literary life of Henry Fielding went out with little
honor, as honor goes before the gilded world. But the splendors of his prime are for him a certain guaranty of immortality. And always and ever, while honest men of letters tug
at the oar in the ink sea, his name will be to them an inspiration, his life an honor to their craft and an invitation to
the sacrifices that advance civilization, however little profit
they garner from the world they benefit and ennoble at such
terrible personal cost.

Flaubert, Gustave (Rouen, France, Dec. 12, 1821; Croisset,
May 8, 1880). The father of the novelist was head surgeon
of the Rouen hospital, having his residence in the hospital

building, where the son was born and also a daughter, Caroline. Gustave lived there until he was eighteen, when he went to Paris to study law. From an early age he was fond of literature, and wrote little plays when he was eleven years old, which he acted with his young companions.

The friends of his childhood and youth were few, but their mutual affection lasted till death cut them short. These included Ernest Chevalier, Louis Bouilhet, the poet, and Alfred Le Poittevin. Maxime Du Camp was a friend of later years. He had chosen to study law rather than medicine, although he had no particular taste for the legal profession, and had not then thought of devoting himself to literature. But he idled over his studies, dreamed and scribbled, and visited studios and salons, where he met Pradier, Victor Hugo, and other distinguished men who were interested in the young man. He made a trip to Corsica and the Pyrenees, writing a record of this journey that showed traits of the "master traveler" that he afterward became.

In 1845 the elder Flaubert died; the following year Gustave's only and beloved sister died, and the young student decided to leave Paris and the study of law, and to dwell with his mother at Croisset, near Rouen, in a pleasant house overlooking the Seine. From this time (1846) he determined to devote his time to literature, and he wrote the first draught of The Temptation of Saint Antony, which he did not finish till many years later.

In 1849 Flaubert made a journey to the East, where he collected much material used later in his romances. After 1846 he lived chiefly at Croisset for thirty-four years, working furiously, with little relaxation. He had assumed the guardianship of his dead sister's little daughter and worked for his mother and the child. Among his friends were MM. Sainte-Beuve, Jules Sandeau, Théophile Gautier, the De Goncourt brothers, George Sand, and Alphonse Daudet.

From 1850 to 1856 Flaubert planned and wrote *Madame Bovary*. This great realistic and analytical romance appeared first in the *Revue de Paris* (1856). Early in the following year the author was compelled to appear before the court in an action brought against himself and his publishers for having produced a work supposedly immoral and irreligious. Flaubert was vigorously attacked by the public prosecutor, but was so well defended by his own lawyer that he was acquitted of the charge of corrupting public morals.

From 1857 he wrote on both *Salammbô* and The Temptation of Saint Antony; and *Salammbô*, the result of immense literary and archeological study, appeared in 1862. This work was a marvelous reconstitution, more than half intuitive, of a civilization practically unrecorded in history. He then began a novel of contemporaneous manners, entitled *Sentimental Education* (1869).

During the Franco-Prussian War of 1870, and for some time thereafter, the political condition of France, and the moderate success of *Salammbô* and *Sentimental Education* (moderate compared to the tremendous success of *Madame Bovary*), besides a tendency to epilepsy, from which Flaubert had suffered from early years, affected unfavorably the novelist's mental and physical health. He lost his mother in 1872; his two lifelong friends, Le Poittevin and Bouilhet, were both dead, his friendship with Maxime Du Camp was broken; and finally he lost part of his fortune in coming to the assistance of his niece and her young husband, who had been unfortunate in pecuniary affairs. His chief consolation was in the affection and tender care of this niece, Madame Commanville, and the touching friendship that existed between himself and George Sand. She sustained his drooping spirits and often cheered him to something of his old gaiety, and wrote him indefatigably the most charming elder-sisterly letters.

Flaubert found also some comfort in the growing talent of his young disciple, Guy de Maupassant, to whom he taught the art of writing, and in whom he foresaw a glorious successor to himself.

He worked in these later years more tirelessly than ever, finally completing, in 1874, that Temptation of Saint Antony which had obsessed all his life and which may fairly be called "the temptation of Flaubert." In 1874 his play, The Candidate, written in 1847, was produced at the Vaudeville Theater in Paris, but was not successful. It was not his first dramatic effort, as he had already written a sort of lyric fairy play, The

Castle of Hearts (Le Château des cœurs), which was first published in his posthumous works.

In 1877 Flaubert published a volume entitled Three Tales (Trois contes) and then set himself to writing the work which was of all his productions the dearest to his heart—Bouvard and Pécuchet. Exhausted by his toil on this unique work of philosophy, strung on a mere thread of story, he died without finishing it. A monument, sculptured in high relief, composed of a medallion portrait of Gustave Flaubert with an allegorical female figure below it, the work of the sculptor Henri Chapu, was erected by the city of Rouen, in 1890.

Fogazzaro, Antonio (Vicenza, Italy, March 25, 1842). His father took part in the defense of his native city against the Austrians in 1848, during the War of Liberation, while his mother busied herself making cockades for the soldiers. Their home in truth was the rallying-place for Vicenza patriots; and amid this influence Antonio began to learn his numbers. In time he entered the Liceo, where he came under the poetical guidance of Giacomo Fanella, the abbot, who incited his students to the study of Æschylus and Lucretius among the ancient poets and to Heine among the modern. The latter exercised a strong hold over the imagination of Fogazzaro, as also did the poetry of Byron in French. However, Fogazzaro was slow in developing his genius for writing, and the early part of his career was that of an ordinary lawyer. At length he ventured into verse with Miranda (1874), a metrical romance, and two years later published Valsolda, a volume of poems. There was a Wordsworthian simplicity and pathos about these verses which added a genuine and wholesome note to modern Italian poetry. Despite his success as a poet, Fogazzaro turned his attention to novel writing, and his first attempt, Malombra (1881), augured well. Then followed Daniele Cortis (1885), Il Mistero del Poeta (1888), and the first romance of his trilogy, Il Piccola Mondo Antico (1896), which has been translated into English as The Sinner (1907). This attracted the attention of French critics, whose notice created a prodigious demand for it. Not since I Promessi Sposi had any Italian novel created such a sensation, and its author was hailed as the legitimate successor of Manzoni, whom he reveres as his literary master. The second story of the trilogy, Il Piccola Mondo Moderno (The Man of the World), appeared in 1901, and the last, *Il Santo (The Saint)*, in 1905. This one aroused universal discussion because of its treatment of the Roman Catholic Church, and it was consequently placed upon the Index Expurgatorius.

Ford, Paul Leicester (Brooklyn, N. Y., March 23, 1865; New York City, May 8, 1902). When a child a fall from a nurse's arms permanently injured his spine and dwarfed his growth. This accident prohibited an ordinary course of education, and the boy was put under private tutors. Paul had, naturally, a brilliant mind, and his love of study was pronounced from the first. Gordon L. Ford, his father, was for many years the publisher of the New York Tribune, as well as a collector of rare books; and from him the young student obtained a large amateur printing outfit, which he learned to operate. As early as 1876 he partly set up a revised edition of the Webster Genealogy, by Noah Webster, with his own name on the title-page as editor. He also ransacked his father's splendid library, one of the finest private collections in the metropolis, and thus gleaned a vast amount of unusual information while yet a lad. Travel was another source of delightful knowledge to him, and he traversed much of the United States and of Europe. American colonial history especially appealed to him, and his investigations in that field proved invaluable. His exhaustive edition of the Writings of Thomas Jefferson (1892) was followed by the equally admirable Writings of Thomas Dickinson (1895); then in the same spirit he wrote The True George Washington (1896) and The Many-Sided Franklin (1899). He also edited the New England Primer (1897) and The Federalist (1898), and issued many pamphlets relating to American historiography. As a skilled bibliographer he made the catalogue (1896) of the James Lorimer Graham Library, bequeathed to the Century Association, and compiled biographies of Hamilton and of Franklin. At the time of his death he was editor of The Bibliographer, which he founded. As a writer of fiction he was singularly successful, and in this field produced: *The Honorable Peter Stirling* (1894), The Great K. & A. Train Robbery (1897), The Story of an Untold Love (1897), Tattle-Tales of Cupid (1898), Janice Meredith (1899), Wanted: A Matchmaker (1901), and Wanted: A Chaperon (1902). His last work was a return to the realm of our Colonial history: Journals of Hugh Gaine, Printer (1902).

Fothergill, Jessie (Cheatham Hill, Manchester, England, June 7, 1851; Berne, Switzerland, July 28, 1891). She was the eldest child of Thomas and Anne Fothergill, a middle-class couple who, when their daughter was quite young, re-moved to Bowdon, in Cheshire, about ten miles from Man-chester. Here her father continued his small cotton industry till 1866, the year of his death. Shortly after this bereavement the family went to live in Littleborough, near Rochdale. Jes-sie's education was begun in an insignificant private school in Bowdon, and was finished in a Harrogate seminary. Alto-gether her life was like that of most English girls in narrow, provincial circumstances, but she made use of her environment in the novels she afterward wrote, and her study of the condi-tions of the cotton-mill workers bore fruit. Her stories deal mostly with moorland life, the factories of Lancashire and Yorkshire, together with highly-wrought descriptions of the power of music. Character portrayal was her strong point. In 1874 Miss Fothergill had an unexpected and welcome opportunity to spend some time in Germany, and upon her return to England, spurred on by her enthusiasm and by need of money, she wrote her first novel, Healey (1875). Encouraged by its reception, she attempted another, Aldyth (1876), and the proceeds of these two books enabled her to go to Düsseldorf with a party of friends. It was during this sojourn that she developed her extraordinary passion for music, which is ap-parent in every chapter of her next and most famous novel, *The First Violin* (1877). Thenceforth her life was devoted to literature and travel on the continent of Europe. The rest of her books were entitled: The Wellfields (1880); Kith and Kin (1881); Made or Marred (1881); One of Three (1881); Peril (1884); Borderland (1888); The Lasses of Leverhouse

(1888); From Moor Isles (1888); A March in the Ranks (1890) and Oriole's Daughter (1893).

Fouqué, Friedrich Heinrich Karl, Baron de la Motte (Brandenburg, Germany, February 12, 1777; Berlin, January 23, 1843. His grandfather and his father served in the Prussian army, and the little Friedrich, an only child, was godson and namesake of the great King. He was educated chiefly at home by tutors, one of whom, August Hülse, fostered his pupil's literary taste. Law was taken up at Halle, but in 1794 he quitted that study to become an *über completer cornet* in the cuirassier regiment commanded by the Grand Duke of Weimar. Thus equipped, he went through the unfortunate campaign of the Rhine, and for some years led a life divided between military duties and literature. Important among the former were his deeds at the battle of Lützen, in 1813, when he twice narrowly escaped death. Subsequently he was disabled by an accident to his horse while bearing a secret despatch, and was honorably discharged from the army with the rank of major of cavalry and the decoration of the Johanniter orden. From 1831 to 1842 he lectured at Halle on modern history and poetry. At the beginning of his career as a man of letters he studied assiduously the Spanish and Italian poets, and filled his mind with Norse legends. Under the pseudonym of Pellegrin he brought out his first effort, Dramatische Spiele (1804), and the Schlegels were his publisher-sponsors. Thus highly encouraged he produced plays, poems, and romances, especially Alwin (1808), which won the praise of Richter. From this time forth he dropped his pen-name, and under his own wrote Sigurd der Schlangentöter (1808), founded on the Nibelungenlied. In 1811 he published several plays and the chivalric romance, Der Zauberring (The Enchanted Ring). During the next three years his pen was very prolific, and he founded Der Musen, a periodical. But in 1814 he reached the height of his genius, for then appeared in its four parts his crowning achievement, the Jahreszeiten. The first part was the ever-lovely *Undine*, the second contained Die bliden Hauptlente, the third instalment was Aslanga's Ritter mit Algin und Jocunda, and the fourth part was *Sintram*, which takes its place for perpetual charm beside his *Undine*. In 1814 he published also a romance, Die Fahrten Thiodolfs des Isländers, which he regarded as his best work. Fouqué was certainly one of the most industrious and popular writers of the early nineteenth century, but he lived to see the decay and end of the Romantic cult, of which he was a prime figure.

Fowler, Ellen Thorneycroft (England, 1873). She is the eldest daughter of the Right Honorable Sir Henry Fowler, who, during 1894-'95, was the Secretary of State for India. In childhood she amused herself by writing verses and stories, in this fashion chronicling the events of her domestic and social life. Next she figured as a contributor to the "poet's corner" of the local weekly, repaid merely by seeing herself in print; then she began sending her verses to sundry magazines, and many were accepted. These fugitive bits of work with others were finally gathered into a thin volume, Verses Grave and Gay (1891); and she repeated the experiment in Verses Wise and Otherwise (1895). Next came a collection of short stories, Cupid's Garden (1897). After this a friend urged her to try her hand at a more sustained piece of fiction, and within four months she had completed her first sensational success, Concerning Isabel Carnaby (1898), which proved a clever society study, written with unusual verve. Then followed a volume annually: *A Double Thread* (1899), The Farringdons (1900), Sirius and Other Stories (1901), Fuel of Fire (1902), and Place and Power (1903). In the latter year she married Alfred Lawrence Felkin, and collaborated with him on Kate of Kate Hall (1904). Another novel from her pen alone was In Subjection (1906).

France, Anatole, the pseudonym of Jacques Anatole Thibault (Paris, April 16, 1844). He is the son of Jacques Thibault (1805–1865), a well known bookseller. He was educated at the Collège Stanislas, and in 1876 was appointed librarian to the Senate, an office he still occupies. Choosing to pursue a literary life, he soon became known from his critical contributions to La Vie Littéraire, Le Globe, Les Débats, La Revue des Deux Mondes, La Revue de Paris and other periodicals. His first book was a biography of Alfred de Vigny, published in 1868. This was followed by Poëmes dorés (1873), and Noces corinthiennes (1876); and in 1878 by a novel, Tocaste et le chat maigre, which was well received. In 1881 his novel, Le crime de Sylvestre Bonnard, was crowned by the French Academy, and established his reputation.

Other novels now followed in quick succession: Les désirs de Jean Dervieu (1884); Le livre de mon ami (1885); Nos enfants (1885); Balthazar (1889); Thaïs (1890); Les opinions de Jerome Coignard (1893); L'étui de nacre (1894); and Le lys rouge (1896). The last, translated into English as The Red Lily, was at once crowned by the Academy and pronounced his greatest work. It is the story of a heartless coquette who pretends to love two men, who love her, and loses both of them; it stands by itself in modern fiction as a study of woman's fickleness. Its author was elected, in the same year, a member of the Académie Française in succession to the Comte de Lesseps.

Frederic, Harold (Utica, New York, August 19, 1856; Henley-on-Thames, England, Oct. 19, 1898). He was the son of Henry De Motte Frederic, who was killed in 1858; the younger man was of Dutch, French, and New England ancestry. He attended the public schools in Utica until his fourteenth year, when he began to study for a draughtsman. When twenty years old he became a reporter on the staff of the Utica Herald, of which he became editor in 1880. Two years later he left this place to take charge of the Albany Evening Journal, and in 1884 went to Europe as special correspondent of the New York Times, with headquarters in London. During this connection he traveled much, being sent cn special missions to Russia, Ireland, Germany, etc.

Mr. Frederic began his literary career, outside of newspaper work, by the publication, as a serial in Scribner's Magazine, of a novel entitled Seth's Brother's Wife (1887), which at once brought him into notice as a forceful and interesting writer. This was followed by other novels and descriptive and historical works in the following order: The Lawton Girl (1890); In the Valley (1890); The Young Emperor: William II of Germany (1891); The Return of the O'Mahoney (1892); The New Exodus: a Study of Israel in Russia (1892); The Copperhead (1893); Marsena, and Other Stories of the War Time (1894); *The Damnation of Theron Ware* (1896).

This last work, a brilliant analysis of religious life and experience in what may be called the American middle class, was recognized as one of the ablest efforts of the time and gave its author a high place in the domain of letters. The New Exodus, the result of his visit to Russia, is a study of Anti-Semitism. His later works, some of which were posthumous, were: March Hares (1896); Gloria Mundi (1898); and In the Market-Place (1899), none of which reached the level of *Theron Ware*.

Freytag, Gustav (Kreuzburg, Silesia, Germany, July 13, 1816; Wiesbaden, April 30, 1895). He studied at the universities of Breslau and Berlin, and became docent of the German language and literature at the former, but resigned in 1844 and went to Leipzig and Dresden. In 1848 he returned to Leipzig and, jointly with Julian Schmidt, succeeded Kuranda as editor of the Grenzboten, which he conducted till 1861, and again from 1867 to 1870. In 1854 he was appointed councilor of the court and lecturer to the Duke of Gotha. In 1879 he removed to Wiesbaden, where he resided until his decease.

Freytag's earliest literary works are dramatic. His drama Die Valentine appeared in 1846, and the comedy Die Journalisten (The Journalists) in 1853. In 1855 was published his first novel, *Soll und Haben*, which gained for him a wide popularity and was translated into many languages, appearing in its English dress as *Debit and Credit*. In 1859 was produced a tragedy Die Fabier (The Fabians), in 1863 Die Technic des Dramas (The Technic of the Drama), and in 1864 another novel, Die verlorene Handschrift (The Lost Manuscript). From 1859 to 1867 were published several historical works, collected in four volumes in the latter year under the title of Bilder aus der deutschen Vergangenheit (Pictures from the German Past). Between 1870 and 1880 also he published a series of six novels, illustrative of German life from the time of the Romans down to the Napoleonic wars, which were ulti-

mately collected under the title Die Ahnen (Our Ancestors).
An autobiography, Erinnerungen aus meinem Leben (Recollections from my Life), was published in 1887, with a
collected edition of his works in twenty-two volumes.

Gaboriau, Émile (Saujon, Charente-Inférieure, France,
Nov. 9, 1833; Paris, Sept. 28, 1873). He was first employed
as a clerk in the office of a notary, then as a volunteer in a cavalry regiment, and later became secretary to Paul Féval. He
began his literary career with sketches of theatrical, military,
and fashionable life, published in the lesser Parisian journals,
and later collected under various titles, as Ruses d'amour,
Les comédiennes adorées, Mariages d'aventure, etc. In 1866
he published in Le Pays a story of crime entitled l'Affaire
Lerouge, which brought him into notice, and this was followed
by a series of similar works which gave him a European reputation as a reviver of the romances of rascality. Gaboriau
made a careful study of the Paris police system, and his stories,
which exhibit a thorough acquaintance with all phases of criminal life, are written with apparent ease and full of interesting
incidents.

Among his other works are: *File No. 113* (1867); Le Crime
d'Orcival (1867); *Monsieur Lecoq* (1869); Les esclaves de
Paris (1870); La vie infernale (1870); La clique dorée (1871);
La corde au cou (1873); L'argent des autres (1874); Le petit
vieux des Batignolles (1876); La dégringolade (1876). The
last mentioned three works were posthumous. In 1872 Gaboriau, in collaboration with Hippolyte Hostein, dramatized
L'Affaire Lerouge in five acts, adapting for it an episode in
Monsieur Lecoq.

Galdos, Benito Perez (Las Palmas, Canary Islands, May
10, 1845). After a preliminary education at home, he was sent
to Madrid to study law, but soon developed a taste for art,
especially for painting. Living in Madrid during the revolutionary period, he began to write political and literary articles
in El Contemporáneo, El Parlamento, La Nación, La Revista
de España, and other periodicals. In 1871 he published a
historical romance entitled El Audaz, and in 1872 a second

one, entitled La Fontana de Oro, which, however, was written in 1867.

Having now found his vocation in romance, Galdos produced rapidly a series of historical novels dealing with Spanish history, which, under the general title of Episodios Nacionales, are divided into two series, each of ten volumes. The first series, finished in 1875, includes the following: Trafalgar; La corte de Carlos IV; El 19 de marzo y el 2 de mayo; Bailén; Napoleon en Chamartin; *Saragossa;* Gerona; Cádiz; Juan Martin el Empecinado; La batalla de los Arapiles.

The second series, finished in 1880, comprises: El equipaje del rey José, Memorias de un cortesano de 1815; La segunda casaca; El grande Oriente; 7 de Julio; Los cien mil hijos de San Luis; El terror de 1824; Un voluntario realista; Los apostólicos, Un faccioso mas y algunos frailes menos.

In 1876 Galdos began a series of Novelas españolas contemporáneas, the vogue of which has been even greater than that of the National Episodes. Among these are: Doña Perfecta (1876); La familia de Léon Roch (1878); *Marianela* (1878); Gloria (1880); El amigo manso (1882); El doctor Centeno (1883); La de Bringas (1884); Tormento (1884); Lo prohibido (1885); Fortunata y Jacinta (1887); Miau (1888); La incognita (1889); Torquemada en la hoguera (1889); Realidad 1890); Ladesheredada (1891); and Angel Guerra (1891).

Having established his reputation as the first and most prolific of Spanish novelists, Galdos sought next to conquer the drama, but, though he met with some success, his plays are inferior to his novels. Chief among them are: Realidad (1892); La loca de la casa (1893); La de San Quintin (1894); Doña Perfecta (1900); Electra (1900).

In 1886-'90 Galdos was a deputy in the Cortes for Guayama, one of the districts of the Island of Puerto Rico. In 1897 he was received into the Spanish Academy.

Galt, John (Irvine, Ayrshire, Scotland, May 2, 1779; Greenock, April 11, 1839). His father, captain of a West Indiaman, removed his family to Greenock when John was about ten years old. The boy had received a desultory education at home and in the Irvine grammar school, and at Greenock was put first into the custom-house and then into a mercantile house. Delicate and sensitive as a child, he had early formed a love for ballads and story-books, and he soon found his way to the public library and a literary society, and to contribute to a local newspaper.

After some years of mercantile life, partly in Greenock and partly in London, he entered at Lincoln's Inn, but never was called to the bar. In 1809 he set out on a commercial mission to the Continent, and traveled nearly three years in Southern Europe and the Mediterranean countries, publishing the result of his observations on his return in Voyages and Travels, and Letters from the Levant. He sailed from Gibraltar to Malta with Lord Byron and Mr. John Hobhouse, and afterward visited the poet in Constantinople and in Greece.

Soon after his return he married Elizabeth, daughter of Dr. Tilloch, editor of The Philosophical Magazine and proprietor of The Star newspaper, on which Galt was for some time employed. He published in 1812 a Life of Wolsey, edited in 1814–'15 the New British Theatre, and compiled from 1816–'20 the Life and Studies of Benjamin West. A tragedy entitled The Appeal was acted a few nights at Edinburgh, and The Earthquake, a novel, met with little favor; but another, entitled The Ayrshire Legatees, which appeared in Blackwood's Magazine in 1820–'21, turned the popular tide in his favor.

He now produced stories in rapid succession, among them: Annals of the Parish (1821); Sir Andrew Wylie (1822); Ringham Gilhaize (1823); The Spaewife (1823); Rothelan (1824); The Entail (1824); The Omen (1825); and The Last of the Lairds (1825), all stories of Scottish life.

In 1826 he visited Canada as the agent of the Canada Company, a large corporation for the purchase of crown lands, and founded the town of Guelph; but, in consequence of a difficulty with the company, returned to England in 1829 and resumed his literary labors. In 1830 he published his novel Lawrie Todd: or, The Settlers in the Woods, a graphic account of pioneer life in the New World, incorporating some of his own experiences. In the same year he published a Life of Lord Byron, in 1833 the Autobiography of John Galt, and in

1834 the Literary Life and Miscellanies of John Galt, for which William IV sent him two hundred pounds.

Lawrie Todd was followed by other novels, Southennan, Boyle Corbet, Stanley Buxton, The Member, The Radical, Eben Erskine, and The Lost Child, of very unequal merit. In 1834, poor and paralyzed, Galt found a home with a sister in Greenock, where he dictated compositions after he had lost the use of every limb. In 1836 he edited, with an introduction, Forty Years Residence in America, exemplified in the Life of Grant Thorburn (the original of Lawrie Todd), Seedsman, New York, written by himself.

John Galt is described as more than six feet in height, of herculean frame when in health, small piercing eyes, straight nose, long upper lip, and finely rounded chin.

Gaskell, Elizabeth Cleghorn (Lindsey Row, now part of Cheyne Walk, Chelsea, London, Sept. 29, 1810; Holybourne, near Alton, Hampshire, Nov. 12, 1865). She was the daughter of William Stevenson, originally a Unitarian minister, who gave up theology to devote himself to agricultural pursuits, and who finally settled in London as keeper of records to the Treasury. Her mother, daughter of a Mr. Holland, of Sandle Bridge, Cheshire, died within a month after Elizabeth's birth, and the child was sent to Knutsford, Cheshire, to the care of Mrs. Lumb, sister of Mrs. Stevenson. Her aunt was poor, living in a modest house with an old-fashioned garden on the heath; but she had other relatives in Knutsford, among them her uncle Peter Holland, grandfather of the present Viscount Knutsford, a country physician.

Knutsford, a quaint little country town fifteen miles from Manchester, supplied her later with the materials for her pictures of life at Cranford. Here she spent all her early life, making an occasional visit to London, where she stayed with her uncle, Swinton Holland, in Park Lane. When fifteen years old she was sent for two years to a school at Stratford-on-Avon, where she studied Latin, French, and Italian. She afterward spent two winters at Newcastle-on-Tyne, and one in Edinburgh, where her youthful beauty was so much admired that painters and sculptors asked her to sit for her portrait.

Her father died in 1829, and three years later, Aug. 30, 1832, she married at Knutsford the Rev. William Gaskell, minister of the Cross Street Unitarian Chapel in Manchester. Her marriage was a happy one, her husband being the confidant of her literary life, and occasionally coöperating in her literary labors.   In 1838 when William Howitt announced his intention of publishing his Visits to Remarkable Places, Mrs. Gaskell offered to contribute an account of Clopton Hall, near Stratford.   This, written in 1840, was her first known publication.   In 1841, on a Rhine tour, she made the acquaintance of William and Mary Howitt, which ripened into an intimacy that lasted during life.

In 1844 the Gaskells lost their only son, William, and, to assuage his wife's grief, Mr. Gaskell advised her to write. The result was her first novel, Mary Barton, which, after being declined by many publishers, was bought by Chapman and Hall for one hundred pounds, and published in 1848 anonymously.   It immediately achieved a great success, was translated into many languages, even the Finnish, and made her reputation.   The new writer was eagerly welcomed by Dickens, and invited to contribute to Household Words, then about to begin.   In the first number, March 30, 1850, she began a story entitled Lizzie Leigh, which was concluded April 30th.   She contributed frequently afterward both to it and to All the Year Round, her stories being collected later in various forms.   In 1851–'53 she published in Household Words a series of original papers which were republished in book form in the latter year under the title Cranford.   They are delightful chapters of real life tinged with the most delicate sentiment, and constitute, says Lord Houghton, "the purest piece of humoristic description that has been added to British literature since Charles Lamb."

Her principal works of fiction, besides those mentioned, are: Moorland Cottage (1850); Ruth (1853); North and South (1855); Round the Sofa (1859); Right at Last (1860); Sylvia's Lovers (1863); Wives and Daughters (1866). Most of her works were republished in this country.

In 1850 Mrs. Gaskell made the acquaintance of Charlotte Brontë, with whom she was intimate until the latter's decease

(1855). In 1857 she published an elaborate biography of the author of Jane Eyre, in two volumes, giving many interesting details of her private life.

Gautier, Théophile (Larbes, France, Aug. 31, 1811; Paris, Oct. 23, 1872). The great apostle of Romanticism and of the much debated doctrine of "art for art's sake" was the son of Jean-Pierre Gautier, who was employed in the Internal Revenue service. His mother, Adélaïde-Antoinette Cocard, was a charming woman, whose influence on her son was highly beneficial. The family did not remain long in the South after Théophile's birth, but removed to Paris—henceforth the lad's home as it was of the man—in 1814, at the time when Napoleon abdicated at Fontainebleau and was removed to Elba.

Gautier very early displayed one of his characteristic traits; an insatiable love of reading. At five years of age he read with facility, and from that day was known as an omnivorous reader: everything was grist to his mill, encyclopedias and dictionaries, novels and books of travel, history and art, naught came amiss to him; and in his memory, readier and more retentive than that of most men, he stored what he acquired, to turn it to account in the innumerable volumes and articles which later came from his busy pen. He was first sent to the Collège Louis-le-Grand, one of the most famous in Paris, but the life of a French schoolboy in the institutions of that period was somber and dull to a degree. Gautier pined and fretted until his father removed him and sent him to the Collège Charlemagne as a day-pupil. There he met the lad who remained his intimate friend until death, Gérard de Labrunie, better known under his pseudonym of Gérard de Nerval, under which he published striking tales of true Romanticist character and tone.

While still at school, Théophile Gautier exhibited so marked a vocation for art that he was enrolled in the studio of Rioult, and there experienced the Romanticist influence which, it is to be noted, developed more rapidly and more fully among painters than even among writers. Victor Hugo, who had finally abandoned the pseudo-classical style of his earliest poetic efforts, had quickly attained the position of leader of the movement, and he was as a god to the fiery generation of artists who saw in him the greatest genius France had ever brought forth. Gautier's admiration for him was well-nigh idolatry, and when the aspiring youth was finally presented to the poet he at once became his most ardent and his most enthusiastic supporter. Nor did that admiration ever diminish although literary taste changed and Romanticism passed away. To the very last Gautier sang the praises of his master in poesy, and contributed very largely, by his articles and his books, to strengthen the fame of the author of Hernani.

Without abandoning painting, Gautier felt inspired to write verse, and, like Hugo, he at once wrote admirably, unlike most of his comrades of that day, to whom it sufficed to produce rich rhymes and strange periods. Already Gautier exhibited the power and the accuracy which were later to influence so profoundly the Parnassian school of writers.

It was in the memorable year 1830 that he published his first volume of verse. The time was ill chosen, for the minds of men were stirred by revolutionary ideas, and they had no thought to spare for poetry amid the storms of politics and the crashing of thrones. The book, therefore, passed almost unperceived amid the tumult of the first of "the glorious days of July," yet not wholly so. Gautier shortly produced a purely romantic poem, Albertus, a fantastic composition after the manner of the Germans, whose notions were greatly in favor with the new school. But already, spite of his enthusiasm for Romanticism, and all it meant to his ardent generation, Gautier saw the ridiculous side of much that was being done, and in his next work, La Jeune France, he indulged in well-merited sarcasm at the expense of the more exaggerated followers of Hugo. Then came the book which at once made him famous—the unforgettable *Mademoiselle de Maupin*, which scandalized many and transported others with delight. The celebrated Preface, in particular, attracted attention and excited enmity by its brilliant challenge to the conservative ideas which still largely ruled and which it was the ambition of the Romanticists to destroy.

At this time an event happened to Gautier which he believed to be a great misfortune: he was compelled by the necessities of life to enter the ranks of writers for the press, and thenceforth he remained a newspaper man to the end of his life. Sad, indeed, and almost despairing, are the lines he wrote on this occasion: a farewell to poesy and art. But Gautier was mistaken: the new departure to which he was compelled was to prove the making of his influence and the benefit of art. The press gave him precisely the means he needed to act on the public on the one hand and on the artists and writers on the other. He reached a far wider public and performed a far more important work than he could have done had he, as he desired, remained a free lance. Nor did the exacting requirements of his new profession prevent his publishing many independent works, as well as many which first appeared in instalments in the public press. Fortunio, one of his best tales, came out in 1838; La Comédie de la mort, in verse, appeared in 1838.

Gautier was devoured by the desire to see foreign countries. His fellow-Romanticists were entirely satisfied to write about Spain, Italy, and the East, without stirring from the boulevards and the Latin quarter; but Gautier longed to see foreign lands with his own eyes. His ambition was further stirred by a rapid trip to Belgium, in search of the originals of Rubens's splendid women, and in 1840 he went to Spain, the land of his dreams. The result was the most remarkable book of travels which France had yet produced. It was a new mode of vision and description which Gautier revealed in this delightful and fascinating account of his journey. Chateaubriand and Lamartine had already revolutionized the method of writing books of travel, but neither of them possessed the special aptitudes and the peculiar training of Théophile Gautier. A thorough artist, like his illustrious predecessors, he had had a more careful training in the science of observation: he saw more accurately, more closely than they; and in this respect, with the command of the largest vocabulary known among authors of that period, he was bound to produce a wholly new and wholly remarkable work. His Voyage en Espagne (1843) was the first and best of the series, although the Voyage en Italie, Constantinople, and the Voyage en Russie run it very closely indeed. In these books Gautier displayed the peculiar characteristics of his talent: a rare power of observation, of discrimination in the selection of effective details, the power to reproduce accurately whatever he saw, whether that was architecture, painting, costume, or manners. His descriptions are invariably brilliant and vivid, felicitous in the choice of words, rich and warm in color. His marvelous vocabulary enabled him to carry out the principle he afterward so ardently advocated, that there is but one word in the language to describe definitely a given thing or effect. Consequently all his books of travel possess a directness and a sense of life which then were rarely met with in literature.

Gautier was a Romanticist, undoubtedly, but he worked more like a realist: his use of detail, carefully chosen, his striving after exactness, his endeavor to depict faithfully, were not Romanticist traits, but true realistic features. He has been reproached with never penetrating beneath the surface, and the reproach is just; on the other hand, Gautier never set up to be a psychologist, an analyst of sentiments and passions; he was entirely content, like his companions in the school, to represent the external without seeking to discover to the reader the occult motives and working forces. Hence, while he tells in incomparable language of the picturesqueness of Spain, of the charm of Venice, of the strangeness of Constantinople, of the barbaric splendors of Russia, he does not inform his reader with regard to the character of the races, or attempt to explain, by reference to the moral side of the nation, the results obtained by it in art in any form. Nor does he concern himself in the least with the political or social conditions: these do not interest him. And that is chiefly because he sees in civilization a corrupting force, against which he would react with all his might. He is no admirer of material progress: an artist to the core, he curses the civilization which introduces a dead level of uniformity in costume, which destroys the picturesque for the sake of the practical, which substitutes the utilitarian for the beautiful. And civilization manifests itself chiefly, in his view, in the civil institutions, in the religious forms, in the industrial developments: railways and steamers, stores and hotels, law-courts and prisons. He prefers the simpler but richer life of the good old days of chivalry and romance.

Another reason is that from the outset of his career Gautier was the devoted worshiper of ideal beauty, and his effort was continual to discover beauty wherever it might lurk. Beauty, according to him, does not reveal herself to all men, but only to those who have eyes to see and hearts capable of appreciating the revelation. Civilization is the reign of ugliness; politics are a moral hideousness; institutions, save those of days long vanished, are abominations which enslave man and crush in him the sense of the beautiful. Civilization is the mad hunt for wealth, coarse, material wealth; it is devoid of any trace of idealism, and in idealism alone is Beauty beheld.

His sensational novel, *Mademoiselle de Maupin*, is, in truth, naught but a Hymn to Beauty, albeit more sensual than ideal, but in principle it states already what was to the end the object of Gautier's striving and the aim of his teaching. His books of travel develop this idea more vigorously and more brilliantly, in some respects; his earlier poems contained it, and his last volume of verse is a masterly exposition of it. That he was sensual at times is undeniable, but he never was gross; his sensuality was that of the artist, not of the voluptuary; he cared not so much for the fleshly as for the divinely beautiful; he expressed this with singular felicity when he declared truly that he ever preferred a fine statue to the loveliest woman.

As a teacher of the Beautiful, then, undoubtedly Gautier did his best and most lasting work. He taught first the public and then the artists, and both needed it. The public, because it cared for none of the higher things of life and looked upon art as waste of time and money; the artists, because in the flush of Romanticist success extravagance and wild nonsense and incorrectness of expression were accepted as manifestations of genius. It was Gautier's task to elevate the general public to a proper understanding of the mission and the beneficent effects of art, and to train the artists to respect grammar and sense while still producing works of rare poetic worth.

Accordingly, in all his writings the dominant note is the cult of beauty. Even when he launches into pure fiction, as in his Fortunio, still one of the most popular of his tales, in Le Roi Candaule, in Militona, in *Le Capitaine Fracasse*, the search for the beautiful is the main motive. He enjoys, indubitably, the fun of romance, the exhilaration of composing works which will captivate the fancy; but the main purpose is ever visible. He insists that his reader shall appreciate the gorgeousness of Oriental display, or the splendor of female loveliness, or the charm of architecture of the days of Louis XIII. These things are the important ones; the romance is the gilding of the artistic pill which the *bourgeois* must swallow for the welfare of his esthetic nature.

In his criticisms of literature the same object is apparent. He does not hesitate to condemn even writers who are admired by his school if these fail to fulfil the conditions of highest art; he denounces exaggeration, abominates deformity, renounces the cult of the grotesque. He understands it, and can discover some good in the authors of the earlier part of the seventeenth century; but he lays bare ruthlessly their faults and shortcomings. Les Grotesques did not wholly please the admirers of the group he mercilessly scored; and while he bestowed generous praise upon Victor Hugo, whose glorious verse ever transported him with enthusiasm, he failed not to condemn the imitators of the master, who, lacking his transcendent genius, merely imitated his faults and made them worse.

It was perhaps as the apostle of the doctrine of "art for art's sake" that Gautier exercised the most lasting influence upon French poetry, for while the work of Victor Hugo inspired Leconte de Lisle, Sully-Prudhomme, Hérédia, and Baudelaire, it was the teaching of Gautier which gave the Parnassian school its principles and enabled it to produce works of such rare perfection. Briefly, that doctrine is simply that Art is an end in itself not a means to an end. The artist has not to consider the results of his work, the moral results, since art and morals have two wholly different realms. This has been contested and will certainly be debated still, but the point is that Gautier firmly believed what he preached. The artist was bound to present his subject worked out to the point of perfection, or as nearly that point as he could manage. Whether the subject was high or low mattered comparatively little: the important part was the perfection of form, which renders Beauty visible. Hence, infinite care, patient labor, no more wild effusions, no more random attempts at effect, but resolute striving for the very best. In the poems of Leconte de Lisle is seen the result of the doctrine: perfection of form, singularly high sense of beauty, intense esthetic satisfaction, combined with subjects for the most part profound and noble in themselves. In the poems of Baudelaire, on the other hand, the evil of the doctrine is apparent, for Baudelaire deliberately chose filth and corruption for the basis of his work. The form is superb, the language wondrous, the imagery unsurpassed, the poetry unquestionable, but it is all poisonous, noxious, evil. Gautier himself illustrated his doctrine in his last volume of poems: Emaux et camées, in which there is not a single piece which does not evidence his principles and set them forth in perfection. But Gautier did not care for the low and the vile, and his love of Beauty led him rather to the ideal than to the gross, hence his verse is preferred by the true lover of poetry to the dark and sensual richness of Baudelaire.

It is, then, especially as a teacher that Gautier is great even now. The age of Romanticism has passed away; modern generations cannot feel the enthusiasm which Hernani and other plays of that classic awoke in Gautier and his contemporaries. The fantastic fiction of those by-gone days leaves the modern reader cold. Time has stripped of their glamor the heroes that compelled admiration when Gautier was young; they stand before us in all their littleness and weakness, mere marionettes, unendowed with life. But the real service that Gautier rendered his country and his fellow-countrymen is lasting; he taught the cult of Beauty; and as he advanced in years he saw that it was not, as he had so long believed, inconsistent with material progress, with the advance of civilization. More than any other man, it may be, he trained the French public to an appreciation of art in its manifold manifestations, and led artists to a more thorough and a more sane understanding of their task.

He died in 1872, just after the close of the Franco-Prussian War, having been in Paris throughout the siege, of which he has left accounts of unequaled interest. His principal works besides those already named are: Une nuit de Cléopatre; Jettatura; Le roman de la momie; Spirite; Ménagerie intime;

Tableaux de siège; Portraits contemporains, and Histoire du romantisme.

Glasgow, Ellen Anderson Gholson (Richmond, Virginia, April 22, 1874). She is the daughter of Francis Thomas and Anne Jane (Gholson) Glasgow. Her paternal ancestor, Arthur Glasgow, came to America some time previous to the American Revolution. Ellen was educated privately at home, and may be almost said to be self-taught. She began early to write verse and finished a novel when a girl, which she never offered for publication. After contributing to periodicals, she wrote, before her twenty-first year, a novel entitled The Descendant (1897), which at once brought her into notice.

This was followed by Phases of an Inferior Planet (1898); The Voice of the People (1900); The Freeman and Other Poems (1901); The Battleground (1902); *The Deliverance* (1904); The Wheel of Life (1906); The Ancient Law (1908).

Miss Glasgow's strongest book, *The Deliverance*, is a story of life in Virginia since the Civil War. Two of Miss Glasgow's novels have been translated into German.

Godwin, William (Wisbeach, Cambridgeshire, March 3, 1756; London, April 7, 1836). The son of a dissenting minister and the seventh of thirteen children, he was brought up in the strictest Puritanical principles. He was physically puny as a child, but intellectually precocious. His schooling began at a dame's school at Guist, Norfolk, where his father had settled about 1760, and in 1764 he entered the school of Robert Akers at Hindolvestone, where he became an usher in 1771. His father died in 1772, and in the following year William went with his mother to London, and soon after entered Hoxton Academy where, though a Calvinist, he formed the philosophical opinions as to materialism and necessity to which he adhered through life.

In 1777 he preached at Yarmouth and Lowestoft in summer, and in 1778 became minister of a congregation at Ware, Hertfordshire, where he came under the influence of Joseph Fawcet, a follower of Jonathan Edwards and a strong republican. In 1779 he removed to London, and in 1780 became minister of a congregation at Stowmarket, Suffolk, where his faith in Christianity was shaken by study of the French philosophers. Two years later he had a disagreement with his congregation, and went to London to try authorship.

His first publication was a Life of Chatham (1783), which was followed by pamphlets, articles, and contributions to the Annual Register, of which he was at one time conductor. He now dropped the title of Reverend and entered into politics, which brought him into contact with Sheridan and other Whig politicians, though he would not accept offers of support as a party writer. In 1793 he published Enquiry Concerning Political Justice and its Influence on Morals and Happiness, in which he advocated an intellectual republic founded on universal benevolence, which made him known as the philosophical representative of English radicalism. This was followed in 1794 by a novel entitled *Things as they Are: or, The Adventures of Caleb Williams*, which was suggested partly by his opinions as to the falseness of the common code of morality. Though designed to illustrate the views set forth in his Political Justice, the interest of the story is so predominant that the social ideas of the author are entirely overlooked. The story, which has many striking situations, was dramatized by George Colman the Younger as The Iron Chest and successfully produced in 1796 in London.

In 1796 Godwin made the acquaintance of Mary Wollstonecraft, author of the Vindication of the Rights of Woman, who was living as Mrs. Imlay in the literary circle frequented by him. She had previously formed in Paris a connection with an American named Imlay, who deserted her. After giving birth to a child, and failing in an attempt at suicide, she returned to England and sought relief from her trials in literature and in the promulgation of radical ideas. As she and Godwin held similar ideas about marriage, they lived together for six months, when they married for prudential reasons, March 29, 1797. The marriage was kept quiet awhile, Godwin occupying an apartment about twenty doors from that of his wife. Mrs. Godwin gave birth to a daughter, Aug. 30, 1797, and died Sept. 10th following. The daughter, Mary, became, in 1816, the second wife of the poet Shelley.

Godwin, thus left in charge of his infant daughter and of Mary Wollstonecraft's daughter by Imlay, returned to his studies and to society in 1798, and in 1801 married a Mrs. Clairmont, who proved a querulous wife and a harsh step-mother. Godwin's Memoirs of the Author of the Vindication of the Rights of Woman (1798) is a feeling tribute to the memory of his first wife, but describes the details of her life with a minuteness which subjected him to considerable censure. In the next year he published a second novel, entitled St. Leon, purporting to be the autobiography of a philosopher who has become immortal by the discovery of the elixir of life. It contains many passages of fine description and true pathos, but has some incredible situations and was not so successful as Caleb Williams. His other novels are: Fleetwood (1805); Mandeville (1817); Cloudesley (1830); and Deloraine (1833). Among other works are the tragedies Antonio (1800) and Falkener (1807); Life of Chaucer (1803-'04); Lives of John and Edward Phillips (1815); History of the Commonwealth of England to the Restoration of Charles II (1824-'28); and Lives of the Necromancers (1834).

Godwin was much embarrassed in his later years pecuniarily and had difficulties with his wife, who brought him a son, William, in 1804. He had now five children to support: two of Mary Wollstonecraft's, two Clairmonts, his wife's children by her first marriage, and his own child by her. In 1805 he lived in Hanway Street, where Mrs. Godwin carried on business as a bookseller and publisher, he contributing children's books, small histories, and compilations under the name of Edward Baldwin. In the latter part of his life he obtained a clerkship in the Record Office. In 1832 his son William died, and he himself followed four years later. In 1851 his remains and those of his first wife were removed to Bournemouth, Hampshire, and buried in the same grave with Mrs. Shelley.

Goethe, Johann Wolfgang von (Frankfort-on-the-Main, August 28, 1749; March 22, 1832). Astrologers have pointed out as significant of Goethe's brilliant and fortunate career that the hour of his nativity was high noon when the Sun was in Virgo, and Jupiter and Venus were in the ascendant. His father, Johann Kaspar, having traveled extensively in Italy and France, practised law at Frankfort, and at the age of thirty-eight married Katharina Elisabeth Textor, a girl of eighteen. He took her to live at the house of his widowed mother, who, although more than eighty years of age, still managed her excellent property and her well-trained household. The oldest child seems to have inherited some of the characteristics of both parents: from the young mother natural vivacity, vivid imagination, quick wit; from the father a determined will, strong ambition, consciousness of his powers and deserts, a hot temper, and a sense of duty. As the boy increased in years he had a sister and a brother to play with, but few other companions. His mother told him fairy stories, which cultivated his poetic sensibilities. His father, a man of unusual culture, delighted in his early unfolding intellectual abilities, and kept him hard at his studies. The Christmas puppet-shows, which were performed for the delectation of the children in the upper rooms of the big house, awakened the theatrical instinct of the lad. He had access to his father's extensive library and he read German translations of Télémaque, Tasso, and Ovid, Robinson Crusoe, and other books, as well as the German writers of his own day.

As time went on he had instruction in Latin, Italian, and Greek, as well as in French. The father, though he objected to games of cards, taught his children to dance. He liked to read aloud to the family circle, and sometimes from books that were wearisome to them. In January, 1759, a battalion of French soldiers through a ruse took possession of Frankfort, and Goethe saw his father's newly ordered mansion given over to a foreigner, Lieutenant Thoranc, who ruled it with a high hand. Frau Goethe made the most of the trying circumstances by taking French lessons of the Lieutenant's interpreter, and young Goethe enjoyed greater freedom than he had ever before known. The foreigners introduced theatrical representations, and the boy had all the tickets he desired, his grandfather being the chief magistrate. He came also into close contact with one or two painters whom the French Count employed, and thus he learned some of the practical methods of art. He had already begun to experiment in German verse, and as his familiarity with French increased he tried his hand at the classic Alexandrine couplets.

After the house was evacuated by the French Lieutenant, young Goethe once more took to his tasks with regularity. He learned English in about a month's time, and had lessons in mathematics, drawing, and in music. He learned to play the flute. About this time he conceived the notion of a romance in the form of family letters, cleverly introducing the various languages he was studying, even Hebrew, which was opening to him the treasures of the Old Testament. He also took part in theatricals and played important rôles. His father was ambitious for him to become a lawyer, and directed his studies to that end. He practised fencing, rode horseback, but never had a chance to swim. A few years later he became an adept in skating. He would have been very glad to become a member of the Arcadian Society, but his application was rejected. He had unfortunately acquired a reputation of associating with bad companions, the result of the French occupation. He gives some account of this humiliating experience in his Truth and Poetry.

When he was sixteen his father sent him to the University at Leipzig. He confided to his sister that he should devote his time to the study of belles-lettres, rather than the law, which he detested. The instruction offered seemed to him like dry husks, causing intellectual dyspepsia. He fell into a state of melancholy, and his health was affected. He grew discouraged about his poetry, disaffected with the Church, and the only consolation he found was in Nature. His friend Schlosser arrived and reawakened his interest in writing. He sent home poems in German, French, English, and Italian. He usually wrote in French or in English, often ending his letters with verse.

Schlosser stayed at an inn kept by a family named Schönkopf. Goethe there met the daughter of the house, Anna Katharina, who appears in his autobiography as Annette or Kättchen. In order to distract attention from what was to both of the young people a serious affair, he pretended to be desperately in love with another person, and to please this someone else he dressed and conducted himself in a way that excited ridicule. After a while he wearied of the deception and declared himself openly Annette's lover.

Lessing's Laokoön appeared, and had a great influence upon the young poet. Oeser's lectures on Art also stimulated him. It was many years before he definitely decided that he would not become an artist, and all his life he amused himself with painting, etching, and other forms of creative expression. At Leipzig he fought a duel with a theological student and was wounded in the arm. He indulged in many escapades, some of them not very creditable. He kept up his interest in theatrical productions and acted with Constanze Breitkopf in Lessing's newly published Minna von Barnhelm, being exceptionally clever in comic parts. Yet when Lessing came to Leipzig Goethe designedly kept out of his way, and the two never met. His fits of jealousy made his "Kättchen" miserable. Finally, when he found that she was more inclined to his friend, J. G. Kanne, he released her and gave her handsome parting gifts. His grief at her defection, his irregular life, his too great indulgence in coffee and beer, and a severe cold, made worse by his breathing of poisonous fumes while etching, brought on a hemorrhage and made an invalid of him. He determined to leave Leipzig.

On his return to Frankfort he sketched and etched, wrote poetry and studied law desultorily. He became interested in alchemy, and set up a small laboratory in his room. In the autumn of 1768 some of his songs, with Breitkopf's melodies, were published, but without the poet's name. About eighteen months later, after his health was reëstablished, he went to Strasburg. He wrote a friend that the Heavenly Physician had rekindled the fire of life in his body, and that courage and joy were once more his. Marie Antoinette passed through Strasburg on her way to Paris, and Goethe wrote a French poem in her honor, but the savage criticism of a Frenchman cured him of any pride that it might have caused him. He still paid comparatively little attention to the law, but was for the time interested in chemistry. He fell under the influence of the strange and erratic Herder, a pupil of Kant; but Herder cared little for French literature and still less for Goethe's verse. With the exception of a few years of misunderstanding, their friendship lasted till Herder's death.

While at Strasburg Goethe fell in love with Frederika Elisabetha, daughter of Pastor Brion of Sessenheim. She had blue eyes, delicate features, a short nose, pretty neck, and abundant hair. Goethe cut her name and his on a tree, as he had when he was in love with Kättchen. He felt that he had to decide between his self-development and his love. The story of this affair—which one of his biographers calls "his first great renunciation"—is known even in the smallest particulars. Before he broke the chains that fettered him he spent nearly a month at Sessenheim in daily and almost hourly communion with the lovely girl who fairly worshiped him. He painted the pastor's carriage, and made baskets, read Homer in a Latin translation, began to translate Ossian, and collected folk-songs.

On his return to Strasburg he finished his doctoral dissertation, but it was not accepted on account of its irreligious tendencies. By a compromise he was granted promotion as a "licentiate," which in some parts of Germany was equivalent to being a Doctor of Law. At Strasburg he was recognized as a genius, but of erratic, irregular, and dangerous habits. An interesting anecdote connects him with Strasburg. One day as he was sitting with some friends, enjoying a distant prospect of the cathedral, he remarked that the tower was not finished, and suggested what should have been done to complete it. An organ-builder present who knew the plans assured him that he was correct.

On his way home he stopped at Mannheim, and was greatly impressed by the fine museum of antiquities there. He began to practise law at Frankfort, but had only two cases in seven months. His spare time he spent in playing the violoncello and reading Shakespeare and Ossian. Under the influence of Shakespeare he wrote the first draught of Götz von Berlicheingen. He still yearned for the fair Frederika, but was resolved to crush the sentiment. He left her broken-hearted, and she remained true to him all her days.

In the summer of 1772 at his father's desire Goethe went to Wetzlar to get a deeper insight into the mysteries of the

Imperial Law court. At first he found the town "lonely, empty, and barren," but in time he made a host of acquaintances— young men who came from all parts of Germany for the same purpose. At the Inn they established a Rittertafel (singing society). He was called "Götz der Redliche" (the fluent). At Wetzlar he tried to translate Goldsmith's Deserted Village, and began his poem, The Wanderer. He met here Charlotte Sophie Henriette Buff, a fair and charming blonde, witty and full of life, virtuous, religious, and industrious. Goethe did not know at first that she was engaged to his friend, Kestner, the Secretary of Legation. In his ever susceptible heart passion ripened quickly. Kestner had perfect confidence in his Löttchen, and Goethe kept him informed of the exact state of his own feelings. But at last the situation became unendurable. Goethe tore himself away without a formal farewell. In August, 1772, he left Wetzlar, and went mainly on foot to Ems. Thence he went down the Lahn in a boat until he reached the Rhine, at Ehrenbreitstein. Here he made a visit at the beautiful home of Frau de la Roche. He was greatly pleased with her charming seventeen-year-old daughter, Maximiliane. Had not Löttchen's memory been too fresh in his mind it would have been a case of love at first sight. After this visit he was wont to confide all his thoughts and feelings to Frau de la Roche, whom he called "mamma."

After his return to Frankfort the news reached him that Lessing's young and brilliant friend whom he had met at Wetzlar had killed himself in consequence of an unhappy love-affair. His own desperate love for Löttchen and this young man's tragedy he wove into the double fabric of The Sorrows of Young Werther. In September, 1773, he wrote to Kestner: "I am working at a romance, but it goes slowly." About the time he was finishing the first part of Werther he made the experiment of seeing whether he could endure stabbing himself with a sharp dagger. The famous romance was finished in March, 1774, and published anonymously, though his name appeared in the Catalogue. At first Kestner and his wife were greatly offended at the freedom which Goethe had taken in depicting their lives, but afterward they fully forgave him. Goethe himself served as model for a literary work; his friend

Klinger depicted him as the Doctor in his story, The Suffering Wife. Götz, which was published at the expense of his friend Merck, was winning for the poet golden opinions. It was given on the stage at Berlin with great success. He had also in mind his drama of Mahomet, having got hold of the Koran while at Wetzlar. The figure of the Wandering Jew and that of Faust were flitting before his mind even at this early period. He wrote in a week's time his Clavigo to please Anna Sibylla Munch, a charming girl of seventeen. He wished to prove that within the strict limitations of the classic drama he could move freely. Clavigo was his first book to be printed with his name. *Werther* was published anonymously. For a time he thought seriously of marrying Anna, but he was still too fond of his freedom. The great Swiss mystic, Lavater, to whom Goethe had sent a number of silhouettes, and was greatly drawn, came to visit him at Frankfort. With Lavater, Basedow the educator, and Schmoll, Goethe made an excursion down the Lahn to Lahneck and Coblentz, on the way producing several fine poems. He went as far as Thalehren-breitstein, where he was obliged to borrow money of Madame de la Roche. Her daughter had married Brentano, a widower with five children, and Goethe felt in honor bound not to see her very frequently. After his return, Klopstock came to visit him, and he read to the author of The Messiah several scenes from Faust. This year he first essayed painting in oil "with the greatest zeal, reverence, and hope." He painted Schlosser a fire-screen with Virgil's head, but found he could not do "great things." *Werther* was beginning to create an immense sensation. Numbers of impassioned young men were moved to follow its hero's example as the simplest way of settling their unhappy love-affairs .

In December, 1774, Goethe met for the first time Captain Ludwig von Knebel, who was traveling with Prince Constantin of Weimar and his brother, the heir apparent. This was really the turning-point of the poet's life. Shortly afterward he was taken to the new and fine house of the Schönemanns. He had up to that time refused to go there, rather glorying in his reputation of being *une grosse bête*, or, as he called himself, "the Bear." But he was immediately infatuated with the

fair young daughter, Anna Elizabeth, who in his correspondence is known as "Lili." She was a blonde, with great dark
blue eyes, delicate, gentle features, and a fascinating smile.
She sketched and painted and wrote poems. His usual jealousy began to show itself. Goethe could not bear to think
of any woman whom he loved either attentive to others or less
passionate than himself. This affair dragged along until the
arrival of the Schönemanns' friend Frau Delph from Strasburg. She took the matter in hand and betrothed the young
couple. "Take each other's hands," she said. There were
kisses and passionate embraces, gifts and great enthusiasm
at first. But Goethe did not relish losing his freedom, and
the Schönemanns did not at all approve of such a lover for the
wealthy young girl. Goethe grew more jealous; Anna became
resentful, and the inevitable happened. All this time he was
keeping up a passionate and sentimental correspondence with
Louise von Stolberg, the sister of the young Countess Stolberg.
Goethe never had seen her, but he confided to her many of
his inmost feelings. With the Stolbergs he finally went to
Strasburg, all of them dressed in true *Werther* costume—blue
coats, yellow waistcoats, and round gray hats. At Karlsruhe
he met the Princess Louise von Darmstadt, the bride of the
Duke of Weimar. He called her an angel, picked up some
flowers that fell from her corsage and kept them. While there
he visited his sister, who was unhappily married. She urged
him to give up Lili, but he still felt drawn to her. On the top
of the Saint Gothard Pass he ardently kissed a golden heart
which she had given him.

At Strasburg the susceptible youth saw a silhouette of Frau
von Stein, and it affected him so much that he did not sleep
for three nights. When he reached home he had to explain
to Lili as he best might his rude absence and his neglect to
write her during the excursion. A period of storm and stress
followed. One night, as he tells in his "Life," he slept out on
the Mühlberg. He was tempted to leave Frankfort without
his parents' permission, but he had no money to carry out this
scheme. In September, 1775, he was at Offenbach with Lili,
and wrote the Bundeslied, which was sung as a quartet. On
his return to Frankfort, in order to buy Lili a present he

borrowed money of Jacobi, which was recovered with some difficulty seven years later. Someone told Lili of his treatment of Frederika Brion, and the final rupture came on the nineteenth of October. He had just written the scene in Auerbach's cellar. Goethe went to a masked ball, stayed all night, and danced minuets assiduously with a beautiful girl who had a cough. The Grand Duke of Weimar on his way through Frankfort again sought out Goethe and invited him to Weimar. There was then no thought of a long stay. The carriage promised did not come. Goethe, who had said good-by to his friends, kept in hiding, slipping out only at night, wrapped in a long mantle, to visit the girl of the minuet. While in this seclusion he worked on Egmont, but as he was beginning to grow too fond of this unknown girl he departed suddenly with the intention of visiting Italy. At Strasburg, where he made a short stay, Frau Delph wished him to marry a daughter of a nobleman named Von Wrede.

The carriage for Weimar found him at Strasburg. He reported to the Grand Duke early in November and took up his residence at the House of Privy Councillor Von Kalb. He was not very cordially welcomed by the court. Indeed, that he was willing to stay at all has been the wonder of his biographers. The town was forlorn and dreary. The palace had been burned. He was regarded as an interloper. Not being a "noble" he had to eat at the marshal's table. He met almost from the first with both open and secret opposition. But the Prince called him "Du," and he soon found himself deeply interested in Frau Charlotte von Stein. She was the mother of seven children, she was ill and unhappy; but she had great, soulful eyes and she knew how to manage him. The Stolbergs came and begged him to go with them to Hamburg and meet their sister, but the Duke objected.

The story of Goethe's activities at Weimar would fill pages. He revived the exploitation of the old Immenau mines; he built roads; he reformed the little army; he built the theater and personally supervised the productions of plays and operas. He exerted an elevating influence on the Grand Duke, who in the exuberance of his youth was at first inclined to be dissipated. The Duke gave him a garden and a furnished summer-house on the Ilm. It had a porter's lodge and kennels and bee-hives. He wrote Lila in praise of conjugal love; also his drama The Brother and Sister.

When the Duke went incognito to Frankfort, he urged Goethe's parents to let their son enter his service, promising him perfect freedom and a salary of one thousand two hundred thalers a year. Goethe and the Duke took an excursion that lasted several months, and when they returned to Weimar Goethe's position was assured. He still painted pictures and executed several remarkable portraits; he worked also at his etching. He studied botany and geology, lived very simply, drank no coffee and little wine; slept on a straw mattress with slight covering and took a cold bath even in winter.

He began Wilhelm Meister and finished Tasso, which was inspired by his relations to Madame von Stein. He was always breaking into passionate expressions of love for this lady, whose husband was certainly complaisant, though sometimes she would banish him from her presence. He was happy in his activities, in spite of all opposition. He wrote Lavater that the duty which he had undertaken was growing daily dearer to him. He confessed that in Frau von Stein he found the compendium of mother, sister, and sweetheart. She was "the ideal of his soul."

In 1781 he founded a school for knitting and embroidery for the poor children of soldiers, which proved a success. He grew more and more interested in botanical studies, and was beginning to formulate the ideas that afterward grew into his treatise on the coloring of flowers.

After years of this varied activity he began to yearn for a change and he resolved to go to Italy. Having arranged with the Leipzig publisher, Göschen, to issue a complete edition of his works in eight volumes, for which he was to receive an honorarium of two thousand thalers, he got leave of absence from the Duke, and without letting anyone know where he was going set out in September for the longed-for land of enchantment. The story of his experiences may be read in his charming Italian Journeys, where he tells of his leisurely trip down the Italian lakes, his three weeks in Venice, and his inspiring months in Rome. Especial enjoyment he found with the painter Tischbein, who painted a remarkable portrait of him surrounded by fragments of broken marbles. He was crowned by the Arcadian Society under the name of Megalio. He also became intimately acquainted with Angelica Kaufmann. The Prince of Waldeck, with whom he climbed Vesuvius, invited him to accompany him through Albania and Dalmatia, but he declined. With the painter Kniep he visited Sicily and described it in the diary he kept for Frau von Stein. On the way he revised his plan of Tasso. On his return to Rome he began once more his researches into the art of the ancients. He made new acquaintances which greatly delighted him.

But the Grand Duke began to clamor for his return, and on June 18, 1788, without even stopping to see his mother, he arrived once more at Weimar. He found Frau von Stein greatly changed. He himself had been so long absorbing new experiences that he was a different man. The bond between them was broken. While the coldness between them was daily increasing it happened that a young woman of humble origin, Christiane Sophie Vulpius, met him one day in the park and presented a petition. She was twenty-three, short, with pretty blue eyes, a well-shaped nose, full lips, a round face and long light hair. Goethe had once before noticed her in an artificial-flower factory, where he was showing the Prince of Darmstadt about. Goethe became interested in her, and established her in his summer house; then about a month after his return he announced her as his wife though without any formal ceremony. He still occasionally saw Frau von Stein, but never again as before. Schiller, whom Goethe had met in Stuttgart in 1777, came to Weimar attracted by the divorced Charlotte von Lengefeld. At first there was not much sympathy between them. Goethe was willing to patronize him, but not to be his friend.

The Duke gave Goethe a new dwelling, which was planned in the Italian style and suitable to contain his collections of art treasures and natural curiosities, and he was busily engaged in putting this in order. He was also printing the last volume of his collected works and thinking of publishing his Roman Elegies and his Epigrams. The Duke planned to build a new court theater, of which Goethe should be the director. He accompanied the Duke in the campaign of 1792 and voluntarily exposed himself to fire so as to experience the sensation of that particular danger. The four months of his absence were filled with many delightful episodes: reunions with old friends and meetings with distinguished persons. When he reached Weimar again he took hold with renewed zeal of the unfinished house and the affairs of the new theater, where he prepared to produce the masterpieces of Shakespeare and of the French stage. He was also busy with his version of Reynard the Fox, and various plays for the stage, as well as his scientific investigations, especially those relating to optics and anatomy.

In the following June, Voss, the translator of Homer, reached Weimar, and Goethe paid him especial attention; but Voss did not approve of the meter of the poet's Reinecke. This same year he accepted joyfully Schiller's invitation to collaborate on the projected journal, Die Horen, which was destined to accomplish so much for German literature. This was the beginning of a delightful friendship which ended only with Schiller's untimely death, in 1805. At Eisenach, where Goethe had a long series of conversations with him, he read to the elder poet his Roman Elegies, revealed to him his plans about the theater and a Musenalmanach, and encouraged him to finish some of his pieces for the stage. For ten years the friendship with Schiller, which has been called Der Dioskuren-bund—the alliance of Castor and Pollux—served as the highest inspiration to both men. At Weimar Goethe instituted his Friday evenings, where all the brightest spirits congregated. Goethe also was a frequent guest at the Dowager Duchess's, where he found special delight in the charming young Henriette von Wolfskeel-Reichenberg, who played and sang like an artist.

At Karlsbad, where he went to get relief from a persistent and painful swelling of the cheek, he had a lively love-affair with the beautiful Jewess, Marianne Meyer. He wrote several of his Märchen, and undertook to contribute to the Horen a translation of Benvenuto Cellini's Autobiography. He was also deeply engaged in the study of architecture. In September, 1795, he was grievously afflicted in the death of his second son. His eldest, August, was about seven. A pretty picture is given of the great Goethe, accompanied by the little lad in mountaineer's dress, and answering the naïve questions which his curiosity prompted. The prototype of this may be seen in Felix in Wilhelm Meister. Toward the end of the year the happy thought occurred to him to publish a collection of epigrams under the title Die Xenien. Schiller collaborated with him, and the work made a great sensation. In Schiller's company he wrote within nine days the first five cantos of his beautiful idyl, Hermann und Dorothea. When it was finished he sold it for one thousand thalers in gold to the Viewegs. It made a universal success.

By this time Goethe had grown extraordinarily stout, and it is said that his personal appearance militated against his popularity with the royalties that visited Weimar. Accordingly he withdrew himself a good deal from society and devoted his days to composition and other intellectual work, his nights to astronomy. The early days of the new century were disturbed by severe illness; his life was despaired of. He almost lost the sight of one eye. This discipline caused him to put his son August on a safer social basis by formally legitimizing him. He still took an active interest in the theater, for which Schiller was furnishing his masterpieces. The University at Jena, especially its library, occupied him. He found time to write his Eugénie, in which he expresses his own personal sorrow at the loss of a child. Four times death had visited his household since his eldest son was born. Schiller's death was a great loss to him. When he heard the news he burst into uncontrollable weeping.

In October, 1806, Weimar was overrun by the French; even Goethe's house was not spared. Christiane's presence of mind probably saved his life. As a recognition of this service he resolved to make her his legal wife in the sacristy of the court chapel. This ceremony took place on the 19th of October, but it was not easy for the court circles to forget what her position had been. This year he made the acquaintance of his old friend Max Brentano's daughter, Bettine, who cherished a passionate admiration for him. She was full of life and vivacity, and Goethe greatly enjoyed her presence.

She did not hesitate to confess her love for him. It became rather embarrassing, and he had to repress her. When in September his mother died, Goethe sent Christiane to Frankfort to regulate her estate, which was very much reduced. He received only twenty thousand gulden. A few days later Goethe was presented to Napoleon, who made his famous remark, "Voilà un homme!" He and Goethe had a lively conversation about literature and especially the drama. Napoleon presented Goethe with the insignia of the Legion of Honor. The Emperor Alexander, who was most friendly to him, made him a member of the Order of Saint Anne. This year his Faust was presented to the world, arousing great admiration and wonder. The following years were troubled by frequent and severe illnesses which he tried in vain to overcome by visits to various "cures." While he was mortified by the treatment which the court ladies accorded Christiane, he found some consolation in the success of his son August. The Duke gave him one sign of favor after another.

When the news of the entry of the allied armies into Paris reached Weimar, Goethe was confined to the house with rheumatism. Having somewhat recovered, he spent some time at Frankfort, where he entered into very friendly relations with the brilliant and artistic Marianne von Willemer, who inspired him to write some of his most charming songs, those included in his Divan. In 1816 Goethe was decorated with the great cross of the White Falcon, an order reëstablished by the Grand Duke with appropriate ceremonies. The question of a constitution arose. Goethe was opposed to the freedom of the press and to popular government. He felt that they stood in the way of a really strong management of affairs. In June of this year Christiane passed away, and about a year later the control of his house was handed over to his son's wife, Ottilie.

More and more was Goethe recognized as the great glory of the city and the state. Even Frankfort, which when he sold his house there had lost the opportunity of making him an honorary citizen, proposed to erect a memorial to him. At Marienbad, where he went for his health in 1823, he fell passionately in love with Ulrike Levezow, and it was rumored that he would marry her. But this plan fell through. He became more and more engrossed in music and was enraptured with the playing of the talented Szymanowska, who inspired one of his most beautiful poems.   In January, 1817, he resigned his office as director of the Weimar theater.   As the years went on pilgrims from all parts of the world came to him, attracted by his great fame as poet, artist, philosopher, scientific man, and critic.   These years were saddened by the dissonance between August and Ottilie, and by August's pathetic mental illness. The burning of the Weimar theater in March, 1825, seemed to him an evil omen, but he showed all his old energy in having it rebuilt, so that it might be in readiness for the Grand Duke's jubilee.   He was then engaged in making arrangements for a new edition of his works, and it was entrusted to the Cottas, who offered him an honorarium of sixty thousand thalers and a royalty.   On the occasion of the Grand Duke's fiftieth anniversary a medal was minted in honor of the friend who all these years had been so closely allied to the ducal pair.   All sorts of honors were heaped upon him.   Jena gave him the degree of doctor.   His Iphigenia was performed at the theater and was published in a memorial edition.   When Goethe entered the ducal box the whole audience saluted him.   When the curtain rose a bust of the poet, crowned with laurel, was seen.

His latter years were filled with activity.   He was still busied with the second part of Faust.   Shortly after he had finished the Classic Walpurgisnacht, in the spring of 1829, the young composer Mendelssohn made him a visit and played to him many of his compositions.   Goethe gave him some of the manuscript of the Faust.   In October of that year August died in Rome.   Thorwaldsen sculptured a memorial stone for him.   In spite of failing health Goethe still worked at Faust and on his autobiography.   Among the foreigners who came to see him were Thomas Carlyle and Sir Walter Scott, also George Bancroft.   On the morning of March 22, 1832, he held Ottilie's hand and engaged in lively conversation with her; but even as he talked his speech failed him.   At noon he settled himself in a corner of his chair and peacefully passed away. He was laid next Schiller in the ducal tomb.   The house where he lived so many years is still kept as he left it, and has been a shrine for multitudes of pilgrims.

Taken all in all, Goethe was the greatest of all the Germans of his age. His sentimentality, which we cannot help regarding as a weakness, was in no small measure the effect of the age in which he lived. But the assuredness with which he advanced on his career, the breadth of his views, the brilliance of his intellect, the variety of his activities, mark him as one of the greatest men of all time.

Gogol, Nikolai Vassilievitch (Pultowa, Russia, March 31 (N. S.), 1809; Moscow, March 2 (N. S.), 1852). He was educated in a public gymnasium at Pultowa and in the lyceum at Niejinsk. In 1831 he received the appointment of teacher of history in the Patriotic Institution, and three years later that of professor of history in the University of St. Petersburg. This position he resigned at the end of a year, to devote himself to literature, and in 1836 left Russia and lived the next few years chiefly in Rome.

Gogol had published previously Evenings at a Farmhouse, a collection of tales and sketches of rural life, which met with much favor, and a drama entitled The Inspector, in which the corruption and venality of public officials were severely criticized. In 1837 he wrote a novel, *Dead Souls*, which was published in 1842 and translated into English under the title of *Home Life in Russia* (1854). It narrates the adventures of a rascal named Tchitchikoff, who goes about purchasing the rights of proprietors to "dead souls," that is, serfs recently dead, whose names have not yet been taken from the government rolls. "When I have obtained the names of some thousands of serfs," he said, " I shall carry my deeds to some bank in St. Petersburg or Moscow, and raise a large sum on them; then I shall be a rich man, and in condition to buy real peasants in flesh and blood."

Toward the end of his life Gogol fell into a state of religious melancholy, and eulogized some of the abuses he had before satirized, thus losing the favor which he had won from the Liberals. In this condition he burned all his unpublished manuscripts, which he declared were written under the inspiration of the devil, and among which were the concluding parts of *Dead Souls*. In 1857, a certain Dr. Zahartchenko, of Kieff, published a continuation of it.   An English translation of the entire work, by Isabel F. Hapgood, entitled *Tchitchikoff's Journeys: or, Dead Souls*, was published in New York in 1886. Gogol's complete works, comprising tales, dramas, and poems, were published in four volumes in Moscow, 1862.

Goldsmith, Oliver (Pallas, near Ballymahon, Longford, Ireland, Nov. 10, 1728; London, England, April 4, 1774).   His father, the Rev. Charles Goldsmith, a clergyman of the Established Church, married in 1718 Ann, daughter of the Rev. Oliver Jones, master of the Diocesan School at Elphin, and to them were born five sons and two daughters.   Henry, the eldest son, was distinguished both at school and college, but made an early and imprudent marriage, and retired upon a curacy as his only means of subsistence.   Another brother, John, probably died young; Charles went to the West Indies; and Maurice was a cabinet-maker in Dublin.   The two sisters, Catharine (Mrs. Hodson) and Jane (Mrs. Johnstone), lived and died at Athlone.

Oliver, the second son and fifth child of this marriage, was born seven years after the birth of the first.   The slender resources of the parents had been exhausted in the education of Henry, and his father had determined to bring Oliver up to trade, but his mother, who saw the bent of his mind, persuaded her husband to give him a learned education.   Oliver was of singular habits of mind, and distinguished for an odd, irregular application of his early talents.   He was sometimes grave and thoughtful, at others gay and frolicsome even to excess.   Remarkably active and athletic, he excelled in physical exercises, especially in ball-playing, of which he was very fond.   He began to scribble verses before he was eight years old, his early attempts at rhyme affording much amusement to the family.

After some preliminary teaching, Oliver was placed under the care of the Rev. Mr. Griffin, master of the school at Elphin, then was sent to Athlone School for two years, and later to the school of the Rev. Patrick Hughes, at Edgeworth Town, County Longford, where he remained until ready for the university.   In 1744 he entered Trinity College, Dublin, as a sizar or poor scholar, a class of students whose position was then

Portrait of Oliver Goldsmith

Photogravure after the painting by Sir Joshua Reynolds

Portrait of Oliver Goldsmith

Photogravure after the painting by Sir Joshua Reynolds

highly disagreeable, they being obliged to wear a dress indicative of their condition and to perform many menial services. Goldsmith submitted with reluctance to these humbling conditions, and was often reduced to great straits, but by borrowing, pawning his books, and writing ballads contrived to keep his place. In 1749 he was admitted to the degree of Bachelor of Arts, and was persuaded to prepare for the Church; but when, two years later, he presented himself to the Bishop of Elphin, for ordination, in a pair of scarlet breeches, he was rejected. He then became a tutor in a gentleman's family, and after a few months bought a horse and set out to see the world with thirty pounds in his pocket, but soon returned home destitute. An uncle then gave him means to study law, and he set out for London with fifty pounds, which he lost in gaming in Dublin. At the end of 1752 he was sent to study medicine in Edinburgh, where he spent two winters hearing lectures; but near the end of his second term, burdened with debts and hunted by bailiffs, he fled to the Continent. After nearly a year at Leyden, he went to Paris to study chemistry, but soon set out to make the tour of the Continent. He wandered through parts of Germany, Switzerland, and Italy, usually on foot, supporting himself in various ways, as described in the story of the Philosophical Vagabond, in *The Vicar of Wakefield*. At Padua, where he remained several months, he took his medical degree, and in 1756 he returned to England, friendless and penniless.

His history during the next two or three years is somewhat obscure; he was for a time an assistant to a chemist in London, then tried to practise medicine in Southwark; next was usher in a school at Peckham, and finally settled down as a literary hack in London. By 1759 he began to attract attention as a writer through articles in The Critical Review, The British Magazine, The Lady's Magazine, The Busybody, The Bee, and other periodicals. His first acknowledged work, An Inquiry into the Present State of Polite Learning in Europe, brought him into public notice. Soon after he contributed to the Public Ledger the famous Chinese Letters, republished (1762) under the title of The Citizen of the World, which improved both his reputation and his finances. He emerged from his garret, took rooms in Fleet Street, and made acquaintance with many prominent men, including Percy, Smollett, and Dr. Johnson, with whom he contracted a warm and lasting friendship. Burke, who had been at college with him, and Hogarth were his frequent visitors, and he formed an intimacy with Sir Joshua Reynolds which ended only with Goldsmith's life. He was admitted also to the famous Literary Club at its institution.

In 1764 Goldsmith published his History of England, in a Series of Letters from a Nobleman to his Son, which won the praise of being the most finished and elegant summary of English history yet written. In the next year appeared The Traveller, a poem detailing impressions received during his wanderings on the Continent. *The Vicar of Wakefield* was written simultaneously with The Traveller, but was not published until 1766. The manuscript had been sold in advance for sixty pounds, to save its writer from the bailiffs. This now famous story is marked by a simplicity of style, a truth of circumstance, an adherence to nature, an easy change of incident, and a bright and clear delineation of character, which place it among the foremost productions of fiction. It has, says Mitford, "the truth of Richardson, without his minuteness; and the humor of Fielding, without his grossness: if it yields to Le Sage in the diversified variety of his views of life, it far excels him in the description of the domestic virtues, and the pleasing moral of the tale."

In 1767 Goldsmith began writing for the stage, producing The Good-Natured Man, which, though only partly successful when played at Covent Garden Theatre, brought him five hundred pounds. His second comedy, She Stoops to Conquer, was more successful and brought him not only fame but a large pecuniary reward. Even this was far from meeting his needs, as his association with the learned, the gay, and the opulent brought new wants and the necessity of a more elaborate style of living. He worked hard, but he found the need of money increasing at a rate which rendered all hope of relief from his labors entirely desperate. In 1774, on his return from a visit to the country, he fell ill of a low fever, under which his overtaxed powers gave way, and he died in the forty-sixth year of his age. His friends were deterred from honoring

his remains with a public funeral in Westminster Abbey by the
disclosure of his embarrassed affairs; for, though it was calculated that he had earned in the fourteen years of his literary
life more than eight thousand pounds, he died with an indebt-
edness of about two thousand pounds. He was buried privately
in the Temple Church burial-ground, but as no memorial was
erected, the place is now uncertain. His friends erected a
monument to his memory in Westminster Abbey, with a Latin
inscription by Dr. Johnson; and in 1837 a marble slab with an
English inscription was placed in the Temple Church.

Goldsmith's works, besides those already mentioned, include: Life of Voltaire (1759); Life of Richard Nash, Esq.,
of Bath ("Beau Nash," 1762); Edwin and Angelina: or, The
Hermit (poem, 1765); Beauties of English Poetry (1767);
Poems for Young Ladies (1767); Life of Lord Bolingbroke
(1770); Life of Thomas Parnell (1770); The Deserted Village
(poem, 1770); The Haunch of Venison (poem, 1771); The
Grecian History (1774); Retaliation (poem, 1774); and A Sur-
vey of Experimental Philosophy (1776). Goldsmith's essays
were collected and reprinted during his lifetime. The first
collection of his poems appeared in London in 1780. There
are many reprints and translations of his works in France and
Germany. Biographies of him have been written by Mitford,
Prior Irving, John Forster, and others.

Grand, Sarah, the pseudonym of Frances Elizabeth Clarke
McFall (Donaghadu, County Down, Ireland, 1855). She is
the daughter of Edward John Bellenden Clarke, an officer in
the Royal Navy, and of Margaret Bell, daughter of the late
George Henry Sherwood, Rysome Garth, Yorkshire, and granddaughter of Robert Bell, Humbleton House, Yorkshire. Educated privately, she married, when but sixteen years old, Lieut.-
Colonel McFall, of the Royal Army, and accompanied him to
the East, where she spent five years, visiting India, China, and
Japan. In 1891 she traveled in the United States.

Her first publication was a novel entitled Ideala, written
when twenty-six years old. It was followed by *The Heavenly
Twins* (1893), said to have been written even earlier, but to
have long awaited a publisher.

Other works by her are: Our Manifold Nature, a collection of stories (1894); The Beth Book (1897); The Modern Man and Maid (1898); Babs the Impossible (1900).

Mrs. McFall lives in Kensington, London. She is very active in the woman's movement in England, and has served as president of the Society for Woman's Suffrage and of the Woman's International Progressive Union, and as vice-president of the Scottish Association for the Promotion of Woman's Public Work.

Grant, James (Edinburgh, August 1, 1822; London, May 5, 1887). He was the eldest son of Captain John Grant, of the 92d Gordon Highlanders, and grandson of James Grant, of Corrimony, an advocate. Through his mother, a Watson of Overmains, he was closely related to Sir Walter Scott, the Swintons of Swinton, and other prominent families. In 1833 Captain John Grant was ordered to Newfoundland, and took his three sons with him. After six years in American barracks, James returned home with his father, who resigned in 1839, and obtained an ensigncy in the 62d foot. In 1843 he resigned and entered the office of an architect in Edinburgh, where he became a skilful draughtsman. But his bent was for literature, and in 1845 he published a story entitled The Romance of War, followed by a sequel, The Highlanders in Belgium (1847), and The Adventures of an Aide-de-Camp (1848).

He now became a voluminous writer of military and historical romances, dealing largely with Scottish history, some of which had a large circulation in a cheap form. Among these are: Walter Fenton: or, The Scottish Cavalier (1850); *Bothwell: or, The Days of Mary, Queen of Scots* (1851); Jane Seton (1853); Harry Ogilvie (1856); Dick Rodney (1862); Second to None (1864); The White Cockade (1867); Under the Red Dragon (1872); Playing with Fire (1887); Love's Labor's Won (1888), etc.

He published also many historical works, among them Memoirs and Adventures of Sir W. Kirkaldy of Grange (1849); Memorials of the Castle of Edinburgh (1850); Memoirs of Sir J. Hepburn (1851); Memoirs of Montrose (1851); Cavaliers of Fortune: or, British Heroes in Foreign Wars (1859); British Battles on Land and Sea (1873); Illustrated History of India (1876); Old and New Edinburgh (1880); History of the War in the Soudan (1885-'86); and The Tartans of the Clans of Scotland (1886).

Grant was an authority on military affairs, and was frequently consulted by the War Office concerning technical matters. He was of strong religious susceptibilities and in 1875 embraced the Roman Catholic faith.

Grant, Robert (Boston, Jan. 24, 1852). He is the son of Patrick and Charlotte Boardman (Rice) Grant, his father having been a merchant in Boston. His grandfather, a Scotchman, settled in Boston in 1800 and married a daughter of the Hon. Jonathan Mason, a United States Senator. Robert was educated at the Boston Latin School and at Harvard University, where he was graduated in 1873 and was the class poet. He took a post-graduate course in philology, received the degree of Ph.D. in 1876, and, after three years in the Law School, that of LL.B. in 1879.

After practising law in Boston several years, he became in 1888 a member of the Board of Water Commissioners and in 1889 its chairman. In 1893 he was chosen Judge of the Probate Court and Court of Insolvency for Suffolk County, Mass., an office which he still holds. He has been, since 1895, an overseer of Harvard University.

Judge Grant began his literary work when in college, and has kept it up throughout his official career, winning a permanent place among the best writers of the day. His writing is marked by grace of expression, careful portrayal of character, and a certain quiet humor which appeals to every reader. Besides numerous short contributions to periodicals, he has published several volumes of verse and many novels, some of which have been very successful. Among his works are: The Confessions of a Frivolous Girl (1880); The Average Man (1883); The Knave of Hearts (1885); Mrs. Harold Stagg (1890); The Carletons (1891); The Reflections of a Married Man (1892); The Opinions of a Philosopher (1893); The Bachelor's Christmas, and Other Stories (1895); The Art of Living (1895);

The North Shore of Massachusetts (1896); Search-Light Letters (1899); *Unleavened Bread* (1900); The Undercurrent (1904); The Orchid (1905); The Law-breakers (1906).

Judge Grant married, July 3, 1883, Amy Gordon, daughter of Sir Alexander Tilloch Gordon, G.C.M.G., of Montreal, Canada, and granddaughter of John Galt, the Scottish novelist. In the same year he delivered a poem, entitled Yankee Doodle, at the Phi Beta Kappa reunion at Cambridge; and in 1886 another, The Oldest School in America, at the two hundred and fiftieth anniversary of the Boston Latin School. Both of these were published.

Gras, Felix (Malemort, Vaucluse, France, May 3, 1844; Avignon, March 4, 1901). He was educated at Beziers, but returned when seventeen years old to his father's farm, whence he was sent in 1864 to Avignon, and articled to Jules Giéia, a lawyer and a man of letters. His master was a member of the Félibrige, or brotherhood of Provençal poets and writers, founded in 1835 by Joseph Roumanille for the revival of the Provençal as a literary language. Roumanille, called the father of the Félibrige, was Gras's brother-in-law, and he was thus brought into intimate connection with many men of letters, including Frédéric Mistral, Brunet, Aubanel, Mathieu, and others.

After much desultory work, Gras published in 1876 an epic poem in twelve cantos, entitled Li Carbounie, which won him the first place among the Provençal writers of the younger generation. This was followed by Tolosa, an epic, descriptive of the crusade of Simon de Montfort against the Albigenses (1882), and a collection of short poems, Lou Roumancers Provençal (1887). A collection of prose stories, Li Papalino, describing in racy style the loves and hates, the sensuality and the superstitions of the Papal Court at Avignon, met with much favor, but his greatest popular success was *Li Rouge dóu Miejour* (*The Reds of the Midi*), which was first published in New York in 1898 in an English translation by Mrs. Catharine Janvier. A year later Gras wrote sequels to it entitled The Terror and The White Terror.

In 1891 he succeeded Roumanille as Capoulié or President of the Félibrige and held the position until his death

Gray, Maxwell (Newport, Isle of Wight, England, 18—). The pseudonym of Mary G. Tuttiett, daughter of the late F. B. Tuttiett, M.R.C.S., and Eliza Gleed. She began her literary life as a general writer, contributing essays, poems, and stories to periodicals, but finally made a more ambitious effort, which resulted in a novel published in 1879, entitled The Broken Tryst. This attracted very little attention, but her second novel, *The Silence of Dean Mailland*, published in 1886, at once gave her reputation and standing in the world of letters.

Her later novels are: The Reproach of Annesley (1888); In the Heart of the Storm (1891); An Innocent Impostor (1892); The Last Sentence (1893); A Costly Freak (1893); Sweethearts and Friends (1897); The House of Hidden Treasure (1898); Ribstone Pippins (1898); The World's Mercy (1900); Four-leaved Clover (1901).

She has published also several volumes of poems, including: Westminster Chimes (1889); Lays of the Dragon-Slayer (1894); and The Forest Chapel and Other Poems (1899).

Green, Anna Katherine, the maiden and literary name of Mrs. Charles Rohlfs (Brooklyn, New York, Nov. 11, 1846). Her father, James Wilson Green, a lawyer, removed to Buffalo in 1857, and Anna Katherine, after preliminary studies in the public schools of Brooklyn and Buffalo, was sent to Ripley Female College, Poultney, Vermont, where she was graduated in 1867. She returned in time to Brooklyn and engaged in literary work, writing short stories and poems, but did not attract notice until 1878, when the publication of a novel entitled *The Leavenworth Case*, illustrating the danger of dependence on circumstantial evidence, at once made her reputation. Many hundred thousand copies of it were sold and it was translated into most modern languages. It was dramatized and played in 1891-'92, her husband taking the leading part, that of Harwell.

In 1884 Miss Green married Charles Rohlfs, an actor, associated for several years with Edwin Booth and other tragedians, and the couple soon after made their home in Buffalo. In designing furniture for his own house, Mr. Rohlfs developed a distinctive style, now known by his name, which has found patronage both in this country and in Europe.

Anna Katherine Green's published works include, besides that mentioned: A Strange Disappearance (1879); The Sword of Damocles (1881); Hand and Ring (1883); X. Y. Z. (1883); The Mill Mystery (1886); 7 to 12 (1887); Behind Closed Doors (1888); The Forsaken Inn (1890); A Matter of Millions (1890); The Old Stone House (1891); Cynthia Wakeham's Money (1892); Marked "Personal" (1893); Miss Hurd: An Enigma (1894); Dr. Izard (1895); That Affair Next Door (1897); Lost Man's Lane (1898); Agatha Webb (1899); The House in the Mist (1905); The Millionaire Baby (1905); The Woman in the Alcove (1906); The Chief Legatee (1907); The Mayor's Wife (1907).

She has published also two volumes of poems, The Defense of the Bride, and Other Poems (1882), and Risifi's Daughter, a drama (1887).

Greene, Sarah Pratt McLean (Simsbury, Hartford County, Connecticut, July 3, 1856). The daughter of Dudley and Mary (Payne) McLean, she received her education at Mt. Holyoke Seminary, and was for a time at Madison University. In 1887 she married, in St. Louis, Missouri, Franklin Lynde Greene, son of Judge Greene, of Fremont, Ohio, and lived at various places in the West. After the decease of her husband and two sons, she returned to the East, and her home is now in Roxbury, Mass.

Mrs. Greene began her literary career by contributing short stories to Harper's Magazine and other periodicals, but first became known in 1880 by her novel *Cape Cod Folks*, which made considerable talk at the time because well-known Cape Cod people were recognizable in its characters. These persons brought suits for damages, and their true names were removed from later editions of the book. *Cape Cod Folks* was followed by: Towhead (1883); Some Other Folks (1884); Last Chance Junction (1889); Leon Pontifex (1890); Stuart and Bamboo (1897); The Moral Imbeciles (1898); Vesty of the Basins (1900); Flood Tide (1901); Winslow Plain (1902).

Gréville, Henri, the pseudonym of Alice-Marie-Céleste Henri, Madame Durand (Paris, Oct. 12, 1842; Boulogne, May 26, 1902). She received a good education at home and was conversant with several languages when she went to St. Petersburg with her father, who had been appointed professor of the French language and literature in the university and law school in that city. She rapidly acquired the Russian language and made a study of the manners and customs of the country, and had already published, under the chosen pseudonym, several novels in Russian periodicals, when she married M. Durand, a French professor in the school of law in St. Petersburg. In 1872 she returned to France and wrote many novels, romances, and other works, especially on matters connected with Russian life, in the Revue des Deux Mondes, the Journal des Débats, Figaro, La Siècle, Le Temps, etc.

Among her numerous works the following are best known: *Dosia* (1876); L'Expiation de Savelli (1876); La Princesse Ogheroff (1876); Les Koumiassine (1877); Susanne Normis (1877); Sonia (1877); La Maison de Maurèze (1877); Nouvelles russes (1877); Lucie Roday (1879); Cité Ménard (1880); L'Heritage de Xénie (1880); Le Moulin Frappier (1880); Les Degrés de l'échelle (1881); Rose Rozier (1882); Une Trahison (1882); Louis Breuil (1883); Un Crime (1884); Les Ormes (1884); Cléopâtre (1886); La Fille de Dosia (1887); Nicanor (1887); Frankley (1887); Comédies de paravent (1888); La Seconde Mère (1888); Un Mystère (1890); Aurette (1891); Péril (1891).

Griffin, Gerald (Limerick, Ireland, Dec. 12, 1803; Cork, June 12, 1840). His father, a brewer, was of an old family of the sept of Ui Griobhtha, a name which he changed to Griffin. Gerald was educated at Limerick, where he began early to contribute poems and critical articles to the local press. In 1820, when he was seventeen years old, his parents emigrated to Pennsylvania, and he went to live with an older brother, William Griffin, M.D. (1794–1848), at Adare, near Limerick. Determined to devote himself to a literary career, he went in 1823 to London with a tragedy entitled Aguire, of which he was unable to dispose. Aided by John Banim, he supported himself several years in a precarious way by contributions to The Literary Gazette and other periodicals, and gradually acquired reputation as a brilliant magazine writer.

In 1827, at the suggestion of Banim, he tried fiction, publishing his Holland Tide, together with three other stories, which met with a good measure of success. In the same year he returned to Ireland and completed the first series of Tales of the Munster Festivals, intended to illustrate traditional observances of the peasantry in the south of Ireland. These tales, of which three volumes were published, were followed by a novel entitled *The Collegians,* founded on occurrences in Munster, issued anonymously in 1829. This story, called by the Irish Nation one of the most perfect prose fictions in the world, is the original of Boucicault's drama The Colleen Bawn: or, The Brides of Garry-Owen, first played at the Adelphi Theatre, London, Sept. 10, 1860. A popular edition of the novel published in 1861, illustrated by Phiz, was renamed The Colleen Bawn: or, The Collegian's Wife.

In 1830 he published a volume of tales illustrative of the Five Senses, and another entitled The Rivals. About this time he entered as a law student in the University of London. He published also a second series of the Tales of the Munster Festivals, followed by: a historical novel entitled The Invasion (1832); Tales of My Neighborhood (1835); The Duke of Monmouth (1836); and Talis Qualis: or, Tales of the Jury Room (1842).

In 1838 Griffin returned to Limerick and became a member of the Roman Catholic society of Christian Brothers, a body devoted to teaching, and discharged the duties incumbent on the position until his decease. In 1842 his tragedy of Gisippus: or, The Forgotten Friend, which had been persistently declined during his life, was successfully produced at Drury Lane Theatre, with Macready in the principal rôle and with Helen Fancit as Sempronia. Osborne Davis, of the Irish Nation, calls it the "greatest drama written by an Irishman."

Gerald Griffin's novels and poems, collected and edited by his brother, were published in 1842–'43, and his poetical and dramatic works in 1857–59.

Grossi, Tommaso (Bellano, Lake of Como, Italy, Jan. 20, 1791; Milan, Dec. 10, 1853). He was destined for the Church, but was early infected by the revolutionary ferment in Italy, and determined to devote himself to literature. In 1820 he published a poem entitled Ildegonda, a half-romantic, half-classic production, which was much admired. This was followed by I Lombardi alla prima crociata (1826), which is mentioned by Manzoni in his novel, I promessi sposi. Under the influence of Manzoni's novel, Grossi tried his hand at fiction, and the result was the historical romance *Marco Visconti*, which brought him fame at home and made him known abroad through translations into English, French, and German. It was the beginning of the historical novel in Italy, and has always been popular.

It was followed by another novel, Ulrico e Lida, which, though replete with a delicate appreciation of nature and graceful sentiment, was not so successful. In 1848 Grossi celebrated in verse, though somewhat prematurely, his country's enfranchisement, but he died before the full fruition of his hopes. His collected works were published in Milan in 1854, under the title Vita ed opere di Tommaso Grossi (Life and Works of Tommaso Grossi).

Guerrazzi, Francesco Domenico (Leghorn, Italy, Aug. 12, 1804; Cinquantina, near Cecina, Sept. 27, 1873). Deprived of a mother before he had known her, and brought up by a rude and austere father, with whom he quarreled when he was only fourteen years old, he had for a long time to contend with loneliness and poverty. He paid his way while studying law at the University of Pisa, by reading proofs, translating books, and by teaching pupils older than himself. When twenty years old he took his degree of Doctor of Laws and, having become reconciled with his father, opened an office in Leghorn. Brought up on Machiavelli, and an enthusiastic admirer of Byron, whom he had met at Pisa, he took to literature as a means of propagating his liberal political opinions.

His first romance, La Battaglia di Benevento (1827), produced a lively sensation and brought him into public notice;

and his Elogio di Cosimo del Fanti (1828) caused his confinement for six months at Montepulciano. In the next year he became associated with Mazzini in founding the Indicatore livornese, which was soon suppressed. In 1831 and in 1833 he was again imprisoned, the last time at Portoferraio. There he wrote, in 1834, L'Assedio di Firenze (published in Paris, 1836), a historical novel full of patriotic fervor. Upon his discharge from prison he settled in Florence, where he became a successful lawyer.

In 1848 Guerrazzi was elected a deputy, and on the overthrow of the Capponi Ministry, in 1849, he was chosen a triumvir with Mazzini and Montanelli. Afterward, on the flight of the Grand Duke, he was proclaimed dictator. His violence in this position irritated the people, and on the restoration of the Grand Duke, public opinion turned against him. He was arrested and iniquitously prosecuted, and in spite of his admirable defense, Apologia della vita politica di F. D. Guerrazzi (1852), he was condemned, after three years' imprisonment, to the galleys, but finally was permitted to select Corsica as a place of perpetual banishment. There he wrote *Beatrice Cenci* (1854), La Torre di Monza, and Fides.

Restored to liberty and action by later events, he went to Genoa, where he wrote Il Buco nel Muro, a humorous work. In 1862 and 1865 he sat in the Parliament of Turin. Though Guerrazzi wrote the purest Italian, his style was bitterly intemperate, Byronic in impulsiveness, and occasionally blasphemous. Other novels by him are: Veronica Cybo (1844); Isabella Orsini (1844); Marchese di Santa Prassede (1853); and Pasquale Paoli (1860), the last dealing with the fall of Corsica. His collected works in fifteen volumes were published at Milan in 1877.

Habberton, John (Brooklyn, N. Y., Feb. 24, 1842). From 1850 to 1859 he lived with an uncle in Illinois, where he attended a high school, and then, returning to New York, learned typesetting in Harper and Brothers' publishing-house. In 1862 he enlisted in the Union Army and at the close of the Civil War was mustered out as First Lieutenant. After several years in the Harpers' counting-room he undertook publishing on his own account in 1872, but failed. He was subsequently literary editor of The Christian Union, 1874–'77, and staff editor of the New York Herald, 1877–'92. His earliest book, *Helen's Babies*, after being declined by various publishers in New York, Boston, Chicago, and elsewhere, was issued by a Boston house in 1876 and reached a circulation of more than two hundred and fifty thousand copies in the United States. It was reprinted by eleven English publishers and also in the British colonies, and was translated into French, Italian, Spanish, Danish, German, and Bohemian. In the same year he published The Barton Experiment and The Jericho Road, and in 1877 five more books, all of which were popular but by no means repeated the success of his first book. He continued to be a very prolific author for a series of years, among his other books being a novel, Brueton's Bayou (1886), which was highly praised by The London Academy; Who was Paul Greyson? (1881); Life of George Washington (1883); All He Knew (1890); and *Trif and Trixy* (1897). In 1880 he produced a drama in four acts, entitled Deacon Cranket, which was played more than five hundred times. He also edited, with introductions, two volumes of selections from The Spectator.

Hackländer, Friedrich Wilhelm von (Burtscheid, Germany, Nov. 1, 1816; Starnbergersee, Bavaria, July 6, 1877). He wrote several books on military life that made him famous in his native country. The first two, Bilder aus dem Soldatenleben and Das Soldatenleben im Frieden, both published in 1844, established him as a humorous writer and led to an invitation to travel with Baron von Taubenheim in the Orient. Two books of travel resulted from this journey. Hackländer took active part in the Piedmont campaign of 1849, and the result was another book of military life, Das Soldatenleben im Krieg. In 1855 he founded the popular weekly, Ueber Land und Meer, at Stuttgart, where he passed the remainder of his life. He wrote several plays, of which Der Geheime Agent (1850) was a permanent success and was translated into several languages. His novels were, Handel und Wandel (1850) and *Forbidden Fruit* (*Namenlose Gesichten,* 1851), the latter achieving great popularity in Germany.

Haggard, Henry Rider (Bradenham, Norfolk, England, June 22, 1856). He is the son of W. M. R. Haggard, of Bradenham Hall, and on being sent to the Ipswich Grammar School he prepared himself for a clerkship in the Foreign Office. At nineteen he received an appointment on the staff of Sir Henry Bulwer and accompanied that official to Natal as secretary in 1875. The next year he went to the Transvaal on the Special Commissioner's staff and was shortly made Master of the High Court of the Transvaal. Retiring from the Colonial Service in 1879, he returned to England, where he married. Events in Natal then requiring his presence to secure his property, he once more went to South Africa, and the important engagements of Hilldrop, Majuba Hill, and Laing's Neck took place not far from his own house, in which the treaty of retrocession was subsequently signed. Disgusted with the colonial policy at this period, he went back to England, and in 1882 published Cetywayo and his White Neighbors, in which book is narrated the results in South Africa of the irresolute action of the British Government. He lost fifty pounds on this literary venture, and Dawn, his first novel (1884), brought him only ten pounds. Undiscouraged by his small amount of literary success he published The Witch's Head in the same year, his gains in this venture amounting to fifty pounds. In 1885 he was admitted to the Bar, his legal career beginning in the Probate and Divorce Court. In the leisure evenings of his first term he employed himself in writing *King Solomon's Mines* (1885), a work which made him immediately famous. *She* (1887); Jess (1887); and Allan Quatermain (1887), were as phenomenally successful as *King Solomon's Mines*, and Maiwa's Revenge (1888), written in a single fortnight, continued the tale of its author's triumphs. Later fiction by him includes among other works: Cleopatra: The World's Desire (with Andrew Lang, 1890); The Wizard (1896); Montezuma's Daughter; and The People of the Mist. Of a very different nature are: The Last Boer War (1899), reprinted in the United States as A History of the Transvaal; A Farmer's Year (1898); and A Gardener's Year (1905). In these later works it is apparent that greater pains have been taken in the composition, and it should be said of Cleopatra that the author visited Egypt to study the setting for the tale. A recent critic traces a certain kinship between Mr. Rider Haggard and Disraeli and Bulwer, saying: "In these Byronic novelists, who preserved for their heroes the dear corsair expression, half savage, half soft, love of the romance of pure adventure was handed down across Dickens and Thackeray, and in an indirect way Bulwer and Disraeli are the progenitors of the Ouidas and Rider Haggards of a later age."

Halévy, Ludovic (Paris, France, Jan. 1, 1834; May 8, 1908). The son of Léon Halévy, adjunct professor of literature in the École Polytechnique, the nephew of Jacques François Halévy, the famous operatic composer, he began his career in the Civil Service under the Duc de Morny. While still in that situation he wrote several librettos to various comic operas by Offenbach, Bizet, and Morny, but was unsuccessful until he began to collaborate with Meilhac. Together they wrote the librettos of Offenbach's La belle Hélène (1865); Barbe bleu (1866); La grande duchesse (1867); La Périchole (1868); and Bizet's Carmen (1875), while in Frou-Frou (1869) they achieved one of the greatest theatrical successes of their century. So well did they blend their brilliant talents that it is impossible to separate the work of one from that of the other. The two men, however, did much writing independently, Halvéy producing the three satirical novels, Monsieur and Madame Cardinal (1873); Les petites Cardinals (1880); La famille Cardinal (1883); and L'abbé Constantin (1882); Criquette (1883); Mademoiselle Duval, and lesser fiction. His most important work is L'abbé Constantin, a pure, sweet story of French provincial life, which has been widely read and admired not only in France but in England and America as well, various English translations of it having appeared. Its moral tone is irreproachable and its representation of French character was more or less a revelation to the bulk of English and American readers. Halévy was elected to the French Academy in 1884, but although he continued to mingle freely with his literary and artistic contemporaries he wrote but little during the last eighteen years of his life. In 1868 he was married to Mademoiselle Bréguet. His friend, Jules Claretie, has characterized him as one of the inspirers of French literature.   A complete edition of the dramatic works of Halévy and Meilhac has appeared in Paris in recent years.

Hamerton, Philip Gilbert (Laneside, Shaw, Lancashire, England, Sept. 10, 1834; Boulogne-sur-Seine, France, Nov. 4, 1894).   Left an orphan in his tenth year, he was educated at the grammar schools of Burnley and Doncaster and was placed with a clergyman to be prepared for Oxford; but, owing to his reluctance to sign the Thirty-nine Articles this design was relinquished.   He possessed independent means, so he resolved upon following art and authorship.   He traveled and painted in Scotland, and in 1855 published a collection of descriptive verse entitled The Isles of Loch Awe, and Other Poems. In 1858 he married Mademoiselle Eugénie Gindriez, a union which proved most harmonious, although he was an Englishman and was more or less of a freethinker, while she was a Frenchwoman and a devout Roman Catholic.   In 1862 he settled in the neighborhood of Autun, France, where much of his life was spent till shortly before his death.   As a painter he would most probably never have risen much above mediocrity, and it was a fortunate circumstance that about this time he published A Painter's Camp in the Highlands (1862), which not only attracted immediate notice in England and America, but resulted in his becoming a valued contributor to English periodicals, and succeeding Palgrave as art critic on the Saturday Review.   In 1869 he established The Portfolio, a high-class art journal, to which he contributed, among other articles, a series of papers with etchings by himself, entitled The Unknown River, which appeared in book form (1870) with a dedication to his American friend, Horatio Nelson Powers.   In 1869 he published *Wenderholme*, a story of Lancashire and Yorkshire, which possesses great charm of descriptive detail, as does Marmorne (1878), a novel issued under the pseudonym of Adolphus Seagrave.   His later fiction is well planned, with faithful characterization and original humor, and it displays entire familiarity with French architecture and landscape.   But it was as an essayist that he made his chief impression on his time, and in The Intellectual Life (1873) he succeeded in the difficult task of writing a collection of didactic essays that should win popularity among thoughtful readers. Indeed the volume had a distinct formative influence upon the young people of its day and is still perused with interest. Among later volumes were: Round My House (1876), a faithful study of French social life; Modern Frenchmen (1878), which helped materially in establishing cordial relations between French and English; Human Intercourse (1882); French and English (1890). He left an autobiography brought down to the date of his marriage, and in 1897 it was completed and published by his widow. Her portion of the work reveals the entire sympathy which existed between them and is a remarkable example of idiomatic English written by one who knew nothing of English when she was married and whose residence in Great Britain was very brief.

Harben, William Nathaniel (Dalton, Ga., July 5, 1858). He was the son of Nathaniel Parks Harben, a Southern planter, and was educated privately and at Crawford High School in his native town. For several years he engaged in business, but in 1888 he entered the literary field with a translation from the German, and then began the writing of short stories which were favorably received north and south. He traveled extensively abroad, spending much time in Paris and London, and was an associate editor of The Youth's Companion (1891–'93). His first novel, White Marie, appeared in 1889 and discusses slavery from a Southern point of view. It was followed by: Almost Persuaded (1891); A Mute Confessor (1892); and The Land of the Changing Sun (1893), the last-named not only appearing in book form but serially in a thousand journals controlled by the American Press Association. He has since passed much of his time in New York, and has given his whole time to literary work, contributing short stories to the magazines and writing many novels, some of which are: The Woman Who Trusted (1901); Westerfelt (1901); *Abner Daniel* (1902); The Georgians (1904); Mam' Linda (1907). His style long ago caught the popular fancy, and his novels and short sketches, which are marked by clever dialogue and description, as well as skilful construction, find a host of appreciative readers. He married, in 1896, Maybelle Chandler of Benson, S. C.

Hardy, Arthur Sherburne (Andover, Mass., Aug. 13, 1847). His early education was obtained at a school in Neufchâtel, Switzerland. He then prepared for college at Phillips Academy, Andover, spent a year at Amherst College, and in 1869 was graduated at the United States Military Academy at West Point with the commission of artillery lieutenant. After serving a short time as an instructor of artillery tactics at West Point he resigned from the army in 1870 and was professor of civil engineering at Iowa College (1870–'73). In 1874 he studied scientific bridge construction in Paris, was made professor of civil engineering in the Chandler Scientific School of Dartmouth College, and was professor of mathematics at Dartmouth from 1878 to 1893. From 1897 to 1899 he was Minister-resident and Consul-general to Persia and Minister-plenipotentiary to Greece, Rumania, and Servia, 1899–1901, and to Spain 1902–'03. He published Elements of Quarternions (1881) and several other text-books in applied mathematics, but to the literary world he is known as novelist and poet. In 1883 he published a strongly original novel, But Yet a Woman, which attracted much favorable notice both for its polished style and delicate delineation of character. It was succeeded by *The Wind of Destiny* (1886) a psychological tale as popular as its predecessor. *Passe Rose,* a semi-historical romance of the days of Charlemagne, appeared in 1889 and met with very general admiration. Subsequent books by him were: Life and Letters of Joseph H. Neesima; Songs of Two (1900), a collection of verse; His Daughter First (1903). In 1898 he married Grace Aspinwall, a daughter of Henry C. Bowen, long the publisher of The Independent, and in later years resided at Woodstock, Conn.

Hardy, Thomas (Dorchester, Dorset, England, June 2, 1840). Articled at sixteen to an ecclesiastical architect of Dorchester, he studied later at King's College, London, and in 1863 won a prize from the Royal Institute of British Architects for an essay upon Colored Brick and Terra-Cotta Architecture. He practised his profession under Sir Arthur Blomfield in London from 1862 to 1867, and his familiarity with architectural details has left its mark upon his novels. His first novel, Desperate Remedies, was put forth in 1871, and shows his genius in the formative period. A far better piece of work is Under the Greenwood Tree (1872). The next year he gave up architecture in order to devote himself entirely to literature, and wrote and published A Pair of Blue Eyes. During 1874 his novel *Far from the Madding Crowd* was issued serially and anonymously in the Cornhill Magazine and was by many persons attributed to George Eliot, since no other living author was esteemed capable of writing it. It was followed by The Hand of Ethelberta (1876) and *The Return of the Native* (1878), the last-named his finest work, in the opinion of many critics. Since its publication its author has written a long series of books, mainly fiction, including: The Trumpet Major (1880); A Laodicean (1881); Two on a Tower (1882), wherein a very complicated situation is delineated; *The Mayor of Casterbridge* (1886); The Woodlanders (1887); Wessex Tales (1888); A Group of Noble Dames (1891), a collection of short stories; *Tess of the D'Urbervilles* (1891), a work which maintains throughout a firm grip upon the reader's sympathies; Life's Little Ironies (1894), a series of gloomy short stories; Jude the Obscure (1895), a harrowing tale displaying the most pitiless analysis of character; and The Well-Beloved (1897). Throughout his work appears constantly the author's fondness for his native region, which he calls Wessex; and his appointment in 1894 as one of the county magistrates reveals the Dorset appreciation of his genius. The Wessex edition of his novels was issued in 1895, and he has since published Wessex Poems (1899), a collection of his verse of many years; Poems of the Past and Present (1901); The Dynasts: A Drama of the Napoleonic Wars (1904-'08). His verse is of interest on account of its authorship, but scarcely otherwise, since it lacks spontaneity and its fetters are seen to cramp his powers of expression.

Harland, Henry (Sidney Luska) (St. Petersburg, Russia, March 1, 1861; London, England, Dec. 20, 1905). He received his education at the College of the City of New York and Harvard University, and after some years spent in European travel as a correspondent, and as a clerk in the Surrogate's Office in New York City, he removed to London, which thenceforth continued his home. He edited The Yellow Book for several years from 1894, a quarterly periodical founded for the purpose of disseminating somewhat advanced views upon art. Adopting at the outset of his career the pseudonym of "Sidney Luska," he published under it several works of fiction: As It Was Written (1885); Mrs. Peixada (1887); My Uncle Florimond (1888); The Yoke of the Thorah (1887); Mr. Sonnenschein's Inheritance (1888); and some others, dealing with Jewish life in the United States. These achieved some popularity in this country, but are now nearly forgotten. In 1890 he stopped abruptly all writing of this purely ephemeral nature, and after waiting three years put forth the carefully written Mademoiselle Mirs, in entire contrast to any preceding work of his. Its delicate beauty of workmanship is repeated in Grey Roses (1895); Comedies and Errors (1898); the widely popular novel, *The Cardinal's Snuff-Box* (1900); and The Lady Paramount (1901). These later works were especially well received by the English public.

Harland, Marion (Amelia County, Va., Dec. 21, 1831). Her maiden name was Mary Virginia Hawes. She was educated in good schools and began writing for publication at the age of fourteen. In 1856 she married the Rev. Edward Payson Terhune. Much of her literary activity has been given to editorial work and writing on household topics. She conducted the magazine Babyhood for two years, and later The Home-Maker, and departments in Wide Awake, St. Nicholas, and the Philadelphia North American. Her departmental work has also included a School for Housewives, published simultaneously in twenty-five newspapers. Her novels are: The Story of Mary Washington; *Alone;* Moss-Side; The Hidden Path; Judith; Handicapped; Nemesis; At Last; Helen Gardner's Wedding-Day; Jessamine; With the Best Intentions; True as Steel; Sunnybanks; My Little Love; A Gallant Fight; The Royal Road; His Great Self; Mr. Wayt's Wife's

Sister; Eve's Daughters; When Grandmamma Was New; Dr. Dale; The Distractions of Martha.

Harris, Joel Chandler (Eatonton, Ga., Dec. 8, 1848; Atlanta, Ga., July 3, 1908). He began his career as a printer's apprentice, then studied law and practised his profession for a time in Forsyth, Ga., doing some editorial work meanwhile. In 1876 he was appointed a member of the staff of the Atlanta Constitution, becoming editor-in-chief in 1890. It was in this journal that his famous negro-dialect stories first appeared, and in 1880 the earliest volume of these studies of Afro-American folk-lore was collected with the title of Uncle Remus, His Songs and His Sayings. Nights with Uncle Remus was published in 1884: and later books were: Mingo and Other Sketches (1884); Free Joe and Other Georgian Sketches (1888); Daddy Jake (1889); the juveniles, Little Mr. Thimblefinger (1894) and Aaron in the Wildwoods (1897); Chronicles of Aunt Minervy Ann (1899); *Gabriel Tolliver* (1902); Told by Uncle Remus (1905). More than one critic has pointed out the fact that in the Uncle Remus stories the old plantation negro seemingly evolves a philosophy of his own to the effect that in the long run weakness wins, and perhaps thus expresses a certain revolt from the conditions surrounding himself. The most helpless of all animals, the rabbit, is thus made victorious over the wolf, the fox, and the bear. To Southerners his stories appealed not as something entirely new but as an accurate presentation of what had long been familiar, while to Northern readers they revealed conditions of existence quite foreign to anything of which they had had personal experience. For some time the figure of Uncle Remus was supposed to be drawn from a definite original the author had known; but Mr. Harris at last explained that the portrait was a composite of several old plantation negroes whom he had encountered at various times. The Uncle Remus tales themselves are characteristic folk-lore stories originating in Africa and transplanted to America, and Mr. Harris's merit lay not merely in his perception of their literary value and his skill in giving them color and atmosphere, but in his presentation of story-teller and listener in addition to the story itself. Uncle Remus, however, was not

Mr. Harris's only creation, for Aunt Minervy Ann and Daddy Jake, to name no others, are distinctly original personages.

Harrison, Constance Cary (Fairfax County, Va., April 25, 1846). She was educated by private governesses; in her girl-hood, during the Civil War, she lived in Richmond, Va., and afterward went to Europe with her widowed mother to com-plete her studies in music and languages. In 1867 she married Burton Harrison, a lawyer who had been private secretary to Jefferson Davis. They went to New York, which has since been Mrs. Harrison's residence, although she has traveled ex-tensively and spent much time in London, Paris, and other European cities. In addition to her novels she has written many short stories and several comedies, including translations from the French. Her novels are: Golden Rod (1880); Helen Troy (1881); Bar Harbor Days (1887); *The Anglomaniacs* (1887); A Daughter of the South (1892); Sweet Bells out of Tune (1893); A Bachelor Maid; An Errant Wooing (1895); A Merry Maid of Arcady; A Son of the Old Dominion (1897); Good Americans (1898); A Princess of the Hills (1901); The Unwelcome Mrs. Hatch; Latter-Day Sweethearts (1906).

Harte, Francis Bret (Albany, N. Y., Aug. 25, 1839; Cam-berley, Surrey, England, May 5, 1902). He removed to Cali-fornia in 1854 and for three years engaged in gold-digging and teaching school; then, getting employment as a compositor on the Golden Era, began writing for it sketches that secured local attention. He soon became its assistant editor and sub-sequently editor of the Weekly Californian; was secretary of the United States Mint in San Francisco, and from 1868 to 1870 edited the Overland Monthly, which he founded. His short stories and his poems had by this time given him a national fame and he was for a year professor of literature in the Uni-versity of California. He had already published The Lost Galleon, and Other Poems (1867); and Condensed Novels (1867); while his poem of The Heathen Chinee was known to nearly everyone. He then removed to New York in order to give himself entirely to literary pursuits, but after a time he held consular posts at Crefeld, Germany, 1878–'80, and at

Glasgow, 1880–'85, and after 1885 he made his home in London. He was one of the most prolific authors of his time. Among the more important of his many books were: East and West Poems (1871); The Luck of Roaring Camp, and Other Sketches (1871), which contains the best of his short stories; *Gabriel Conroy* (1876); Two Men of Sandy Bar (1876); The Twins of Table Mountain (1879); Flip (1882); A Sappho of Green Springs (1896); Barker's Luck (1896); The Three Partners (1897); Under the Redwoods (1901). Bret Harte was at his best in describing the conditions of life in lawless communities beyond the borders of ordinary American civilization, and his delineations of adventures of all kinds were as sympathetic as they were frank. That his characters were often disreputable troubled him very little; he regarded them quite impersonally, assuming no responsibility for their actions, and not at all caring to point a moral. A note of exaggeration ran through his descriptions of Californian doings and sayings, but the essential truth of his accounts was easy to recognize, nevertheless, and they usefully supplement more matter-of-fact history. During his long residence in London, he made for himself a wide circle of English friends, and his later books enjoyed in England a rather larger measure of appreciation than in his own country.

Hartner, Eva, the pen-name of Emma von Twardowska (Germany, 1850). Her writings, although very popular in Germany, are little known elsewhere, and nothing of importance is known regarding her life. Her *Severa* appeared in 1881.

Hauff, Wilhelm (Stuttgart, Württemberg, Nov. 29, 1802; Stuttgart, Nov. 18, 1827). He received a desultory education and from 1820 to 1824 studied theology at Tübingen; in the last year of his life he became editor of the Stuttgart Morgenblatt and married. His first volume, Märchenalmanach (1826) met with speedy success on account of its dramatic humor, as also did his Mitteilungen aus den Memoiren des Satans (1826), and Der Mann im Monde (1826). The last-named book was a parody upon the work of the novelist, H. Clauren, under whose name it appeared, with the result that Clauren's most loyal admirers were deceived as to its authorship. Lichtenstein (1826), one of the best of his works, is a still popular romance and includes a striking series of historical portraitures of men and customs. Among other writings of his were: Phantasien im Bremer Ratskeller (1827); and Das Bild des Kaisers, and *Peter Munk*, known in English as *The Iron Heart*. All his works evince rare ability, and German literature lost much by his untimely death. Frequent editions of his books have been put forth, and after the lapse of three generations he remains as popular an author as ever.

Hawthorne, Julian (Boston, Mass., June 22, 1846). He was the only son of the famous novelist, Nathaniel Hawthorne, and studied at Harvard University (1863–'67). He passed two years in the study of civil engineering at a Real-Schule in Dresden, Saxony, and from 1870 to 1872 was a hydrographic engineer in the New York Dock Department. Two years more in Dresden followed, and from 1874 to 1881 he made his home in London, where he contributed much to reviews and magazines and was for two years on the staff of the Spectator. In 1882 he returned to the United States, and has since engaged in journalism and other general literary work. He married Minnie Amelung in 1870, and Hildegarde Hawthorne, the eldest of their seven children, has already attracted favorable notice as essayist and critic. While Julian Hawthorne was in the employ of the Dock Department his resolution to cultivate literature was made. Several short stories and sketches written by him in 1871 were so well received that he definitely determined upon giving up his profession of engineering. In 1873 his first novel, Bressant, appeared, and there was a general disposition to regard his work kindly. Idolatry (1874) was respectfully received, and a later novel, Garth (1877), was recognized as a marked advance in literary style. It was followed by many more works of fiction. Among them were: Mrs. Gainsborough's Diamonds (1878); Sebastian Strome (1879); *Archibald Malmaison* (1879), a weird and gruesome tale; Fortune's Fool (1883); Dust (1883); The Great Bank Robbery (1887); and Love is a Spirit (1898). In 1884 he published Nathaniel Hawthorne and His Wife: A Biography. Later works of a general character were Confessions and Criticisms (1886); American Literature (1891); History of the United States (1899).

Hawthorne, Nathaniel (Salem, Mass., July 4, 1804; Plymouth, N. H., May 19, 1864). He was descended from Puritan ancestry, his earliest American progenitor, William Hathorne, having accompanied Winthrop in the *Arbella* in 1630, settling in 1636 in Salem. The novelist's father (1776–1808), also Nathaniel, was a sea-captain who married Elizabeth Manning of Salem. Of their three children Nathaniel was the second. On her husband's death his widow took her children to her father's and later to her brother's at Raymond, Me. He was graduated from Bowdoin College in 1825, where his especial friends had been Longfellow and Franklin Pierce, afterward President. Returning to Salem, he led a secluded life, writing and destroying much likewise. *Fanshawe*, his first book, was issued anonymously in 1828, his name first appearing appended to four Tales in an annual for 1831, *The Token*. The first collection of Twice-Told Tales was published in 1837, but despite Longfellow's appreciative review they attracted little attention. For two years (1839–'41) Hawthorne served as weigher in the Boston Custom-house and was surveyor at the Custom-house in Salem (1845–'49). In the intervening years he had spent some months in the famous socialistic community of Brook Farm, had married Miss Sophia Peabody of Salem in 1842, and set up housekeeping in the Old Manse in Concord. He had also published a second series of Twice-Told Tales and two volumes of sketches entitled Mosses from an Old Manse. Before leaving Salem (1849) he had written the first draft of *The Scarlet Letter*, which his friend, James T. Fields, the publisher, advised him to extend. This was done, and the first edition of five thousand copies was sold in two weeks. Both in England and America the tale was received with the most flattering enthusiasm. In the same year (1850) Hawthorne moved to Lenox, Mass., where he wrote *The House of the Seven Gables* (1851). He then lived for some months at West Newton, Mass., where he wrote *The Blithedale Romance* (1852) and The Snow Image, and Other Tales (1852). His friend Pierce, now

President, offered him the Liverpool consulate, which was accepted, and Hawthorne accordingly spent seven years abroad, the first five years employed in his consular duties. In 1860 he published *The Marble Faun*, issued in England as *Transformation*. He returned to America just prior to the Civil War and settled again in Concord in the house since known as Wayside. The last book issued in his lifetime was Our Old Home, a series of impressions of England. He left behind him the fragmentary tales: The Dolliver Romance; Dr. Grimshawe's Secret; and *Septimius Felton*, as well as several volumes of English, French, and Italian Note-Books, all of which were ultimately published. In the generation which has elapsed since his death no diminution of his fame may be noted. His style is unique in its literary quality, and he has come at last to be fairly classed among the great masters of English prose.

Hay, John (Salem, Ind., Oct. 8, 1838; Newbury, N. H., July 1, 1905). He was graduated from Brown University in 1858 and at once began the study of law in the office of Abraham Lincoln in Springfield, Ill. He did not practise after gaining admission to the bar, in 1861, but became one of the President's private secretaries, and during the Civil War period served for a time in the field and was brevetted lieutenant-colonel. From 1865 to 1867 he was secretary of legation at Paris and subsequently at Madrid; on returning to America he was for five years on the editorial staff of the New York Tribune, in which he published his Pike County Ballads, reprinted in book form in 1871. He married, in 1875, a daughter of Amasa Stone of Cleveland, in which city he then made his home and devoted himself to literary work, interrupted only by his service as First Assistant Secretary of State (1879-'81). In March, 1897, he was appointed Ambassador to Great Britain by President McKinley, a selection that met with general approval. While serving in this capacity he did much to establish cordial relations between his own country and England, and his diplomatic experience was of great value to him when he became Secretary of State in August, 1898. Grave and difficult questions came before him while he held this office and were handled with rare skill. During the Boxer outbreak in China he succeeded in obtaining justice for the Chinese. He negotiated and signed the Hay-Pauncefote Treaty of 1901, and warmly supported the Hague Conference and the Anglo-Japanese Treaty of 1902, his main diplomatic achievement probably being the maintenance of the "open-door" policy in China. In addition to the Pike County Ballads he was the author of a second volume of Poems (1890); Castilian Days (1891); and he collaborated with John G. Nicolay in the preparation of a ten-volume life of Abraham Lincoln (1890), a painstaking and authoritative biography. In 1883 a striking anonymous novel, entitled *The Bread-winners*, was published serially in the Century Magazine, the authorship of which was attributed to him and never definitively denied by him.

Hay, Mary Cecil (Shrewsbury, England, 1840 or 1841; Worthing, Sussex, England, July 24, 1886). She was the daughter of Thomas William Hay, a well-known clockmaker of Market Square, Shrewsbury, and his wife, Cecilia, and in that picturesque town the earlier portion of her career was passed. Some years after her father's death she removed with her mother and two sisters to Worthing, in Sussex, which thenceforth remained her home. Her first novel, entitled Kate's Engagement, was published in book form in 1873 after first appearing serially, like nearly all of her books. Hidden Perils (1873); Victor and Vanquished (1874, originally printed with the title Rendered a Recompense), followed this and were moderately successful, but her best known, and, according to some critics, her best novel, was *Old Myddelton's Money* (1874). Still other critics have esteemed The Arundel Motto (1877) very highly, because of its careful characterization and genuine humor in addition to its finish of style. Other among her novels that may be named are: The Squire's Legacy (1875); Nora's Love Test (1876); For Her Dear Sake (1880); Missing, and Other Tales (1881); Lester's Secret (1885); and A Wicked Girl, and Other Tales (1886). The proofs of the last-named book were corrected while its author was suffering from a painful malady which endured for the last year of her life. While Miss Hay's fictions all attained a fair share of success in her own country they were far more popular in the United States and Australia. They all displayed the practised hand of the professional novelist, and were always well told, wholesome tales which never failed to give pleasure to the reader.

Hearn, Lafcadio (Santa Maura, Ionian Islands, July 27, 1850; Tokyo, Japan, Sept. 27, 1905). The son of an English father and a Greek mother, he was educated in England and France and came to the United States in 1869, engaging in journalism in Cincinnati, New Orleans, and New York, successively. He lived at St. Pierre in Martinique 1887–'89, and in 1890 went to Japan, where he was naturalized under the name of Yakumo Koizumi and received the appointment of lecturer in English literature at the Imperial University of Tokyo. His earliest books were Stray Leaves from Strange Literature (1884); Some Chinese Ghosts (1886); Chita: A Memory of Lost Island (1889), a story displaying rare powers of description; Two Years in the French West Indies (1890), which acquired new interest after the destruction of St. Pierre by a volcanic eruption in 1902; and *Youma* (1890). Hearn's later books are almost exclusively concerned with Japanese themes and reveal more fully than any other works, in English, at least, the complexities of Japanese character and social conditions. Among them are: Glimpses of Unfamiliar Japan (1894); Out of the East (1895); Japanese Inner Life (1897); Kokoro (1896); Kotto (1902); Gleanings in Buddha Fields (1897). As an interpreter of the mystic and exotic he displayed rare power.

Hewlett, Maurice Henry (London, Jan. 22, 1861). As the eldest son of Henry Gay Hewlett, of Shaw Hill, a man with a passion for medieval customs, furnishings, and chronicles, he inherited the antiquarian tastes and talent which were early to make him conspicuous. From the London International College, Isleworth, he went to Oxford, but left at nineteen years of age, without obtaining a scholarship, and applied himself to "blackletter" law. Of this academic period he has said: "I wasted my time. I dreamed. I tried to do things too big for me, and threw them up at the first failure. I diligently pursued every false god. I don't think I was very happy, and I am sure I was very disagreeable." He was admitted to the bar in 1890, but failing health drove him to Italy, where he recovered strength and devoted himself to the study of recondite phases of the life and thought of the Middle Ages. On his return to England he was appointed lecturer on medieval times at University College and at South Kensington Museum. Not until he had passed his thirtieth year did he begin his now well known interpretation of Italian life during the Middle Ages and the period of early Renaissance. In 1895 appeared his first book, Earthwork out of Tuscany, a series of studies the fruit of his sojourn in Italy. The next year he received from the English Government his appointment as Head of the Land and Revenue Records, an office he still retains. Official routine has been counterbalanced by brilliant incursions into the field of letters. Three books, The Masque of Dead Florentines (1895), Songs and Meditations (1897), and Pan and the Young Shepherd (1898), preceded his first great success, *The Forest Lovers* (1898). Then came Little Novels of Italy (1899), containing such gems of short-story writing as the Madonna of the Peach-Tree and The Duchess of Nona. *Richard Yea-and-Nay* (1900) followed and created a sensation on both sides of the Atlantic. But Hewlett was not thereby induced to become prolific, and he gave his literary *credo;* "A writer who is worth anything accumulates more than he gives off, and never lives up to his income." Since his romance of Richard the Lion-Hearted he has produced the following: New Canterbury Tales (1901); Fond Adventures (1903); The Queen's Quair (1904); The Road in Tuscany (1904); The Fool Errant (1905); and The Stooping Lady (1907).

Heyse, Johann Ludwig Paul (Berlin, March 15, 1830). He is the son of Karl Wilhelm Ludwig Heyse, the noted philologist, and was educated at the Frederick William Gymnasium of his native city, and at the universities of Berlin and Bonn. Following his father's example, he applied himself to philology, and in 1852 traveled to Italy to continue his researches. Before this, however, he had produced a fanciful tale, Der Jungbrunnen (1848) and a tragedy on the story of Francesca da Rimini

(1851), both of which evinced the influence of the Romantic school. In 1854 he reprinted his epics, Urica (1851) and Die Brüder (1852), and they aroused so much interest and discussion that in May, 1854, King Maximilian of Bavaria invited the young author to make Munich his permanent home. Obeying the royal summons, he lived in that city for a number of years, and there he married the daughter of the eminent art critic, Franz Kugler. Frequent visits to his favorite land of Italy resulted in his living most of the time in his later years on the banks of Lake Garda. Love for that country is apparent in a number of his productions. In 1855 he published four novelettes in one volume, two of which were acknowledged masterpieces; and from that time Heyse has dominated the short story in Germany. The best collection of his fiction in this form is Das Buch der Freundschaft (1883), and the most famous single example is L'Arrabbiata. Of his more sustained fiction the noteworthy novels are: Kinder des Welt (1873); *Im Paradiese* (1875), translated into English as *In Paradise;* Merlin (1892); and Ueber allen Gipfeln (1895). As a poet he is known principally by Thekla (1858), a noble performance.

This dominant and versatile mind in German literature has given numerous dramas to the stage, among which may be mentioned: Meleager (1854); Die Sabinerinnen (1859); Elizabeth Charlotte (1860); Ludwig der Bayer (1862); Hans Lange (1866); and Maria von Magdala, which had a success in America during the season of 1902. Altogether his works comprise upward of forty volumes. He has also made masterly translations of Leopardi, Giusti, and other Italian poets. His reminiscences, Jugenderinnerungen und Bekenntnisse, appeared in 1900.

Hichens, Robert Smythe (Speldhurst, Kent, England, Nov. 14, 1864). He was the eldest son of the Rev. Canon Hichens, rector of St. Stephen's, near Canterbury, and was educated at Tunbridge Wells, Clifton, and at the Royal College of Music. After a brief experience as a musician, during which he wrote and published many lyrics, some recitations, and several short stories, he resolved to turn his attention entirely to literature, and spent a year at the London School of Journalism. In time he became a member of the staff of the London World, and wrote miscellaneous articles. A trip to Egypt in 1893 for his health resulted in a burning ambition to become a novelist; and while in that land of Pharaohs he conceived the idea for An Imaginative Man (1895), and in his later stories he fondly returned to the "Dark Continent" for background and color. But his first success was his brilliant satire on the English esthetes headed by Oscar Wilde, *The Green Carnation* (1894), which was published anonymously, and had a tremendous vogue. Other novels followed rapidly: After To-morrow (1895); New Love (1895); The Folly of Eustace, and Other Stories (1896); Flames (1897); The Londoners: A Farce (1898); The Slave (1899); Tongues of Conscience (1900); The Prophet of Berkeley Square (1901); Felix (1902); The Woman with the Fan (1904); *The Garden of Allah* (1905); The Black Spaniel (1905); The Call of the Blood (1906); and Barbary Sheep (1907).

One of his critics has acutely said: "None of Hichens's contemporaries is his superior in keen, witty analysis of character, in subtlety of feeling, in all the arts of modern story-writing." Mr. Hichens collaborated with Wilson Barrett in the successful play Daughters of Babylon, and was co-dramatist of The Medicine Man, produced by Sir Henry Irving, and of Becky Sharp, a stage version of Thackeray's Vanity Fair.

Hoffmann, Charles Fenno (New York City, 1806; Harrisburg, Pa., June 7, 1884). He was the son of Judge Josiah C. Hoffmann and younger brother of Ogden Hoffmann, both well known in legal circles. At six years of age he was sent to a Latin grammar school, and remained there for three years; next he attended an academy in Poughkeepsie, N. Y., from which he ran away because of the severe discipline. After that he had a private tutor. When twelve years old he lost his leg through an unfortunate attempt to leap from a pier to a passing steamboat. Three years later he entered Columbia College, where he spent three years, leaving before graduation. He studied law in Albany, and was admitted to the bar in 1827. Disliking the legal profession he quitted it within a few years to join Charles King on the New York American, a journal to which he had from time to time contributed anonymously. In 1833 he established the Knickerbocker Magazine, but gave it up and became the editor of the American Monthly, which he continued to conduct for some time. Its pages contained much of his prose work and poetry, and his first novel, Vanderlyn, appeared serially in it during 1837. Meanwhile he wrote two books which were the outcome of his wanderings in search of health: A Winter in the West (1835) and Wild Scenes in Forest and Prairie (1837), both of which achieved considerable popularity. But his most important prose contribution to literature was the story, *Greyslaer: A Romance of the Mohawk* (1840), founded upon the murder in Kentucky of Colonel Sharpe by Beauchamp. As a poet, Hoffmann composed several lyrics and songs, which have obtained a lasting place in their class. Of such are Rosalie Clare, Monterey, and Sparkling and Bright. His volumes of verse include: The Vigil of Faith (1842); The Echo (1844); Lays of the Hudson, and Other Poems (1846); and Love's Calendar, and Other Poems (1848). For three years prior to his losing his mind he edited The Literary World (1846–'49). From the latter year till his death (1884), he was an inmate of the Harrisburg insane asylum.

Holland, Josiah Gilbert (Belchertown, Mass., July 24, 1819; New York City, Oct. 12, 1881). He began the study of medicine in 1840, at the Berkshire Medical College, Pittsfield, Massachusetts, and four years afterward received his degree. Settling in Springfield, Massachusetts, he began practise, but patients were few and needy, so he was compelled to cast about him for a more lucrative occupation. With genuine Yankee perseverance and versatility he taught a district school, became a traveling writing-master, and then turned daguerreotypist. After a time editorial work appealed to his ambitious fancy, and he established The Bay State Courier, which ran its course in six months. Subsequently he taught school in Richmond, Virginia, and held the place of superintendent of public schools at Vicksburg, Mississippi, during a period of sixteen months. In 1849 he was once more on his native ground as associate editor of the Springfield Republican; and in 1851 was able to purchase an interest in that journal. This he sold in 1866, but not until his work under the pseudonym of "Timothy Titcomb" had made it a widely known and popular newspaper. First to appear was his series of Letters to Young People Married and Single, which attracted a multitude of readers, and was brought out in book form in 1858. "Timothy Titcomb" became a household name; his varied experiences and sympathy with work-a-day life fitted him well for his rôle of kindly, humorous adviser, whose morality was impeccable. To this period of Dr. Holland's career also belongs his History of Western Massachusetts (1855); The Bay Path (1857); Bitter-Sweet: A Poem in Dramatic Form (1858); Gold Foil (1859); Miss Gilbert's Career (1860); Letters to the Joneses (1863); Plain Talk on Familiar Subjects (1865); and the Life of Lincoln (1865). Before he left Springfield for Europe, in 1868, Dr. Holland had also won distinction as a popular lecturer. Returning from abroad, where he had traveled for two years, he founded Scribner's Monthly, in 1870, and it absorbed successively Hours at Home, Putnam's Magazine, and Old and New. Ultimately it became the present Century Magazine, which was conducted by Dr. Holland up to his death. Among other activities he was president of the Board of Education of New York City, and chairman of the board of trustees of the College of the City of New York. His later works comprise mainly novels and poems, of which mention may be made of Kathrina (1868); Arthur Bonnicastle (1873); The Mistress of the Manse (1874); The Story of Sevenoaks (1875); and Nicholas Minturn (1876). His complete poetical works were published in 1879.

Holmes, Oliver Wendell (Cambridge, Mass., August 29, 1809; Boston, October 7, 1894). From the Phillips Academy at Andover, Mass., he went to Harvard College in 1825, and was graduated four years later. Several poetic flights were attempted during these days, but none was memorable. A year after graduation, however, he wrote Old Ironsides for the Boston Advertiser, and it made him famous. For a short while he applied himself to law at the Harvard Law School, but abandoned it for medicine, which he studied here and in Paris, returning home in 1836 to take his medical degree at his *alma mater.* The same year saw the publication of his first collection of verses, among which were Evening, by a Tailor, and The Height of the Ridiculous. Between 1838–'40 he filled the chair of anatomy and physiology at Dartmouth College, and on June 15, 1840, he married Amelia Lee Jackson. Together they settled in Boston, where he eventually established a medical practise, but in 1847 he became Parkman Professor of anatomy and physiology at Harvard University, an appointment he held for thirty-five years; and from 1882 he was Professor Emeritus. As a physician he was the first to prove the infectiousness of puerperal fever, and produced the following scientific works: Lectures on Homeopathy and Its Kindred Delusions (1842); Currents and Counter-Currents in Medical Science (1861); and Border-Lines in Some Provinces of Medical Science (1862). But it was by his humorous essays that he became known throughout the English-reading world. In 1857 the first number of the Atlantic Monthly presented to the public the first chapter of The Autocrat at the Breakfast Table, which appeared in book form the next year. Its two companion compositions, The Professor at the Breakfast Table (1860) and The Poet at the Breakfast Table (1871–'72), went through the same channel of publication. To fiction he contributed three noteworthy novels in *Elsie Venner* (1861); *The Guardian Angel* (1868); and *A Mortal Antipathy* (1885). Other prose works are: Soundings from the Atlantic (1864); Mechanism in Thought and Morals (1871); two volumes of essays: John Lothrop Motley (1879) and Ralph Waldo Emerson (1884), memoirs of unequal merit. Two of his last books, Our Hundred Days in Europe (1887), a record of a Continental tour, and Over the Tea-Cups (1890), a final collection of essays, are full of his undiminished, undimmed wit. Incidentally, during his trip abroad, in 1886, Cambridge, Oxford, and Edinburgh Universities conferred honorary degrees upon him. To return to his poetry, the best known and universally admired examples are: The Chambered Nautilus (his own favorite); The Iron Gate; The Voiceless; Sun and Shadow; The Last Leaf; The Wonderful One-Hoss Shay; The Schoolboy; Parson Turell's Legacy; and The Moral Bully. His principal volumes of poetry appeared in the following order:

Urania (1846); Astræa (1850); Songs in Many Keys (1861); Songs of Many Seasons (1875); The Iron Gate and Other Poems (1880); and Before the Curfew and Other Poems (1888).

Homer, according to Herodotus, the poet who is the fountain-head of European literature, lived during the ninth century before Christ, and this period is the one most commonly accepted by critics, though many modern authorities contend that he existed several centuries earlier. Of the date of Homer's birth and life, however, probably no record, real or pretended, ever was known. Even his very existence has been doubted, and his name has been variously interpreted to signify "hostage," "companion," and "blind," and again to mean "connector of lays" or "compiler." There are eight so-called Lives of Homer extant, but all are manifestly spurious, and exhibit a curious medley of superstitions fashioned from minor poems attributed to him. These legends set forth the rigmarole that Homer was the son of the river Meles and the nymph Critheis, and was therefore called Melesigenes; that he wandered from city to city in Asia Minor, reciting and occasionally "teaching" his poetry for bread; that he immortalized in his poems those who treated him kindly, sometimes bestowing precious manuscripts upon his benefactors; and that he finally died on the Island of Ias, under circumstances foretold by an oracle. This last story comes from a lost work of Aristotle, and relates how some young fishermen propounded a riddle which Homer could not solve; thereupon he composed his epitaph and died three days afterward. It is well known that seven ancient cities—Smyrna, Rhodes, Colophon, Salamis, Chios, Argas, and Athenæ—contended for the honor of being his birthplace. The earliest mention of the name of Homer is found in a fragment of the philosopher Xenophanes, who flourished in the sixth century B.C., and the oldest direct reference to the *Iliad* and the Odyssey are in Herodotus, who quotes from both epics. Many minor poems, such as the Margites, the Batrachomyomachia (Battle of the Frogs and the Mice), about thirty Hymns, and several Epigrams, have been attributed to Homer, as well as many lost works, like the so-called Cyclic Epics. But as early as the third century B.C. this list was restricted by the most discerning commentators to the *Iliad* and the Odyssey alone. Then, later, the skeptical *chorizontes*, or Separators, arose and denied Homer the authorship of the Odyssey; and numerous celebrated scholars have held the same belief; while in 1795 the entire system of Homeric criticism was revolutionized by F. A. Wolf, who asserted that both epics were not originally complete, independent poems but a series of poems by different writers—Homer and others— the whole being connected by Pisistratus about 540 B.C. Since this theory was advanced, however, several of Wolf's strongest arguments have been refuted. But this is certain: to the Greek nation Homer was Bible, Shakespeare, Milton, and Domesday Book in one; and to the modern mind he is the supreme epic poet of European literature.

Hope, Anthony, the pen-name of Anthony Hope Hawkins (London, Feb. 9, 1863). He was educated at Marlborough, and at Balliol College, Oxford, where he won honors in classics and obtained his master's degree. He was also president of the Oxford Union. He read law in the Middle Temple, was admitted to the bar in 1887, and three years later published his first novel. This was successful, as was every book that followed it, and in 1894 he gave up practise to devote himself wholly to writing. He visited the United States in 1897, and found his wife in Miss Elizabeth Sheldon, of New York. They have one son and one daughter. Besides his novels, Mr. Hawkins has written several successful plays and the Dolly Dialogues. His novels include: A Man of Mark (1890); Father Stafford (1891); Mr. Witt's Widow (1892); *The Prisoner of Zenda* (1894); The Chronicles of Count Antonio (1895); The Heart of Princess Osra (1896); Phroso (1897); Simon Dale (1898); Rupert of Hentzau (1898); The King's Mirror (1899); Quisante (1900); The Intrusions of Peggy (1902); The God in the Car; Tristram of Blent; Double Harness; A Servant of the Public; Sophie of Kravonia; and Tales of Two People (1907).

Howard, Blanche Willis (Baroness von Teuffel) (Bangor, Maine, July 21, 1847; Munich, Germany, Oct. 7, 1898).

From a high school in her native city she went to a boarding-school in New York, where she completed an ordinary course of education. She began writing in her teens, but published nothing of note until 1875, when her breezy story, One Summer, brought her name before the public. Some time later she obtained a commission from the Boston Transcript, and sailed for Europe. From 1878 most of her time was spent in Stuttgart, where in 1886 she became editor of a magazine published in English. In 1890 she married the Baron von Teuffel, a physician attached to the German court. She won a place in social circles, and her home was a refuge for her young countrywomen studying music or art in Germany. Most of her work has been translated into the principal European languages. It includes: One Year Abroad (1877); Aunt Serena (1880), *Guenn: A Wave on the Breton Coast* (1882); Aulnay Tower (1886); The Open Door (1889); No Heroes (1893); A Fellowe and His Wife (1892), written in collaboration with William Sharp; Seven on the Highway (1897); and two posthumous novels, Dionysius the Weaver's Heart's Dearest (1899) and The Garden of Eden (1900).

Howells, William Dean (Martin's Ferry, Ohio, March 1, 1837). He was the son of William Cooper Howells, a printer and a Swedenborgian, and the boy was brought up to follow both the trade and the faith. Between 1840 and 1849 the family lived in Hamilton, Ohio, and here and in other towns young Howells passed through his apprenticeship as typesetter, reporter, and editor on various newspapers. Meanwhile he found time to become familiar with the best authors and with several modern languages, and to make skilful use of his mother tongue. After serving on Columbus and Cincinnati journals, he wrote in 1860 a campaign life of Abraham Lincoln, a task that secured him the Consulate at Venice, Italy, where he remained till 1865. On his return to the United States he was connected successively with the New York Tribune, Times, and Nation, and eventually went to the Atlantic Monthly, of which he was editor-in-chief from 1871 to 1881. Leaving Boston, he again made his home in New York City, where for a period he conducted the department called The Editor's

Study in Harper's Magazine, and in December, 1900, revived
The Easy Chair in that periodical, the latter department having
closed at the death of George William Curtis. By general
consent he is the foremost exponent of the realistic school of
fiction devoted to interpreting American life. Though best
known as a novelist, he has written poems, travel books, bio-
graphical and literary essays, and several short comedies.
Among his many books are: Venetian Life (1866), Italian
Journeys (1867), Their Wedding Journey (1871); A Foregone
Conclusion (1875); The Lady of the Aroostook (1878); The
Undiscovered Country (1880); *A Modern Instance* (1882); A
Woman's Reason (1883); *The Rise of Silas Lapham* (1885);
The Minister's Charge (1886); Tuscan Cities (1886); Modern
Italian Poets (1887); A Hazard of New Fortunes (1889); A
Boy's Town (1890); Criticism and Fiction (1891); The Quality
of Mercy (1892); A Traveler from Altruria (1894); The Land-
lord at Lion's Head (1897); A Ragged Lady (1899); Their
Silver Wedding Journey (1899); Literary Friends and Ac-
quaintance (1900); Heroines in Fiction (1901); Literature and
Life (1903); London Films (1905); and Between the Dark and
the Daylight (1907).

Hughes, Thomas (Uffington, Berks, England, Oct. 20, 1822;
Brighton, England, March 22, 1896). He was the second son
of John Hughes of Donington Priory, Newbury, Berkshire.
After attending school at Twyford from 1830 to 1833, he was
sent in February, 1834, with his elder brother to Rugby, and
was educated under the famous Dr. Thomas Arnold. On
December 2, 1841, he matriculated at Oriel College, Oxford,
and he was graduated B.A. four years later. He was called
to the bar at Lincoln's Inn in January, 1848, and became a
member of the Chancery Bar. Subsequently he offered himself
as a fellow-worker to the little band of Christian Socialists, and
soon was esteemed as a social reformer. This activity led to
a seat in the House of Commons for Lambeth in 1865–'68,
and for Frome from 1868 to 1874, and as a member of Parliament he advocated the cause of the working classes, especially
those of trade-unions, and the amendment of the law of master
and servant. As late as 1893 he aided in the passing of the

Industrial and Provident Act. Since June 23, 1869, he had been Queen's Counsel, and this, together with his various public services, promoted his humanitarian dream of a better understanding between capital and labor, to teach the true value and strength of coöperation. Akin to this ambition was his well-known experiment in establishing in 1880 a profit-sharing community at Rugby, Tennessee. Though this idealistic project came to naught, Hughes liked the United States, sympathized with the National cause during the Civil War, and formed a strong bond of friendship with James Russell Lowell. In July, 1882, he was appointed a county court judge in England. From the time of its inception he had been interested in the Workingman's College in London, and from 1872 to 1883 he was at its head. As a writer, Hughes is best known by his incomparable *Tom Brown's School Days* (1856), which was evidently written from his own experiences at the famous Rugby School. He also contributed to fiction: The Scouring of the White Horse (1858) and Tom Brown at Oxford (1861). To biography he gave: Alfred the Great (1869); A Memoir of David Macmillan (1882); Life of Bishop Fraser (1887); and David Livingstone (1889). His miscellaneous works were: A Lecture on the Slop System (1852); An Account of the Lockout of Engineers (1860); Religio Laici (1861); The Cause of Freedom (1863); Memoir of a Brother (1873); Lecture on the History and Objects of Coöperation (1878); The Manliness of Christ (1879); Rugby, Tennessee (1881); and Vacation Rambles (1895).

Hugo, Victor-Marie (Besançon, France, Feb. 26, 1802; Paris, May 22, 1885). This great French writer—poet, patriot, novelist, friend of humanity—was the son of Count Joseph Leopold Sigisbert Hugo, of the Revolutionary and the Napoleonic wars. His early years were passed in Corsica, Paris, and Italy, and he began to study classic literature when very young, wrote verse when ten years of age, and at thirteen produced some creditable poetry about Roland and his chivalry. By the time he was eighteen he had written a tragedy entitled Irtamène; a drama, Inez de Castro; and Athalie, another tragedy. He determined to devote himself to literature, and his odes on The Statue of Henri IV, The Virgins of Verdun, and Moses on the Nile were crowned at the Floral Games of Toulouse. Chateaubriand called him *l'enfant sublime* ("the sublime child"). In 1822 the young poet married Adèle Foucher whom he had always known and loved.

In 1819 Victor Hugo founded a journal—Le Conservateur littéraire—in collaboration with his two brothers, and many of his poems appeared therein. His first volume of poems was published in 1822, attracting wide attention and winning high praise. This was followed by the crude but promising story, Bug-Jargal, *Hans of Iceland* (1823), and the second and third volumes of poems. In 1827 the poet published a drama, with Oliver Cromwell as its hero, in the preface to which he advocated the abolishment of the stilted, artificial style of the classic French school of dramatic writing. At this time the romantic style held sway in every department of art, and Hugo became its chief representative in the drama. He wrote Amy Robsart, Marion Delorme, and Hernani. These achieved brilliant success as dramatic masterpieces, though the public censor (under Charles X) forbade continuance of the representation of Marion Delorme. In 1832 Le roi s'amuse was produced for one night only, and then interdicted, public opinion assigning as a reason the fact that it represented monarchs in a very unflattering light. Previously to these events Hugo had received pensions from the Government for his literary work, but after the prohibitory orders regarding his plays he resigned all his pensions.

From 1829 to 1843 he wrote Lucrèce Borgia, Marie Tudor, and Angelo, three prose dramas; Ruy Blas, Les Burgraves, and Esmeralda, the latter an opera. Le dernier jour d'un Condamné (The Last Day of a Condemned Man, 1829) is an analysis of the last hours of a man that had been condemned to death, and was intended as a solemn protest against the infliction of the death penalty.

Hugo's great romance of the Middle Ages, *Notre Dame de Paris*, was published in 1831, and another volume of poems appeared in the same year, followed in the next ten years by many volumes of prose and poetry. He had gradually changed from his early royalist sympathies to a radically revolutionary point of view, notwithstanding which Louis Philippe made him an officer of the Legion of Honor in 1837. In 1841 he was elected to the French Academy, and in 1845 became a member of the Chamber of Peers. In this capacity he made, in 1847, an eloquent plea for the return of the political exiles, occasioned by a petition from Jerome Bonaparte for permission to come back to France.

After the Revolution of 1848 Hugo accepted without protest the republican form of government, and was chosen to represent the city of Paris in the Constituent Assembly in June of that year. Two months later he founded the political journal, L'Evenement, for which he and his sons, his friend Theophile Gautier, and other freethinkers wrote. In this publication he strove to preserve absolute independence, and advocated measures belonging to both the Right and the Left, among the latter the abolition of the death penalty. In 1849 he demanded the dissolving of the Constituent Assembly. In the same year he was chosen as one of the deputies from Paris to the National Assembly, and soon came out boldly against the administration of Louis Napoleon, who had been chosen President in 1848. In July, 1849, he broke away from the reactionary party, the cause of dissension being the project for public assistance, and later that year he tried to oppose the intervention to overthrow the Roman Republic. He had become by this time the leader of the Democratic party in all public matters, and an orator idolized by the masses, though he encountered many gibes and sneers from the upper classes because of his conversion to republicanism, his own early royalist and Napoleonic poems being quoted freely against him.

Hugo was a bitter enemy to Louis Napoleon, and shortly before the *coup d'état* of the latter he made a fiery speech against any reéstablishment of an empire. After the *coup d'état* (Dec. 2, 1851) Hugo was one of the first to fall under the ban of the new Emperor. On the 11th he was banished from Paris and went to Belgium; thence he traveled to England, and finally settled on the island of Guernsey, where he lived until the fall of the Second Empire (1870).

Between 1852 and 1870 this author produced many great

works of poetry and prose, the greatest of these being *Les Misérables* (1862), regarded by many critics as the most remarkable work of fiction in any language. It was published simultaneously in eight different cities and in nine languages. Other works belonging to this period are a translation of Shakespeare's plays into French (1864); *Toilers of the Sea* (1866); and *The Man who Laughs* (*L'homme qui rit*, 1869).

After the fall of the Empire Hugo returned to France, and was in Paris throughout the famous siege in the Franco-Prussian war, being appointed a member of the Committee of Public Safety.

In 1874 appeared another of his great romances, *'Ninety-three*, a story of the French Revolution, published in eight languages, and from 1875 to 1877 he published numerous speeches, public letters, the Story of Napoleon III and his *coup d'état*, and a charming and intimately personal work, The Art of Being a Grandfather, which won the world's admiration.

On the eightieth birthday of the great French writer the nation turned out to do him honor, and brother writers all over the world hailed him as their master.

Ingelow, Jean (Boston, Lincolnshire, England, March 17, 1820; Kensington, England, July 20, 1897). She was the eldest child of William Ingelow, a well-to-do English banker, and his Scotch wife, whose family hailed from Aberdeenshire. She was educated at home. When she was quite young the family removed from Lincolnshire to Ipswich, but most of her long life was spent in London, where she moved in a circle that included Tennyson, Ruskin, Froude, Browning, Christina Rossetti, and other authors. As a young girl she contributed anonymous verses under the pseudonym "Orris" to various magazines, but it was not until Tennyson found some "charming things" in her first volume, A Rhyming Chronicle of Incidents and Feelings (1850), that she gained any exceptional notice. Even such kindly encouragement could not inspire her to "set fire to the Thames," and the general public failed to recognize her poetic ability till 1863, when she published her first volume of Poems, which contained High Tide on the Coast of Lincolnshire, 1571, one of the finest modern ballads in the language. This volume of verses had an extraordinary success; it reached a fourth edition in the year of publication, and by 1879 had attained its twenty-third printing. Two other series of her poems were issued respectively in 1876 and 1885. Much of her versification shows the influence of Wordsworth and Tennyson, but it possesses a lyrical charm of its own. Another talent of hers was that of writing children's stories, and her best work in this line will be found in Stories Told to a Child (1865); in a group published in 1867, comprising Little Rie and the Rosebuds, The Suspicious Jackdaw, The Grandmother's Shoe, The Golden Opportunity, Deborah's Book, The Minnows with Silver Tails, The Moorish Gold, and The Wild-Duck Shooter; and in A Sister's Bye-Hours (1868); Mopsa the Fairy (1869), The Little Wonder-Horn (1872), The Little Wonder-Box (1887), Very Young, and Quite Another Story (1890). As a novelist her best effort was *Off the Skelligs* (1872). She also wrote in fiction Studies for Stories (1864) and Fated to be Free (1875). Her complete poems were published in one volume in 1898.

Irving, Washington (New York City, April 3, 1783; Irvington, N. Y., Nov. 28, 1859). His father, a Scotchman, came to the United States with an English wife, and engaged in trade. Young Irving attended private schools in the city of his birth from 1787 to 1799, and in 1801 entered a law office, where he remained three years. In that time, in fact as early as 1802, he began contributing under the pseudonym of Jonathan Oldstyle, to the Morning Chronicle, then edited by his brother. Failing health obliged him to go to Europe in 1804, and his sojourn lasted until 1806. From January to October, 1807, he edited, with his brother William and J. K. Paulding, Salmagundi: or, the Whim-Whams and Opinions of Launcelot Langstaff, Esq. This short-lived imitation of the Spectator was followed in 1809 by his humorous History of New York, supposedly written by Diedrich Knickerbocker. It brought him reputation and money, and he gave up any lingering ideas of law he may have entertained. In 1812 he was on the staff of Governor Tompkins of New York, and in 1813-'14 he was assistant editor of the Analectic Magazine of Philadelphia. Beginning with 1810 he had been a silent partner in his brother's mercantile firm, and in 1815 he went to Liverpool to look after its interests. Three years afterward the firm failed and Irving turned to literature. He published the Sketch-Book of Geoffrey Crayon (1819), which contained the two American classics, *Rip Van Winkle* and *The Legend of Sleepy Hollow*. Between the years 1820 and 1825 he traveled in Europe, visiting the Rhine and stopping at Paris, and in this period he produced Bracebridge Hall (1822) and Tales of a Traveller (1824), two volumes of sketches and short stories. In 1826 he went to Madrid as an *attaché* to the United States Legation, and there he remained for three years. Taking full literary advantage of his position, he examined the Spanish archives and wrote such works as History of the Life and Times of Columbus (1828); A Chronicle of the Conquest of Granada (1829); Voyages and Discoveries of the Companions of Columbus (1831); and The Alhambra (1832), the latter being written, from data on hand, while the author was Secretary of the United States Legation in London, 1829–'32. He returned to the United States in the latter year and received a wide and warm welcome, for his countrymen realized his services as literary representative in Europe of their hitherto unpretentious world of letters. With him he brought the double honor of the medal of the Royal Society of Literature (1830) and the degree of LL.D. from Oxford (1831). From 1842 to 1846 he was United States Minister in Spain, and after rendering that service he retired to Sunnyside, his beautiful countryseat on the Hudson. The most noteworthy of his later productions were: Oliver Goldsmith (1849); Mahomet and His Successors (1850); Wolfert's Roost (1855); and his monumental Life of Washington (1855–'59).

Jackson, Helen Maria Fiske Hunt (Amherst, Mass., Oct. 18, 1831; San Francisco, Cal., Aug. 12, 1885). She was a daughter of Nathan W. Fiske, who was professor first of languages, then of philosophy, at Amherst College. From the female seminary in Ipswich, Mass., where she received her early education, she was sent to the school of the Rev. John S. C. Abbott in New York City. When twenty-one years old she married

Major Edward B. Hunt, of the United States Engineers, who was killed in October, 1863, while experimenting with a submarine invention at the Brooklyn Navy-Yard. Shortly after this tragic occurrence the widow lost their only child, and she began writing serious poems by way of consolation. Many of these appeared under her pen-name "H. H." in periodicals and attracted attention to their author, who then resided at Newport, R. I. In 1870 she published a volume of Verses, some of which were praised by Emerson as possessing "rare merit of thought and expression." Thenceforth she became a prolific writer of miscellaneous prose and verse. President Arthur appointed her a special commissioner to examine into the condition of the mission Indians of California, and this led to her plea for better treatment of the red man, both in A Century of Dishonor (1881) and in her best romance, *Ramona* (1884). Meanwhile, in 1876, she had been married again, this time to William S. Jackson, a banker of Denver, Col. But her literary work went on unabated. She wrote many tales for children and several good novels. The one-time sensational Saxe Holme series of stories was attributed to her, but she always denied its authorship. Her undisputed works included: Bits of Talk (1873); Bits of Travel (1873); Mercy Philbrick's Choice (1876); Hetty's Strange History (1877); Nelly's Silver Mine (1878); Letters from a Cat (1880); Mammy Tittleback and Her Family (1881); and the posthumous Sonnets and Lyrics (1886).

Jacobs, William Wymark (London, Sept. 8, 1863). He was the son of William Gage Jacobs, a wharfinger at Wapping, where the family resided for some years, and here William, Jr., became familiar with the environment and peculiarities of sailor life, which he has used with such successful results in his humorous fiction. Indeed, as a boy he had determined to be a sailor, but one experimental cruise destroyed its attraction for him forever. After a private-school education, he entered the civil service at sixteen years of age, and four years later became an official in the Post Office Savings Bank, where, to quote his own whimsical words, he spent his days "reckoning up other people's money rather than counting my

own." But like many another he found the civil service a
stepping-stone to literature, for at twenty-one he wrote an article
for the Blackfriar's Magazine, which was conducted by his
fellow-clerks. This maiden effort was distinctly modeled on
the style of Max Adeler; nevertheless, there were calls for more.
Once he sent an article to a popular weekly paper that had offered
a prize of five shillings for the best contribution, and he won
the honorarium. Soon another paper made him a modest
offer for a series of articles, which appeared during a period
of four years. Success was slow; but one day he sent a story,
entitled A Case of Desertion, to Jerome K. Jerome, then editor
of To-day. This was accepted at once with a demand for
more like it, which resulted in the series of twenty-one stories
afterward published as Many Cargoes (1896). Thus at a
stroke he achieved a long-sought reputation. His water-side
characters were comparatively new in fiction, and the Thames
below London found an able delineator, one who knew the
life *intime* of the little craft that ply up and down the old river.
Stories of the coasting-trade are his forte. Among them may
be mentioned: The Skipper's Wooing (1879); Sea Urchins
(1898); A Master of Craft (1900); Light Freights (1901); *At
Sunwich Port* (1902); The Lady of the Barge (1902); Odd Craft
(1903); Dialstone Lane (1904); Captains All (1905); and Short
Cruises (1907).

James, George Payne Rainsford (London, Aug. 9, 1801;
Venice, May 9, 1860). He was the son of Pinkstan James,
an officer in the Navy and a physician, and was educated at
a school in Putney, where he evinced an aptitude for languages,
readily acquiring French and Italian, and gaining some knowledge of Persian and Arabic. As a youth he traveled consider-
ably on the Continent and became acquainted with Cuvier,
Darwin, and other eminent contemporaries. For a while he
led the life of a man of fashion in London, but about 1827 he
devoted himself to historical study and romance-writing after
the manner of Scott, who had encouraged his literary impulse.
Eventually he developed into the most prolific author of his
era, and in some respects became one of the most successful.
More than a hundred novels are credited to him, and the British

Museum Catalogue enumerates sixty-seven titles under his name. Many of these have been repeatedly reprinted. But fiction was only a part of his work, for he produced a number of popular historical studies, edited memoirs, collections, and letters, and wrote poetry and plays. On the strength of his reputation as a historian, his friends secured him from William IV the post of historiographer royal, and in that capacity he published pamphlets on such topics as History of the United States Boundary Question (1839) and the Corn Laws (1841). About 1850 he was appointed British consul in Boston, and two years later he was transferred to Norfolk, Va. In 1856 he was made consul at Venice, where he died suddenly of apoplexy. His first novel, Richelieu, was written in 1825 and published in 1829. Best-known among his subsequent romances were: Darnley (1829); De l'Orme (1830); Philip Augustus (1831), Delaware (1832), later re-issued as Thirty Years Since; *Henry Masterton* (1832); The Gypsy (1835); Attila (1837); The Man-at-Arms (1840); The King's Highway (1840); Agincourt (1844); Arabella Stuart (1844); The Smuggler (1845); Henry Smeaton (1851); and Ticonderoga (1854). His historical works included: Charlemagne (1832); Memoirs of Great Commanders (1832); Life of the Black Prince (1836); Memoirs of Celebrated Women (1837); Lives of Eminent Foreign Statesmen (1838-'40); The Life and Times of Louis XIV (1838), Life of Richard I (1842); A History of Chivalry (1843); Life of Henry IV of France (1847); Dark Scenes from History (1849); John Jones's Tales from English History (1849); and An Investigation into the Murder of the Earl of Gowrie (1849). His long poem, The Ruined City, appeared in 1828, and his two plays—Blanche of Navarre and Camaralzaman—were produced respectively in 1839 and 1848.

James, Henry (New York City, April 15, 1843). His father, who bore the same name, was an eminent Swedenborgian clergyman. Following private education in New York, Henry and his elder brother, William, the psychologist, were taken in 1855 to Europe by their parents, and attended schools in Switzerland, France, and England until 1860. On his return to this country Henry entered the Harvard Law School (1862), but the lectures of James Russell Lowell had more attraction for him than the course of jurisprudence. For several years he experimented with a literary style, produced a few short stories, and, with William Dean Howells acting as his sponsor in the world of letters, devoted himself to authorship. The *cognoscenti* quickly recognized the art of his work, but not till the publication of *Daisy Miller* (1878) did he gain the attention of the general reading public. Meanwhile, he had again visited England, where he continued to live, making only occasional trips to his native land. At first his manner of writing was simple and pleasant, but, steeping himself in the subtleties of the French and Russian psychological schools of novelists, he began using their methods, and he is now recognized as the leading representative of analytical fiction in English. Being essentially cosmopolitan, and treating national characteristics and types from a neutral standpoint in such stories as The American (1877), The Europeans (1878), and *The Portrait of a Lady* (1881), he has been called the creator of the "international novel." As a critic, biographer, and essayist he has taken high rank for his keen appreciation, perception, and delicacy. Among his noteworthy novels are: Roderick Hudson (1875); Confidence (1878); An International Episode (1879); A Bundle of Letters (1879); The Diary of a Man of Fifty (1880); Washington Square (1881); The Bostonians (1886); The Princess Casamassima (1886); The Tragic Muse (1890); The Other House (1897); What Maisie Knew (1897); The Two Magics (1898); In the Cage (1898); The Awkward Age (1899); The Sacred Fount (1901); The Wings of the Dove (1902); The Ambassadors (1903); and The Golden Bowl. Two of his achievements in biography are Nathaniel Hawthorne (1879) and William Wetmore Story and His Friends (1903). Of his critical and miscellaneous works, the following may be mentioned: French Poets and Novelists (1878); Portraits of Places (1884); A Little Tour in France (1884); and The American Scene (1906).

Jerome, Jerome Klapka (Walsall, Staffordshire, England, May 2, 1859). The elder Jerome owned the Jerome Pit in the Cannock Chase Colliery, where an inundation deprived him of his mines when his son was only four years old. Thereupon the family removed from the fringe of "the Black country" to London. Both parents had died by the time Jerome was fourteen. He was compelled to leave the Philological School at Marylebone, and secured employment in the Euston offices of the London and Northwestern Railway. A clerkship grew exceedingly distasteful in four years, and so he set his mind on becoming an actor, which he forthwith did at Astley's Theatre, London. Here he remained for nine months, and among other prodigious feats played four rôles in Mazeppa, being twice killed before the last act. Subsequently, twelve months' experience in the provinces extinguished the charm of the footlights. In that year he had played every conceivable part. At this juncture he turned to journalism, having long had a penchant for writing tales and sketches, which, however, had been steadily rejected. Now he became a "liner"; but six months of receiving three halfpence a line for accepted contributions suggested a change of occupation, and he ventured to teach. Another six months over and he was again a journalist. Then in succession he tried advertising, canvassing, shorthand, and finally entered the office of a solicitor, where he remained until his success as an author warranted his giving up all for literature. From 1892 to 1897 he edited The Idler jointly with Robert Barr, and between 1893 and 1897 he conducted To-day. Noteworthy among his varied books are: On the Stage—and Off (1888); Stageland (1889); Idle Thoughts of an Idle Fellow (1889); Three Men in a Boat (1889); Ruth (1890); Novel Notes (1893); John Ingerfield and Other Stories (1893); A Prude's Progress (1895); The Rise of Dick Halward (1896); Sketches in Lavender (1897); The Second Thoughts of an Idle Fellow (1898); The Observations of Henry (1901); *Paul Kelver* (1902); Tea-Table Talk (1903); Tommy & Co. (1904); Susan in Search of a Husband (1906); and The Passing of the Third Floor Back (1907). Several of his comedies and farces have won approval, as Barbara (1886); Sunset (1888); Wood Barrow Farm (1891); Mac Haggis (1897); and Miss Hobbs (1900).

Jewett, Sarah Orne (South Berwick, Maine, Sept. 3, 1849). When she was twenty years old she made her début in the

Atlantic Monthly, to which magazine she has been a frequent contributor ever since. Her literary efforts have been devoted mainly to short stories of New England life. She has traveled extensively in the United States, the West Indies, and Europe, and is a member of the Lyceum Club, London. The honorary degree of Litt.D. was conferred upon her by Bowdoin College. Most of her books are collections of unconnected stories and sketches. The first, Deephaven, was published in 1877. Her other works include: *A Country Doctor* (1884); A Marsh Island (1885); Betty Leicester (1889); The Life of Nancy (1895); and A Tory Lover (1901).

Johnson, Samuel (Lichfield, England, Sept. 18, 1709; London, Dec. 13, 1784). His father, Michael Johnson, was a bookseller, whose shelves were ransacked early by Samuel, who learned his letters at a dame-school, and his Latin at the Lichfield Grammar School. Though by nature indolent and desultory, he entered Pembroke College, Oxford, in 1728, but left it three years later without receiving a degree. While there, however, he distinguished himself as one possessing a mind filled with varied knowledge, and as a Latin scholar. At the end of 1731 his father died, leaving him a paltry twenty pounds, and the following year he became an usher in a school at Market Bosworth. He soon left this, and, going to live with a friend in Birmingham, he set to work on an abridged translation of Loba's Voyage to Abyssinia, which appeared in 1735. On July 9th of the same year he married a widow—his beloved "Tetty"—twenty years his senior. Her small fortune enabled them to open a boarding-school for young gentlemen at Edial Hall. Pupils were few, but David Garrick was one of them. The institution failed, and Garrick and Johnson journeyed to London, both master and pupil practically penniless. Subsequently Johnson returned for his wife. Hard as his lot had been hitherto, it was worse in London, at least until he began earning a pittance by writing for Cave's Gentleman's Magazine, and editing its Parliamentary debates reported by William Guthrie, in 1738. From 1740 to 1743 he wrote them himself under the caption Debates in Magna Lilliputa. Meanwhile he had published his poem, London (1738), after the manner of Juvenal's third satire. In 1744 appeared his sympathetic Life of Richard Savage, and in the following year Miscellaneous Observations on Macbeth. The year 1747 witnessed the issuance of his Plan for a Dictionary of the English Language, which was completed eight years later (April, 1755). Another adaptation of Juvenal, The Vanity of Human Wishes, written in 1748, was published in 1749, and in February of that year Garrick produced his tragedy Irene, which he had laid aside in 1736. This brought Johnson three hundred pounds, but scant encouragement to follow the drama. Between 1750 and 1752 he wrote his semi-weekly Rambler, which gave him the rank of impressive moralist. Three days after its last issue (March 14, 1752), his wife died. He was then in the midst of his lexicographical labors, and despite all work his struggle with adversity continued—indeed, it was undiminished until he reluctantly accepted a pension in 1762. In 1756 he issued his proposal for an edition of Shakespeare, which was not given to the public till 1865. Meanwhile he wrote the Idler (1758–'60), and in 1759 composed *Rasselas* within a week, to defray the funeral expenses of his mother. In 1763 he met James Boswell, who was to become his inimitable biographer, and in 1764 he was one of the original members of the Literary Club, which included Burke, Goldsmith, and Reynolds. In 1765 he formed the memorable friendship with the Thrales, who ministered to his comfort for sixteen years. All through that period composition was onerous to Johnson, his conversation offering him a more desirable outlet for his ideas. Nevertheless, he wrote the following: The False Alarm (1770); Thoughts on the Late Transactions respecting the Falkland Islands (1771); Tour to Scotland and the Hebrides (1773); The Patriot (1774); Tour to Wales (1774); Taxation no Tyranny (1775); Journey to the Western Islands (1775); Political Tracts (1776); and Lives of the Poets (1779–'81). Posthumously appeared Prayers and Meditations (1785); Sermons (1788–'89); and Diary in North Wales (1816).

Johnston, Mary (Buchanan, Botetourt County, Va., Nov. 21, 1870). Miss Johnston was educated at home, as her health was delicate throughout childhood and early youth. Having free range of a fine library, and being interested in the colonial history of her native State, her studies and general reading had always a decided leaning toward historical subjects, the fruit of which was shown in later years by the appearance of her two fine novels of colonial Virginia, Prisoners of Hope (1898) and To Have and to Hold (1899), both of which attained great popularity. Other novels were Audrey (1902), which was dramatized soon after its appearance in book form; Sir Mortimer (1904); The Goddess of Reason (1907).

Johnston, Richard Malcolm (Powellton, Hancock Co., Ga., March 8, 1822; Baltimore, Md., Sept. 23, 1898). He came of good old Virginian stock, and was brought up on his father's large plantation. In 1841 he was graduated with first honors at Mercer University, and after teaching for a year he was admitted to the bar, and in 1843 began the practise of law in Sparta, Ga. For ten years he was a law partner of Linton Stephens, a younger brother of Alexander H. Stephens. In 1857 three flattering offers were made him: one of a judgeship in the northern circuit of his State; another the presidency of Mercer College; and a third the professorship of *belles-lettres* in the University of Georgia. Deep-rooted love of literature led him to make the last opportunity his choice, and he held the chair till the outbreak of the Civil War, in which he served as a Confederate officer. In those troublous days he managed to open a boys' school at Rockby, Ga., which became famous throughout the Southern States. This institution was afterward removed to Baltimore County, Md., where its founder lived and worked from 1867 till his death. Though his creative literary ability evinced itself late in life, he produced many admirable stories of the rural life of middle Georgia. Certain humorous phases of it find in him an unexcelled delineator. His first effort was Georgia Sketches (1864); then came the Dukesborough Tales (1871), which caught and held public attention. Works in similar vein were: Old Mark Langston (1884); Two Gray Tourists (1885); Mr. Absalom Billingslea and Other Georgia Folk (1888); Ogeechee Cross-Firings (1889); Widow Guthrie (1890); The Primes and Their Neighbors (1891); The Chronicles of Bill Williams (1891); Mr. Billy

Army in the Civil War, and was wounded at Drury's Bluff. He attended public schools in this country, and several terms at the universities of Heidelberg and Paris. From 1868 to 1882 he served as correspondent for various newspapers, being stationed sometimes at Washington and sometimes at Paris. He has lived for some years in retirement on his farm in Maryland. His novels include: *The Money-Makers;* Trajan; History of a Sentimental Young Man; The Aliens; The Iron Game; The Players; Fortune-Wreckers; and A Yankee Crusoe.

Kennedy, John Pendleton (Baltimore, Md., Oct. 25, 1795; Newport, R. I., Aug. 18, 1870). He was the son of wealthy parents, and was graduated at the University of Maryland (then Baltimore College) in 1812. During the second war with England he served in the United States Army, then studied law, and in 1816 was admitted to the bar. He was a delegate to the State Legislature 1821-'23, and a member of Congress 1837-'39 and 1841-'45. In 1846 he again sat in the Maryland House of Delegates, of which he was elected speaker, and during the administration of President Fillmore he was Secretary of the Navy. While acting in this capacity he despatched Commodore Perry's expedition to Japan, and the second Arctic expedition of Dr. Elisha K. Kane. Retiring from active politics, he contributed to the political discussions in the newspapers of the period, and when the Southern States seceded he sent out an appeal to the citizens of Maryland, in which he showed how little the State had to gain by secession and how much by remaining in the Union. He made several trips abroad and had a wide literary acquaintance both in his own country and in England. He was especially intimate with Thackeray; but the story that he contributed a chapter to The Virginians at the request of Thackeray himself has little, if any, foundation in fact. He resided much of his life in Baltimore, his home being a literary center. In 1867 he was United States commissioner to the Paris Exposition, and at his death he bequeathed his library and papers to the Peabody Institute of Baltimore. The degree of LL.D. was conferred on him by Harvard University in 1863. In collaboration with Peter Hoffman Cruse he published in 1818-'19 The Red Book, a periodical partly modeled after Irving's Salmagundi. His other literary works include: Swallow Barn: A Sojourn in the Old Dominion (1832); *Horse-Shoe Robinson: A Tale of the Tory Ascendancy* (1835); Rob of the Bowl, a third historical romance (1838); Quodlibet (1840); Memoirs of the Life of William Wirt (1849); The Blackwater Chronicle (1853); Narrative of an Expedition of Five Americans into a Land of Wild Animals (1854); Mr. Ambrose's Letters on the Rebellion (1865); and At Home and Abroad (1872). Kennedy's novels, while somewhat loosely constructed, form valuable supplements to the historical literature of Maryland and Virginia, and after the lapse of seventy years retain much of their early popularity and may still be read with interest.

Kimball, Richard Burleigh (Plainfield, N. H., Oct. 11, 1816; New York City, Dec. 28, 1892). He was educated at Dartmouth College and in Paris, studied law and practised his profession in Waterford, N. Y., and later in New York City. He projected the Galveston and Houston Railroad, the first railroad in Texas, and from 1854 to 1860 was president of the company. Much of his literary work was devoted to the writing of essays. His novels include: *St. Leger: or, The Threads of Life* (1850); Was He Successful? (1863); The Prince of Kashna (1864); and Henry Powers, Banker (1868).

Kingsley, Charles (Holne, Devon, England, June 12, 1819; Eversley, Hampshire, England, Jan. 23, 1875). He was the eldest son of the Rev. Charles Kingsley (d. 1860) and was educated at King's College, London, and Magdalen College, Oxford. In July, 1842, he was made curate of Eversley, and shortly after his marriage to Miss Fanny Grenfell, in 1844, he became rector of the same parish. For several years he threw himself heartily into endeavors to improve the condition of the laboring classes, both morally and physically, and his novels, *Alton Locke, Tailor and Poet* (1850), and Yeast (1851), reflect the intensity of his opinions at that period. His attitude might then have been described as that of a Christian Socialist, but his views would now be considered conservative, and in later life he was more nearly Tory than Radical. In 1853 he published *Hypatia*, in which striking story Christianity is shown at odds with the fading Greek philosophy, and in 1855 *Westward Ho!* his most characteristic if not his greatest book. From 1860 to 1869 he was professor of modern history at Cambridge, but he was not altogether successful in this office, his methods being rather those of the historical novelist than the trained inquirer. In 1864 he became involved in a painful controversy with John Henry Newman, the immediate cause being his rash assertion that "Truth for its own sake never had been a virtue with Roman Catholic clergy," and his attributing this opinion to Newman especially. Following Newman's protest Kingsley issued a pamphlet entitled, What, then, does Dr. Newman mean? which in its turn brought forth Newman's famous Apologia pro Vita Sua. Failing health now overtook Kingsley, and *Water Babies* (1863) was the last book written when he was really at ease. He found relief in travel, and in 1869 became canon of Chester, and in 1873 of Westminster. He was widely known as a lecturer on natural history and kindred topics, and he visited the United States in 1874, delivering many lectures; but he fell seriously ill at Colorado Springs and did not long survive his return to England in August. He was a man of quick sympathies and wide interests, but never was a systematic thinker, his beliefs being instinctive rather than being reasoned out. As reformer, preacher, novelist, and poet he occupied a high place in the history of his immediate time. Among his books not already mentioned are: The Saint's Tragedy (1848), a religious drama in blank verse; Glaucus: or, The Wonders of the Shore (1855); *Two Years Ago* (1857); Andromeda, and Other Poems (1858); Town and Country Sermons (1861); *Hereward the Wake* (1866), a very spirited historical romance; Madame How and Lady Why (1869); At Last: A Christmas in the West Indies (1871); Town Geology (1872); Lectures Delivered in America (1878).

Kingsley, Henry (Barnack, Northamptonshire, England, Jan. 30, 1830; Cuckfield, Sussex, May 24, 1876). He was the third son of the Rev. Charles Kingsley (d. 1860) and was educated at King's College, London, and Worcester College, Oxford, but left the university in 1853 to accompany some fellow-students to the Australian gold-fields. At the end of five years spent in unremunerative employment he returned to England and in 1864 married his cousin, Sarah Maria Kingsley, and settled near Henley-on-Thames. He had already turned to good account his Australian experiences in *The Recollections of Geoffry Hamlyn* (1859), which speedily brought him fame, and in 1861 it was followed by the even more spirited tale of *Ravenshoe*, usually considered his finest work. Austin Elliot, appearing in 1863, was translated into French by Daurand Forgues in 1886. Later works of his include: The Hillyars and the Burtons: A Story of Two Families (1865); Leighton Court (1866); Silcote of Silcote (1867), a tale of much rugged power both in narrative and in characterization; Mademoiselle Mathilde (1868); Stretton (1869); The Harveys (1872); Valentin: A French Boy's Story of Sedan (1872); Reginald Hetherege (1874); The Grange Garden (1876); and Fireside Studies (1876), a series of ably written critical essays on Marvell, Addison, and other writers. The greater part of his work displays vigor and freshness, and as a novelist he must be placed before his more celebrated brother, Charles. He was editor of the Edinburgh Daily Review (1869–'70), a Free-Church paper; and during his editorship, the Franco-German war occurring, Kingsley went abroad as correspondent. He was present at the battle of Sedan, Sept. 1, 1870, and was the first Englishman to enter the town after its capture by the German forces. After giving up his place on the Review he settled in London, where he wrote many of his novels, removing later to a country home in Sussex.

Kipling, (Joseph) Rudyard (Bombay, Hindustan, Dec. 30, 1865). He is the son of John L. Kipling, long associated with schools of art at Bombay and Lahore, India. He was educated at the United Service College, Westward Ho, Devon; and his schoolboy experience at that institution was long afterward utilized in his narrative of Stalky & Co. (1899). On his return to India he was attached to the editorial staff of the Lahore Civil and Military Gazette (1882–'87) and the Allahabad Pioneer (1887–'89), contributing to these papers many Anglo-Indian verses and sketches. His Schoolboy Lyrics (1881) was published by his father, and the son followed it by publishing on his own account Departmental Ditties (1886) and Plain Tales from the Hills (1888), as well as Soldiers Three; The Gadsbys; Wee Willie Winkie and Other Stories, in 1889. He was now well known throughout India, but visiting England and America failed at first to secure a publisher. By 1890, however, he had become famous, and although his popularity has undergone variations as to intensity, his right to occupy a place among foremost English authors of the twentieth century is uncontested. In 1892 he married the sister of his American friend Wolcott Balestier, and from 1892 to 1896 he lived at Brattleboro, Vt., writing before and during this period Life's Handicap (1890); *The Light that Failed* (1891); Barrack-Room Ballads (1892); The Naulahka (with Balestier, 1892); Many Inventions (1893); *The Jungle Book* (1894); Second Jungle Book (1895); The Seven Seas (verse, 1896); and *Captains Courageous* (1897). Still later books have been The Day's Work (1891); Kim (1901); Just-So Stories for Children (1902); and Puck of Pook's Hill (1906). In 1908 he received the degree of Doctor of Letters from Cambridge University. As a prose writer he is at his best when dealing with life and its conditions in India, and the precise nature of that life he has impressed upon the minds of his countrymen as no one before him has done, while in his ballads of the barrack-room he has interpreted the mind and heart of the British soldier with amazing faithfulness and entire sympathy. The brutality of the barracks, the coarse but picturesque slang of the soldiers' mess, are reflected in his pages with vigor and audacity, and while they may repel the over-fastidious they attract the broad-minded student of humanity. As a poet his verse ranges from the spirited doggerel of the barrack-room ballads to the nobility of the Recessional, written for the Queen's Jubilee in 1897. Much of his work is ephemeral from its nature, but not a little seems destined to endure. His vogue is naturally greatest in his own country, but it is almost equaled by his American popularity.

Kirk, Ellen Olney (Stonington, Conn., Nov. 6, 1842). Her maiden name was Olney. Some of her early writings were issued under the pseudonym Henry Hayes. She received her education at Stratford, Conn., and in 1879 married John Foster Kirk. She has contributed many short stories, reviews, and essays to magazines, and has published the following novels: Love in Idleness (1877); Through Winding Ways (1880); A Lesson in Love (1883); A Midsummer Madness (1884); *The Story of Margaret Kent* (1886); Sons and Daughters (1887); Queen Money (1888); A Daughter of Eve (1889); Walford (1890); Ciphers (1891); Maidens' Choosing (1892); The Story of Lawrence Garth (1895); A Revolutionary Love Story (1898); The Revolt of a Daughter (1898); Dorothy Dean (1899); Dorothy and Her Friends (1900); Our Lady Vanity (1901); A Remedy for Love (1902); Good-bye, Proud World (1903); The Apology of Ayliffe (1904); and Marcia (1907).

Kjelland, Alexander Lange (Stavanger, Norway, Feb. 18, 1849). He studied at the University of Christiania, but, although admitted to the bar in 1872, never practised his profession. In 1889 he edited the Stavanger Avis, and in 1901 became burgomaster of his native place. He is classed among the best interpreters of Norse thought and feeling, and his longer stories are not only faithful presentations of Norwegian life and character, but are noteworthy as animated individualizations of the city of Stavanger itself. As a satirist he bears some resemblance to Thackeray, but his satire is as good-humored as it is keen. His studies of Norwegian life are realistic, and his style is both polished and incisive, every sentence being constructed with an eye to the general effect. His earliest book, Novelletter (1879), written while he was the prosperous manager of a brick-and-tile kiln, betrays the influence of Daudet upon his style, as does also Nye Novelletter (1880); Garman og Worse (1880, English translation by Kettlewell 1885) is to some extent autobiographical, and Arbeidsfolk (1881) is concerned with Socialism to some extent. Other fictions by him are: *Elsa* (1881); Skipper Worse (1882); Gift (1883); Fortuna (1884); Sne (1886); Sankt Hans Fest (1887); Jakob (1891). He has also published several comedies: Homeward Bound (1878); Three Pairs (1886); Betty's Guardian (1887); and Professors (1888). His dramas are inferior to his novels.

Laboulaye, Edouard René Lefèbvre de (Paris, France, Jan. 18, 1811; Paris, May 25, 1883). Early taking up the study of law, he gave his attention particularly to Continental legal history, and when but twenty-eight he became eminent in his profession by the publication of his important work, Mémoire sur l'histoire de la propriété foncière en Occident (1839). Two years later he became an advocate in the Royal Court of Paris and published an essay on the life and doctrines of Frederic Charles de Savigny. This was followed in 1843 by his Recherches sur la condition civile et politique des femmes and Essai sur lois criminelles des Romains (1845); works which not only met with appreciative attention among legal scholars but contributed to revive in the author's own country the study of legal history. In 1849 he was made professor of comparative jurisprudence in the Collège de France. He was greatly interested in American history and institutions, and his lectures to his countrymen during and after the period of the American Civil War were very popular. His ironical Paris en Amérique (1863) reached its thirtieth edition in Paris and was translated into English. Other political satires were the Contes bleus (1864); Nouveau contes bleus (1865); and Le prince Cariche (1865); the last of which passed through successive editions and was an important factor in the fall of the Third Napoleon. Among other works of Laboulaye's were his very notable Histoire politique des États-Unis, 1620–1789 (1855–'66); Études contemporaines sur l'Allemagne (1856); La liberté religieuse (1858); *Abdallah*, a still popular Arabian romance (1859); Les États-Unis et la France (1862); L'État et ses limites (1863); Étude sur la politique de M. de Tocqueville (1863); La république constitutionelle (1871). He was a prolific contributor to French reviews and journals, and he translated into French Walter's Law Proceedings of the Romans; Channing's social writings and Slavery in the United States; and also Benjamin Franklin's Memoirs and Correspondence. His personal appearance was very attractive, and this and his pleasing address contributed to draw around him at his legal lectures many persons who had no particular interest in the study of law.

Lamartine, Alphonse Marie Louis De Prat de (Milly, near Macon, France, Oct. 21, 1790; Paris, March 1, 1869). He was reared in the Catholic faith, and his early education was received from his mother. At twenty he went to Italy, remaining two years, and on the fall of Napoleon entered the Garde Royale, but soon quitted it and after Waterloo mixed freely in Parisian society. His first book, Méditations poétiques (1820), proved very popular, its romantic lyricism being new to French verse, but his Nouvelles méditations (1823), and Harmonies (1829), hardly repeated the excellence of the first work. He entered the Diplomatic Service in 1820, being then appointed to the Naples Embassy, and on his way thither married at Geneva a young English girl, Marianne Birch, who had both beauty and wealth. Transferred to Florence in 1827 he remained there five years, and in 1829 was elected to the Academy. He was originally a liberal Royalist, but leaned more and more to republicanism under Louis Philippe, and in 1734 entered the Chamber of Deputies as member from Bergues. In this decade he published Souvenirs d'Orient (1835); Jocelyn (1836); Chute d'un Ange (1838); and Recueillements (1839). His greatest prose work, the Histoire des Girondins, was issued as a whole in 1847, and its brilliant rhetoric helped to precipitate the Revolution of 1848. When that broke out in February Lamartine became one of the foremost public men in France and as Minister of Foreign Affairs enjoyed for a few months an extraordinary popularity. But though a distinguished man of letters he was unpractical, and the insurrection of June caused his popularity to disappear almost instantly. In January, 1849, he received only a few thousand votes for the Presidency, and three months later he was unable to secure even an entrance to the Legislative Assembly.

His political career had involved him in many expenses, and he now set about to retrieve his affairs by writing. In addition to *Graziella* (1852), which embodies some of his early Italian experiences, he published Confidences (1849); Nouvelles confidences (1851); Histoire de la Restauration (1852); Histoire de la Turquie (1854–'55); Histoire de la Russie (1855); as well as lesser biographical and miscellaneous works. Lamartine was by temperament wholly unfitted for historical work demanding careful investigation and impartiality, and his histories have little value. In 1867 Napoleon III granted him the income from 500,000 francs, an action which was made a party matter by extreme Republicans, who reproached Lamartine for accepting it.

Lang, Andrew (Selkirk, Scotland, March 31, 1844). He was educated at St. Andrew's University and Balliol College, Oxford, and was elected a fellow of Merton College, Oxford, in 1868. He is one of the most industrious as well as one of the most prolific of living authors, and he has distinguished himself in several branches of scholarship. Of especial importance are his: Custom and Myth (1884); Myth, Ritual, and Religion (1887); The Making of Religion (1898); and Magic and Religion (1901). With Prof. Butcher he prepared a translation of The Odyssey (1879) and, with Messrs. Zeuf and Myers, of the Iliad, while from the French he has translated Aucassin and Nicolette (1887). Among his volumes of society and other verse may be cited: Ballades in Blue China (1880); Grass of Parnassus (1888); and Helen of Troy (1882); while as a novelist he is favorably known by: The Mark of Cain (1886); *The Monk of Fife* (1895); Pickle the Spy (1897); The Companions of Pickle (1898); and The Disentanglers (1902). He is also an essayist of ability, as evinced by his Letters to Dead Authors (1886); Lost Leaders (1889); Letters on Literature (1889); and Essays in Little (1900), and has edited Perrault's Popular Tales and several volumes of fairy tales, and among the many miscellaneous works of his should be named a Life of Lockhart (1896); History of Scotland from the Roman Occupation, vol. I (1900); Prince Charles Edward (1900); John Knox and the Reformation (1905); Homer and His Age (1906); and Alfred Tennyson (1901). His residence has been in London throughout his literary career, and he was for many years on the editorial staff of the Daily News.

Lepelletier, Edmond-Adolphe de Bouhélier (Paris, June 26, 1846). He was educated at the Bonaparte Lycée, and became a lawyer, but made no attempt to practise his profession, turning instead to journalism and writing for the newspapers. In 1868 he joined the brilliant group then engaged in editing Nain Jaune, and in the following year he suffered a month's imprisonment on account of an article attacking the administration of Baron Haussmann. He was in the army during the campaign of 1870–'71, and saw active service. After the war he returned to journalism, editing one paper after another and becoming involved frequently in affairs that could be adjusted only according to the *code duello*. Several of his duels resulted seriously. In 1886 he was an unsuccessful candidate for Parliament. His novels are: L'Amant de Cœur (1884); Le Supplice d'une Mère (1884); La-i-tou (1885); Les Morts Heureuses (1886); Claire Everard (1888); *Madame Sans-Gêne*.

Le Sage, Alain-René (Brittany, Dec. 13, 1668; Boulogne, France, Nov. 17, 1747). His father and his maternal grandfather were lawyers. At fourteen he was left an orphan, and was sent by an uncle to the Jesuit college at Vannes. There, by his aptitude for humanistic studies, he attracted the notice of the principal, the Abbé Bochart, by whose advice he soon began at Paris the study of law. In 1694 he married Marie-Elisabeth Huyard, a *bourgeoise* of Paris. After the birth of his first child, René-André, well-known as the actor Montmesnil, he gave up the law for the profession of letters. About 1695, an annuity of six hundred pounds was bestowed upon him by the Abbé Jules de Lyonne, and this comfortable income he received regularly for many years. The Abbé died in 1715, and in this year appeared the first part of the work by which posterity knows Le Sage, *Gil Blas*. He began his literary ventures in 1695, by translations from the Greek, work criticized by Sainte-Beuve as talent wasted on matters too remote, but which, nevertheless, performed the double office of providing for his family and forming his style. So well was this latter object attained that when he revised these translations, forty years later, he hardly altered the language. It was his friend the Abbé who directed his thoughts to the wealth of material in the literature of Spain. The Spanish Succession was "forcing all imagination toward the Pyrenees," and it was even more natural for him than for Molière and Corneille to ransack Spanish sources for the foundations of his plays. He was, however, no mere borrower or servile imitator. By force of his genius, he impressed his own personality as a dramatic author upon his completed productions, in translation, adaptation, and invention. He carefully preserved the fine points of the originals, but the brilliance and charm of his mind gave new life to old, and often dull, works. Though gentle in character, in his dramas he was a keen satirist of men, and his popularity suffered, with the pit, on that account. But he had a great success at court, and it was recognized that in Turcaret he gave to the French people the finest bit of comedy since Molière. He declined election to the Academy, contented, he said, that his works should represent him among his countrymen. He was proud and independent, but a man without reproach, devoted to his family, his profession, and his religion. He became quite deaf, and spent his last years at Boulogne, surrounded by loving children and his devoted wife. Of his numerous works, the most notable are: The Point of Honor (Le Point d'honneur, 1702); Don César Ursin (1707); Crispin: The Rival of His Master (Crispin rival de son maître, 1707); The Lame Devil (Le Diable Boîteux, 1707); Turcaret (1708); *Gil Blas* (4 vols., 1715-'35).

Lever, Charles James (Dublin, Ireland, Aug. 31, 1806; Trieste, Austria, June 1, 1872). He was the second son of James Lever, a Dublin architect, but, in spite of his typically Irish genius, came of English descent on both sides of the house. He was educated at private schools and at Trinity College, Dublin, and subsequently studied medicine in Germany and also pursued this study on returning to Dublin in 1830. In 1833 his parents died and the same year he married Miss Catherine Baker. As she brought him little property, and his medical practise and inheritance from his father were not sufficient to balance his entire lack of economy and his heavy losses at the gaming-table, his affairs were soon in a disastrous condition, and in this strait he turned to literature as a means of livelihood. He was already a contributor to the Dublin University Magazine, and the first instalment of his novel, Harry Lorrequer, which appeared in that periodical for Feb.

1837, at once brought him popularity. He was attached to the British embassy at Brussels (1840-'42), and in April, 1842, returned to Dublin to undertake the editorship of the University Review, in which his rollicking tale of *Charles O'Malley* (1840) had been published. This was followed by Jack Hinton, the Guardsman (1843); *Tom Burke of Ours* (1844); Arthur O'Leary (1844); The O'Donoghue (1845); and The Knight of Gwynne (1847). All of these works are marked by the highest animal spirits, a marvelous fund of anecdote, and vigorous character-drawing, but display little art or form. Lever's passion for cards kept him continually poor, yet when in 1845 he resigned his editorship and went to Brussels he drove about in his carriage although reduced to his last fifty pounds. He settled in Florence in 1847, where he wrote The Martins of Cro' Martin, Roland Cashel (1850) and The Dodd Family Abroad (1853), stories superior in a literary way to his earlier tales, but not so well received by the public. At this period of his career his pen was especially active, and Maurice Tiernay (1852) and Con Cregan (1849) may be named among his fictions issued at this time. In 1857 he was made British Consul at Spezzia, the duties of his post requiring very little of his time. Here he remained for ten years, the principal novels produced in this decade being: The Fortunes of Glencove (1857); Davenport Dunn (1859); Tony Butler (1865); and Sir Brook Fosbrooke (1866), his own favorite among his works. Lord Derby gave him in 1867 the consulship of Trieste with the remark, "Here is six hundred a year for doing nothing, and you are just the man to do it." But Lever did not like Trieste nor its climate, and the death of his wife made his stay there distasteful. He, however, still continued to write fiction, the best of the novels written at the close of his career being The Bramleighs of Bishop's Folly (1868) and That Boy of Norcott's (1869). In the last-named there was still perceptible some of the vigor and fire of *Charles O'Malley*.

Lewald, Fanny (Madame Stahr) (Königsberg, Prussia, March 24, 1811; Dresden, Saxony, Aug. 5, 1889). She was the daughter of a Hebrew merchant, but at sixteen she became a Protestant Christian, with his consent, and with him she traveled extensively. In 1841 she published, in Europe, her first novel, Der Stellvertreter, and in 1845 visited Italy, where she met the German scholar, Adolf Stahr, whom she married in 1855. She subsequently traveled much in England and other countries, and her home in Berlin presently became the meeting-place of many intellectual persons. She took an active part in raising the status of women, uniting with Jenny Hirsch in 1869 in editing Die Fraunwelt, a periodical devoted to spirited advocacy of women's rights. In defense of this principle she wrote Osterbriefe für die Frauen (1863) and Für und wider de Frauen. She was a voluminous author, and among her many novels were: *Hulda* (1874); Klementine (1842); Jenny (1843); Diogena (1848); Wandlungen (1853); Mädchen von Hela (1860); Nella (1870); Die Erlöserin (1873); Neue Novellen (1877); Helmar (1880); Stella (1884). A volume of reminiscences, entitled Zwölf Bilder aus dem Leben, appeared in 1888; but her autobiography, Meine Lebensgeschichte, had been published as early as 1861–'63.

Lewis, Matthew Gregory (London, England, July 9, 1775; at sea, May 14, 1818). He was the son of Matthew Lewis, Deputy Secretary at War and owner of extensive estates in Jamaica, and while he was a schoolboy his parents separated. The son remained on good terms with both parents and frequently conveyed messages between them. He visited Weimar in 1792, where he met Goethe, and in 1794 became an attaché of the British Legation at The Hague. A perusal of Mrs. Radcliffe's Mysteries of Udolpho inspired him at this time to write *Ambrosio: or, The Monk* (1795), but the indecencies of the text excited so much adverse criticism that many of the objectionable passages were consequently omitted from the second edition. Lewis sat in Parliament for Hindon, Wiltshire, in 1796–1802. His father died in 1812; the whole of his great property became the son's possessions, and he twice made the trip to Jamaica to attend to his landed interests there. While returning from Jamaica a second time he died of yellow fever. He was a small man with singular, projecting eyes, and is said to have looked like a schoolboy all his life. He moved in the best society, and although called a bore by Scott and Byron, what is more certain is that he was amiable and benevolent and a good son to his parents under very trying circumstances. He did not favor emancipation, but he was a friend of Wilberforce and did well by his slaves in Jamaica. He had a knack of versifying, and some of his poems which he set to music of his own were not far behind those of Moore's. Among his many plays, most of which were produced at Drury Lane and Covent Garden theaters, were: The Castle Spectre (1798); Rolla (1799); The Love of Gain (1799); The East Indian (1799), subsequently called Rich and Poor; Alphonso, King of Castile (1801); Adelgitha (1807); and Timour the Tartar (1812).

Lie, Jonas Lauritz Edemil (Eger, near Drammen, Norway, Nov. 6, 1833). At the age of five he went with his family to Tromsö, where his childhood was passed in daily familiarity with the details of life in a northern seaport that found their reflection in his novels long afterward. At the University of Christiania Ibsen and Björnson were his fellow-students, but his own inclinations were not then toward literature, and after being admitted to the bar in 1858 he settled as a solicitor in Kongsvinger. In 1860 he married his cousin, Thomasine Lie, and in 1866 published a volume of poems. At thirty-five he gave up his profession, and in 1870 he put forth a romance entitled The Visionary, which was successful, and the Norwegian Government gave him a traveling stipend. He published Tales and Sketches from Norway (1872); The Bark Future (1873); and *The Pilot and His Wife*, the most widely circulated of all his novels and the one that in the opinion of most critics placed him at the head of Norwegian novelists. He received the poet's pension from the Government, and spent some years in Germany and Paris, the Parisian capital finally becoming his home. Among his novels of the last quarter century are: Thomas Ross (1878); Rutland (1881); Go Ahead! (1882); A Maelstrom (1884); The Daughters of the Commodore (1886); Troll I and II (1891–'92); Niobe (1893); When the Sun Goes Down (1895); Maisa Jons (1900); When the Iron Curtain Falls (1902). Very many of his fictions have been translated into French, German, and other languages, and his popularity in his own country has been unbounded. The truthfulness of his descriptions, his unaffected pathos, and his moral force have endeared him to his countrymen, while his delicate psychology and convincing character-analysis have compelled the admiration of the most diverse critics. His return to Norway in 1893, after a twelve years' absence, was made the occasion of a national festival. Although Paris continued to be his permanent home, his later summers were spent at his villa in the Tyrol.

London, Jack (San Francisco, Cal., Jan. 12, 1876). He is the son of John and Flora London, and was educated at the Oakland High School and the University of California, but was obliged for pecuniary reasons to leave the University in his freshman year. He went to the Klondike region in 1897, but returned the next year on the death of his father, the task of supporting the family now falling upon him. He had already acquired a great fund of experience obtained as a seaman before the mast and as a tramp in the United States and Canada, and his adventures supplied him with abundance of literary material. His first magazine article appeared in the Overland Monthly for January, 1899, and his first book, The Son of the Wolf, was published in 1900. Since then he has been much before the public as author, socialist lecturer, and journalist. In April, 1900, he married in Oakland Bessie Madern, and in Chicago, 1905, Charmian Kittredge. The strongly virile quality of his writing has secured a wide reading for much of his work, and many to whom his books were not familiar read with interest his war correspondence during the Russo-Japanese conflict. Among his many books are: The God of His Fathers (1901); A Daughter of the Snows (1902); The Children of the Frost (1902); The People of the Abyss (1903); *The Sea Wolf* (1904); The War of the Classes (1905); White Fang (1907); The Iron Heel (1907); and The Road (1907).

Longfellow, Henry Wadsworth (Portland, Me., Feb. 27, 1807; Cambridge, Mass., March 24, 1882). He was a son of the Hon. Stephen Longfellow and his wife, Zilpah Wadsworth Longfellow. He was educated at Portland Academy and Bowdoin College, and was graduated in 1825. He then studied and traveled extensively abroad, and from 1829 to 1835 was professor of modern languages and librarian at Bowdoin. He was then offered the professorship of modern languages at Harvard College, and in order to fit himself more fully for this he spent a year in Scandinavia, Germany, and Switzerland. On his return at the close of 1836 he was established as Smith professor of French and Spanish literature at Harvard, which chair he resigned in 1854, and at his suggestion James Russell Lowell was appointed his successor. Longfellow's first printed verses, The Battle of Lovell's Pond, appeared in the Portland Gazette of Nov. 17, 1820, but his first book, Coplas de Jorge Manrique, a translation from the Spanish, was not issued until 1833. This was followed by Outre-Mer (1835), a series of sketches not unlike Irving's Sketch-Book; by *Hyperion* and his earliest collection of original verse, Voices of the Night (1839). Longfellow married in 1831, Miss Mary Potter, of Portland, who died with her child in Rotterdam in 1835, and is commemorated in his poem, Footsteps of Angels. The next year he met Miss Frances Appleton at Interlachen, from whom he drew the picture of Mary Ashburton in *Hyperion*. They were married in 1843, and the bride's father, Mr. Nathan Appleton, then gave them the well known Craigie House, in Cambridge, which continued to be the poet's home for the rest of his life. In this house Mrs. Longfellow was accidentally burned to death in 1861. In 1847 he published Evangeline, his own favorite among his poems, a romance in hexameter verse which still retains its early popularity. Among other volumes of his verse are: The Spanish Student (1843), a pleasing dramatic experiment; The Golden Legend (1851); Hiawatha, which has since appeared in many languages (1855); The Courtship of Miles Standish, also in hexameter (1858); Tales of a Wayside Inn (1863), a translation of Dante's Divine Comedy (1867-'70); New England Tragedies (1868); Three Books of Song (1872); Aftermath (1873); The Hanging of the Crane (1874); The Masque of Pandora (1875); Kéramos (1878); and Ultima Thule (1880). In 1849 he published a prose tale entitled Kavanagh, which received respectful notice by reason of its authorship, but which has no strong points and is practically forgotten. Longfellow's popularity at home and abroad was very great during his lifetime, and although it is more clearly perceived now than formerly that his genius was adaptive rather than creative, he still remains the most generally beloved of American, perhaps of English writing poets. In 1884 his bust was placed in Westminster Abbey, he being the only American author to be thus commemorated. He left five children: Charles, who served as a cavalry lieutenant during the Civil War; Ernest, an artist of distinction, Alice, Edith, and Annie.

Loti, Pierre (Louis Marie Julien Viaud) (Rochefort, France, Jan. 14, 1850). He was of Huguenot ancestry, entered at seventeen the naval school, La Borda, and rose in his profession till in 1898 he resigned as lieutenant. His pseudonym is said to have originated in his extreme shyness in early youth, which led his comrades to call him after the Loti, the Indian flower that blossoms almost unseen. He evinced little love for books or study, and not till 1879 did he write his first romance, Aziyadë, which, like much of his subsequent writing, appears to be autobiographical. On leaving Tahiti in 1880 he published a Polynesian romance first entitled Rarahu, but afterward Le Mariage de Loti, while the scene of his next book, Le roman d'un spahi (1881), was Senegambia. To this succeeded a group of short studies, Fleurs d'Ennui (1882); Mon Frère Yves (1883), one of his most characteristic works; Le pécheur d'Islande (1886), a novel of life among Breton fisherfolk; Le Kasbah (1884), an Algerian tale; *Madame Chrysanthème* (1887); and Au Maroc (1890). Still other works of Loti's were: Le roman d'un enfant (1890); Fantôme d'Orient (1892); Le désert (1895); Galilée (1895); and Ramuntcho (1897), a story of the Basque country. In May, 1891, he was elected to the French Academy. The charm of his impressionist pictures has been very generally recognized, while the vague melancholy pervading his work is felt to fall upon one in time. The closely personal character often given to his work by a Continental author reaches its extreme example in Loti, and few English or American readers can understand or sympathize with deep feeling so inextricably associated with the willingness minutely to record its varied aspects. His earliest books abounded in these semi-autobiographic confessions, the beauty and melody of which have only half reconciled the Anglo-Saxon reader to their peculiar quality of unreserve. When all is said, however, it must be admitted that Loti is not only one of the most original prose writers of his time, but, in the matter of literary style, one of the most beautiful also.

Lover, Samuel (Dublin, Feb. 24, 1797; St. Heliers, Jersey, July 6, 1868).   He was the eldest son of a Dublin stockholder and was educated privately, his aptitude for music being especially remarkable from childhood.   When placed in his father's office he found his tasks distasteful, and a rupture with his father followed.   He then turned his attention to painting, particularly to miniature portraiture, and in 1828 was elected to the Royal Hibernian Academy.   Long before this his talent as a song-writer had brought him the friendship of the poet Moore, and in 1826 he put forth the best known of all his ballads, Rory O'More.   In 1831 appeared his first book, Legends and Stories of Ireland, and in 1832 exhibited at the Dublin Academy a miniature of Paganini, which was highly commended.   In 1835 he established himself in London as a miniature-painter, and became at once a favorite in literary and artistic circles of the metropolis.   In 1837 he published his first novel, Rory O'More, and as if he were not already sufficiently distinguished as musician, painter, poet, and novelist, he dramatized the tale with such success that it held the stage more than one hundred nights.   He also wrote several other dramas and operas.   Songs and Ballads was published in 1839, and his best known novel, *Handy Andy*, in 1842.   L. S. D., his third novel, appeared in 1844, but is now known by its later title, Treasure Trove.   Failing eyesight presently forced Lover to relinquish painting, and to make up for the consequent loss of income he arranged an entertainment called Irish Evenings, consisting of a monologue, of songs, recitations, and stories of his own.   This was well received in England and was repeated in Canada and the United States in 1846.   Except in Boston, he won success during his American tour, in the course of which he wrote one of his most popular songs, The Alabama.   He subsequently wrote librettos for two operas by Balfe, and after his second marriage, in 1852, he confined himself chiefly to song-writing. Lover was one of the most versatile men of his generation. The genuine Irish quality of the first two of his novels is likely to find for them appreciative readers for a long time.

Ludlow, James Meeker (Elizabeth, N. J., March 15, 1841). He is a descendant of William Ludlow, who emigrated from Shropshire, England, and was one of the founders of Southampton, L. I. He was graduated at the College of New Jersey, now Princeton University, in 1861, and three years later at Princeton Theological Seminary. He was ordained by the presbytery of Albany in 1865 and was pastor of the First Presbyterian Church in Albany in 1864–'68, and of the Collegiate Reformed Church at Fifth Avenue and Forty-eighth Street, New York City, in 1868–'77. From 1877 to 1885 he was in charge of the Westminster Presbyterian Church in Brooklyn, N. Y., and since 1886 he has been pastor of the First Presbyterian Church at East Orange, N. J. In 1881 he made an extended trip through the Orient and the Holy Land, and not far from this time began contributing frequently to religious papers and periodicals, and in 1883 published his first book, A Man for A' That: or, My Saint John. This was followed by a Concentric Chart of History (1885); *The Captain of the Janizaries*, a story of the fall of Constantinople (1886); A King of Tyre, a story of 300 B.C. (1891); That Angelic Woman (1892); A Baritone's Parish (1896); The Age of the Crusades, a historical work (1897); Deborah (1901); Incentives for Life (1902); Sir Raoul (1905); and Jesse Ben David (1907). *The Captain of the Janizaries* is probably his best known work, but Deborah, and A King of Tyre, to mention no others, have enjoyed an extensive popularity as well. Dr. Ludlow received the degree of D.D. from Williams College in 1872 and of L.H.D. from Princeton University in 1890, and in 1885 was offered the presidency of Marietta College, which he declined. In 1865 he married Emma J. Orr.

Lyall, Edna (Ada Ellen Bayly) (Brighton, England, March 10, 1859; Eastbourne, England, Feb. 9, 1903). She was the daughter of Robert Bayly, a barrister, who died when she was but eleven, and after the death of her mother, three years later, she lived with her sister, the wife of Canon Crowfoot of Lincoln. She was hardly ten when she began writing, and her first book, Won by Waiting (1879), was written very soon after she left school. It deals with home life in France and England, and was succeeded by *Donovan* (1882), written at intervals during three years, which at first was received but coldly. Its sequel, We Two (1884), proved so popular that the predecessor began to be called for, and *Donovan* soon became what it has since remained, the most popular of all her works. In September, 1884, she removed to Eastbourne, Sussex, which was her home for the rest of her career, and here her later books were written. These include: In the Golden Days (1885); Knight Errant (1887); Autobiography of a Slander (1887); Derrick Vaughan, Novelist (1889), a record of some of Miss Bayly's own literary struggles; A Hardy Norseman (1889); Doreen (1894); How the Children Raised the Wind (1895); Autobiography of a Truth (1896); Wayfaring Men (1897); Hope the Hermit (1898); In Spite of All (1901); The Hinderers (1902). Her works still have a wide circulation in the United States as in her own land and are all pleasantly written, displaying at times considerable force in character analysis, as well as vigor of narrative.

Maartens, Maarten, is the pen-name of Joost Marius Willem van der Poorten-Schwartz (Amsterdam, Holland, Aug. 15, 1858). He passed his childhood in England and his school years largely in Germany. Returning to Holland, he studied law at the University of Utrecht. From 1883 to 1884 he was a lecturer on law at the University, which gave him the degree of LL.D. He has also received the honorary degrees of LL.D. and Litt.D. from the universities of Aberdeen and Pennsylvania respectively. He lives at Zonhenval Castle, near Doorn, Holland, though he spends much of his time in London and in Paris and on the Riviera. He is an honorary member of the Authors Club of New York. His publications are: The Sin of Joost Avelingh (1890); An Old Maid's Love (1891); A Question of Taste (1891); *God's Fool* (1892); The Greater

Glory (1894); My Lady Nobody (1895); Her Memory (1898); Some Women I Have Known (1901); My Poor Relations (1903); Dorothea (1904); The Jailbird, a one-act play, produced at Wyndham's Theater, London, in 1904; The Healers (1905); The Woman's Victory (1906); and The New Religion (1907).

Maarten Maartens, unlike his fellow-artists in Holland, has taken English rather than French life as his model. Recognizing that he never could obtain a wide audience by writing in the Dutch language, Mr. Maartens determined from the first to produce his novels in English. He sent his first work, The Sin of Joost Avelingh, to many London publishers, and upon their declination of it he published it at his own expense. Having an excellent plot it pleased a great many readers. In God's Fool he produced a work that, for cleverness of plot, subtlety of allegory, strength of character-drawing, and literary finish is a masterpiece worthy of Thackeray. In his subsequent work Mr. Maartens has rarely fallen below this high standard, and he holds a secure place among the novelists of the world. The London Spectator said of him: "Like the painters of his own country, Mr. Maartens is remarkable for the fidelity and finish of his pictures. Like them, too, he is most at home in depicting the most ordinary occurrences of the most ordinary every-day life. He propounds no philosophical questions; he avoids all storm and passion; but his characters do live in a way in which few novelists succeed in making their characters live."

McCutcheon, George Barr (Tippecanoe County, Indiana, July 26, 1866). He was educated in the public schools of Lafayette, Ind., and in Purdue University at the same place. He acquired journalistic experience as a reporter and city editor on Lafayette newspapers. He wrote many novels before he produced one that found a publisher. This was Graustark, which appeared in 1900. It met with instant success, and two weeks after publication was being dramatized and translated. The other novels of Mr. McCutcheon are: Castle Craneycrow (1902); The Sherrods (1903); Brewster's Millions (1903); The Day of the Dog (1904); Beverley of Graustark (1904); Nedra

(1905); The Purple Parasol (1905); Cowardice Court (1906); Jane Cable (1906); The Flyers (1907); and The Daughter of Anderson Crow (1907). Brewster's Millions was dramatized, and in this form it has achieved unusual popularity, in England as well as in America.

"Mr. McCutcheon," says Paul Wilstach in the Bookman of New York, "is a story-teller, not a stylist, a rhetorician, or a philosopher. But he has a tale to tell which he embellishes with taste and discretion, really astonishing fertility of imagination, and sufficient sense of human nature to bring the characters and story near to the reader without making them commonplace."

MacDonald, George (Huntley, Aberdeenshire, 1824; Sept. 18, 1905). This Scottish novelist and poet was educated at Aberdeen University, and he studied for the ministry at the Independent College, Highbury, London, but owing to illness gave up preaching for writing. His first works were in poetry. Encouraged by his wife, he tried fiction, publishing *David Elginbrod* in 1862, considered by many the best of his novels. His other works of fiction that may be mentioned are: Alec Forbes of Howglen (1865); Annals of a Quiet Neighborhood (1866); The Seaboard Parish (1868); Robert Falconer (1868); Wilfrid Cumbermede (1871); Malcolm (1874); Thomas Wingfold, Curate (1876); The Marquis of Lossie (1877); Sir Gibbie (1879); What's Mine's Mine (1886); Lilith (1895); and Salted with Fire (1897). He wrote also many stories for the young, and several religious works. In 1872-'73 he made a lecturing tour through the United States, where his works had become very popular among religious people. In later years he spent the winters at Bordighera, Italy, in a house built for him by an admirer of his genius.

Mr. Gilbert Chesterton, the English critic, said of him: "If we test the matter by strict originality of outlook, George MacDonald was one of the three or four greatest men of nineteenth-century Britain." "His novels," said W. Garrett Horder, "were, to a large extent, sermons in disguise. He took little trouble about the plot, and in nearly every story there was one character through which the author communicated his thought to the reader." The great lesson he strove to inculcate was the fatherly idea of God, and the present prevalence of this idea is due more to his novels than to its expression in all the theological works written upon the subject, if not, indeed, in all the sermons upon it.

Mackenzie, Henry (Edinburgh, Scotland, August, 1745; Edinburgh, 1831). He was educated at the University of Edinburgh, and became an attorney, practising first in his native city, and subsequently in London. He was an ardent Tory in politics, writing many tracts in defense of the principles of that party, for which he was rewarded in 1814 by appointment to the office of Comptroller of Taxes for Scotland, a place which he retained until his death. His house was the center of the literary circle of Edinburgh. Lord Cockburn called him "one of the Arbitri Elegantiarum of Old Edinburgh."

His literary productions are: *The Man of Feeling* (1771); The Man of the World (1773); The Prince of Tunis: A Tragedy (1773); and Julia de Roubigné (1773). He edited two periodicals, The Mirror and The Lounger, and contributed many essays and miscellaneous articles to these and to other publications. He was also the author of several biographies.

Lord Cockburn said of him: "The title of *The Man of Feeling* adhered to him ever after the publication of that novel; and it was a good example of the difference there sometimes is between a man and his work. Strangers used to fancy that he must be a pensive, sentimental Harley; whereas he was far better—a hard-headed, practical man, as full of worldly wisdom as most of his fictitious characters are devoid of it, and this without in the least impairing the affectionate softness of his heart."

"The principal object of Mackenzie in all his novels," says Sir Walter Scott in his Life of Mackenzie, "has been to reach and sustain a tone of moral pathos by representing the effect of incidents, whether important or trifling, upon the human mind, and especially on those which are not only just, honorable, and intelligent, but so framed as to be responsive to those finer feelings to which ordinary hearts are callous."

Macleod, Fiona. (See SHARP, WILLIAM.)

Macquoid, Katherine Sarah (Kentish Town, England, 1840). She is the daughter of the late Thomas Thomas and Phœbe Gadsden. In 1851 she married Thomas Robert Macquoid, an artist, who has illustrated most of her books of travel. She and her husband live at Tooting, South London. Besides Miss Macquoid's books descriptive of her European travel, and many stories in magazines, she has written among others the following novels: Patty (1871); Diane (1875); Little Fifine (1881); Her Sailor Love (1883); A Strange Company (1885); *At the Red Glove* (1885); Joan Wentworth (1886); Miss Eyon of Eyoncourt (1892); The Story of Lois (1898); A Ward of the King (1898); His Heart's Desire (1903); and also several juveniles.

In her youth she visited France, and was deeply impressed with the romance of that country. Mr. Lewes, afterward the husband of George Eliot, advised Mrs. Macquoid to write French stories, because he believed in the value of early impressions. She acted upon his advice, with the result that much of her fiction relates to France.

Mrs. Macquoid's first notable success was Patty, which appeared serially in Macmillan's Magazine in 1870. This attracted the admiration of John Morley, who became a friend of Mrs. Macquoid and an encouraging critic of her subsequent work. *At the Red Glove* is commonly regarded by readers as the cleverest of her stories. Before its publication in book form it appeared serially in Harper's Magazine.

Major, Charles (Indianapolis, Ind., July 25, 1856). He was educated in the common schools, and is engaged in the practise of law at Shelbyville, Ind. His novels are: When Knighthood was in Flower (1898); Bears of Blue River (1900); *Dorothy Vernon of Haddon Hall* (1902); A Forest Hearth (1903); Yolanda (1905); A Maid of Burgundy (1905). The first-named novel was dramatized shortly after its production in book form, and achieved success on both sides of the Atlantic. *Dorothy Vernon* also was dramatized, but was not so successful as the former.

Malot, Hector Henri (La Brouille, France, March 20, 1830; Paris, Aug. 12, 1907). He turned from the law, for which he was educated, to authorship. At first his work was that of a hack editor, journalist, and playwright. Finally, however, he launched forth with the first of a trilogy of novels intended to depict a cycle of family life. Under the general title of Victims of Love, he produced Lovers (1859), Husband and Wife (1865), and Children (1866). A host of novels followed, of which the first that achieved noteworthy success was Sans Famille (1878). This was crowned by the French Academy, and published in the United States under the title of No Relations. Other novels are: Baccara (1886); *Conscience* (1888); Justice (1889); and Complices (1892).

In 1895 M. Malot announced in Le Temps that he had abandoned novel-writing, having discovered that this was in the case of an old author simply the exploitation of a name to which time had given commercial value, and that persistence in it was due either to senile obstinacy or to avariciousness. "Not with pen in hand, but rather with silver in hand, do those die who write to the last," he said.

M. Malot was true to his resolve, and rounded out his literary career by writing in 1896 a literary biography entitled The Romance of My Romances.

Manzoni, Alessandro (Milan, Italy, March 7, 1785; Milan, May 22, 1883). The name of Manzoni stands preëminent in the Italian literature of the first half of the nineteenth century. It may be questioned whether the artistic primacy belongs to him or to Foscolo or to Leopardi; but as regards effective influence upon the literary currents of his time, none can compare with him.

Yet no one less than he strove to gain this celebrity and this prestige; his life was quiet and serene, and kept its course, not solicitous of honors or of fame, like a beautiful river of clear water.

He was the son of Count Pietro Manzoni and of Giulia Beccarra, daughter of the famous author of the work, *Of Crimes and of Penalties;* his earliest known literary production was a poem of democratic spirit in *terzina rime,* in the manner of Monti, written when he was fifteen, but not published. Having gone to France in 1805, he frequented the refined and intellectual society of the capital, where his freethinking tendencies were confirmed by the "Encyclopedists"; but doubt and scepticism were not congenial to his tranquil and gentle character, which sought support for its noble aspirations in a fixed and well-balanced moral system.

In a poem of 1807, On the Death of Carlo Imbonati, immediately recognized by Foscolo, and praised in his notes to the Ode Dei Sepolcri, Manzoni defines this system in brief:

> "to keep the hand pure
> And the mind; so much to experience
> Of human things as may be needful
> Not to o'ervalue them; ne'er to be servile;
> Ne'er to make a truce with aught that's vile;
> The holy truth never to betray; nor ever utter word
> That gives applause to vice or scorn to virtue."

When he wrote this, his conversion to the Catholic religion had not begun, but it is clear that little was lacking to it. Before returning to the faith of that religion, he had been converted to its morality; for his nature inclined him to that order and that spiritual equilibrium which it promotes. With it his literary production at this period was in harmony; thus in the poem in blank verse entitled Urania, though there is heard again the echo, a little labored and formal, of Monti's poetry, the subject is spiritual and the moral tone modest and refined. Vain is the favor of the Muses to the poet if the Graces, symbol of delicacy, refinement, and sobriety, do not accompany the song.

When he returned in 1810 to Milan he had become a convert to the Catholic religion, partly through the influence of the amiable Henrietta Blondel, who had recently become his wife, and who, herself a convert from Protestantism to Catholicism, had acted as a gentle spur to his own convictions.

From this time began the true period of original activity in Manzoni's art. The conflict between his Christian nature and his theories no longer existed, since he had found in the Catholic religion a credibility which wonderfully assured him; and his genius had full play in all its potency. The first fruits of his conversion were the Sacred Hymns, in which the happy convert interpreted Christianity in harmony with the humanitarian philosophy of the century, or, rather, as he says, sought "to bring back to religion those grand, noble, and humane sentiments that naturally spring from it." Full of lyric fire and finely elaborated, the five sacred hymns, The Resurrection, The Name of Mary, The Nativity, The Passion, and Pentecost, opened a new field to Italian poetry, which, abandoning the everlasting mythologic themes and the prevailing rhetorical forms dear to the classicists, and taking from foreign romanticism its best, became more true, more spiritual, more human, seeking in its own neighborhood the best and most interesting material; for, according to the great Lombard, literature should propose to itself "the useful for its purpose, the true for its subject, and the interesting for its means."

In 1821, when the news of Napoleon's death reached Milan, Manzoni wrote, in three days, his ode *The Fifth of May*, not free from slight defects, but of lofty and magnificent inspiration, especially at the close, where he invokes God to repel "from the weary dust of the hero every evil word." The ode was translated into many languages, among others into German by Goethe. [A fine English translation by William Dean Howells was published in his Modern Italian Poets, 1887.] It hastened the author's fame; the Sacred Hymns had not had a large circulation at first; and his tragedy, The Count of Carmagnola, published the previous year, had little more. In 1823 he issued a second tragedy, Adelchi.

In the dramas he set aside the famous "Aristotelian" unities of time and place, and with them every other rule and norm not "founded in the reason of art and in harmony with the nature of the dramatic poem." He aimed at reproducing faithfully what is called historical and local color; to this end he studied with all diligence for the first of his tragedies the usages of war and the conditions and quality of the soldiers of fortune of the fifteenth century, to whose number Carmagnola belonged; for the second he reviewed the events of the last years of the Longobard domination and the condition of the Italians under that domination. To the dialogue, to the style, to the language, he gave more simplicity and naturalness than had theretofore been deemed appropriate by writers of tragedy. He introduced the chorus as the lyrical expression of the emotion awakened by the part of the action represented. In fine, he considered the supreme intent of dramatic action to be education and instruction. All this he discussed and defended in the prefaces to the two tragedies and in a letter in French to a French gentleman; the tragedies themselves he accompanied with historic notes and the second with also a learned discussion On Some Points of the Longobard History in Italy.

But in the Carmagnola, the love of historic truth made the poetic expression somewhat cold; and in the Adelchi, the latter overlay the former, so that to Goethe the one seemed too historic, the other not historic enough. Thus, in practise Manzoni failed of his purpose; the representations of the two noble works, which were ill adapted for the stage, were failures. Yet the tragedies live, not so much because of having broken with the Aristotelian unities, or of having taken the dialogue away from the domain of rhetoric, as because of the lyric elements diffused in most beautiful poetic passages, in the speech of certain characters, and in the magnificent choruses, which—especially the chorus of Ermengarde in the Adelchi— are among the best lyric strains of the Italian Parnassus.

In the tragedies, too, is diffused the Christian sentiment of the Sacred Hymns; Adelchi, indeed, does not seem to be of that hard Longobard race that held it "glory to be pitiless"; of these years are also the beautiful Observations upon Catholic Morality, in which he sought to place in relief with simplicity and close argument the humane beauty and the civic stability emanating from Catholicism.

Having now arrived at the finest maturity of his years and his genius, having achieved success in criticism and in poetry, Manzoni turned his mind to romance—a species of literature which till then had not been treated successfully in Italy. Ugo Foscolo, it is true, in the Last Letters of Jacopo Ortis, had published a kind of epistolary romance upon the model of Goethe's Werther, rich in artistic quality and patriotic spirit, but not properly a romance; nor did it, in many respects, attain its purpose. Among other points, the fine patriotic enthusiasm that dominates it removes it too far from that proportioned objectivity that every novel should have.

In 1821 Manzoni began to publish parts of his romance *I Promessi Sposi* (*The Betrothed*), which was to make him famous throughout Europe and remain one of the masterpieces of Italian literature. The book was published in 1827 at Milan; but the first edition, which contained many fine things afterward suppressed, and others which were then inartistic but were fully developed by him later, was for public reasons only recently restored; thus giving evidence of Manzoni's grand artistic conscience, and the moral sensitiveness of his Christian spirit.

In the first edition (1827) the book was full of constructions purely literary, abounded in inappropriate and affected elegancies, and contained erroneous and dialect expressions; often they betrayed the native of Lombardy who had lived long beyond the mountains. Dissatisfied with this, the author, after many years of study and effort, taking pains to come into direct and immediate contact with Florentine speech, succeeded in reducing his novel to the form in which we now read it, that is, in choice Tuscan, with simplicity, with naturalness, with vivacity; this revision appeared from 1840 to 1842.

Even in its first form, however, *I Promessi Sposi* had shown itself as the masterpiece it is, and men of various and opposing schools had united in warm praise of it; the romanticists and the classicists vied in attributing to themselves the merits of the book, but ended with acknowledging that Manzoni had chosen the best features of the two schools and harmonized them in the characteristically Italian equilibrium of his subtle intellect.

It is difficult to reconstruct the external story of *I Promessi Sposi:* we propose to speak of the part of inspiration which came to it from without; for he was a man to resolve and assimilate all extraneous elements into perfect unity. Moreover, he always acknowledged having learned much from Walter Scott. In his work, Manzoni found, among other features, men and women of humble rank as heroes and heroines of romance, such as were to be his betrothed lovers, Renzo and Lucia.

The general idea of the romance—the action of which takes

place from 1628 to 1631—came to the author in reading the Milanese History of Ripamonti, which gives a picture, if not complete, yet minute and varied, of that age midway between civilized and barbarous, modern and feudal, honest and corrupt.

Around the two humble protagonists of the romance, who, in truth, are the least noteworthy, moves a varied and vivid throng of powerful feudal lords, of monks, of priests, of men of arms and of students, of officials, and of townspeople. The portraiture of certain characters is wonderful, as, for example, those immortal personages, the Innominato, Padre Cristoforo, Don Abbondio, and Cardinal Federico Borromeo. The psychology, minute and subtle (possibly too subtle and minute), is above all praise; especially, because through it runs an irony, kindly and yet slightly bitter, a humor delicate and profound, almost new in Italian literature.

The book, translated immediately into almost all the languages of Europe, became popular and was imitated—imitated, that is to say, as far as imitation is possible of a work of that nature, whose greatest value is not in the plot and in external coloring, but in the minor psychologic life that informs it. And therefore, among all the historic romances that swarmed in Italy after *I Promessi Sposi*, there remain as records of the patriotic and psychologic thought of the time those of Guerrazzi, of D'Azeglio, and also of Grossi; but one alone, The Confessions of an Octogenarian, by Ippolito Nievo, is still read as if it were of yesterday.

This serves to show that even if belonging to a false kind, masterpieces are of permanent value; the genius of the author redeems and saves them.

And that historic romance is a false kind, Manzoni himself, with wonderful courage and with keen insight, undertook to prove in his essay, Of Historic Romance and in General of the Mingled Components of History and of Invention. In writing his two tragedies and his romance he had believed that he could harmonize history and fiction, and he had succeeded to the limit of the possible. But later he came to believe that that class was hybrid; and he did not hesitate to show, with calm and keen argument, the absurdity of the attempt, which had been the greatest effort of his literary life. He condemned not only the tragedies, but the romance. This is a proof, not solely of his profound critical acumen, but, better and more, of his sound and fearless conscientiousness as a man and a writer.

Serene and secure in his domestic life, not always fortunate, an enemy to all excess, he was a Catholic and a patriot at a time when country and religion; through the malignity of men and of events, seemed to occupy opposing camps. And his political poems, though they have not the impetuous fire of Berchet, the Tyrtæus of Italy, speak, as from a height, of the rights of country and of nationality. Even in 1814 he expressed in a line the aspirations of Italy to unity and independence, a line not beautiful, but still famous:

"We shall not be free if we are not united."

And later when the Pope proclaimed the excommunication, he, the poet of the Sacred Hymns, a Senator of the Kingdom, did not hesitate to place himself among the excommunicated by his vote for Rome as the capital of Italy.

Not enough account is taken of this by those who, some decades ago, tried to represent him as a bigot and a timid friend of his country because too much a friend of religion. Even in literary criticism this charge was emphasized and exaggerated, not without some responsibility on the part of Carducci, who was not yet free from some classic and republican prejudice. But these and many others afterward proved themselves in the wrong; those who had been constantly his ardent enemies thus reconsecrating his glory as a man and an author. The same poet of the third Italy, invited to speak at a national commemoration of the great Lombard, attributed to certain "evil birds," that took their flight beneath the grand pinions of the "Lombard eagle," the origin of those darts that he had turned against them.

Manzoni is, and will always remain, a pure and grand national glory; he will remain so by the intrinsic merit of his works, by the influence he exerted upon his time, and because he restored to Italian literature that universality which it had not known since the Cinquecento.

And now, when the inedited pieces of his work are appearing in a complete edition, that glory is growing more circumstantiated, even as to matters of minor account, shines ever more brilliantly, and, instead of losing by too minute and close examination, is acquiring more and more solidity and breadth of influence.

Marlitt, E., the pen-name of Eugénie John (Arnstadt, Germany, Dec. 5, 1825; Arnstadt, June 22, 1887). Her father was a merchant, but he neglected his business for drawing, and as her mother spent in reading novels the time she should have devoted to the house, the family was reduced to poverty. The Princess of the country, however, patronized Eugénie, and sent her to Vienna to fit herself for an operatic career. But when she made her début, she sang out of tune, owing to a cold which had affected her hearing. She withdrew to her home in mortification. The Princess continued her benefaction by making Eugénie her companion and reader. But the girl was unhappy. She had a morbid mind, and was offended at being thrust in the background by the petty nobility, who were intellectually beneath her. Her bitterness was increased by a hopeless attachment she formed at court, and she became so irritable that her patroness was forced to retire her upon a small pension. Shortly after this the Princess lost her fortune and was compelled to discontinue the stipend. Then Eugénie, made desperate by growing deafness, adopted the pseudonym of E. Marlitt and took up novel-writing to support herself. After one partial success and one failure, she achieved great popularity with Gold-Else, which appeared serially in the Gartenlaube during 1866, and was published in book form in 1868, in which year her masterpiece, *The Old Mam'selle's Secret*, also appeared. Countess Gisela was published in 1869, and *A Little Moorland Princess* in 1872. In these charming stories, however, she seems to have exhausted her experiences and observations; her later novels, written in her family circle, contain mechanical characters and strained incidents. "In most of her tales," says S. Baring-Gould, "she managed to introduce a *kranke Seele* ('morbid soul'), and it need hardly be said from whom she painted it. Her stories are sensational, she carries on the reader's interest from beginning to end, and she has considerable descriptive skill, but her novels do not . . . provoke thought, and show no deep insight into character. She can show hate changed into love, but not a moral transformation."

Marryat, Frederick (Westminster, now in London, July 10, 1792; Langham, Norfolk, Aug. 9, 1848). In the intervals when he was not running away to sea, he picked up something of an education at private schools. At the age of fourteen he was permitted to enter the navy. He served in the famous *Impérieuse* under the daring admiral, Lord Cochrane, and in two years and a half of service took part in more than fifty engagements. In 1818 he received a medal for at least a dozen gallant rescues, and in 1824-'25 commanded with distinction in the Burmese war. He also invented a code of signals. With this rich naval experience he began writing sea-stories in 1829. His first book, Frank Mildmay, was rightly criticized for a fault usual in the initial attempt of a novelist: it contained material enough for several books. His subsequent stories, however, improved rapidly in point of construction. In the fifty-six years of his life he wrote twenty-five novels, among the most notable of which may be mentioned: Peter Simple (1834); Jacob Faithful (1834); The Pacha of Many Tales (1835); *Mr. Midshipman Easy* (1836); *Japhet in Search of a Father* (1836); Snarleyyow (1837); Masterman Ready (1841); The Children of the New Forest (1847); and *The Little Savage*, a posthumous work published in 1848. He edited the Metropolitan Magazine, in which a number of his novels appeared serially. His biography has been written by his daughter, Florence, also a novelist of ability. The Encyclopædia Britannica says of his novels: "They were in the first flush of their success when Dickens was a youth, and they have an interest in the history of literature as forming an important link between Smollett and Fielding and the author of Sketches by Boz." James Hannay says of Marryat: "Patriotism, manliness, firm friendship, good faith, kindliness— these are his 'ideals'; and the scenes in which they appear are bathed in the jolliest humor . . . and every-day sympathy, exhilarating as sunshine itself."

Martineau, Harriet (Norwich, England, June 12, 1802; Ambleside, June 27, 1876). She was of Huguenot ancestry, and was early converted to Unitarianism, and while in her teens contributed articles to the organ of that denomination. The family fortune disappearing in a mercantile failure, she turned to authorship for support. Although interrupted much by sickness, before her death she had produced thirty-six books, besides thousands of literary articles of various kinds. She set out to popularize political economy and other scientific and philosophical subjects by writing works of fiction, largely juvenile, to illustrate their principles. The mother of Victoria, afterward Queen of England, read with her daughter the whole of Miss Martineau's tales illustrating political economy, with the result that Victoria as Queen was able to take an unusually intelligent interest in the economic revolution wrought in the early part of her reign. In mature life Miss Martineau became an agnostic; she avowed her opinions on religion in a book, Eastern Life, Past and Present (1848). Becoming a disciple of Comte, she wrote a condensation of her master's Positive Philosophy in 1853. Her chief work of fiction is *The Hour and the Man* (1840), a novel founded on the history of Toussaint L'Ouverture. Of her other novels may be mentioned: Deerbrook (1839) and The Crofton Boys (1841). Visiting America (1834–'35), she wrote a work in 1837 entitled Society in America, which created a great deal of comment on this side the Atlantic, both adverse and favorable. Miss Martineau also wrote a monumental historical work entitled History of England During the Thirty Years' Peace, covering the period following the battle of Waterloo (1815).

Miss Martineau in her retirement at Ambleside proved that she was not an empty theorist, by applying scientific principles of agriculture to her estate with results that excited the wonder and envy of the old-school farmers of the neighborhood.

Maturin, Charles Robert (Dublin, Ireland, 1782; Dublin, Oct. 30, 1824). He was educated at Trinity College, Dublin, and took orders in the Anglican Church, and later became curate of St. Peter's, Dublin, where he achieved a reputation for eloquence. He published his first three novels under the pseudonym of Dennis Jasper Murphy. They were ridiculed by the public and press, but Sir Walter Scott saw in them evidences of genius, and recommended the author to Byron, with the result that Maturin was enabled to place a tragedy, entitled Bertram, on the stage of the Drury Lane Theater with Kean in the hero's rôle. This play was the first and only dramatic success of the author. Two following tragedies were flat failures. Then he turned again to fiction, producing: Women (1818); *Melmoth the Wanderer* (1820); and The Albigenses (1824), which was intended to be the first of a series of romances illustrating periods of European history, and gave promise that the author might yet curb the extravagance of his imagination, which no one more clearly than he recognized had impaired his previous work. He died during the year, however, and his name is now almost forgotten, save for one remarkable novel, *Melmoth*, of which George Saintsbury, the critic, says: "Although long, and marvelously involved with tales within tales, *Melmoth* is a powerful book, which gave something more than a passing shudder to its own generation (it especially influenced Balzac) and which has not lost its force even now."

Melville, Herman (New York City, Aug. 1, 1819; Sept. 28, 1891). He was educated at the Albany Classical School, but went to sea in 1836; he returned in 1837 and taught school until 1840; then he went to sea again in January. He ran away from the ship at Marquesas Islands, 1842, and was rescued after four months' captivity among the cannibal Typees. He became a clerk in Honolulu for a time, and returned to America in 1844. He told the story of his experiences at sea and his romantic captivity in *Typee* (1846). The book created a sensation; it was believed that the author was drawing the long bow. Philarètre Chasles, a French critic, said: "Mr. Melville's style is so ornate, his Rubens-like tints are so vivid and warm, and he has so strong a predilection for dramatic effects, that one does not know exactly how much confidence to repose in his narrative. We do not take, except *cum grano salis*, his florid descriptions." Titus Munson Coan, however, avers Melville's fidelity to truth. He says: "My father, the Rev. Titus Coan, went over Melville's ground in 1867 and . . . he told

ine that the descriptions were admirably true and the characterizations faultless in the main.   The book is a masterpiece,
the outcome of an opportunity that will never be repeated.
Melville was the first and only man made captive in a valley
full of Polynesian cannibals, who had the genius to describe
the situation, and who got away alive to write his book."

Typee was followed by a number of other novels, of which
Omoo (1847), White Jacket (1850), and *Moby Dick* (1851) may
be mentioned as dealing with Melville's experiences in the
South Pacific.   Of these works Henry S. Salt writes in the
Gentleman's Magazine: "Naturalness is, on the whole, Melville's prime characteristic. . . . His narratives are as racy
and vigorous as those of DeFoe, Smollett, or Marryat; his
character-sketches are such as only a man of keen observation
and humor could have realized and depicted.   Moreover, there
is a large-souled humanity in Melville which differentiates
him entirely from the mere artist or littérateur."

During the Civil War Melville wrote a number of stirring
patriotic poems, reckoned by the critics as among the best produced in that period.

Mendoza, Diego Hurtado de (Granada, Spain, 1503; Madrid, April, 1575).   He was a younger son of the Mendoza
to whom the government of Granada was entrusted when it
was wrested from the Moors.   Being destined for the Church,
he was sent to the University of Salamanca, where, some time
between 1520 and 1525, he wrote the novel which made him
famous, *Lazarillo de Tormes*.   Persuading his father to permit
him to join the army, he served with the Spanish troops of
Charles V in Italy.   Here he attended lectures in the universities of Bologna, Padua, and Rome.   Entering the Diplomatic Service, he was sent as Ambassador to Venice.   Here
he began collecting manuscripts, among others the first complete text of Josephus.   In 1547 he was sent as special pleni-
potentiary to Rome; in 1554 he was recalled to Spain.   Shortly
after this Charles V abdicated in favor of Philip II.   Mendoza
was not a favorite with this monarch, who seized the occasion
of Mendoza's quarrel with a courtier to banish him from the
court.   Mendoza spent the remainder of his life at Granada

in study and literary work, writing poetry, preparing a history of the Moorish insurrection in Granada of 1568–'70.

Lazarillo de Tormes was not published until 1553, when it was printed anonymously in Antwerp. Next year it was reprinted at Burgos, Spain. Parts of it were condemned by the Inquisition, and later editions were expurgated of these passages. The work is notable as being the first "picaresque" novel, or story of rambling adventure, of which Le Sage's Gil Blas, and, to a certain extent, Cervantes's Don Quixote, are classic examples. The work was so popular that continuations of it were written after Mendoza's death by less capable authors.

Meredith, George (Hampshire, England, Feb. 12, 1828). He was born of Welsh and Irish parentage (to which is traced the so-called "Celtic spirit" of his works). He was educated in Germany, where he laid the foundations of a classic erudition upon which he has builded ever since, to the delight of the cultured and the confusion of the unlearned among his readers. Returning at the age of fifteen to England, he spent the next five years of his life learning types of rustic character and the natural life and features of the countryside. At twenty he went to London to study law, but soon abandoned it in favor of literature. He began as a poet. He married the widowed daughter of Thomas Love Peacock, and dedicated to his brilliant father-in-law his first volume of verse. To the same satirical novelist has been traced the whimsical spirit of Meredith's first work in fiction, The Shaving of Shagpat (1856). His first novel proper, however, was peculiarly his own—*The Ordeal of Richard Feverel* (1859). In the beauty of its love-passages he never has surpassed it—indeed, it may be challenged that no author has done so. Evan Harrington (1861) is a semi-humorous novel based on the theme of whether it is possible for a tailor to be a gentleman. Meredith's wife died in 1863, and he went to live with the Rossettis and Swinburne. But in no sense did he become a dilettante. Rather, he entered upon an arduous career of journalism, as publishers' reader, leader-writer for newspapers, review editor, and translator. He published Sandra Belloni in 1864, and Rhoda Fleming in 1865.

In 1866 he went as correspondent for a London newspaper to the seat of war in Italy between that country and Austria. In behalf of Italian independence he wrote (1867) Vittoria, a sequel to Sandra Belloni. Marrying again, he settled in Surrey, whence he journeyed weekly to his tasks in London. In 1871 he wrote Harry Richmond, a novel of romantic adventure which is popular with many readers who are bewildered by his other epigrammatic philosophical works of fiction. Beauchamp's Career (1876) is a political novel, the consummate art of which is shown by the Liberalism it inculcates, although the author has studiously refrained from expressing his own views. The next large novel he wrote is *The Egoist* (1879), a searching presentation of man's selfishness. *Diana of the Crossways* (1885) established the author as the leading novelist of England. On the death of Tennyson, in 1892, Meredith was elected president of the British Society of Authors. On his eightieth birthday, February 12, 1908, he received congratulations from his fellow-authors throughout the civilized world.

"His methods we may dispute," says Henry Copley Green, in the Atlantic Monthly; "his excess of analysis we may find an insult to the reader's insight and a veil over his character's will, yet Mr. Meredith's thought is so hot with life, his prose so poignant with poetry, that even for his faults men may thank him in the coming days when his spirit of laughter and stoicism, of fire and brave intelligence, shall be loved by every adventurer in the magic land of English letters."

Mérimée, Prosper (Paris, France, Sept. 28, 1803; Cannes, Sept. 23, 1870). His parents were painters of some celebrity, and his father was also the author of a History of Painting in Oil, which was translated into English. A knowledge of English distinguished Prosper at college, and his life-long interest in English men and letters dates from his childhood, when he heard Northcote, Hazlitt, and others discuss them at his father's house. After leaving college he began the study of law, but soon turned to language and literature. To Greek, Spanish, and English he gave much attention, and later he learned Russian, which he called the most beautiful language of Europe, not excepting Greek. He also studied theology, architecture, numismatics, magic, and even scientific cookery. But, more than in all else, he was interested in the manifestations of the human soul in character and life. For lyric poetry he had no taste, but epic poetry, that embodied sentiment and incident, he read with enjoyment. The list of his friends would include the names of the most illustrious men of his time in Europe and some of the most distinguished women. His long friendship and correspondence with the Comtesse de Montijo is also a part of his literary life, for she aided him in many ways, chiefly in selecting the topics for his Spanish histories and novels and in obtaining access to original documents. He received appointments successively to the post of Chief of the Cabinets of Marine, of Commerce, and of the Interior. He was also made Inspector of Historic Monuments, including manuscripts, buildings, etc., treasures which France was in danger of losing. In connection with this work he visited Spain in 1830 and saw for the first time the future Empress, Eugénie de Gusman, daughter of the Comtesse de Montijo, then four years old. She became his pet and his pupil. When she also became his sovereign it is said that, with his oath of allegiance, he vowed never to make a recommendation to her of a person or a measure. His intimate relations with the imperial family gave him great prestige, which he never used to his own advantage. The Empress shed tears of joy on his election to the Senate. He was a member of the Academy of Inscriptions and of the French Academy. His correspondence was voluminous, his Letters being among the classics of France, the country of polished letter-writers. He had no religious faith, though he thought it probable that there was a God. During his last years he performed many acts of kindness for impecunious artists by obtaining orders for them; for the families of old friends, by editing posthumous works; not despising the writing of memorial notices for the comfort of a friend's widow or children. His health had been affected by the disturbed state of his country, and the declaration of war in 1870 rent his heart. The ultimate fate of the Empress caused him intense anxiety. He withdrew to Cannes, and there died. Among his last utterances were the words: "I bleed to-day for the humiliations of the French. However weak and ungrateful they may be,

I love them always." Among his numerous works, the following are notable: Jacquerie (1828); Mateo Falcone (1829); A Chronicle of the Time of Charles IX (Chronique du temps de Charles IX, 1829); The Malcontents (Les mécontents, 1830); Colomba (1840); Arsène Guillot (1844); *Carmen* (1845); History of Don Pedro I, King of Castile (L'Histoire de Don Pedré I, Roi de Castile, 1848); Historical and Literary Sketches (Mélanges historique et littéraires, 1855); Letters to an Unknown (Lettres à une inconnue, 1873; second series, 1875); Letters to Panizzi (1881).

Mitchell, Donald Grant (Norwich, Conn., April 12, 1822). He was graduated at Yale in 1841, from which institution he received in later years the degree of LL.D. He studied law in New York, and spent one year as United States consul in Venice (1853–'54). Since then he has lived on his farm of Edgewood, near New Haven, Conn. Adopting the pen-name of Ik Marvel, he embarked upon a literary career. Among his works may be noted: Reveries of a Bachelor (1850); Dream Life (1852); Rural Studies (1867); *Doctor Johns* (1866); English Lands, Letters, and Kings (1889); American Lands and Letters (1897).

Mr. Mitchell's distinctive literary form is that of the romantic reverie. Annie Russell Marble, writing in the Atlantic Monthly, says: "The best reveries by Ik Marvel are gentle visions of mild happiness and sorrow; there is day-dream for the youth, aspiration for the man, retrospect for the aged. Speaking through these reveries of domestic life is an undertone of delight in nature. My Farm of Edgewood (1863) was well summarized as 'practical enough for an agriculturist, yet romantic enough for a poet.'"

Moore, George (Ireland, 1853.) He began his literary career as a poet, but, owing to the severe criticism meted out to his early volumes of verse—Flowers of Parnassus (1877) and Pagan Poems (1881)—he turned his attention to fiction and criticism. His most noted novels are: A Mummer's Wife (1884); *Esther Waters* (1894); *Evelyn Innes* (1898); and Sister Teresa (1901)—a continuation and to some extent a re-writing of *Evelyn Innes*. It is characteristic of the author's devotion to literary style that only recently (in 1908) he declared his purpose to re-write *Evelyn Innes,* which he evidently considers his masterpiece. Yet this story is one that has been especially praised for its art. Says a writer in the Book Buyer of New York: "*Evelyn Inness* is a study of the struggle between the spirit and the flesh, between the Church and the world, . . . a tragic, intensely human, delicately wrought record. Mr. Moore has not chosen his characters and incidents to suit himself and facilitate his task; he has recorded them as they came, and only his consummate craft, his minute yet encompassing psychological insight has carried him through." This painstaking care in writing Mr. Moore learned from the French literary artists, Flaubert and Maupassant. In his earlier novels—A Mummer's Wife and *Esther Waters*—he followed the realistic method of Zola.

Mr. Moore is a member of that circle of Irishmen who are attempting to revive the Erse, the ancient language and literature of their nation. With the Irish poet William B. Yeats and others, he founded the Irish Literary Theatre at Dublin. In one of his more recent works, The Untilled Field (1903), a collection of stories presenting the unhappy condition of Ireland, he charges the Roman Catholic Church with killing the "joy of life" among the Irish, and proposes that they revert to their ancient pre-Christian paganism.

Mr. Moore is a dramatist of ability; his chief play is The Strike at Arlingford (1894).

Moore, John (Stirling, Scotland, 1729; Richmond, England, 1802). He studied at the University of Glasgow; was apprenticed to a surgeon; and served in military hospitals in the Netherlands during the war of the Austrian Succession. He settled at Glasgow as a physician, but, after two years of practice there, traveled on the Continent with the young Duke of Hamilton. On a later journey he witnessed early scenes of the French Revolution, which he described in a Journal published in 1793-'94, and quoted frequently by Thomas Carlyle in his French Revolution. He wrote three novels: *Zeluco* (1786); Edward (1796); and Mordaunt (1800).

Zeluco, says Thomas Green in his Diary of a Lover of Literature (1810), "is well contrived to purge the selfish and malignant passions by exhibiting the hideous effect of their unrestrained indulgence." Byron, in the introduction to his Childe Harold, says that in planning the poem he intended to make his hero "a modern Timon, perhaps a poetical Zeluco." Of Moore's general powers as a writer of fiction Thomas Carlyle wrote in the Edinburgh Encyclopædia: "As a novelist he showed no extraordinary felicity in the department of invention, no great power of diversifying his characters, or ease in conducting his narrative. The main quality of his works is that particular species of sardonic wit with which they are indeed perhaps profusely tinctured, but which frequently confers a grace and poignancy on the general strain of good sense and judicious observation that pervade the whole of them."

Moore, Thomas (Dublin. Ireland, May 28, 1779; Devizes, Wiltshire, England, Feb. 25, 1852). Trinity College, Dublin, having been opened to Roman Catholics in 1793, Moore, who was of that faith, entered the institution, and won an enviable reputation for scholarship. In 1799 he went to London as a student of law at Middle Temple. He brought with him a translation of the Odes of Anacreon, and, by means of his social attributes, he obtained leave of the Prince of Wales to dedicate it to his Royal Highness, and secured subscriptions for its publication from half the fashionable world. He was appointed Registrar of the Admiralty at Bermuda in 1803, but after a year's sojourn in the islands, leaving a deputy in office, he traveled through the United States. He returned to England in 1804, and devoted himself to literature. The Bermuda office proved to be no sinecure; for in 1818 the deputy defaulted for six thousand pounds, and Moore fled to Paris to escape the debt for which he was held responsible. In 1822 the amount was compounded at one thousand pounds, which Moore paid by the help of Lord Lansdowne, and returned to England. Moore's last years were harassed by the misconduct of his sons, and by financial embarrassment, for, although he received extraordinary prices for his works, and, after 1833, an annual pension of three hundred pounds, he was most im-provident. Tempted by need, he engaged to write a history of Ireland, receiving payment in advance. The work was not suited to his abilities. He was too conscientious in making investigations, and, after laboring many years at it, he left it uncompleted. For the last seven years of his life he was a total wreck. Moore's chief works are: The Poetical Works of the Late Thomas Little—a pseudonym which he early dropped (1801); Irish Melodies—original words set to old Irish airs (10 nos., 1807-'34); Lalla Rookh (1817); The Loves of the Angels (1835); *The Epicurean* (1827); Life of Lord Byron (1830); Travels of an Irish Gentleman in Search of a Religion (1833); History of Ireland (1835-'46).

It has been the fashion to disparage Moore; but, as Stopford Brooke points out in his A Treasury of Irish Poetry, "the man whose work Byron frankly admired, who received letters of thanks and appreciation from readers in America, Europe, and Asia, whom the Italians, French, Germans, Russians, Swedes, and Dutch translated, whose Lalla Rookh was partly put into Persian, to whom publishers gave three thousand pounds for a poem before they had even seen it—can scarcely be treated with indifferent contempt. A contemporary verdict, when it is almost universal, counts."

More, Hannah (Stapleton, near Bristol, England, Feb. 2, 1745; Clifton, England, Sept. 7, 1833). She was the fourth of five daughters of a schoolmaster, and, showing precocious ability, received every encouragement to engage in a literary career, one admirer even securing her independence by settling an annuity upon her. She visited London in 1774, where she made the acquaintance of Garrick, the actor, for whom she wrote a tragedy, Percy, which was produced in 1777 with great success. After Garrick's death her mind took on a more religious tone; she published Sacred Dramas in 1782; Slavery (1788); Thoughts on the Manners of the Great (1788); and An Estimate of the Religion of the Fashionable World (1791). She then turned her attention to practical means of averting the influence upon the common people of the atheistic and revolutionary doctrines of Thomas Paine and his school, writing many tracts in homely language, which were circulated by the millions. The most famous of these is The Shepherd of Salisbury Plain. In 1808 she published anonymously *Cœlebs in Search of a Wife*, a tract in the guise of a story. She devoted her old age to philanthropic work, especially to improving the condition of the poor children in her neighborhood. Her home was a shrine of good deeds, whither philanthropists made pilgrimages from all parts of the world. She retained all her faculties within two years of her death.

Morier, James Justinian (Smyrna, 1780; England, 1849). He was educated at Harrow, and in 1807 was appointed secretary to Sir Harford Jones's mission to the court of Persia. On May 7, 1809, he set out homeward with despatches from Teheran; and the publication of a book (1812) giving an account of his journey made him famous. It was translated into French and German. He returned to Teheran in 1810 as secretary of legation under Sir Gore Ouseley, and, after the latter's retirement, was British representative at the Persian court. He was recalled in 1815, was pensioned in 1817, and thereafter devoted his time wholly to literature. His success was sufficient to elicit from Sir Walter Scott the judgment that he was the best novelist of the day. His novels are: *The Adventures of Hajji Baba of Ispahan* (1824); Zohrab, the Hostage (1832); and Ayesha, the Maid of Kars (1834).

Morris, William (Walthamstow, near London, March 24, 1834; London, Oct. 3, 1896). He was educated at Marlborough School and at Exeter College, Oxford. In early manhood he was affected by the Catholic impulse then moving among the cultivated classes of England, but he fell under the influence of Carlyle, Ruskin, and Kingsley, and his spiritual aspirations were turned in the direction of humanitarian ideals. In 1854 and 1855 he visited France, going the second time with Burne-Jones, the artist. These trips influenced him to become an architect. He also tried painting; but in 1861 he settled upon the designing of artistic furniture and household decorations, having Burne-Jones and Dante Gabriel Rossetti as his associates. This firm was dissolved in 1871, Morris continuing the business alone. In 1890 he established the Kelmscott Press for the making of beautiful books. Theodore L. De Vinne, the American printer, says of him: "He seems to have been the first of moderns to see that typography was a manly art that could stand on its own legs without crutches lent by sister arts, and that it should be treated and clothed in manly fashion." He grew wealthy as well as famous from his businesses, which he conducted, as far as modern conditions permitted, upon the methods of the medieval guilds. In 1885 he became an active socialist, writing and speaking for the socialistic cause, and contributing to it of his wealth.

His first books were poetry. As he had small power of invention, he took old tales and told them in verse. From the simple charm of his narrative manner he was early recognized as the "modern Chaucer." His chief poetical works are: The Defence of Guinevere (1858); The Life and Death of Jason (1867); The Earthly Paradise (1868); The Story of Sigurd the Volsung (1877). He originated a new literary form, a romance within archaic prose interspersed with verse. Of this the most notable examples are: The House of the Wolfings (1889); The Roots of the Mountains (1890); The Story of the Glittering Plain (1891); The Wood Beyond the World (1894); *Child Christopher* (1895); The Well at the World's End (1896); and The Water of the Wondrous Isles (1897).

He wrote much in verse and prose for the cause of socialism: Art and Socialism (1884); Chants for Socialists (1885); Useful Work *v.* Useless Toil (1885); A Dream of John Bull (1888); and News from Nowhere (1891). He also translated into English verse Virgil's Æneid (1876) and Homer's Odyssey (1887), and performed a prodigious amount of literary work in introducing medieval romances and the Scandinavian sagas to English readers.

Justin McCarthy, in his History of Our Own Times, says: "Nothing can be more beautiful, tender, and melancholy than some of his sweet, pathetic stories. . . . He has such a story-teller's power as one might suppose suited to absorb the evening hours of some lady of medieval days." William Butler Yeats, the Irish poet, says of Morris: "All he writes seems to me like the make-believe of a child who is re-making the world, not always in the same way, but always after its own heart."

Mühlbach, Luise (Klara Müller Mundt) (Neubrandenburg, Jan. 2, 1814; Berlin, Sept. 26, 1873). She was the daughter of a burgomaster, and in 1839 married Theodor Mundt, subsequently an author and university professor. She was an extremely prolific writer of sensational novels, mainly historical, which were eagerly read by the patrons of circulating libraries, and not a few of them enjoyed great popularity in England and the United States as well, through the medium of translations. In one year alone she wrote a dozen volumes for the circulating libraries; but naturally such rapid composition precluded any special excellence of style. In spite of their want of artistic finish, her romances nevertheless display much descriptive merit. All were published under the pseudonym of Luise Mühlbach, and among the best of her earlier romances was Aphra Behn (1849). Others that may be noticed were: Emperor Joseph II and his Court (1855, 9th ed. 1866); Queen Hortense (1856, 5th ed. 1861); *Marie Antoinette and her Son* (1867); Emperor Alexander and his Court (1871); *Berlin and Sans-souci* (8th ed. 1882); *Henry VIII;* Empress Claudia, Princess of Tyrol (3d ed. 1867).

Mulock, Dinah Maria (Stoke-upon-Trent, England, April 20, 1826; Shortlands, Kent, Oct. 12, 1887). In 1865 she married George Lillie Craik, editor, author, and professor of English literature in Queen's College, Belfast. Mrs. Craik, however, is known in literary history as Miss Mulock, under which name she achieved her maiden success, the novel *John Halifax, Gentleman* (1856). Other notable works of hers are: A Life for a Life (1859); Christian's Mistake (1865); A Noble Life (1866); Woman's Kingdom (1868); *A Brave Lady* (1870); Young Mrs. Jardine (1879); King Arthur (1886). Miss Mulock was also a poet, and some of her poems, such as Philip, My King, hold a place in the anthologies.

Of *John Halifax, Gentleman*, Margaret O. W. Oliphant says: "This work, which relates the history of a good man's life and love, has but little incident, and no meretricious attractions, but it attained the higher triumph of securing the public attention and sympathy by its pure and elevated feeling, fine perception of character, and subdued but admirable literary power."

Louisa Parr, in Woman Novelists of Queen Victoria's reign, writes of Miss Mulock: "She never posed as a brilliant, impassioned writer of stories which tell of wrongs, or crimes, or great mental conflicts. Her teaching holds high the standard of duty, patience, and the unquestioning belief that all that God wills is well."

Murger, Henri (Paris, France, March 24, 1822; Jan. 28, 1861). He was the son of a concierge and at fifteen entered a notary's office, but finding his duties there distasteful he presently became secretary to Count Leo Tolstoi, a place which afforded him much leisure for writing as well as independence. For a decade or more he led an irregular, irresponsible career among artists and students, and he is commonly supposed to portray himself as Rodolphe, the hero, in his *Scènes de la vie de Bohême* (*Bohemian Life*, 1848). The details of existence in the Latin Quarter with its strange blending of high spirits with squalor and vice are faithfully reflected in Murger's pages, and to him, perhaps more than to anyone else, is due the identification of Bohemia as a moral condition rather than a precise locality. Dissipation, in his estimation, was preferable to cleanly living, and his career ended in an insane asylum. He wrote much in verse as well as prose, and many of his lyrics possess great beauty. Several of his songs have been translated by Andrew Lang in Ballads and Lyrics of Old France. Murger's *Bohemian Life* remains his prose masterpiece, Les Buveurs d'eau (1854) approaching it most nearly in excellence. Among other works of his were: Scènes de la vie de jeunesse (1851); Claude et Marianne (1851); Adeline Protat (1853); Madame Olympe (1859); Les nuits d'hiver (1861); and Les Roueries de l'Ingénue, which he left unfinished at his death.

Murray, David Christie (West Bromwich, Staffordshire, England, April 13, 1847; London, Aug. 1, 1907). He obtained his education at a private school in his native place, and began active life as a reporter on the Birmingham Morning News, then edited by his friend George Dawson. He had already made his mark as a descriptive reporter when in 1873 he went

to London to serve on the Daily News.   He was subsequently
employed on the staff of the London World, and during the
Russo-Turkish war was special correspondent of the Scotsman
and the London Times.   Returning to England, he soon gave
up journalism for fiction-writing, his first extended story, A
Life of Atonement, appearing in Chambers' Journal in 1879.
Joseph's Coat was printed the next year, and at the time of his
death he had written about thirty novels, as able and spirited
as they were deservedly popular.   Among them were: Val
Strange (1881); By the Gate of the Lea (1882); *The Way of
the World* (1884); Aunt Rachel (1886); A Dangerous Catspaw
(with Henry Murray, 1888); The Weaker Vessel (1888); Time's
Revenge (1893); In Direst Peril (1894); A Rogue's Conscience
(1896); This Little World (1897); A Race for Millions (1898);
and Despair's Last Journey (1901).   In 1897 Mr. Murray
published My Contemporaries in Fiction, a generously appreciative as well as discriminating study of the work of his novel-
writing confrères.

Norris, Frank (Chicago, Ill., 1870; San Francisco, Cal.,
Oct. 25, 1902).   He was educated at the University of California, and at Harvard University, studied art in Paris, 1887–'89,
and was correspondent in South Africa for the San Francisco Chronicle at the period of the notorious Jameson raid.
In 1896–'97 he edited the San Francisco Wave, and he was
war correspondent in Cuba for McClure's Magazine in 1898.
The painful realism of his first novel of importance, McTeague
(1899), first brought him into general notice, and his next novel,
Moran of the Lady Letty (1900), was concerned with a vigorous
recital of adventures off the California coast.   The Octopus
(1901), a strongly conceived story, is an impressive arraignment
of Californian railway methods and their oppressive bearing
upon the growing and transportation of wheat, and was widely
circulated.   *The Pit*, dealing with commercial contests over the
exchange of wheat, ran serially in The Saturday Evening Post
in 1902–'03, and was issued in book form in the last-named
year.   At the time of Mr. Norris's death he was literary adviser
in a publishing-house in New York City.

Norris, William Edward (London, England, Nov. 18, 1847). He was the son of a former chief justice of Ceylon, and was educated at Twyford, Hants, a school then in charge of the present dean of Durham, G. W. Kitchin, and at Eton. On leaving Eton he planned to study modern languages in preparation for diplomatic service, but gave up this idea, and, though subsequently called to the bar at the Inner Temple, he never practised his profession. A story, Monsieur Badeau, sent to the Cornhill Magazine, so greatly attracted the notice of its editor, Leslie Stephen, on account of its marked ability, that he not only accepted the tale, but encouraged Mr. Norris to attempt the composition of a novel. His novel, Heaps of Money, in which appears the strong character of Mainwaring, was published in 1877, and was followed by Mademoiselle Mersac, which ran serially in the Cornhill for 1889, and Matrimony (1880), perhaps the book with which his name is most closely associated in the minds of a majority of readers. All his stories are noteworthy for their discriminating character-analysis, quiet humor, and finish of style, and the greater number of them have been first issued serially. James Russell Lowell was an enthusiastic admirer of Norris's novels, reading several of them in the last months of his life. Among his books written after Matrimony are: No New Thing (1882); Thirlby Hall (1883); A Bachelor's Blunder (1885); My Friend Jim (1886); The Rogue (1888); His Grace (1892); A Deplorable Affair (1893); The Dancer in Yellow (1896); The Widower (1898); An Octave (1900); and Lord Leonard, the Luckless (1903).

Ohnet, Georges (Paris, France, April 3, 1848). He was the son of an architect who intended he should become a lawyer, but after the Franco-Prussian war he gave up the law for journalism and was successively attached to the staffs of Le Pays and Le Constitutionnel. His sparkling, attractive style won some attention, and in 1875 his first drama, Regina Sarpi, written in collaboration with Denayrouze, was brilliantly successful at the Théâtre Historique. This was succeeded in 1877 by the drama of Martha, successfully brought out at the Gymnase, and not far from this time he began the series of idealistic fictions to which he gave the general title of Battles of Life.

Serge Panine, crowned by the Academy, appeared in 1881; and subsequently *Le Maître de Forges* (*The Iron-Master*, 1883), dramatized by the author and acted at the Gymnase; La Comtesse Sarah (1883); Lise Fleuron (1884); La Grande Manière (1885); Les Dames de Croix-Mort (1886); Veloute (1888); Le Docteur Rameau (1889); Dernier Amour (1889); Dette de Haine (1891); Le Droit de l'Enfant (1894); Gens de la Noce (1900); and some lesser works. M. Ohnet's novels concern themselves chiefly with the life and customs of the *bourgeoisie* and have attained a wide popularity in the author's own country. Excellent translations of several have appeared in English, and both in England and in America his work has found appreciative readers despite its rather conventional construction and tinge of melodrama. In July, 1885, M. Ohnet was decorated with the Legion of Honor.

Oliphant, Laurence (Cape Town, Cape Colony, August 27, 1829; Twickenham, England, Dec. 23, 1888). He was the son of Sir Anthony Oliphant, Attorney General in Cape Colony. He received a desultory education, and accompanied his parents on a European tour in 1848–'49. In 1851 he went on a hunting expedition in Nepaul with Jung Bhadur, one result of which was his first book, A Journey to Katmandu (1852), and then, going to England with his mother, studied law for a season, presently forsaking his studies for a Russian tour. Of this he wrote in his next book, The Russian Shores of the Black Sea (1853). Between 1853 and 1861 he was in the Diplomatic Service in Washington and in China. He joined the filibuster Walker in Nicaragua in 1856, and had many adventures. Among his writings at this time were Minnesota and the Far West (1855); the Trans-Caucasian Campaign (1856); and The Filibusters (1860). He entered Parliament in 1865, where he did not show any special talent for debate, but his sprightly novel, Piccadilly, first printed in Blackwood's Magazine, and in book form in 1870, was a genuine literary success. By this time it was evident that his want of ballast left him at the mercy of his whims and impulses, and he presently fell under the influence of a noted spiritualist prophet, Thomas Lake Harris, who had established a small community at Brocton, Chautauqua County, N. Y. Obeying Harris's command, Oliphant left Parliament and went to Brocton, where he lived the life of a farm laborer, in entire subjection to the imperious will of Harris. After three years he was allowed by Harris to return to Europe and act as Times correspondent during the Franco-Prussian war, and even to remain in Paris a few years. He there met Miss Alice Le Strange, whom he married, and in 1873 he returned to Brocton with his wife and his mother, both of whom were employed in the menial tasks of the community. Oliphant was now busied with the financial affairs of the settlement and traveled much in its behalf. As late as 1878 he still believed that Harris was an incarnation of Deity, but his mind was now taken up by a project for colonizing Palestine. By Harris's orders his wife had been separated from him and sent to California, but she was at last allowed to join him in a trip to Egypt; and in 1881 Lady Oliphant died in California, where her son had taken her in the hope that she might recover from the illness brought on by the hardships of the life at Brocton. He now shook off the influence of Harris and went to Palestine, where his wife died in 1886. Two years later he married a daughter of Robert Dale Owen, but before they could establish themselves in Palestine he died. He was one of the most brilliant men of his day, but was only partially sane, and the terrible mistakes of his eccentric career resulted from undisciplined thinking and entire lack of self-poise. Among works of his not already named were: *Altiora Peto* (1883); Massollam (1886); Haifa (1889); Scientific Religion (1888); Episodes of a Life of Adventure (1887).

Oliphant, Margaret Oliphant Wilson (Wallyfort, near Musselburgh, Scotland, April 4, 1828; Wimbledon, England, June 25, 1897). In her childhood her parents removed to Liverpool, and there and in Birkenhead her youth was chiefly passed. In 1852 she married her cousin Francis Oliphant, an artist in stained glass, and later accompanied him to Rome, where he died in 1859. She afterward went to Windsor, which was her home for almost thirty years, but resided at Wimbledon for the three years preceding her death. She was left a widow with two sons, and educated them as well as two orphan nieces, from the proceeds of her writings; but the elder son died in 1890, and the second son, with whom she wrote the Victorian Age of Literature, died, after a long invalidism, in 1894. She began to write early in life, her first book, Passages in the Life of Margaret Maitland, appearing in 1849. This was the precursor of several other tales of Scottish life by her which, in the view of some critics, are far more convincing than much of the Scottish fiction popular within the past twenty years. She continued amazingly industrious almost to the last hour of life, producing nearly a hundred books in fiction, history, and general literature, as well as hundreds of contributions to periodicals, the general level of excellence being remarkably high when the amount of work accomplished is considered. The best of all her many novels are the series of five tales comprising the Chronicles of Corlingford, namely: The Rector and the Doctor's Family (1863); *Salem Chapel* (1863); The Perpetual Curate (1864); Miss Majoribanks (1866); and Phebe Junior (1876), and of these *Salem Chapel* and Miss Majoribanks may be placed as chief. Very slightly inferior in excellence and interest to these are Zaidee (1856); Madonna Mary (1866); For Love and Life (1874); Valentine and his Brother (1875); Carita (1877); The Primrose Path (1878); Within the Precincts, a story of Windsor (1879); He that Will Not when He May (1880); Harry Joscelyn (1881); The Ladies Lindores (1883); The Cuckoo in the Nest (1892); The Sorceress (1893); *A House in Bloomsbury* (1894); and Sir Robert's Fortune (1895). Of several tales of the supernatural A Little Pilgrim in the Unseen (1882) is best known, though A Beleaguered City is possibly a better piece of writing; and the group includes also Old Lady Mary and The Open Door (1884). Among miscellaneous works by Mrs. Oliphant are: Life of Edward Irving; A Memoir of Count de Montalembert (1872); The Makers of Florence (1874); The Makers of Venice (1887); The Literary History of England (1882); Royal Edinburgh (1890); and Annals of a Publishing-House (1897). She became popular very early in her literary career, and remained so to the end. She did not possess the power to build up a work of imagination on the largest scale, but her knowledge of character was accurate, and she occupies an honored place among novelists of the second rank. The principal defect of her novels was structural, her plots being sometimes ineffective, while the strain of continuous production for a lifetime appeared in the latter half of a tale with a promising beginning. Her Autobiography was edited by Coghill (1899).

Osborne, Duffield (Brooklyn, N. Y., June 20, 1858). He is the son of Samuel and Rosalie Duffield Osborne, was educated at the Brooklyn Polytechnic Institute and Columbia University, and was graduated at the Columbia Law School in 1881. He was admitted to the New York bar the same year, practised his profession in New York City until 1892, and was assistant secretary of the department of city works, Brooklyn department, 1892-'94. He then spent a year in foreign travel and has since made his home in New York engaged in literary work. For several years he has been secretary of the New York Authors Club. He began a literary career by contributions to Life and Puck in 1885, and in 1888 his first book, an historical romance, entitled The Spell of Ashtaroth, was issued in New York and London and proved popular. Later fictions by him are: The Robe of Nessus (1890); The Secret of the Crater (1902); *The Lion's Brood* (1906); The Angels of Messer Ercole (1907). He has also published many poems and short stories and has edited Livy's Roman History (1898) and Macaulay's Lays of Ancient Rome (1901).

Ouida (Louise de la Ramée) (Bury St. Edmunds, England, 1840; Lucca, Italy, Jan. 25, 1908). When she was twenty years old Mlle. de la Ramée went to London and began to write novels, taking as a pen-name a little sister's childish mispronunciation of her first name. She was successful from the beginning, and speedily became wealthy. Comparatively early in life she took up her residence in Lucca, Italy, where she occupied a fine villa and devoted herself unremittingly, and almost to the exclusion of human associations, to literary production and the care of her numerous dogs and horses. Around Lucca she was known as "The Lady of the Dogs." At one time she domiciled thirty of these animals, but at the same time she had forty horses. If neighborhood traditions may be credited, she once gave every dog in Lucca a dinner, paying the rather large bill cheerfully and promptly, although she was then in debt for the necessities of her own household. Her love of animals was reflected frequently in her writings, notably in A Dog of Flanders. She held persistently aloof from human kind, admitting few visitors and diminishing their number as the years passed. One frustrated romance colored her solitary life. An Italian nobleman paid court to her and won her deep regard, if nothing more; but Ouida fortunately discovered that he was more seriously attached to another and younger lady, whom eventually he married. She dismissed him from her presence and then wrought vengeance upon him by delineating him so unmistakably in her novel *Friendship* that he was obliged to go into retirement. As early as 1894 reports of Ouida's poverty were current, and, owing largely to her own stubborn reticence, these multiplied from year to year until, a few months before her death, they became the sensation of the literary world. It is safe to say that most of these reports were gross exaggerations; but there is no room for doubt that her great income had been frittered away, and that she was often hard pressed for ready money. She was uncommonly generous and charitable, her animal entourage was expensive, and, despite her solitude, her own manner of living was of a grandiose and therefore costly order. There is no occasion now to revive and perpetuate the picturesque stories of her distress which were widely published in England and the United States early in 1907; but it should be recorded that they brought her numerous offers of assistance, which she declined with plain manifestations of the pain inflicted on her by the false reports. She did avail herself, however, of the pension of £150 accorded her by the British Government, and when she died she left neither property nor posthumous works. Her canine companions had been reduced to three. She consigned them to the care of her maid with instructions to feed them as long as possible, and, when she could no longer do so, to shoot them. Her works include: Held in Bondage (1863); Strathmore (1865); Chandos (1866); *Under Two Flags* (1867); Idalia (1867); Tricotrin (1869); Puck (1870); Folle-Farine (1871); A Dog of Flanders (1872);

Pascarel (1873); Two Little Wooden Shoes (1874); Signa (1875); In a Winter City (1876); The Story of a Dream (1877); *Friendship* (1878); Moths (1880); A Village Commune (1881); In Maremma (1882); Bimbi: Stories for Children (1882); Wanda (1883); Pipistrello (1884); The Princess Napraxine (1884); A Rainy June (1885); Othmar (1885); Don Gesualdo (1886); A House Party (1887); Guilderoy (1889); Ruffino (1890); Syrlin (1890); The Tower of Taddeo (1890); Santa Barbara (1891); The New Priesthood (1893); The Silver Christ (1894); Two Offenders (1894); Le Selve (1896); The Massarenes (1897); Toxin, an Altruist (1897); La Strega (1899); The Waters of Edera (1900); Critical Studies (1900); and Street Dust (1901).

Parker, Sir (Horatio) Gilbert (Camden East, Addington, Ontario, Canada, Nov. 23, 1862). He was educated at Trinity College, Toronto, studied theology, and took deacon's orders in the Church of England. His health failing, he went to Australia, withdrew from the ministry and joined the editorial staff of the Sydney Morning Herald. At Her Majesty's Theater in Sydney he produced in 1888 an adaptation of Goethe's Faust, which was successful, as was also The Vendetta, which followed it. Later plays by him were No Defence (1889) and The Seats of the Mighty (1897), a dramatization of his own novel issued the year before. After leaving Australia he traveled widely in the South Sea Islands and Canada. He married in New York City in 1895, Miss Amy Vantine, and he has since resided in England. In 1900 he entered Parliament as member for Gravesend, and he was knighted in 1902. His earliest books were: Round the Compass in Australia (1892); Pierre and His People: Tales of the Far North (1892); Mrs. Falchion (1893); The Trespasser (1893); The Translation of a Savage (1894); and The Trail of the Sword (1895). His novels had been slowly attracting attention during these few years, but his story, When Valmond Came to Pontiac (1896), brought him more definitely forward as an author, and his reputation was further increased by An Adventurer of the North (1895); and the happily entitled romance The Seats of the Mighty (1896), a story of the taking of Quebec. He has

since published The Pomp of the Lavillettes (1897); The Battle
of the Strong (1898); The Lane that Had no Turning (1900);
The Right of Way (1901); Donovan Pasha (1902); A History of Old Quebec (1903); A Ladder of Swords (1904);
and The Weavers (1908). His novels enjoy equal popularity in England and America and their literary quality is of a
high order for the most part.

Pater, Walter Horatio (London, England, Aug. 4, 1839;
Oxford, July 30, 1894). He was the second son of Richard
Glode Pater, a physician in Shadwell, London, who died when
his son was an infant. The family then removed to Enfield,
and Walter was sent to King's School at Canterbury, a locality
which he described lovingly years afterward in his story of
Emerald Uthwart. While at school he read Ruskin's Modern
Painters and manifested a leaning toward art, but showed no
especial literary ability. As an undergraduate of Queen's College, Oxford, he had a shy secluded career, making but few
friends, and after taking his degree he remained in Oxford as
a tutor. He had once thought of taking Anglican orders, and
subsequently of becoming a Unitarian clergyman, but gave
up this intention also, and on being elected a fellow of Brasenose College in 1864, he settled down to a university career.
He had begun to write by this time, and he sent contributions
to the Westminster and Fortnightly reviews, which with other
papers were published in book form as Studies in the History
of the Renaissance (1878). About him in Oxford now gathered
a small circle of men of esthetic tastes, over whom Pater's
influence was very great. These gladly welcomed his *Marius
the Epicurean* in 1885, as did London men of letters also. It
is its author's masterpiece and displays, in the elaborate style
peculiar to him, his conceptions of esthetic existence. Later
volumes published by him were: Imaginary Portraits (1887);
Appreciations, with an Essay on Style (1889); Plato and Platonism (1893); and in 1894 the exquisite study entitled The Child
in the House. After his death appeared his: Greek Studies
(1895); Miscellaneous Studies (1897); Gaston de Latour, a
fragmentary romance (1896); and Essays from the Guardian
(1897). Pater traveled on the Continent, and lived in Ken-

sington and in Oxford by turns, but his work was mainly done in his rooms at Brasenose. He wrote with difficulty, and revised and corrected continually. The result was a style often extremely beautiful in its subtle convolutions, but almost never without a certain hardness which prevents his acceptance with many. He possessed the limitations of a contemplative and somewhat indolent temperament and shrank from overmuch contact with the world or the making of new friends. Like his own Marius, his mind in his latest years appears to have returned to the religious attitude of his youth. His biography has been written by Greenslet (1903), Benson (1906), and Wright (1907).

Payn, James (Cheltenham, England, Feb. 28, 1830; London, March 25, 1898). He was the son of William Payn, clerk of the Thames Commissioners, and after some years at Eton and the Military Academy at Woolwich entered Trinity College, Cambridge, where he made many friendships that were retained throughout his life. While an undergraduate he published two books of verse, Stories from Boccaccio (1852), which was warmly praised in the Spectator; and Poems (1853). In 1854 he married and settled down to follow a literary career. His home was now at Rydal, and Miss Mitford, a friend of his father's, had given him an introduction to Harriet Martineau, his not distant neighbor. Both authors encouraged and advised him and he soon became a frequent contributor to Household Words, and Chambers's Journal, removing to Edinburgh in 1858 on being made editor of the last-named periodical, and continuing in the editorship for sixteen years. The climate of Scotland not agreeing with him, he went to London in 1861, but continued to edit the Journal. He had already published nine books when in 1864 the most popular of all his books, *Lost Sir Massingberd*, appeared serially in Chambers's Journal, whose circulation it increased by twenty thousand copies. From this time Payn was always occupied in novel-writing, and after resigning his editorship in 1874 he became literary adviser to Smith, Elder and Company, and edited for them the Cornhill Magazine, 1883-'96. He thoroughly enjoyed life in London and rarely left the city, saying that for the quarter century preceding 1884 he had taken but three days of consecutive holiday once a year. Few literary men have worked harder than did he, but he found time for friendships new and old, and as editor was especially kind and helpful to young and aspiring authors. He was very generally beloved by his literary contemporaries, and though he suffered much from rheumatism in his later years, the natural sweetness of his disposition remained undisturbed. Though no imitator of Dickens, he was somewhat influenced by the manner of the earlier novelist, and he possessed an animated, fluent style, as well as abundant humor and dramatic force. He was invariably entertaining without aiming to be profound. Among the best of his novels, after *Lost Sir Massingberd*, are: Married Beneath Him (1865); Carlyon's Year (1868); Gwendoline's Harvest (1870); Won—not Wooed (1871); At Her Mercy (1874); By Proxy (1878); What He Cost Her (1877); The Talk of the Town (1885); The Burnt Million (1890); and A Stumble on the Threshold (1892). The Backwater of Life, issued posthumously (1899), with an introduction by Leslie Stephen, discloses much of the writer's personality in its kindly reflections upon topics of the day.

Peacock, Thomas Love (Weymouth, England, Oct. 18, 1785; Halliford, Jan. 23, 1866). His father died soon after the son's birth, and the boy received a desultory training at home and in a private school. Before he was twenty he published two small volumes of verse of no particular excellence. His best work in poetry is to be looked for in the ballads scattered through his novels. In 1812 he formed a friendship with Shelley, which led to his being appointed Shelley's executor with Byron. In 1816 Peacock published *Headlong Hall*, a satirical novel, which sufficiently attested his talent in that branch of fiction and brought him fame as well. Three years later he was appointed to an important post in the East India Company, by reason of his being an able novelist and a careful Greek scholar, and here he remained for thirty-eight years, retiring at last on an ample pension. In 1819 he married Jane Gryffydh, whom he had first met in 1811, but had not seen since. He proposed by letter and was accepted—an affair, as Shelley told him, very like the ending of one of his own novels. *Headlong Hall* was followed by Melincourt (1817); Nightmare Abbey (1818); and Maid Marian (1822). In later years appeared: The Misfortunes of Elphin (1829); Crotchet Castle (1831), his highest attainment in comedy; and Gryll Grange (1861). Peacock will be oftenest recalled as a satirist, his satire not only being good-humored and genial on the whole, but intimately blended with genuine though eccentric humor. His characterizations are seldom or never real personages, but types instead. They serve as mouthpieces for discussion and are not intended to be life-like presentations of humanity. Peacock's work never has gained the popular ear. He must always have been caviare to the general on account of extravagant satire and great wilfulness, and his novels now attract only the curious student or the genuine lover of satire. Collected editions of his principal works appeared in 1875 edited by Cole, and in 1891 edited by Garnett.

Pemberton, Max (Birmingham, England, June 19, 1863). He was educated at Merchant-Taylors School, London, and Caius College, Cambridge, and was on the staff of Vanity Fair in 1885. He edited Chums, a boys' periodical, 1892–'93, and was editor of Cassell's Magazine in 1896–1906. His first novel, The Iron Pirate, was published in 1893, and since then he has been an indefatigable purveyor of fiction. Among his books may be named: The Sea-Wolves (1894); The Impregnable City (1895); The Little Huguenot (1895); A Gentleman's Gentleman (1896); Christine of the Hills (1897), a spirited romance of Dalmatian life; The Garden of Swords (1899); The House Under the Sea (1902); My Sword for Lafayette (1906); The Diamond Ship (1907); The Lodestar (1907); and *The Footsteps of a Throne*. His stories have been popular in his own country and have met with favor in America also, though to a lesser extent.

Phelps, Elizabeth Stuart (Mrs. Herbert D. Ward) (Boston, Mass., Aug. 31, 1844). She is a daughter of the Rev. Austin Phelps and his wife, Elizabeth Stuart, and was baptized Mary Gray, but received her mother's name in 1852. She was educated in private schools in Andover, Mass. In 1857 her first story appeared in the Youth's Companion. She inherited literary talent on both sides, her father being an author and a professor in Andover Theological Seminary, and her mother a writer of note in her day, the daughter of Rev. Moses Stuart, a theological writer. She began writing for Harper's Monthly in 1864, but her first short story that attracted general attention was The Tenth of January, printed somewhat later in the Atlantic Monthly. In 1868 she published the Gates Ajar, which made her immediately famous and passed through twenty editions in one year. Nearly one hundred thousand copies were sold in the United States, and as many more in Great Britain, and it was translated into many languages. It was attacked from many pulpits, and was the theme of much discussion, but at the present day the theological views it maintained would not be considered radical. This was soon followed by: Men, Women, and Ghosts, a collection of short stories (1869); The Silent Partner (1871), a tale descriptive of the hardships endured by mill-operatives; and The Story of Avis (1877), which still remains among the best of her books. For forty years she has been constantly before the public as an author with something very definite to say, and a very individual way of saying it. She has interested herself in many of the reform movements of her time, such as temperance, the advancement of women, and anti-vivisection, and her writings have faithfully reflected their author's decided opinions. Her style is forcible and original, and her character-drawing sharp and clear, if not in every case convincing, while the moral issues involved in her novels are always ably presented. She has written several juvenile books, and two volumes of refined and thoughtful verse: Poetic Studies (1875) and Songs of the Silent World (1885). Among the more important of her other books are: An Old Maid's Paradise; Sealed Orders (1879); Friends (1881); Doctor Zay (1882); A Singular Life (1894); The Supply at St. Agatha's (1896); The Story of Jesus Christ: An Interpretation (1897); Walled In (1907); Loveliness; Donald Marcy. In 1888 she married Herbert D. Ward, with whom she wrote Come Forth (1890) and The Master of the Magicians (1890). For many years she has made her home in Newton Centre, Mass. She published an autobiographical volume in 1896.

Phillpotts, Eden (Mount Aboo, India, Nov. 4, 1862). He is the son of Captain Henry Phillpotts, of the British army in India, and he was educated in Plymouth, England. Entering the Sun Fire Insurance office at eighteen as a clerk, he remained there till 1890. He then removed to London, where he studied acting for a time; but discovering his lack of ability in that direction he turned his attention to literature. His long residence in Devonshire gave him entire familiarity with its scenery and people, and in his novels he has done for Devon much the same service that Thomas Hardy has rendered for Wessex. The tragic element in them is almost as strong as in Hardy's novels, and their descriptive coloring is a reminder of Blackmore without being in any sense an imitation. His earlier fictions were: A Tiger's Cub (1892); Some Everyday Folks (1893); and Down Dartmoor Way (1894). These were soon followed by Lying Prophets (1896) and Children of the Mist (1898), both of which were extremely successful and placed their author among the foremost of living English novelists. His later volumes include: a collection of tales of schoolboy life, The Human Boy (1899); *Sons of the Morning* (1900); The Striking Hours, a volume of short stories (1901); The Good Red Earth (1901); The River (1902); My Devon Year (1903); The Golden Fetich (1903); The American Prisoner (1904); The Farm of the Dagger (1904); Knock at a Venture (1905); The Secret Woman (1905); The Portreeve (1906); Doubloons (1906); The Whirl-wind (1907); The Folk Afield (1907); The Mother of the Man (1908); and The Human Boy Again (1908). Mr. Phillpotts married in 1892 Miss Emily Topham and for some years has made his home at Torquay on the coast of South Devon.

Poe, Edgar Allan (Boston, Mass., Jan. 19, 1809; Baltimore, Md., Oct. 7, 1849). Both his parents were actors and they were playing at the Federal Street Theater in Boston at the time of his birth. On the death of Mrs. Poe, who outlived her husband a short time, Edgar was adopted into the family of John Allan, a business man of Richmond, Va. He was a handsome, precocious child, and was spoiled by over-indulgence on the part of the Allans, who sent him to school in Richmond and afterward at Stoke-Newington in London for five years. Returning home in 1820, he studied under a tutor and was for a time a student in the University of Virginia. His gambling debts were now so heavy that Mr. Allan would not allow him to return to the University, but retained him in his own counting-room, a post which the youth soon deserted and, going to Boston, published there Tamerlane and Other Poems (1827). He then served two years in the army, was honorably discharged and effected a reconciliation with Mr. Allan. He published Al Aaraaf and other verses in 1829, and the next year his adoptive father obtained an appointment for him at West Point Military Academy. There he neglected his duties, and in six months was dismissed by court-martial. He was now penniless and could expect no further aid from Mr. Allan, who died not long afterward, making no mention of him in his will. Thrown entirely on his own resources, he presently found friends and won a prize of $100 offered for the best prose story by the Saturday Visitor, his story being entitled A Manuscript Found in a Bottle. In 1836 he married his cousin, Virginia Clemm, and for the rest of his life he led an irregular existence, sometimes fairly prosperous and again not far removed from actual want, his drinking habit causing him much mental and physical suffering. As editor of the Southern Literary Messenger he was at his best, since the work was congenial and he was developing critical powers of a high order. For several years from 1837 he alternated between Philadelphia and New York, publishing in the latter city, in 1837, his story of *The Narrative of Arthur Gordon Pym.* He was editor of Graham's Magazine in 1840, then went to Fordham, N. Y., where his wife died in 1847, and two years later he died of alcoholism in a Baltimore hospital. Long before his death his rank as a master of melodious verse was generally recognized, and his skill in the construction of the short story was acknowledged also. Among the most notable of his prose tales are: *The Fall of the House of Usher;* The Gold Bug; Ligeia; and Silence; and his most characteristic poetry is to be found in the collection Poems (1831) and The Raven and Other Poems (1845). As poet and prose writer Poe still commands the admiration of the severest critics. His appeal is made to the artistic sensibilities; the average person knows him only as the author of The Raven and The Bells. In foreign countries he has been much admired and studied and there are French, German, and Spanish editions of his works. His biography has been written by George E. Woodberry (1885) and others.

Porter, Jane (Durham, England, 1776; Bristol, May 24, 1850). She was the daughter of William Porter, an English army officer, who died in 1779, and soon after this event her mother removed to Edinburgh with her three children—Jane, Anna Maria, and Robert. Here they made rapid progress at school, but in order to develop the artistic tastes of Robert they subsequently removed to London, where they mingled in the artistic and literary circles of the metropolis. The younger sister began a long career of authorship at fifteen, but Jane, whose abilities developed more slowly, did not publish her first book, *Thaddeus of Warsaw*, till 1803. This gained immediate popularity and by 1810 had reached a ninth edition. In a German translation it gained the notice of Kosciusko, who sent the author his commendations, and the tenth edition was dedicated to his memory. As a recognition of her talent the King of Würtemberg constituted Miss Porter a lady of the chapter of St. Joachim. In 1810 she published *The Scottish Chiefs*, which not only had very great success in Scotland but was translated into German and Russian, was proscribed by Napoleon, and even reached India. Its popularity has continued to the present almost unabated, it having been reprinted nine times between 1816 and 1882, and it is in constant demand in American public libraries. Among later and lesser works of hers are: The Pastor's Fireside (1815), a novel which was reissued as lately as 1880; Duke Christian of Lüneberg (1824); Coming Out (1828); and The Field of Forty Footsteps (1828); but Sir Edward Seaward's Diary (1831), long attributed to her, was written by her eldest brother, William Ogilvy Porter, a physician in Bristol. Miss Porter wrote several plays, but they met with no success. Till her mother's death in 1831 she lived chiefly at Thames Ditton and Esher. She and her sister then settled in London, where she went much into society. In her latest years she appears to have been in pecuniary difficulties, and in 1842 she was awarded a pension of fifty pounds from the literary fund. In 1844 she received a rosewood chair from American authors, publishers, and booksellers as testimonial of their admiration of her talents. She died at the home of her brother in Portland Square, Bristol, and in Bristol Cathedral is a tablet to her memory and that of her brothers Robert and William, and her sister Anna Maria, whom she outlived by nearly twenty years.

Prentiss, (Mrs.) Elizabeth Payson (Portland, Me., Oct. 26, 1818; Dorset, Vt., Aug. 13, 1878). She was a daughter of Edward and Ann Payson and after attending schools in Portland and in Ipswich, Mass., she taught school herself in Portland and in Richmond, Va., 1840–'43. In 1845 she married the Rev. George L. Prentiss, then pastor of the South Congregational Church, New Bedford, Mass. She accompanied him to New York City in 1851 on the occasion of his call to the Mercer Street Presbyterian Church, and there her home continued to be for the rest of her life. At sixteen she had begun contributing verse and prose to the Youth's Companion, but her first book was the juvenile tale, Little Susy's Six Birthdays (1853), the earliest of the Susy Books, long so popular in the nursery. She continued active as a writer of juvenile tales for a quarter of a century, among her books of this character being: Little Threads; Fred, Maria, and Me (1868); The Old Brown Pitcher (1868); The Story Lizzie Told (1870); Aunt Jane's Hero (1871); and Gentleman Jim (1878); while among her volumes intended for older readers were: *Stepping Heavenward* (1869); The Home at Greylock (1876); Pemaquid (1877); and Avis Benson (1879). *Stepping Heavenward* was her most popular book, more than one hundred and fifty thousand copies being sold in the United States, and probably as many more in other countries, it being translated into French, German, Norwegian, Swedish, and Italian. A strong religious character marks all her work, but she avoided the presentation of doctrinal questions, and a saving sense of humor is always apparent. She also wrote several hymns which have been greatly prized. See her Life and Letters by George L. Prentiss (1882).

Prévost D'Exiles, Antoine François (Abbé Prévost) (Hesdin, Artois, France, April 1, 1697; Chantilly, Nov. 23, 1763). He came of a good family, was educated in Jesuit schools, and at sixteen enlisted in the army. At the close of the war of the Spanish Succession he returned to the Jesuits and, if some accounts may be trusted, joined the order only to leave it presently for the army. An unsuccessful love affair drove him again to the cloister, and in 1720 he took the vows in the Benedictine community of St. Maur. Here he spent the next seven years in study, preaching, and teaching, till at last his unstable disposition once more drove him into the world, and this time he remained self-exiled in Holland and England several years, a period which he devoted to literary work. In 1734 he returned to Paris, assumed the habit of a secular priest, and was for a time almoner of the Prince of Conti, then established himself near Chantilly, where he passed his time in almost constant literary composition. The earliest of his novels, Mémoires d'un Homme de Qualité, appeared in 1728, his famous novel *Manon Lescaut* being included in the seventh volume of this work, to which it is in some sort an appendix. Other fictions by him were: Cléveland (1731–'38); Le Doyen de Killerine (1735–'40); and Histoire d'une Grecque Moderne (1741). He left about two hundred works, but only *Manon Lescaut* survives. This has been the theme of drama and opera, of countless paintings and statues, and, despite its small amount of literary art, it holds its place by reason of its entire truth and dramatic effectiveness. When Richardson's Pamela appeared in 1740, Prévost immediately recognized its literary importance, and two years later his French version of it was published in London. He translated Richardson's Clarissa Harlowe in 1751, and in 1753 began the translation of the English novelist's Charles Grandison. While waiting for Richardson's completion of the last-named tale, he founded with Rousseau the Journal Étranger, the purpose of which was to diffuse in France a better knowledge of English and German literature. On this he labored as editor as well as translator, much to the advantage of Richardson's work. His Richardsonian tasks were indeed labors of love, for he perceived in his contemporary's writing a completer expression of what he had himself endeavored to portray. His life was written by Harisse (1896).

Pushkin, Alexander Sergéivitch (Moscow, Russia, 1799; 1837). Although Pushkin was a noble by birth, there was a strain of African blood in him from a maternal ancestor. His education, according to the custom of his time and rank, was wholly in French, such knowledge of his native country as he gained during early childhood being derived from nursery tales and songs. When he was twelve years old he entered the Imperial Lyceum at Tsarskoe-Selo, where he soon attracted attention by contemptuous neglect of his required studies, and the display of traits that afterward made trouble and fame for him. The boy was obnoxiously opinionated, but his epigrammatic way of expressing himself extorted admiration from even those who were stung by his taunts, and there was further ground for tolerating him in his pronounced gift for poetic diction. One of his poems, published when he was only fifteen, was received with serious approbation, not merely as the effusion of a promising child, but as a finished work of art, and in the following year, 1815, another poem, Recollections of Tsarskoe-Selo, made his name known to all literary Russia. By the time he was graduated, in 1817, he was a recognized figure in Russian literature, and he was elected to membership in the Arzamas, a society that included all the successful writers of the period. A diplomatic career was open to Pushkin, for he was appointed to a clerkship in the Ministry for Foreign Affairs, but he was no less opinionated as a young man than he had been as a boy, and he was rather more free and forceful in expressing his opinions. As his political opinions were especially objectionable and, from the bureaucratic point of view, dangerous, it was necessary to discipline him, and he was sent to Southern Russia in connection with a governmental colonization scheme. His experience there was of incalculable value to his literary career, for he saw life in Bessarabia, the Caucasus, the Crimea, and Odessa, thus gaining incidents and color for his novels and poems. As his opinions underwent no noticeable reformation, he was further exiled, in 1824, to his mother's estate in a remote corner of Russia, where he remained two years. Literary production proceeded apace during this period, and his fame grew with every successive book. Eventually he was permitted to return to the capital, and in 1831 he was re-attached to the Foreign Office for the purpose of writing a history of Peter the Great. Two years later the Government paid him 20,000 rubles for his History of the Pugatcheff Insurrection. Meantime he had married, and in 1837 gossip concerning his wife's relations with d'Anthes, adopted son of the Dutch Ambassador, led to a duel in which Pushkin was killed. His works include: Ruslan and Lyndmila (1820); The Prisoner of the Caucasus; The Fountain of Bakhtchisarai; Eugene Onegin (Yevgen Onyegin, his greatest poem, upon which he worked for nine years, published in 1831); The Gypsies; The Brother of Murderers; Boris Godunoff; Poltava (1829); *The Captain's Daughter* (1836); and Dubrovski (1841).

Quiller-Couch, Arthur Thomas (Cornwall, England, Nov. 21, 1863). His early school-days were passed at Newton Abbott College and Clifton College. Eventually he matriculated at Trinity College, Oxford, and after graduation was appointed lecturer in classics there. He terminated his connection with the University in 1887 and removed to London to take up active literary work. In conjunction with several other writers he founded The Speaker, a weekly periodical devoted largely to literary matters, and he retained an editorial connection with the publication until 1899, although he removed his residence to his native Cornwall in 1891. His life there has been uneventful, but abounding in activity of various kinds. Literary production has gone on at a wholesome rate, his sign-manual, "Q," having come to be indissolubly associated with Cornwall scenes, Cornwall color, and Cornwall character; but he has taken his full share in public affairs, both serious and recreative. In the former sphere he has been appointed to the Magistracy, being a justice of the peace for Fowey, and he is also vice-chairman of the Cornwall Education Committee. His interest in sport centers largely in yachting. He is a member of two clubs and is rear commodore of that at Fowey.

Mr. Quiller-Couch was singularly distinguished in 1897 when he was commissioned to finish the late Robert Louis Stevenson's uncompleted novel, St. Ives. His published works are: Dead Man's Rock (1887); Troy Town (1888); *The Splendid Spur* (1889); Noughts and Crosses (1891); The Blue Pavilions (1891); I Saw Three Ships (1892); The Warwickshire Avon (1892); The Delectable Duchy (1893); Green Bays, verses and parodies (1893); Wandering Heath (1895); The Golden Pomp (1895); Ia (1896); Adventures in Criticism, essays (1896); Poems and Ballads (1896); The Ship of Stars (1899); Old Fires and Profitable Ghosts (1900); The Laird's Luck (1901); The Westcotes (1902); The White Wolf (1902); The Adventures of Harry Revel (1903); Hetty Wesley (1903); Two Sides of the Face (1903); Fort Amity (1904); Shining Ferry (1905); Shakespeare's Christmas (1905); From a Cornish Window (1906); Sir John Constantine (1906); Poison Island (1907); Merry Garden (1907); and Major Vigoureux (1907).

   Radcliffe, Ann (London, England, July 9, 1764; Feb. 7, 1823). Her father's name was Ward. When she was twenty-three years old she married William Radcliffe, then a law-student, who later became editor and proprietor of the English Chronicle. Mrs. Radcliffe's literary productivity covered but a few years, during which she was extremely active. Her success was immediate and very great. She gave vogue to the style of romance founded by Horace Walpole, in which, before the conclusion of the narrative, the reader's wonder is stirred by mysteries eventually explained by natural causes. Her publishers paid her £500 for *The Mysteries of Udolpho*, and £800 for The Italian. These were unprecedented returns for novel-writing at that time, and were not surpassed until the Waverley novels appeared. Nearly all her works were translated into French and Italian. She lived in retirement after 1797, a fact that gave rise to a widely credited rumor that she had become insane from dwelling on the horrors in *Udolpho*. The rumor was an ingenuous tribute to the power of her imagination, but it was apparently far from the facts, for there is no record to show that she was other than well until her final illness. Her works are: The Castles of Athlin and Dunbayne (1789); A

Sicilian Romance (1790); *The Romance of the Forest* (1791); *The Mysteries of Udolpho* (1794); The Italian: or, The Confessional of the Black Penitents (1797); A Journey through Holland and Germany (1795); and Gaston de Blondeville, a historical romance (1826).

Raimund, Golo, pen-name of Bertha Frederich (Hanover, Germany, 1825; 1882). She had a remarkable aversion to personal publicity. Her husband was Eduard Frederich, editor of the Hannoverscher Courier, in which her first works appeared as serials. She adopted the pseudonym Golo Raimund, and, when her novels became popular, she strove further to conceal her identity by an elaborate scheme according to which they were ascribed to a fictitious personage known and "written up" as Georg Dannenberg. Little else is known of her except that she was industrious. Altogether twenty-two novels by her were published. Several went into numerous editions, and some have been translated. The most successful were: *A New Race;* Bauernlehen; Zwei Bräute; Schloss Elkrath; Von Hand Zu Hand; Mein ist die Rache; Zwei Menschenalter; and Ein Deutsches.

Reade, Charles (Ipsden, England, June 8, 1814; April 11, 1884). He was connected intimately for many years with Magdalen College, Oxford, where he took his baccalaureate degree and became a Fellow in 1835. In 1838 he took the Master's degree, was elected Vinerian reader in law in 1842, dean of arts in 1845, and vice-president in 1851. Meantime, in 1842, he had been called to the bar at Lincoln's Inn, and had begun his career as a dramatic author. To the end of his life Reade chose to regard himself as a dramatist rather than as a novelist. The list of his plays, written in collaboration with Tom Taylor, Dion Boucicault, and others, and independently, is long. The most successful was Drink, a dramatization of Zola's L'Assommoir, and another, which was often used by Sir Henry Irving, was The Lyons Mail. He dramatized some of his own novels, and *vice versa*, turned some of his plays into fiction. It was not until he was nearly forty years old that he began novel-writing, and he declared that he did so only after fifteen years of special study of the art. Thereafter he turned out novels quite as abundantly as dramas. Reade never married. His industrious life appears to have been sufficiently varied by the quarrels in which he was constantly embroiled with critics, publishers, and theatrical managers. Somebody was forever invading or neglecting his rights, and he was happiest when fighting to maintain them. There were occasions even when he openly assailed the bench on account of decisions rendered against him. His novels are: *Peg Woffington* (1852); *Christie Johnstone* (1853); *It is Never too Late to Mend* (1856); The Course of True Love Never did Run Smooth (1857); Jack of All Trades (1858); The Autobiography of a Thief (1858); *Love Me Little, Love Me Long* (1859); *White Lies* (1860); *The Cloister and the Hearth* (1861); The Eighth Commandment (1860); *Hard Cash* (1863); *Griffith Gaunt* (1866); *Foul Play* (1869); *Put Yourself in His Place* (1870); *A Terrible Temptation* (1871); *A Simpleton* (1873); *A Woman-Hater* (1877); A Perilous Secret (1883); The Jilt, and Other Tales (1884); and Good Stories of Man and Other Animals (1884).

Reid, Christian, pen-name of Mrs. Frances Fisher Tiernan. She was born in North Carolina, and still resides there. Her novels, which were popular from the first, include: Valerie Aylmer; Mabel Lee; *Morton House;* A Daughter of Bohemia; Miss Churchill; Bonny Kate; Ebb Tide; Nina's Atonement; After Many Days; Hearts of Steel; Hearts and Hands; A Question of Honor; A Summer Idyl; A Gentle Belle; Roslyn's Fortune; A Comedy of Elopement; The Picture of Las Cruces; The Land of the Sun; A Woman of Fortune; and Chase of an Heiress.

Reuter, Fritz (Stavenhagen, Mecklenburg-Schwerin, Nov. 7, 1810; Eisenach, June 12, 1874). He wrote novels, short stories, and poems, the most widely known of which is *In the Year '13*, and attained a high literary reputation. Most of his work is in the Platt-Deutsch dialect.

Richardson, Samuel (Derbyshire, England, 1689; July 4, 1761). His education was limited to elementary schools, from which he was taken at the age of sixteen when he was apprenticed to John Wilde, printer, of London. At the end of his apprenticeship he became his master's foreman, and in 1719 began business on his own account in Fleet Street, removing subsequently to Salisbury Court. When he was well established he married his former master's daughter. That his business was extensive may be inferred from the fact that he printed the Daily Journal, the Daily Gazetteer, the Briton, and the first twenty-six volumes of the Journal of the House of Commons. He did no writing of permanent importance until he had passed his fiftieth year, meantime doing considerable editorial work for other printers in the way of prefaces and dedications. Eventually certain booksellers asked him to write a volume of letters as patterns for young people. This proposal was made to Richardson undoubtedly because of his remarkable faculty for enlisting the confidences of women and his experience in writing letters for them. He was a bashful man, and yet, to the end of his days, he was a kind of father confessor to the women of his acquaintance. In his youth, as he has narrated in one of his introductions, he used to be besought by young men and women to write their love-letters for them, and often he found himself under the necessity of composing a reply to the very letter he had written a few days previously. Richardson regarded the suggestion of the booksellers favorably; but, while he was thinking it over, a story grew up in his mind, and presently he astonished the world by the publication of *Pamela*. The model letters never were written, for the success of the novel led to other work of the same kind. During the last years of his life he held literary court at his residence in Hammersmith, whither needy authors resorted for assistance, which he cheerfully accorded, and admiring women went in droves to hear him read the freshest pages from the novel then in composition. He became a master of the Stationers' Company in 1754, and in 1760 bought a half-interest in the patent of the King's printer. His novels are: *Pamela* (1740); *The History of Clarissa Harlowe* (1748); and *The History of Sir Charles Grandison* (1754).

Richter, Jean Paul Friedrich (Wunsiedel, Germany, 1763; Bayreuth, Nov. 14, 1825). The early death of his father, and, shortly afterward, of his grandparents, left his mother penniless, but she contrived to keep him in the gymnasium at Hof until 1781, when he went to Leipzig to study theology. Having fallen under the influence of Rousseau and the English satirists, he abandoned all ideas of theology and turned his attention to pedagogy, concerning which he had original views.   Finding no opening as a teacher, he tried literature with equally discouraging results, for his first book, Lob der Dummheit, found no publisher until after his death, and his second, Grönländische Progresse, a series of satires on authors (1783), fell flat; and in 1784 he had to run away from Leipzig to escape importunate creditors.   Three years of wandering followed, during which he eked out a bare living as a literary hack.   Then he fell in with people who took his educational ideas seriously, and for nine years he had paying pupils. In that period he wrote and published several books, including satires that established him as a humorist, and the novel, Hesperus, which won for him the ardent friendship of Charlotte von Kalb.   She introduced him to Goethe, Schiller, and others, and, although these leaders received him coldly, he became a favorite figure in Weimar society.   In 1801 he married Caroline Mayer and settled in Bayreuth, where, except for frequent journeys, he spent the rest of his life.   He was noted there for harmless eccentricity, and, although he suffered greatly from failing health and interrupted his writing by much traveling, he completed two novels and several important works on art, politics, and pedagogy. His novels are: Die Unsichtbare Loge (1793); Hesperus (1794); *Titan* (1803); and Flegeljahre (1805).   The Germans call him "Jean Paul the only one!"

Ritchie, Leitch (Greenock, Scotland, 1800; London, Jan. 16, 1865). He resisted early inclinations to literature, which were greatly stimulated by a visit to London, and became a clerk in a bank in his native town, later becoming a merchant's clerk in Glasgow.   At last the call of books became too strong for him and he settled in London, where he applied himself to literary work with the utmost industry.   He wrote thirty original books, and compiled and edited more than fifty others; he founded The Wanderer and the Englishman's Magazine, was editor of The Era and Indian News and associate editor of the London Weekly Review, and was editorially connected with the Westminster, the Quarterly, Chambers' Journal, and other similar publications; and he contributed voluminously to all manner of periodicals. Fiction constituted comparatively a small portion of his writings, many of which were devoted to history and travel. His stories include: Head Pieces and Tail Pieces; Tales and Confessions; *Schinderhannes, the Robber of the Rhine* (1848); The Game of Life (1851); The Magician (1853); Wearyfoot Common (1854); and The New Shilling (1858).

Rives, Amélie (Princess Troubetzkoy) (Richmond, Va., Aug. 23, 1863). Her grandfather, William C. Rives, attained distinction in the diplomatic service. A great part of her childhood was passed in Paris, where her education was conducted by private tutors. Her literary début was made under romantic circumstances; for with one short story, published anonymously, she made an impression that established her as a writer. This was A Brother to Dragons, which appeared in the Atlantic Monthly early in 1888. Three or four other stories from her pen appeared in the magazines in the same year. Then came her marriage to John Armstrong Chanler, followed shortly by the publication of her famous novel, *The Quick or the Dead?* She wrote industriously for several years after this—novels, short stories, and miscellaneous articles. In 1895 she was divorced from Mr. Chanler in South Dakota, on the ground of incompatibility of temperament, and in the following year she married Prince Pierre Troubetskoy, who had considerable repute in Europe as an artist. Since then she has divided her time about equally between her home in Albemarle County, Virginia, and the Prince's estate on Lake Maggiore, Italy. Her novels include: *The Quick or the Dead?* (1888); Barbara Dering (1892); Athelwold (1893); Tanis, the Sang-Digger (1893); Seléné (1905); and Augustine, the Man (1906).

Roberts, Charles George Douglas (Douglas, New Brunswick, Jan. 10, 1860). He was educated in the Fredericton

Collegiate School and the University of New Brunswick. His first employment after graduation was school-teaching, after which he became editor of Goldwin Smith's paper, The Week, at Toronto, which place he held during 1883 and 1884, and resigned to become professor of English and French literature in King's College, Nova Scotia. In 1887 he was appointed professor of economics and international law. Meantime his poems attracted favorable attention, not only in Canada, but in the United States, and his general literary work increased from year to year until 1895, when he resigned his professorship in order to give his time wholly to literature. He went to New York, where he was for a time associate editor of the Illustrated American. Mr. Roberts has published several volumes of verse, as well as books dealing with the history of Canada. His fiction includes: The Raid from Beauséjour (1894); Reuben Dare's Shad Boat (1895); Around the Camp-Fire (1896); The Forge in the Forest (1897); *A Sister to Evangeline* (1898); By the Marshes of Minas (1900); The Kindred of the Wild (1902); Barbara Ladd (1902); The Watchers of the Trails (1904); The Prisoner of Mademoiselle (1905); Red Fox (1905); The Calore Girl (1906); and Haunters of the Silences (1907).

Roche, Regina Maria (England, 1765; 1845). She spent nearly her whole life in seclusion at Waterford, Ireland, where she did her literary work. Her novels are: The Vicar of Lansdowne (1793); The Maid of the Hamlet (1793); *The Children of the Abbey* (1798); The Nocturnal Visit (1800); The Discarded Son (1806); The Houses of Osma and Almeria (1810); The Monastery of St. Colombe (1812); Treothick Bower (1813); London Tales (1814); The Munster Cottage-Boy (1819); The Bridal of Dunamore; Chapel Castle; Contrast; The Nun's Picture; and Traditions of the Castle.

Rousseau, Jean Jacques (Geneva, June 28, 1712; Ermenonville, near Paris, July 2, 1778). The first in the long series of misfortunes that befell this singular man was the death of his mother when he was but a few days old. Many of his subsequent tribulations may properly enough be charged to his own faults, which were glaring to the degree of inexcusability;

but his Confessions record the conviction that his mother's death was his chief calamity, and that he suffered the bitterest remorse for his worst errors. As a child he was sickly, visionary, ultra-sensitive, and had no pronounced taste except for fiction. His father wished him to become a lawyer, and, after some years in ordinary, elementary schools, a place was obtained for him in the office of an attorney, who speedily dismissed him as hopelessly incompetent and irresponsible. Then he was apprenticed to an engraver, who treated him so harshly that he ran away within a year. Rousseau was then sixteen years old, and from that time to the end of his days he was a wanderer. His people had been Protestants for generations, originally Huguenots who had fled to Geneva for religious liberty. Jean Jacques fled to Savoy, a Catholic province, and fell in with a proselytizing priest, who introduced him to Mme. de Warens. She arranged for his further education at a school where it was incumbent on him to profess Catholicism. This he did, and then ran away from school. Penniless, he became a lackey for a nobleman who took a serious interest in him, and for a time it seemed as if the lad might become steady and useful. The nobleman died, and Jean Jacques plunged into dissipation with wild companions. When he had come to the end of his slender resources and suffered sufficiently to feel remorse, he made his way back to Mme. de Warens, who undertook to have him educated for the priesthood. This experiment failed quickly, for the priest to whom he was entrusted could not tolerate his conduct. Then Mme. de Warens, despairing of any other means to subdue his waywardness, became his mistress. This relationship was maintained for several years, interrupted though it was by frequent short journeys on the part of Rousseau. Returning from one of these and finding the lady apparently as faithless as he had been, he left her in a rage and went to Lyons. His education in the interim had been so far advanced that he could presume to teach, and he obtained employment as a tutor. In 1841 he went to Paris to lay before the Academy a new system of musical notation which he had invented. Rousseau had distinct musical gifts, and he had made some study of the art; but evidently he knew less than he thought he did, for the Academy informed him that his invention was neither new nor useful. This failure was not without its bright side, however, for his essay brought him to the notice of many distinguished persons who interested themselves in him and undertook to help him. Thus he obtained the post of secretary to the French Ambassador at Venice, which he held for eighteen months, or until he could no longer endure the slights put upon him by his official superior and intellectual inferior. Returning to Paris in 1745, he became an associate of persons high in the literary world, and at the same time made a mistress of one Thérèse le Vasseur, a cook. She was ignorant and rather stupid, but faithful, and late in life he married her. Meantime she bore him five children, every one of whom, shortly after birth, he conveyed to the Foundling Hospital.

One after another he quarreled with all his friends. He became obsessed with the idea that there were cabals against him, and there is evidence that in some instances he was justified in his suspicions. Deprived of friendly support, he lived in distressing poverty accentuated by frequent failing health. During this period he composed an opera that never came to performance, compiled a musical dictionary, earned a pittance as secretary to a noble lady, and nearly broke down with the anxiety caused by his subsequent employment by her as cashier. Then he became suddenly very famous, for in 1750 he won the Academy prize for an essay on the question whether the progress of science and art contributed to corrupt or improve the morals of mankind. In this declaration he made war upon civilization, and thenceforth he assumed the pose of a reformer. In 1752 he produced a successful opera, Le Devin du Village, of which he wrote both words and music, and made many enemies by the publication of an article advocating Italian music in preference to French. An essay on the origin of inequality among men made a profound sensation in 1753 and increased the number of Rousseau's admirers. He renounced Catholicism and returned to Geneva, where he was cordially received. It was understood that he would resume his citizenship there and take a leading part in affairs, but Voltaire was in Geneva at that period, and Rousseau found that the community was hardly large enough to hold them both. After some further wandering he returned to Paris and found refuge in the Hermitage in the valley of Montmorency, offered to him as a residence by Mme. d'Épinay.

All this time he suffered much from real and imaginary enemies, and in the Hermitage he endured the prosaic tribulation of a mother-in-law's persecution. Largely on account of Thérèse's mother he had to abandon the Hermitage. He was next taken up by the Duke of Luxembourg, under whose patronage he wrote his famous work, Contrat Social. This was condemned by the French Parliament, which expelled him, and he fled to Switzerland only to find himself denied admission to Geneva and expelled from Bern. He found protection under Lord Keith at Neuchâtel, but, on Keith's departure, he had to resume his wandering. Venturing back to Paris he was received with abundant tokens of respect for his genius, but was not allowed to remain. At the suggestion of David Hume, the historian, he went to England; but a quarrel with Hume made his sojourn profitless there, and three years of miserable wandering followed. At last, in 1770, he appeared again in Paris and was permitted to stay. He lived there obscurely, but not in tranquillity, for calumnies were incessantly circulated against him, and he lost friend after friend. Early in 1778 M. de Girardin offered him refuge at Ermenonville, where Rousseau died. His novel, *The New Héloïse* (*Histoire de la Nouvelle Héloïse*), was published in 1760.

Rowson, Susanna (Portsmouth, England, 1761; Boston, Mass., March 2, 1824). She was the daughter of William Haswell, a lieutenant in the Royal Navy, and when she was eight years old she accompanied him on a voyage to America. Their ship was wrecked on Lovell's Island, Massachusetts coast, and they settled in Nantucket; but Lieut. Haswell returned to England on the outbreak of the Revolutionary War. Miss Haswell married William Rowson in London, 1786, and went with him to America in 1793. He became a bankrupt, and she went upon the stage as a means of livelihood. For three years she played in Philadelphia, Baltimore, New York, and Boston, and then taught school in Boston, Medford, and Newton, Mass. Her literary work covered a wide field, including farces and comedies in which she played the leading parts, operas, poems, educational essays, and text-books. Her novels were: Victoria (1786); Mary: or, The Test of Honor; The Inquisitor (1788); *Charlotte Temple* (1790); Lucy Temple: or, The Three Orphans; Rebecca: or, The Fille-de-Chambre; The Trials of the Human Heart (1795); Reuben and Rachel (1798); Sarah: or, The Exemplary Wife: or, Sincerity (1802).

Ruffini, Giovanni Domenico (Genoa, Italy, 1807; England, 1881). Despite his Italian origin, Ruffini ranks as an English writer, all his novels having been written in that language. He was an ardent follower of Mazzini in the movement for Italian unification and freedom from foreign domination. That movement failing, and Mazzini banished, Ruffini, in 1833, fled to England, where he remained until 1842, when he went to France. After the revolutionary movement of 1848 he returned to his native land and plunged into politics. He was elected to the Sardinian Parliament, Genoa at that time being a part of the Kingdom of Sardinia, and in 1849 he was appointed Sardinia's diplomatic representative at Paris. He had not been long at this post when the battle of Novara gave Austria complete supremacy over Sardinia. It appears that Ruffini then finally abandoned hope of a political career, for he returned to England and devoted the rest of his life to literary work, which included novels and an autobiography. His novels were: *Doctor Antonio* (1855); Dear Experience (1858); Lavinia (1860); and Vincenzo (1863).

Russell, William Clark (New York, Feb. 24, 1844). His parents were English, and they returned to their own country during his infancy. He was educated at a private school in Winchester and by tutors at Boulogne-sur-mer. When he was thirteen he entered the British merchant service, and he continued in it until he was twenty-one. At that age he left the sea and devoted his life to writing about it. Besides his novels he has written many short stories and biographies of Nelson and Collingwood. He is married and has two sons and three daughters. His novels are: John Holdsworth, Chief Mate (1874); *The Wreck of the Grosvenor* (1875); The Lady Maud

(1876); A Sailor's Sweetheart (1877); The Frozen Pirate (1877); An Ocean Free-Lance (1878); An Ocean Tragedy (1881); My Shipmate, Louise (1882); The Flying Dutchman (1888); The Emigrant Ship (1894); The Ship, Her Story (1894); The Convict Ship (1895); What Cheer! (1895); Rose Island (1896); The Tale of the Ten (1896); List, ye Landsmen! (1897); The Last Entry (1897); The Two Captains (1897); The Romance of a Midshipman (1898); The Ship's Adventure (1899); Overdue (1903); Abandoned (1904); Wrong Side Out (1904); His Island Princess; and The Yarn of Old Harbor Town (1905).

Sadlier, Mrs. James (Cootehill, Ireland, 1820; 1903). Her maiden name was Mary Ann Madden, under which some of her early works appeared. In 1846 she married James Sadlier, a publisher, in Canada. She is usually ranked as a Canadian writer, much of her fiction being derived from the experiences of Irish immigrants in the Dominion. Besides original fiction she wrote dramas and devotional works, and made several translations. Her novels are: The Red Wand of Ulster; Willy Burke; Alice Riordan (1858); The Orphan of Moscow; The Castle of Rousillon; Benjamin: or, The Pupil of the Christian Brothers; *Bessie Conway;* The Confederate Chieftains (1860); Maureen Dhu (1870); and The Old House by the Boyne (1888).

Saintine, Xavier (Joseph François Boniface) (Paris, July 10, 1798; Jan. 21, 1865). In his youth Boniface gave abundant promise of great attainments in literature, for he won several academical prizes for poetry, and he wrote with the utmost assiduity; but most of his creations, though temporarily successful, proved to have no permanent value. His novel, *Picciola*, which won the Montyon prize of 3,000 francs in 1837, is the only one of his works that has survived. This went through thirty-seven editions during the author's lifetime. He wrote more than a hundred plays under the pseudonym Xavier. Several of his stories were translated. One, The Myths of the Rhine, published in London in 1874, was illustrated by Gustave Doré. Another, Seul, had the extraordinary fate of being published in Boston, Mass. (1845), under the title, The Solitary of Juan Fernandez: or, The Real Robinson Crusoe.

Sand, George (Aurore Dupin, Baronne Dudevant) (Paris, France, July 5, 1804; Nohant, France, June 7, 1876). She was a granddaughter of a natural daughter of Maréchal de Saxe and M. Dupin de Françeuil. Her father was a soldier, of brilliant social and literary gifts; her mother, a Parisian modiste, whose marriage to the young aristocrat, M. Dupin, was not regarded favorably by Mme. Dupin. She was born, she says, "à cheval," between two classes, and to her mingled blood and the divided family sentiment she owed the always warring element of her spirit. Imagination dominated her from infancy; her first doubt of the existence of Santa Claus was an epoch in her intellectual life. A religious crisis, at fifteen, led her to renounce the fortune of her paternal grandmother, and whatever else marked the chasm between her mother—the child of the people—and her father's world. She was placed in the English convent in Paris, where, by her brilliant and daring characterizations of the sisters and her companions, she obtained the nickname of La Diable. After two years she suddenly was seized with an attack of remorse, and, falling on her knees before a picture of St. Augustine, shed burning tears of penitence. This fervor soon passed, but its influence remained. After leaving the convent she resolved to educate herself, and devoured poetry, philosophy, and romance, not omitting religion, which she took from either Jesus Christ or Spinoza. She fed her young mind on Leibnitz, Shakespeare, Byron, and, above all, Rousseau. The result was a moral and intellectual confusion and a melancholy state in which she often resolved to end her life. She once forced her mare, Colette, into the river, but Colette preferred to live, and bounded to the bank. She married Baron Dudevant in 1822, left him, taking her two children, in 1831, and was legally separated from him in 1836. She had attracted attention by her novels, and from that time she wrote systematically —twelve pages a day—and unremittingly, producing an enormous number of novels, reviews, tales, plays, and letters. She collaborated with Jules Sandeau in 1831, and their book appeared under the pen-names, Jules et George Sand. Thenceforward she was Mme. Sand. Her literary life is usually divided into four periods: 1832-'40, the first, in which her novels were marked by a love of poetry and nature; 1840-'48, the second, in which she endeavored to develop a system, and became artificial, although some of her finest work, notably *Consuelo*, was done during this period; 1848-'60, the third, during which, influenced by the Revolution, her productions were largely political and humanitarian; 1860-'76, her last years, but those in which the return to her early romantic manner was most noticeable. The sources of her inspiration were chiefly love, humanity, and nature. Her vivid imagination and acute observation provided her with ample material. Idealization she regarded as the first law of romantic literary creation. Her style was always chaste and elevated, and was the faithful servant of her thought. In 1839 she selected Nohant for her place of residence. There she exercised an unbounded hospitality, continued her literary work, largely for her grandchildren, and there she died. Her numerous works include: *Indiana* (1832); Valentine (1832); Lélia (1833); Letters of a Traveler (Lettres d'un Voyageur (1834); Jacques; *Mauprat; Consuelo;* The Countess of Rudolstadt; Lucresia Floriani; François, the Bastard (François, le Champi); The Devil's Pool (La Mare au Diable); The Little Fadette (La Petite Fadette); The Fine Gentlemen of Bois Doré (Les Beaux Messieurs de Bois Doré): The Marquis of Villemer; The History of my Life (L'Histoire de ma Vie); She and He (Elle et Lui); and Letters to Flaubert.

Sandeau, Léonard Sylvain Jules (Aubusson, France, 1811; Paris, 1883). Like many another French writer, Sandeau aimed at a legal career and, after studying law in Paris, became a journalist. His first literary work of importance was Rose et Blanche, written in collaboration with George Sand. There was nothing sensational in his success, but his reputation grew steadily. In 1853 he was appointed keeper of the Mazarin Library, and in 1858 he was elected to the Academy. Dramatized versions of some of his stories became permanent features of the French stage, and he had a share in preparing them for theatrical representation. His most important novels were: *Madeleine;* Mlle. de la Seiglière (1848); La Maison de Penarvon (1858); and Sacs et Parchemins (1851).

Savage, Marmion W. (Ireland, 1823; 1872). He was for several years editor of the London Examiner, but during most of his career he was a government official stationed at Dublin. His name appears as editor of several legal works. His novels are: *The Bachelor of the Albany;* My Uncle, the Curate; Reuben Medlicott (1852); The Falcon Family (1854); and The Woman of Business (1870).

Schreiner, Olive (Basutoland, South Africa, 1862). She is the daughter of G. S. Schreiner, a Lutheran minister, who was sent by the London Missionary Society to South Africa. She married the Hon. S. C. Cronwright in 1894 and now lives in Hanover, Cape Colony. In 1889 she told the story of her life as follows: "My father was a German, born in Würtemberg. He studied at Basel and went to South Africa as a missionary. My mother is English, the daughter of a Presbyterian minister, and for generations my ancestors have been strict Puritans. I was born in the heart of South Africa, on a solitary mission station. I was many years old before I saw a town. My father died many years ago. My mother has become a Roman Catholic and is living in a convent in South Africa. I came to England for the first time seven years ago and then published *The Story of an African Farm,* which I had written in Africa. The first English edition was published in 1883. I have made stories ever since I could remember; long before I could write I used to scribble on sheets of paper, imagining that I was writing them. I began the story just mentioned when I was hardly more than a child, but left it for some years before I finished it." Her most important work, *The Story of an African Farm,* was published under the pen-name of Ralph Iron. This was followed by: Dreams (1891); Dream Life and Real Life (1893); Trooper Peter Halket of Mashonaland (1897); and An English South African View of the Situation, in which she sympathizes with the Boers (1899). With her husband she wrote The Political Situation (1895).

Schücking, Christoph Bernhard Levin (Clemenswerth, near Münster, Germany, 1814; Pyrmont, Germany, 1883). He received a good education and studied law, which he abandoned for literature. While in charge of the education of the young princes of Wrede in 1842, he met Luise de Gall, whom he married in 1843. He went to Augsburg to edit the Allgemeine Zeitung, and later removed to Cologne, where in 1852 he was on the staff of the Gazette de Cologne. After traveling in England and Italy, he retired to his estate, Sassenberg, near Warendorf and Münster, where he devoted himself to novel-writing. As a rule, his fiction was based on history. His works include: Ein Schloss am Meer (1843); Die Sphinx (1856); Die Geschworenen und ihr Richter (1861); Verschlungene Wege (1867); Feuer und Flamme (1874, English translation, New York, 1876); *Paul Bronckhorst* (1876); Das Recht des Lebenden (1880); and Grosse Menschen (1884). A collection of his works was published in twelve volumes Leipzig (1862); and a second series, also in twelve volumes (1874–'76). His Novels (6 vols.), also appeared in Hanover in 1856–'66. His wife (1815–1855) wrote several novels and collaborated with him in Familien-Bilder and Familien-Geschichten.

Schultz, Amélie Cécile Augustine Jeanne (Paris, 1870). Her father, an officer in the artillery and an inventor, was librarian at the École Polytechnique in Paris. On his death, his daughter turned to her pen for support. The best known of her books are: The Story of Colette (Neuvaine de Colette), which, appearing anonymously in the Revue de Deux Mondes in 1889, attracted attention, and La Famille Hamelin (1891), which was crowned by the Académie Française. Her other books include: Cinq minutes d'arrêt (1889); Les Fiançailles de Gabrielle (1889); Jean de Kerdren (1890); Tout droit (1890); Le Dernier Tour de l'Enchanteur Merlin (1892); Ce qu'elles peuvent (1894); Les Rameaux de François (1895); Entrée dans la monde (1895); Notes de Tunis (1895); Chasse aux alouettes (1895); Petite plage et Bonnets de coton (1896); Entrevue (1897); and La Main de Sainte Modestine (1898).

Scott, Michael (Glasgow, Oct. 30, 1789; Nov. 7, 1835). He studied at the University of Glasgow, became a planter in Jamaica, and then returned to Scotland, where he entered into business and spent the remainder of his life. His novel entitled *Tom Cringle's Log* was published first in Blackwood's Magazine 1829–'33. Subsequently he published in the same magazine The Cruise of the Midge, 1834–'35. Both stories appeared anonymously, and the name of the author was not known until after his death. Their first appearance in book form was in Paris (1836). These books were greatly admired and highly praised by Coleridge, John Wilson, and other noted authors and critics. A writer in the London Literary Journal, twenty years afterward, said: "Two books which we never fail to peruse every year are *Tom Cringle's Log* and The Cruise of the Midge, in which humor and pathos, the most gorgeous descriptions and the most thrilling narrative, so marvelously intermingle."

Scott, Walter (Edinburgh, Scotland, Aug. 15, 1771; Abbotsford, Sept. 21, 1832). The details of his infancy, his lameness, his genius in childhood, his studious and adventurous boyhood, his incomplete education, his adoption of the profession of advocate, may be found in every biography. Scott knew all ranks of society before he published a line. Duchesses, gipsies, thieves, Highlanders, Lowlanders, students, judges, attorneys' clerks, actors, gamekeepers, farmers, tramps—he was at home with all, and he had read everything in literature that most people do not know. It was his fortune to be a poet while England had two kings: George III *de facto*, Charles III and Henry IX *de jure*. Hopeless though the Jacobite cause was, the sentiment lingered; and Scott knew the man who sent the Fiery Cross through Appin in 1745—Invernahyle. A portrait of Prince Charles was one of his earliest purchases. He had seen Burns's birthday ode for a royal Stuart. Yet his youth was contemporary with the French Revolution, which only made him more of a Tory. His infancy dwelt with sad excitement on the British disasters in the American War of Independence. From all this rich experience of men and women, of the European "Twilight of the Gods," of clashing of societies and politics, of war and literature, came the peculiar and original play of his genius. This was ripened probably by a love affair that ended when he was twenty-five—ended as far as hope was concerned, otherwise it closed only with his earthly life. We find its traces in his novels and poems and Journal; it even peeps out in his review of Miss Austen's novels. From living tradition—on the authority of a lady who, having seen her once, loved her to her own death in extreme age—we are able to say that Scott's lost love was "an angel rather than a woman."

As a poet Scott is decidedly out of fashion among our modern *précieux* and *précieuses*, though there is a desirable and probably durable part of his poetry in "the memories he stirs," memories awakened in the minds of his countrymen by the magical names of beloved rivers, lochs, and hills, which he uses as well as Homer employs the more sonorous titles of Greek cities, hills, and streams in his catalogue of the ships. Thus it is that Scott's poetry charms his own folk most, Borderers and Highlanders, carrying them back to legend-haunted burns and ruined towers, where their own ancestors loved and fought and died for their ladies and their kings.

But when we turn to his fiction, and his other prose works, we must admit that Scott was a maker of modern literature as it is to-day. He has very little to say about "problems" of human destiny—problems not to be solved by sword-stroke or lance-thrust. Not that he did not think of them, but because he held that the less said of them the better. There are writers enough to say deep things about questions that nobody can answer; plenty to dwell on the mysterious destinies of mankind. Scott was happier when riding a flooded ford, with the answer to our questionings very near him. In fact, he was born to be a fighting man, and, thwarted by destiny, he was at his best in narrating feats of war, of

> "Old, unhappy, far-off things,
> And battles long ago,"

before lance and sword gave place to rifles and Long Toms.

Scott caused novels to become fashionable. When he published *Waverley*, in 1814, it was said by a friend of his—Mr. Morritt of Rokeby—that only ladies' maids and milliners read novels. In our age, it may almost be said that nobody reads anything extensively but novels. One British publisher, a witness in a recent trial, said that he publishes two novels every week in the year. It is true that other kinds of books are published, but their readers are few in comparison with the readers of stories.

This condition of affairs began with Scott. From 1830 to 1840 a Parliamentary Commission was held on the publishing trade. Eminent publishers gave evidence that it had been usual for men to "form libraries," to buy solid books as they come out. But, they said, since 1814 libraries were no longer formed. This was at the time of the appearance of *Waverley*. Thenceforth, while Scott lived, his novels were bought, two or three novels a year. Everybody read them; the footmen and the maids perused them stealthily by night; everybody talked of them, and poetry, which had been buoyant on a rising market, sank in the scale with histories and other works of learning, except Scott's own Life of Napoleon and Tales of a Grandfather.

Novels, except Miss Edgeworth's, had been despised of men, but Scott opened the sluices for the flood of fiction, which has now swept the sluices themselves into the sea. He himself said: "I have taught many gentlemen to write almost, or altogether, as well as myself," and his imitators were popular. At one stroke he created the historical novel, while all the kail-yard and dialect novels of rustic humor are the children of his rural characters. Dumas and Mérimée and Cooper are also of his offspring. The gate once opened, the novel of fashion, with Bulwer-Lytton's Pelham (which Scott enjoyed); the novel of cockney humor, with Dickens; novels of religious controversy, long forgotten; the satirical novel, with Thackeray; and in fact every sort of novel poured out.

But Scott did more than this: he founded the school of picturesque history, which had a very good run under Michelet, Carlyle, and Froude, though we have no longer historians like these. It was Scott who made the dry old bones of history live and march, who clothed them in flesh and in chain-mail, or in plates of steel, in velvet, silk, and cloth-of-gold; who raised the moth-eaten standard of chivalry, revived their armorial bearings, and replaced the pennoncels on the lances.

His historical portraits, as of James VI, Louis XI, Cromwell, Queen Mary, and Charles II, with a hundred others, reminded the world that the great characters of the past were not mere names, but human beings with passions, humors, and foibles. His erudition was enormous, though it was rather multifarious, as became a romantic historian, than exact. He taught picturesque historians to write as well as he—or even better, so far as style goes. He somewhere blames the historians who have "a boring way of trying to see farther into a millstone than the nature of the millstone permits." That is the way of the modern historian, who does not try to interest and amuse, but to find out what actually happened. The public, like Scott, finds this method "boring," and lightly turns to a novel. The novelist knows exactly what happened. Scott taught us not only that the people of the past were very much alive, but that we must not judge them from our modern pinnacle of knowledge, morality, and religious indifference. Our ancestors had the morals and religion of their time, and Scott took them as they were, and were obliged to be. He is so fair to the party naturally antipathetic to him—Puritans and Covenanters—that he sometimes becomes unfair to his own more picturesque faction, the Royalists. His view of the Catholic Church (though in private he was a sturdy Protestant) is almost always fair and kindly.

It is certain—and it was always perfectly plain to himself and to his other critics—that Scott was a careless writer. He "never learned grammar," he told his son-in-law; moreover, he never knew whither his imagination would carry him. If he invented a plot, some favorite character arose into life within his brain, and rode away with the plot, as Dugald Dalgetty turned *A Legend of Montrose* into the adventures of Dugald Dalgetty.

Readers complain of Scott's want of passion, yet of passion in its purest and strongest phase no man had known more. But if his passion was potent, more potent was his character. He does not deal in embraces, and such descriptions of physical charms and raptures as fill the lines of Burns and Carew and Paulus Silentiarius. "I may not, must not sing of love," says his minstrel; but whoever has read *Rob Roy*, and lost his heart to Diana Vernon, ought to understand. Scott, in Carlyle's phrase, "consumed his own smoke"; which Carlyle never did. In 1797 Scott married Miss Carpenter or Charpentier, to whom he was the fondest and most faithful of husbands. Hogg calls her "a perfect beauty"; small, dark, and piquante, and "a sweet, kind, affectionate creature." Mrs. Scott had humor and high spirits, as one or two of her letters show.

In 1802 appeared his Border Minstrelsy, printed at Kelm by his school friend, James Ballantyne. This was the beginning of a fatal connection. Scott became secretly a printer and publisher; but he had neither the leisure nor the balance for a man of business. He became entangled in the system of fictitious credit; and when a commercial crash came in 1825-'26 he was financially ruined. The poet in him had been acquiring treasures of things old, books and curios; and for these he built Abbotsford, an expensive villa on a bad site, but near the Tweed. He had purchased the land at exorbitant rates, mainly for antiquarian and poetical reasons of association, partly from the old Scottish territorial sentiment. He had kept open house, and had given money with royal munificence. So Sir Walter was ruined; and he killed himself by writing incessantly in the effort to earn enough to pay his creditors. He succeeded, but did not live to see his success. Of his sons and daughters only one left offspring—Sophia, wife of John Gibson Lockhart. Of their children, only one, the wife of Mr. Hope (later Hope-Scott), left issue—Mr. Maxwell Scott, from whom descend a flourishing family.

Scott was not a scientific psychologist, luckily; he did not try, "in a boring way, to see farther into the millstone of personality than the nature of the millstone permits." With passion in the wrong place he had scant sympathy: it is the business of an honorable man, like Ivanhoe, betrothed to Rowena, not to desert her and run away with Rebecca. Scott was much too chivalrous to pry into the *penetralia* of a woman's heart; he could not create a Lady Castlewood, or a Beatrix Esmond, or a Mary Stuart like the Queen in Mr. Hewlett's novel, *The Queen's Quair*. His bad people err on the ruffianly side, not the libidinous. Let us judge him gently; he was not born about 1880; he had the limitations of an age that knew not even railways, much less motors and gramophones. Even in his own day, he was not, as the popular phrase is, "up to date," but he was up to many other dates, from the late Byzantine

Empire, in *Count Robert of Paris*, through the Middle Ages, down to the period of his own youth, and the threatened Napoleonic invasion, described in *The Antiquary*. But in a novel of the period of his own maturity (*St. Ronan's Well*) we see that he "has not found a length." Unlike Jane Austen, he is not quite at home with contemporary society, though he knew it, from the king to the thief. No doubt his great contemporary, whom he admired so much, Miss Austen, wears better, with many readers, than Sir Walter, and may be enjoyed by persons to whom Sir Walter is caviare. Yet in Sir Walter we have an immortal friend, a companion most humorous, chivalrous, kind, and inspiring. For us, time and custom cannot spoil or stale his infinite charm, his undying beneficence.

Seawell, Molly Elliot (Gloucester County, Va., Oct. 23, 1860). She is the daughter of John Tyler Seawell, a nephew of President Tyler. On the death of her father she moved to Washington, D. C. Her story of Little Jarvis took the prize of $500 offered by the Youth's Companion, and her Sprightly Romance of Marsac received the $3,000 prize offered by the New York Herald. Little Jarvis was published in book form in 1890, and The Sprightly Romance of Marsac in 1896. The latter was also dramatized and performed. Miss Seawell's other books are: Midshipman Paulding (1891); Maid Marian (1894), also dramatized; Decatur and Somers (1894); A Strange, Sad Comedy (1895); A Virginia Cavalier (1896); The Rock of the Lion (1897); Gavin Hamilton (1899); The House of Egremont (1901); *Papa Bouchard* (1901); Francezka (1902); Children of Destiny (1903); Fifi (1903); The Château of Monplaisir (1905); The Victory (1906); and The Secret of Tony (1907).

Serao, Matilde (Patras, Greece, 1856). Her father was a political emigrant, and her mother a Greek. She went to Naples and became a schoolmistress; wrote for the Neapolitan papers; and joined the staff of the Capitan Francassa. She married Edoardo Scarfoglio, and founded with him the short-lived Corriere di Roma. Returning to Naples she and her husband established and edited the Corriere di Napoli, and later Il Mattino; and after her separation from him she founded and edited a rival paper, Il Giorno. Her books deal with contemporary Italian life and treat of psychological problems. In spirit as well as in title her Ventre di Napoli (1885) follows Zola's Ventre de Paris. Henry James has characterized her style as follows: "She is a daughter of the veritable South, and a product of the contemporary newspapers, and in some degree doubtless also by inclination she strikes for us, from the first, the note of facility and spontaneity and the note of imitation and practise. Loud, loquacious, abundant, natural, happy, with luxurious insistences on the handsome, the costly, and the flashy, the fine persons and fine clothes of her characters, their satin and velvet, their bracelets, rings, white waistcoats, general appointments, and bedroom furniture. With almost as many repetitions and as free a tongue, in short, as Juliet's nurse, she reflects at every turn the wonderful mixture that surrounds her—the beauty, the misery, the history, the light and noise and dust, the prolonged paganism and the renewed reactions, the great style of the distant and the past, and the generally compromised state of the immediate and the near."

Signora Serao's works include: Cuore Inferno (1881); Leggende Napolitane (1881); Fior di Passione (1883); Piccole anime (1883); La Virtu di Checchina (1884); *La Conquista di Roma* (*The Conquest of Rome*, 1885); and, between 1890 and 1900: Il Paese di Cuccagna (The Land of Cockayne); Addio Amore; All' Erta Sentinella; Castigo; La Ballerina; and Suor Giovanna della Croce. Her Al Paese di Gesù follows the neo-mystic school of Fogazzaro.

Sharp, William (Garthland Place, near Paisley, Scotland, 1856; Sicily, 1905). He was educated at the University of Glasgow, traveled in Australia, settled in London, and married a relative, who was also an author and editor. Mr. Sharp belonged to the Rossetti circle, and wrote a sympathetic study of Dante Rossetti in 1883. He also wrote biographies of Shelley (1887), Heine (1888), and Browning (1889). He was extremely versatile, and achieved distinction as an editor and author, poet and critic. He also wrote under the name of Fiona Macleod.

whose identity he kept secret.   An editor through whose hands a great deal of Fiona Macleod's writings passed, and who was in constant correspondence with the supposed lady, published in the Academy, soon after Mr. Sharp's death, the following: "My correspondent was authorized by Mrs. Sharp to divulge the secret, known previously only within a very small circle, that William Sharp was the writer of every word that proceeded from the pen of 'Miss Fiona Macleod.'   The circumstance will pass into literary history as one of the strangest incidents recorded.   It is perfectly natural to draw a comparison between this case and that of Macpherson and his Ossian; but the comparison would be misleading.   Macpherson invented Ossian for the purpose of passing off certain of his own works as those of the ancient Gaelic bard.   What William Sharp did was quite different.   He was one of those few people who seem to have inherited a dual personality; and he was able to keep its parts entirely separate.   It was as if a man and a woman were joined together in one person." William Sharp's novels, stories, and romances include: Silence Farm (1889); Children of To-morrow (1890); Joseph Severn (1892); *Pharais* (1884); Madge o' the Pool, and A Fellowe and His Wife (with Blanche Willis Howard); In the Gates of the South, and A London Romance (1904).   Wives in Exile, a Comedy in Romance, was published in 1898.   Among his essays are: Ecce Puella, and Other Prose Imaginings (1895); and Studies in Art (1901).   His published poems are: The Human Inheritance: Transcripts from Nature, and Other Poems (1882); Earth's Voices (1884); Romantic Ballads and Poems of Phantasy (1886); Sospiri di Roma (1891); Flower o' the Vine (1894); Vistas, poetic dramas (1894); Lyrical Poems (1901); and Sospiri d'Italia (1904).

Shaw, George Bernard (Dublin, Ireland, July 26, 1856). He settled in London in 1876, devoted himself to journalism, and took an active part in politics.   He also achieved reputation as a platform speaker and political pamphleteer.   His weekly articles on musical subjects, contributed to the London Star (1888–'90), the World (1890–'94), and the Saturday Review (1895–'98), attracted attention, and in 1898 his Perfect **Wagnerite** was published, in which he endeavored to show that the Niebelungen Ring according to Wagner is a kind of glorified socialism. As member of the Fabian Society for the advancement of socialism (the most important society of its kind in London) Mr. Shaw has published many pamphlets and books, including: Fabian's Essays (1889); Fabianism and the Empire (1900); and Fabianism and the Fiscal Question (1900). Between 1880 and 1883 he published four novels: *The Irrational Knot;* Love Among the Artists; *Cashel Byron's Profession;* and The Unsocial Socialist. These were followed by: Plays Pleasant and Unpleasant (2 vols., 1898), consisting of You Never Can Tell; Arms and the Man; Candida; The Man of Destiny; Widower's Houses; The Philanderer; and Mrs. Warren's Profession. His next plays were: The Devil's Disciple; Cæsar and Cleopatra; Captain Brassbound's Conversion; The Admirable Bashville (1901); Man and Super Man (1903); How She Lied to Her Husband (1904); and John Bull's Other Island (1905). His essays on The Quintessence of Ibsenism were published in 1891, and in 1906 Dramatic Opinions and Essays, a reprint of articles contributed by him to the Saturday Review in 1894-'98. These, he says, were "a siege laid to the theater of the nineteenth century by an author who had to cut his way into it at the point of the pen and throw some of its defenders into the moat." Some of Shaw's admirers consider him a social reformer; others, merely a clever jester.

Shelley, Mary Wollstonecraft (London, Aug. 30, 1797; Feb. 1, 1851). She was the daughter of William Godwin and Mary Wollstonecraft. The latter died soon after her birth, and the child was somewhat of a problem to her father, who described her at the age of fifteen as "singularly bold, somewhat imperious and active of mind. Her desire of knowledge is great, and her perseverance in everything she undertakes invincible." In 1812 she met Shelley, the poet, and accompanied him to the Continent. The story of this trip is told in The History of a Six Weeks' Tour, written and published in 1817, and republished with a commentary by Charles Isaac Elton (London, 1894). On the death of his first wife, in 1816, Shelley immediately married Mary Godwin in London. Her history thenceforward was absorbed in that of her brilliant husband. They were seldom apart, and her devotion to him was extreme. A crushing blow was the death of their son, William, in 1819. After Shelley's death in 1822, she returned to London with her three-year-old son, Percy; but she indignantly refused Sir Timothy Shelley's offer to provide for him on condition that she should relinquish her charge of him. At last Sir Timothy relented and settled an annuity upon his grandson. In 1840–'41 Mrs. Shelley and her son traveled in Germany, and in 1842–'43 in Italy. Her fame rests chiefly upon her novel, *Frankenstein* (1818), which was performed as a drama in Paris, and her edition of Shelley's works. She also published Valperga (1823); The Last Man (1826), the story of the destruction of the human race by pestilence, Shelley appearing in its pages as Adrian; Perkin Warbeck, a historical novel (1830); Lodore, a veiled autobiography (1835); and Falkner (1837). Her Rambles in Germany and Italy (2 vols., 1844) were dedicated to her friend, Samuel Rogers. A biography of Mrs. Shelley was written by Mrs. Julian Marshall in 1889. Dr. Richard Garnett writes:

"Nothing but an absolute magnetising of her brain by Shelley can account for her having risen so far above her usual self as in *Frankenstein*. The phenomenon might have been repeated but for the crushing blow of the death of her boy, William, in 1819. From this time the keynote of her existence was melancholy. Her father's pecuniary troubles, and the tone he chose to take with reference to them, also preyed upon her spirits, insomuch that Shelley was obliged at last to intercept his letters. With all this she was happier than she knew, and after Shelley's death she exclaims, with tragic conviction: 'Alas! having lived day by day with one of the wisest, best, and most affectionate of spirits, how void, bare, and drear is the scene of life!' Mary Shelley was a hard student during her husband's lifetime. She read incessantly, without any neglect of domestic duties, acquiring some knowledge of Greek, and mastering Latin, French, and Italian. Of the two romances which she produced during this period, *Frankenstein* is deservedly by far the most famous. Frankenstein's monster, though physically an abortion, is intellectually the ancestor of a nu-

merous family.   The story, which was begun in 1816 in rivalry
with Byron's fragmentary Vampyre, was published in 1818.
Valperga, an historical romance of the fourteenth century, begun in 1820, was printed in the spring of 1822 and published
in 1823, after undergoing considerable revision from Godwin."

Sheppard, Elizabeth Sara (Blackheath, England, 1830;
Brixton, England, 1862).   She was the daughter of an English
clergyman, and on her mother's side was of Jewish blood.
After her father's death, her mother opened a school, in which
the daughter taught music.   She was an accomplished linguist,
knowing Greek, Latin, Hebrew, French, and German.   At the
age of sixteen she began her novel *Charles Auchester*, and sent
the manuscript to Benjamin Disraeli, who said of it: "No
greater book will ever be written upon music, and it will one
day be recognized as the imaginative classic of that divine art."
It was published in 1853.   The character of Seraphael is
supposed to be Mendelssohn.   Miss Sheppard veiled her identity under the name E. Berger.   She also wrote: Counterparts:
or, The Cross of Love (1854); My First Season, by Beatrice
Reynolds (1855); The Double Coronet (1856); Rumour (1858);
and Almost a Heroine (1859).   Round the Fire, a collection
of tales for children, is attributed to her; and she also published
poems.

Shorthouse, Joseph Henry (Birmingham, England, Sept. 9,
1834; London, March 4, 1903).   He was the eldest son of
Joseph Shorthouse, a chemical manufacturer, and was educated at Grove House, Tottenham, where he was a diligent
scholar.   He, however, entered his father's business house and
did not write until he was nearly fifty years of age.   Mr. Shorthouse wrote several books of great charm, but he will probably
always be known as the author of *John Inglesant*, which he kept
for three years in manuscript, and then printed only a hundred
copies for private circulation.   One of these on its appearance in 1881 fell into the hands of Mrs. Humphry Ward, who
recommended it to a publishing house.   It attracted Gladstone's attention, and his praise contributed no little toward
making its fame.   The author was originally a Quaker, but he

entered the Church of England just before *John Inglesant* appeared. A critic has said: "Something of his own stress of religious transition appears in the character of the hero, who is pictured as living in the time of the Civil War, a pupil of the Jesuits, a philosopher, and a Platonist, who is yet true to the National cause. The story, which is deeply mystical and imaginative, has for its central idea the dangers of bigotry and superstition and the necessity of intuitive religion to progress and culture." His other novels and stories are: The Little Schoolmaster Mark: A Spiritual Romance (1885); Sir Perceval (1886); A Teacher of the Violin, and Other Tales (1888); The Countess Eve (1888); and Blanche, Lady Falaise (1891). He also wrote The Platonism of Wordsworth (1881).

Sienkiewicz, Henryk (Wola Okrzejska, Government of Siedlce, Poland, 1846). He prides himself on being born of Lithuanian parents. After receiving an education at the University of Warsaw, he led a wandering life, and joined a community that had been established in California in 1878, the outgrowth of a club of Cracow. This was a settlement including among its members artists, writers, musicians, and actors, among whom were Helena Modjeska and her husband, Count Bogenta Chlaponski. This settlement in the Santa Aña valley proved disastrous, and Sienkiewicz wrote his impressions of California in a series of letters, published in the Polish Gazette of Warsaw under the signature of Litwos. His first book was a humorous story, entitled Nobody is a Prophet in His Own Country (1872); and among his early efforts was a drama, On the Cards, describing party struggles in Galicia. He traveled in Africa; and on returning to Warsaw he became editor-in-chief of a periodical called Slowo (The Word), in which he published a serial from 1880 to 1888, describing the adventures of a group of half savage, half-chivalrous noblemen of the seventeenth century. The great romance was finally completed in thirteen massive volumes. In 1880 he published Pisma, three volumes of village tales in something of the manner of Auerbach and Björnson. Some of his early stories are. Janko the Musician; Nature and Life; and The Old Servant: Shattered, a novel of student life in Kiev, was published before

1881.   Since 1884 Sienkiewicz has enjoyed an almost extravagant reputation in Poland, where he is an idol with the people,
who on his twenty-fifth anniversary as an author presented
him with an estate of three hundred acres and a house in
Russian Poland.   There was also a gala performance at the
theater in Warsaw of a comedy called Pan Zagloba as a Matchmaker.   His novels include: The Tatar Bondage (1880);
With Fire and Sword, and its sequels, The Deluge and Pan
Michael (1886-'88); Without Dogma (1890); The Children
of the Soil (1894); *Quo Vadis* (1895); and Knights of the Cross
(1896).   The latter is written in the old Polish tongue, and
introduces many historical characters.   The novels of the trilogy With Fire and Sword, The Deluge, and Pan Michael are
constructed on a colossal scale and describe the revolts and
struggles of Cossacks, Ukraine Tatars, and Turks against the
Polish Commonwealth, and the submerging of Poland and
Lithuania by the armies of Sweden in 1655.   Of this author,
Edmund Gosse writes:

"It is certainly the great constellation of romances of
seventeenth century history which lifts Sienkiewicz out of the
category of ordinary writers of meritorious fiction.   It is these
fierce, vast panoramas of war which give him for the present
his claim on our attention.   They are in the highest degree
remarkable, and it is much to be desired that he should return
from spheres where others hold more authority than he to this
one province where he reigns supreme.   His three romances
form a cycle of genuine grandeur.   In them he has contrived
to create a huge army of hurrying desperate men, driven over
the monotonous world by storms of vague, homicidal frenzy.
It is not finely and minutely painted.   It is not Tolstoi or
Meissonier; it is rather the work of a gigantic scene-painter
filled with enthusiasm for his work, and standing on a ladder
twelve feet high to paint a hero in a cloud of blood.   It is all
grandiose and magnificent, yet preserved, by an undertone of
poignant melancholy, and by a constantly supported distinction
of sentiment, from the merely melodramatic and tawdry."

Simms, William Gilmore (Charleston, S. C., 1806; 1870).
At an early age he began to write verses and wrote a poem

celebrating the feats of the American army and navy in the War of 1812. His Early Lays and his Lyrical and Other Poems were published in 1827, while he was working with a druggist in Charleston. He was admitted to the bar at the age of twenty-two. In 1828 he became editor of The City Gazette; but his paper, opposing nullification, failed, and he settled in Hingham, Mass., where he wrote Atalantis: a Story of the Sea (1833), which is generally considered his best poem. He also wrote in the same year Martin Faber, the story of a criminal. He returned to South Carolina, became a member of the Legislature, and owned a beautiful plantation, Woodlands, near Midway, S. C., which was looted by Union soldiers during the Civil War. He supported the Southern cause in a weekly newspaper during this period. Edgar Allan Poe called him the best American novelist after Cooper. Mr. Simms was a prolific writer. He wrote histories, biographies, poems, dramas, and historical and romantic novels, the scenes of many of which are laid in South Carolina. The latter include: The Book of My Lady (1833); Guy Rivers (1834); The Partisan (1835); *The Yemassee* (1835); Pelayo (1838); Carl Werner (1838); Richard Hurdis (1838); Border Beagles (1840); The Scout (1841); The Kinsman: or, The Black Riders of the Congaree (1841); Confession: or, The Blind Heart (1842); Beachampe (1842); Helen Halsey (1845); Castle Dismal (1845); The Wigwam and the Cabin (two series, 1845 and 1846); Count Julian (1845); The Damsel of Darien (1845); The Lily and the Totem: or, The Huguenots in Florida (1845); Katherine Walton (1851); Mellichampe (1851); The Golden Christmas (1852); Marie de Bernière (1853); The Maroon and Other Tales (1855); The Foragers (1855); Eutaw (1856); Charlemont (1856); Vasconcelos (1857); and Classique of Kiawah (1860). Among his other works are a History of South Carolina; South Carolina in the Revolution; Civil War in the South; American Loyalists of the Revolution; Morals of Slavery; and biographies of General Marion, General Greene, Captain John Smith, and Chevalier Bayard.

Sinclair, May (Rock Ferry, Cheshire, England, about 1860). She was educated at the Ladies' College, Cheltenham. Of herself she says: "I have lived a very quiet life in the country until the last nine years. I can think best in the country, and work best in town; the former, strange as it may seem, offers too many distractions. I have never been out of England, except for an occasional short visit to Ireland. I began to write novels when I settled in London, nine years ago. Before that I wrote nothing but verse and philosophic criticism. My first published prose article came out in an American review, The New World, in December, 1903, on the Ethical Import of Idealism. I began to write when I was nine years old, but strongly suppressed all my *juvenilia*. My first volume of verse, Hakiketas, and Other Poems (1887), was followed by Essays in Verse (1890). Sonnets and verses appeared in various magazines between 1893 and 1895. My first novel, Audrey Craven, published in 1897, was followed by Mr. and Mrs. Nevill Tyson (1898); Two Sides of a Question (1901); and *The Divine Fire* (1904). A few short stories appeared in Macmillan's, Blackwood's, and Temple Bar." To this list must be added The Judgment of Eve (1906) and The Helpmeet (1907).

Smith, Francis Hopkinson (Baltimore, Md., Oct. 23, 1838). He is an engineer by profession and has built many public works, including the Race-Rock Lighthouse in New London harbor, the Block Island breakwater, the Government seawall around Governor's Island, and the foundation for the Statue of Liberty on Bedloe's Island. He is also a popular lecturer. Mr. Smith has achieved distinction as an artist, especially in water colors and charcoal work. As an author his reputation was established by *Colonel Carter of Cartersville* (1891). His other books include: A White Umbrella in Mexico (1889); A Gentleman Vagabond and Some Others (1895); Tom Grogan (1896); Gondola Days (1897); Venice of To-day (1897); Caleb West (1898); The Other Fellow (1899); The Fortunes of Oliver Horn (1902); The Under Dog (1903); Col. Carter's Christmas (1904); At Close Range (1905); The Wood Fire in No. 3 (1905); The Tides of Barnegat (1906); The Veiled Lady (1907); The Romance of an Old-Fashioned Gentleman (1907); and Peter (1908).

Smollett, Tobias George (Cardross, Dumbartonshire, Scotland, March 19, 1721; Leghorn, Italy, Sept. 17, 1771). His family was of much local importance, and his grandfather, Sir James Smollett, of Bonhill, was a judge and member of the Scots Parliament. Smollett was born on the family estate, the old grange of Dumbarton, and lost his father while young, but was well educated. He wished to enter the army, but his grandfather had procured a commission for his elder brother, and it is said by Sir Walter Scott and other biographers that Smollett revenged himself by describing Sir James in the unamiable character of the old judge in *Roderick Random*. However, he was sent to the University of Glasgow, studied medicine, and was apprenticed to Dr. John Gordon. At an early age he showed his talent for satire and wrote a tragedy called *The Regicide*, which he took to London, hoping, by means of it, to open the road to a literary career. He failed, and was glad to accept the post of surgeon's mate on the Cumberland in Sir Chaloner Ogle's squadron, which joined Admiral Vernon's fleet in the West Indies. While in Jamaica, Smollett fell in love with the daughter of an English planter, Nancy Lascelles, whom he married in England in 1747. In 1750 he got a medical diploma from Aberdeen, and he struggled with the double professions of medicine and literature for several years, chiefly in London. First he tried his hand at pamphlets and shilling satires, such as Advice and Reproof, and wrote the poem Tears of Scotland and a Burlesque Ode on the Loss of a Grandmother. In 1748 he published his novel, *Roderick Random*, which was received enthusiastically. This placed its author nearly in the ranks with Richardson, whose Pamela had appeared in 1741, and Fielding, whose Joseph Andrews had come out in 1742. Indeed, as there was no name on the title-page, the book was even attributed by many to Fielding himself; but in the preface the author distinctly admitted having followed the 'picaresque' method of Lesage. *The Adventures of Peregrine Pickle* appeared in 1751 with immense success, and, like the former story, consisted of a series of loosely connected adventures. Smollett shone in coffee-house society, and was a brilliant member of the brilliant group of wits of that period. After a brief sojourn in Bath as a struggling physician, he returned to London and established himself in an Elizabethan mansion in Chelsea, known as Lawrence House, where Johnson, Goldsmith, Garrick, Wilkie, and John Hunter were frequent guests. Every Sunday he entertained here "unfortunate brothers of the quill," whom he treated with "beef, pudding, and potatoes, port, punch, and Calvert's entire butt beer." Smollett's third novel, *Ferdinand, Count Fathom* (1753), was not only admired, but was frequently imitated. His next work was a translation of Don Quixote (1755), and then he edited a Tory journal, called The Critical Review, which involved him in quarrels and three months' imprisonment on account of an article attacking Admiral Knowles. In 1758 he published his History of England in four volumes quarto, which procured for him the sum of £2,000. In 1760-'61 another novel appeared, *The Adventures of Sir Launcelot Greaves;* and in 1763-'65 he visited France and Italy, where he encountered Sterne, who put the querulous traveler into his *Sentimental Journey* under the name of Smelfungus. Returning to London, Smollett published his Travels in France and Italy (1766), and in 1769 issued a satire on English politics, called The Adventures of an Atom, by Nathaniel Peacock. In failing health, he went, accompanied by his devoted wife, to Italy, where a few months before his death he completed *The Expedition of Humphry Clinker*, which is considered his best novel; and in Thackeray's opinion one of the best in the whole range of imaginative literature. The famous portrait by Verelst, painted in 1756, represents Smollett in "full dress, a stone-colored full-mounted coat with hanging sleeves, a green satin waistcoat trimmed with gold lace, a tye wig, long ruffles and sword, agreeably to the costume of the London physician of his time." Rowlandson, Cruikshank, and Phiz have illustrated his works. Smollett also wrote a farce of sea-life, entitled The Reprisal: or, The Tars of England, which was produced at Drury Lane, Jan. 22, 1757.

"Beneath a very surly exterior," an English critic writes, "there was in **Smollett** a vein of rugged generosity and romantic feeling. His dominant mood is well expressed in his Ode to Independence, published shortly after his death. He was essentially a difficult man, hugging his nationality, a 'proud, retiring, independent fellow,' far more disposed to cultivate the acquaintance of those he could serve than of those who could serve him. He was, as his physician says, '*un uomo di talento svegliato sofferente gli acciacchi della vita umana, ma quasi misantropo.*' He had a marked dislike for modish society. He hated ceremony of any kind, and characteristically compared Roman Catholicism to comedy and Calvinism to tragedy. Of English writers who have any pretension to a place in the first rank, few, if any, are so consistently pagan. The religious point of view never occurred to him. He was no metaphysician like Fielding, and the last word of his philosophy, as expressed in a letter to Garrick, was that the world was a sort of debtor's prison in which 'we are all playthings of fortune.' As a stylist he carried on the robust traditions of Swift and DeFoe."

Souvestre, Émile (Morlaix, France, 1806; Paris, 1854). He was the son of an engineer, studied law, and went to Paris about 1830. He began to write for the stage, and his Siège de Missolonghi was accepted by the Comédie-Française; but he refused to make the required cuts and it was not given. After a few years spent in teaching, editing a journal in Brest called Le Finistère, and in various occupations, he returned to Paris in 1835 and gave himself up to writing novels and plays. He also became professor of style administratif at the École d'administration in 1848, and some of his lectures there were gathered into a book called Causeries historiques et littéraires (1854). His Breton novels gave him much notoriety. In 1854 the Académie Française crowned his book, Un philosophe sous les toits (The Attic Philosopher), published in 1850. "Having retired to the extreme end of a faubourg of the capital," says M. Charton, "in a fourth floor, with a view overlooking several gardens, he worked for eighteen years without relaxation, writing every line with the most scrupulous care and conscientiousness. A tendency to a moral teaching is the most marked characteristic of his romances and novels. Invention and originality are sometimes at fault; but the philosophical intention is never lacking and is accompanied by a simplicity which is natural ornament, and gracious sentiments which render that philosophy delightful."

His works include: Derniers Bretons (1835-'37); L'Echellè des Femmes (1835); Riche et Pauvre (1836); Maison rouge; (1837); Anges du foyer (1838); Mendiant de Saint-Roch (1838); Pasteur d'Hommes (1838); Péronick l'idiot (1838); L'Homme et l'Argent (1839); Pierre sainte de la bruyère (1840); Mémoires d'un sans-culotte bas breton (1841); Pierre et Jean (1842); La Goutte d'Eau (1842); Mât de cocagne (1842); Valise noire (1843); Pierre Landais (1843); Le foyer breton (1844); Réprouves et les élus (1845); Le Monde tel qu'il sera (1846); Un philosophe sous les toits (1850); *Confessions d'un ouvrier (Confessions of a Workingman,* 1851); Au coin du feu (1851); Sous la tonnelle (1852); Sous les filets (1852); Sous les ombrages (1852); Au bord du lac (1852); Pendant la moisson (1852); Dans la prairie (1852); Les Clairières (1852); Scènes de la chouannerie (1852); Récits et souvenirs (1853); Chroniques de la mer (1853); Contes du foyer (1853); Les drames parisiens (1853); Contes et nouvelles (1854); Histoires d'autrefois (1854); and Souvenirs d'un viellard (1854). He also published descriptive books, among which was La Bretagne pittoresque. Trois femmes poëtes inconnues—biographical studies—were published after his death, in 1860. His wife also was a novelist.

Spielhagen, Friedrich Von (Magdeburg, Germany, Feb. 24, 1829). He is the son of an architect, who moved to Stralsund in 1835. Here he spent his early years and also lived in Leipzig, Hanover, and Berlin. He studied medicine, law, and philosophy at Berlin, Bonn, and Greifswald. For a time he taught in a gymnasium in Leipzig. About 1854 he began to write; but his first novels, Clara Ver (1857) and Auf der Düne (1858), attracted little attention. Die Problematischen Naturen (1860) proved a striking success. It reached its eighteenth edition in 1895. His Durch Nacht zum Licht (1861) classed Spielhagen among the best novelists of his country. His other works are: In der zwoelften Stunde (1862); Die Von Hohenstein (1863); In Reih und Glied (1866); Unter den Tannen (1867); Die Dorfkokette (1868); *Hammer und Amboss (Hammer and Anvil,* 1868); Deutsche Pioniere (1870); Was die Schwalbe Sang (1872); Allzeit voran (1872);

Ultimo (1873); Sturmfluth (1876); Platt Land (1878); Das
Skelett im Hause (1878); Quisisana (1880); Angela (1881);
Uhlenhaus (1884); An der Heilquelle (1885); Was will das
Werden (1886); Noblesse Oblige (1888); Ein neuer Pharao
(1889); Sonntagskind (1893); Susi (1895); and Opfer (1900).
An English critic says : "Spielhagen's novels combine two
elements of especial power—the masculine assertion of liberty,
which renders him the favorite of the intelligent and progressive
citizen, and the love of the sea derived from an early residence
at Stralsund, which introduces an element of poetry into his
otherwise rather matter-of-fact fiction and is especially conspicuous in Sturmfluth and Faustulus." H. Lauderbach
writes of Spielhagen as follows: "There is some dead wood
in the long list of his productions; but many works, on the other
hand, are distinguished not only for the elevation and sincerity
of their thought, but for their perfection of form and by a
penetrating sense of nature and life. His books will always
remain a luminous picture of Prussia during the second half
of the nineteenth century." In addition to his novels, Spielhagen has written: Faustulus (1897), a modern prose version
of the Gretchen episode in Faust; a book of travels, Von
Neapel bis Syrakus (1878); and several plays, including Liebe
für Liebe (1875), which was very successful; Hans und Grete
(1876); Gerettet (1884); Die Philosophin (1887); and In eiser-
ner Zeit (1891). Two volumes of Poetry (1892 and 1899) have
also appeared; and also Skizzen, Geschichten, und Gedichte
(1881), and Aus meiner Studienmappe (1891). Aus meinem
Skizzenbuch (1874) and Finder und Erfinder (1900) are reminiscences. Spielhagen's Contributions to the Theory and
Technique of the Novel (1883) and Contributions to the
Theory and Technique of Epic and Drama (1898) are valued
as critical essays.

Spofford, Harriet Prescott (Calais, Me., 1835). She is the
daughter of Joseph N. Prescott and was graduated at the
Putnam free school in Newburyport, Mass. In 1865 she married Richard S. Spofford, a Boston lawyer, and she now resides
in Newburyport. At an early age she contributed to the
Boston papers and magazines, and a story, entitled In a Cellar,

in the Atlantic Monthly in 1859, made her reputation. Her novels and stories include: Sir Rohan's Ghost (1859); The Amber Gods and Other Stories (1863); *Azarian* (1864); New England Legends (1871); *The Thief in the Night* (1872); The Marquis of Carabas (1882); Hester Stanley at St. Mark's (1883); The Children of the Valley (1901); The Great Procession (1902); Four Days of God (1905); and Old Washington (1906). She has also published Poems (1882); The Servant-Girl Question (1884); and Ballads about Authors (1888).

Steel, Flora Annie (Harrow, England, April 2, 1847). She is the second daughter of George Webster of Forfarshire, married a Bengal civilian in 1867, and lived in India from 1867 to 1889. She was Provincial Inspectress of Government India and aided schools in the Punjab. She was also a member of the Educational Committee. Her books, the greater number of which deal with Indian subjects, are: Wide-a-Wake Stories (1884); Miss Stuart's Legacy (1893); From the Five Rivers (1893); The Potter's Thumb (1894); Tales from the Punjab (1894); Flower of Forgiveness (1894); Red Rowans (1895); *On the Face of the Waters* (1896); In the Tideway (1896); In the Permanent Way (1897); Voices in the Night (1900); The Hosts of the Lord (1900); and In the Guardianship of God (1903). Mrs. Steel also published in 1887 a Complete Indian Cook and Housekeeper.

Stendhal, known better by this favorite pseudonym (among other fanciful pen-names) than by his real name of Henri Beyle (Grenoble, France, Jan. 23, 1783; Paris, March 23, 1842). His father was a lawyer, of morose and unpaternal disposition, who early disliked the boy Henri and left him to the care of his stepmother, Séraphie Gagnon, who was also his aunt, his father having married her after the death of her sister, his first wife. This lady Stendhal characterized as a waspish, hypocritical bigot, who compelled him to submit to an authority at once despotic and unreasonable. His other relations were hardly more sympathetic, and they misunderstood the youth's sensitive, ambitious, and ardent nature, so that he grew up feeling himself an isolated being, differing mysteri-

ously from the rest of mankind. He made rapid progress at
the chief school in Grenoble, and in 1799 he went to Paris, and
a little later became connected with the civil and military service in Italy, but followed other less serious pursuits prompted
by his adventurous and romantic disposition and his roving
tastes. In 1830 he received the appointment of French consul
at Civita Vecchia, the exequatur at Trieste having been denied
to him because of his openly avowed sympathy with Italy.
In 1814 he wrote, over the signature of Alexandre César
Bombet, letters from Vienna on Haydn, followed by a Life
of Mozart and by Considerations on Metastasio and the present
state of music in Italy, a later edition of which was published
in 1817, under the name of Stendhal. His other published
works are: A History of Painting in Italy (Histoire de la pein-
ture en Italie, 1817) ; Rome, Naples, and Florence (1817) ;
Promenades in Rome (1829) ; Romanticism in art (Del ro-
mantesmo nella arti, 1819), was written in Italian, for which
language, as well as for all else Italian, he had unbounded admiration. His most famous works are: Love (L'Amour, 1822) ;
Memoirs of a Traveler (1838) ; two romances, *The Red and
The Black* (*Le Rouge et le Noir*, 1831) and *The Chartreuse
of Parma* (1839), the latter a wonderful picture of court life
at Parma and abounding in descriptions of the author's own
adventurous experience as a youthful participant in the battle
of Waterloo and evidence of his intimate knowledge of high
ecclesiastical circles in Rome. Balzac and Sainte-Beuve have
praised this strangely misanthropic being, highly gifted, yet
regarding himself as isolated from the usual ties of love and
affection. His literary reputation has grown steadily since
his death, and he is now estimated as a writer of striking
originality and great power.

Stephens, Ann Sophia (Derby, Conn., 1813; Newport,
R. I., 1886). Her maiden name was Wintherbotham, and she
married Edward Stephens, a printer of Plymouth, Mass. Removing to Portland, Maine, she established the Portland Magazine in 1835 and edited The Portland Sketch-Book; but these
proved short-lived, and she removed to New York, where she
contributed to magazines. Her story Mary Derwent won a

prize of $400 and attracted attention. She edited several magazines and newspapers, and founded the Ladies' World (1843) and the Illustrated New Monthly (1846). Her poem entitled The Polish Boy became a favorite for recitations; and her novels were widely read. The most famous was *Fashion and Famine* (1854), which was translated into French. Her other novels include: Zana: or, The Heiress of Clare Hall, first published in London in 1854, and in New York as The Heiress of Greenhurst in 1857; Sybil Chase (1862); and Ahmo's Plot (1863). In 1854 she made a tour through Europe and the East. Mrs. Stephens wrote a Pictorial History of the War for the Union. A complete edition of her works appeared in 1869 and a new edition of twenty-three volumes in 1886.

Stepniak (child of the steppe), **Sergius** (Hadjatch, Tchernigov, Little Russia, 1852; Chiswick, England, 1895). His real name was Sergius Michaelvitch Kravchinski, and he was of good birth. He was educated at the University of Kiev, was for a time professor there, and was graduated at the St. Petersburg School of Artillery and entered the Forestry Institute. In 1872 he joined the Nihilist circle and began to spread revolutionary ideas among the factory people of St. Petersburg. In 1874 he was arrested, but he escaped and then began a more vehement battle against autocracy than ever, and waxed hot against the brutal methods adopted by the Russian Government against prisoners, and particularly political prisoners. He advocated what was called at one time the Terrorist policy, which aimed at attaining by violence, even by assassination, what could not be accomplished by peaceful methods. Fleeing to Italy, he engaged in conspiracies there, and took an active part in the publication of a paper, The Commune, in Geneva. He also smuggled a press and type into Russia for illegal publications. When the Revolutionists resolved on the death of General Mezentseff, chief of the police, Stepniak, chosen by lot, stabbed him on Aug. 16, 1878; and later he published Life for Life, in justification of the act. From 1879 till 1883 he lived in Switzerland, and then went to London, where he wrote and lectured and was regarded as an agitator who was sincere in his endeavors to effect a change in the attitude of the Russian Government toward reforms. He also lectured in the United States in 1891. Stepniak was killed by an engine at a railway grade crossing at Chiswick, near London. Before his cremation, funeral speeches were made at Waterloo Station by William Morris, John Burns, and Prince Kropotkin. In 1882 his Underground Russia appeared in Italy and in Italian under the name of Stepniak. This striking picture of the political condition of the Russian Empire and the Nihilists was followed by Russia under the Tsars (1885). His other books are: The Russian Storm-Cloud (1886); The Russian Peasantry (1888); *The Career of a Nihilist* (1889); Nihilism as it is (1894); and King Stork and King Log, a study of Modern Russia (1895).

Sterne, Laurence (Clonmel, Ireland, Nov. 24, 1713; London, March 18, 1768). He was the great-grandson of Richard Sterne, Archbishop of York, and his father, an officer in the British army, led a wandering life. At the age of ten this son was sent to school in Halifax, and on the death of his father was left "without a shilling in the world." A cousin, Richard Sterne, helped him go through Jesus College, Cambridge, where he received his B.A. in 1736 and his M.A. in 1740. Sterne was ordained a priest in 1738, and received the parish of Sutton in Yorkshire. In 1741 he married a Miss Lumley and through her influence was presented with the additional living of Stillington. For nearly twenty years he lived at Sutton unheard-of. Parochial duties were hateful to him, and he cared so little about his congregation and so much about sport that one Sunday, when he was walking to church and his dog sprang a covey of partridges, he went home for his gun. He was fond of skating, playing the bass viol, painting and books, and he and his wife often went to concerts and balls. Sterne also shone in coffee-house society. In 1759 appeared the two first volumes of *Tristram Shandy*, which, though published without his name, was known to be his. It had immediate success. Horace Walpole wrote that nothing else was talked of or admired; and when Sterne went to London he found himself a literary lion. For his sermons and a new edition of *Tristram Shandy*, Dodsley paid Sterne £480 and commissioned him to write a new volume every year. In 1760 he removed to Coxwold, in a large cottage, which he named Shandy Hall, and published two new volumes of his famous romance, which were illustrated by Hogarth. In 1762 he went to Paris and returned to England in 1765. For a brief time he resided at Bath, where Gainsborough painted his portrait at one sitting, and then returned to Coxwold. He traveled in France and Italy, and many of his experiences and adventures are described in *A Sentimental Journey* (1768). After being in failing health for many years, Sterne died in his London lodgings soon after his return home. Sir Joshua Reynolds painted him in his clerical gown. An excellent life of Sterne was published by Percy Fitzgerald in two volumes (London, 1864). Sterne, as a sermon-writer was described by a contemporary as "often tottering on the verge of laughter and ready to throw his periwig in the face of the audience." It is said that his wife aided him in their composition.

From an English critic we learn that: "The commonly accepted notion that Sterne drew his wife's portrait in Mrs. Shandy—both were named Elizabeth—has little to support it. Mrs. Sterne had none of Mrs. Shandy's placidity, taciturnity, or stupidity. She was of excitable and bristling temperament, and, while frugal in trifles, lacked capacity for orderly or economical housekeeping. But her husband was never blind to her intellectual ability. Even when smarting under her voluble rebukes and abusing her ill-humor to his friends, he admitted that, 'in point of understanding and finished address,' few of her sex rivaled her."

Sterne did not hesitate to lift whole paragraphs from the works of famous divines for his sermons, nor to borrow and adopt from other authors for his fiction. A great deal of *Tristram Shandy* was taken from Béroalde's Moyen de Parvenir (1599) and Bouchet's Serées (1608); his disquisition on noses was adopted from Bruscambille's Pensées Facetieuses; and he also laid Scarron's Roman Comique under contribution. His works show that he was also indebted to John Dunton's A Voyage Around the World. On this point Sidney Lee says: "But after all Sterne's thefts have been admitted, it is clear that his wealth alike of humor, sensibility, and dramatic instinct enabled him to steal material from all quarters without obscuring his individuality. His style was his own. At its best it is, in Hazlitt's words, 'the most rapid, the most happy, the most idiomatic of any that is to be found. It is the pure essence of English conversational style.' After full account," continues Mr. Lee, "has been taken of Sterne's numerous deflections from the paths of literary rectitude—of his indecency, his buffoonery, his mawkishness, his plagiarisms, his wanton digressiveness—he remains, as the author of *Tristram Shandy,* a delineator of the comedy of human life before whom only three or four humorous writers, in any tongue or of any age, can justly claim precedence. Uncle Toby, Corporal Trim, Dr. Slop, Mr. and Mrs. Shandy, Obadiah, and the Widow Wadman are of the kin—however the degrees of kinship may be estimated—of Pantagruel and Don Quixote, of Falstaff and Juliet's Nurse, of Monsieur Jourdain and Tartuffe. For the guerilla warfare that he incidentally waged in his own freakish fashion throughout the novel on the pedantries and pretenses of learning, he deserves many of the honors that have been paid to Pope and Swift. No modern writer has shown a more certain touch in transferring to his canvas commonplace domestic scenes which only a master's hand can invest with point or interest. It is this kind of power especially that glorifies *A Sentimental Journey.* Defects due to the author's overstrained sensibility practically count for nothing against the artistic and finished beauty of the series of vignettes which Sterne, by his sureness of insight and descriptive faculty, created in *A Sentimental Journey,* out of the simplest and most pedestrian episodes of travel."

Stevenson, Robert Louis (Edinburgh, Scotland, Nov. 13, 1850; Samoa, Dec. 3, 1894). His full name was Robert Louis Balfour Stevenson. For generations his ancestors had been engineers to the Board of Northern Lights, and, after some years of study in schools and under private tutors, Stevenson matriculated at the University of Edinburgh with the intention of adopting the family profession. In 1871 he abandoned the design of becoming an engineer, turned his attention to law, and was admitted to the bar in 1875. Meantime he had written several essays, short stories, and some verse. He became acquainted with several literary men in London, who encouraged him to give his whole attention to writing. Whether or not their advice was decisive, he never undertook to practise law. A canoe-trip in Belgium and France, and a pedestrian tour over other portions of the Continent, gave the material for his first books: An Inland Voyage (1878) and Travels with a Donkey (1879). Some of his best essays were written at this period and published in the Cornhill Magazine and Temple Bar. They attracted little attention at the time, and adequate recognition was not accorded them until some years after they had been collected and published in two volumes—Virginibus Puerisque (1881) and Familiar Studies of Men and Books. During his travels, in 1876, Stevenson met Mrs. Osbourne, an American woman then resident in an artistic colony near Paris. Three years later he heard that she was seriously ill in San Francisco and he decided to visit her. His funds were so low and his resources so slender that he crossed the Atlantic in the steerage, and the continent in an emigrant train. Among the results of this journey were two more books: Across the Plains (1892), and The Amateur Emigrant (1894). He lived in California two years, in which interval, 1880, he married Mrs. Osbourne.

Stevenson never was very robust physically, and by this time his health had become somewhat precarious. His ailment was consumption. Following his marriage was a period of four years during which he traveled almost incessantly in the hope of finding surroundings and climate adapted to his needs. Among other places he tried Davos, the Riviera, Bournemouth, and the Adirondacks. During all this time, as in later years when his illness became a fixed feature of his life and he suffered severely, he worked with the utmost industry and comported himself with a cheerfulness that endeared him to all acquaintances, even to those whose contact with him was only through his books, where his uncomplaining spirit was brightly reflected. In 1888 he undertook another search for health, this time to the South Seas, and found in Samoa the conditions that were best for him. He made his permanent home there and acquired considerable influence among the natives. To the end he continued to write, and when he died he left two unfinished novels. One, St. Ives, was completed by Quiller-Couch, but the other, Weir of Hermiston, was so indubitably Stevenson's masterpiece that no author has ventured to touch it. He was buried on the peak of Mt. Vaea, above Vailima, his Samoan home. Real success did not come to Stevenson until the publication of *Treasure Island*, in 1883, although his immensely popular New Arabian Nights appeared at an earlier date. A considerable portion of his work during the last years of his life was done in collaboration with his step-son, Lloyd Osbourne. His works include two volumes of poetry—Underwoods and A Child's Garden of Verses— and several volumes of essays. His novels are: *Treasure Island* (1883); The Silverado Squatters (1883); *Prince Otto* (1885); *The Strange Case of Doctor Jekyll and Mr. Hyde* (1886); *Kidnapped* (1886); *The Black Arrow* (1888); *The Master of Ballantrae* (1889); *David Balfour*, a sequel to *Kidnapped* (1893); *Weir of Hermiston* (1896); and *St. Ives* (1897).

Stimson, Frederic Jesup (Dedham, Mass., 1855). He was graduated at Harvard in 1876, and at the Harvard Law School in 1878, and was admitted to the bar of New York as well as that of Massachusetts. In 1884-'85 he was assistant attorney-general of Massachusetts; was general counsel to the United States Industrial Commission in 1898–1902; and he is now professor of comparative legislation in Harvard University. His early books were published under the pen-name of J. S. of Dale. His novels and stories include: Rollo's Journey to Cambridge (1879); Guerndale (1882); The Crime of Henry Vane (1884); The Sentimental Calendar (1886); First Harvests (1887); In the Three Zones (1892); Mrs. Knollys and Other Stories (1894); Private Gold (1896); *King Noanett* (1896); Jethro Bacon of Sandwich (1901); and In Cure of her Soul (1906). He has also written books on legal subjects, among which are: American Statute Law (1886); Stimson's Law Glossary (1890); Government by Injunction (1894); Labor in its Relation to Law (1894); Handbook to the Labor Law of the United States (1895); Uniform State Legislation (1896) and The Law of the Constitution: State and Federal (1907).

Stockton, Francis Richard (Philadelphia, April 5, 1834; Washington, D. C., April 20, 1902). He was the son of a Methodist minister, Thomas Hewlings Stockton, was graduated at the Central High School in Philadelphia, and became an engraver, draughtsman, and finally a journalist. He was engaged on the Post in Philadelphia and then joined the staff of Hearth and Home in New York, and later that of Scribner's Monthly. His fantastic tales for children, published in the Riverside Magazine, were issued in book form as The Ting-a-Ling Stories; and, when St. Nicholas was established, he became assistant editor. In this magazine many attractive short stories and serials appeared which were afterward published in book form. Among them are: Roundabout Rambles (1872); What Might Have Been Expected (1874); Tales Out of School (1875); A Jolly Fellowship (1880); The Floating Prince (1881); The Story of Viteau (1881); and The Bee Man of Orm and Other Fanciful Tales (1887). Mr. Stockton also enjoyed a reputation for his humorous and whimsical stories and novels. His The Lady or the Tiger? (1884) attracted much attention and was used as material for a comic opera by Sydney Rosenfeld and produced in New York in 1888. Rudder Grange (1879) was originally published in Scribner's Monthly. His other books include: *The Casting Away of Mrs. Lecks and Mrs. Aleshine* (1886), and its sequel, *The Dusantes* (1886); The Late Mrs. Null (1886); The Hundredth Man (1887); The Great War Syndicate (1889); The Merry Chanter (1890); The House of Martha (1891); The Squirrel Inn (1894); The Adventures of Captain Horn (1895); Mrs. Cliff's Yacht (1896); The Great Stone of Sardis (1897). The Girl at Cobhurst (1898); and A Bicycle of Cathay (1900). The Captain's Toll-Gate was published in 1903 after his death, with a memorial sketch by Mrs. Stockton. An edition of his works in twenty-three volumes was published in 1901-'04.

Stoddard, Elizabeth Barstow (Mattapoisett, Mass., 1823; New York, 1902). She was the daughter of a sea-captain and ship-owner named Barstow, and in 1851 married the poet Richard Henry Stoddard. She began to write poetry for magazines, and her tale entitled My Own Story, published in the Atlantic Monthly in 1860, attracted some attention. She was the author of several novels. *The Morgesons,* published in 1862, was praised by Hawthorne. Its characters are good New England types, and the treatment is realistic. She also published Two Men (1865) and Temple House (1867). Mrs. Stoddard was also the author of a juvenile, called Lolly Dinks's Doings (1874) and many poems. A volume of her verse was published in 1896; and an edition of her works in 1888. Edmund Clarence Stedman says: "Mrs. Stoddard's novels appeal to us through a quality of her own. Written, I think, without much early practise, yet with experience of life, their strong, original style—unmistakable as a human voice—is that of one with a gift, and the writer's instinct produces effects which a mere artist tries for in vain. Style, insight, originality make books like Two Men and Temple House additions not only to the bulk of reading, but to literature itself, as distinct in their field as Wuthering Heights and Margaret, or even as Père Goriot or Richard Feverel, . . . Mrs. Stoddard's other novels, her short stories, her fugitive poems, are marked by the same qualities."

Stowe, Harriet Elizabeth Beecher (Litchfield, Conn., 1812; Hartford, 1896). She was the third daughter of the Rev. Lyman Beecher, and the sister of Henry Ward Beecher. She was educated in her sister's school in Hartford, where she became a teacher at the age of fifteen. In 1832 she removed to Cincinnati with her father, who had become president of Lane Theological Seminary and pastor of the Second Presbyterian Church. In 1836 she married the Rev. Calvin Ellis Stowe (1802-1886), a professor in Lane Theological Seminary, and they frequently sheltered fugitive slaves in their house and assisted them to escape to Canada. In 1850, her husband having been made a professor in Bowdoin College, she removed to Brunswick, Me., and while there she wrote *Uncle Tom's Cabin,* which was published in the National Era, an anti-slavery paper of Washington (June, 1851—April, 1852). When published in two volumes in Boston in 1852, it attracted wide attention. Four editions of more than 300,000 copies were sold in four years; thirty-five English editions were published; and there were 500,000 English reprints and thirty-seven translations. The author dramatized it as The Christian Slave in 1855. As a reply to unfavorable criticisms from the press of the Southern States, Mrs. Stowe published A Key to Uncle Tom's Cabin, presenting the Original Facts and Documents upon which the Story is Founded, together with Corroborative Statements verifying the Truth of the Work (1853). She also published A Peep into Uncle Tom's Cabin for Children (1853). Mrs. Stowe then traveled in Europe with her husband and her brother, the Rev. Charles Beecher, and while in England was presented with a petition for emancipation signed by more than 1,000,000 women of Great Britain and Ireland. Her experiences were preserved in Sunny Memories of Foreign Lands (1854), in which her brother Charles aided. Her next book was Dred: a Tale of the Great Dismal Swamp, another anti-slavery novel (1856). This was re-issued as Nina Gordon in 1866; but its original title was restored in later editions. In 1859 appeared The Minister's Wooing, considered her best work by some critics, among whom was James Russell Lowell, who said: "We are greatly mistaken if it do not prove to be the most characteristic of Mrs. Stowe's works, and that on which her fame will chiefly rest with posterity." Her other novels include: The Pearl of Orr's Island, a story of the coast of Maine (1862); Agnes of Sorrento (1862); Old Town Folks (1869); Pink and White Tyranny (1871); Sam Lawson's Fireside Stories (1871); My Wife and I (1872); We and Our Neighbors (1875); and Poganuc People (1878). Her first publication, A New England Story, written in 1834, was included in a volume of stories called The Mayflower, published in 1849. Mrs. Stowe also wrote Lady Byron Vindicated (1869), a reply to a book published by the Countess Guiccioli, and Men of Our Time (1868). Her other publications include: Geography for My Children (1855); Our Charley and What to do with Him (1858); The Ravages of a Carpet (1864); House and Home Papers, by Christopher Crowfield (1864); Stories about Dogs (1865); Little Foxes (1865); Queer Little People (1867); Daisy's First Winter and Other Stories (1867); The Chimney Corner, by Christopher Crowfield (1868); Little Pussy Willow (1870); Palmetto Leaves (1873); Betty's Bright Idea and

Other Tales (1875); Footsteps of the Master (1876); Bible Heroines (1878); and A Dog's Mission (1881). A selection from her early writings was published in London in 1859 as Golden Fruit in Silver Baskets. From 1868 to 1870 she was co-editor with Donald G. Mitchell of Hearth and Home in New York. Her home was in Hartford, Conn., from 1864 until her death. Her biography was written by her son (1889) and also by Mrs. James T. Fields (1897).

Stuart, Ruth McEnery (Avoyelles Parish, La., about 1850). She was educated in New Orleans and married a cotton-planter, Alfred O. Stuart, after whose death she removed to New York. Her books include: A Golden Wedding and Other Tales (1893); *Carlotta's Intended* (1894); The Story of Babette (1894); Solomon Crow's Christmas Pockets and Others (1896); In Simpkinsville (1897); Sonny (1896); Moriah's Mourning (1898); Holly and Pizen (1899); The Woman's Exchange (1899); Napoleon Jackson (1902); George Washington Jones (1903); The River's Children (1904); and The Second Wooing of Selina Sue (1905).

Sturleson, Snorre (Hvamma, Iceland, 1179; assassinated in 1241). His family traced their descent from the ancient kings of Norway and Sweden and were among the early colonists of Iceland. At an early age he was placed under the tuition of Jan Loptson, grandson of the compiler of the elder Edda, and he was instructed particularly in history, poetry, and mythology. His father died, leaving him well off, and he added to his fortune by marrying at the age of twenty-six a wealthy heiress. Thus he obtained a position of influence and was elected supreme judge or chief magistrate of Iceland. Although he was a master of the laws and civil institutions of his country, his love of intrigue led him to take part in the movement against Norway, where once he had been court poet, and the King Hakon sent secret instructions to Iceland for his arrest, and, if necessary, his assassination. In 1241, therefore, Snorre Sturleson was murdered in his own house. He composed many *drapas*, or laudatory poems, on kings and jarls whom he visited; but his chief work is the Heimskringla, the

Mythic Ring of the World, in which is recorded the history of the Kings of Norway from the earliest period to Magnus Erlingsson in 1177. This was first published in Copenhagen in 1633. Snorre Sturleson is believed to have aided in collecting and arranging the songs of the Elder or *Poetic Edda,* and to have had no small share in compiling the Younger or *Prose Edda,* which treats of Scandinavian mythology and of the language and modes of the ancient skalds. An edition of the *Prose Edda* was published by Professor Rask in 1818. An English translation of the mythological portion is found in Mallet's Northern Antiquities, edited by Blackwall (1847). Rasmus B. Andersen also translated this Edda.

Sue, Marie Joseph Eugène (Paris, Dec. 10, 1804; Annecy, Savoy, July 3, 1857). He was unusually fortunate. His father was one of Napoleon's household physicians, and it is said that the Empress Josephine was his godmother. His father educated him to follow his own profession, and in this capacity he served in the French expedition to Spain under the Duke of Angoulême in 1823. Then, transferred to the navy, he was present at the battle of Navarino in 1828. In 1829 his father died, leaving him a handsome fortune, upon the receipt of which he devoted himself exclusively to letters. At first he tried his hand at sea-stories, somewhat after the manner of Cooper, and published Kernock, le Pirate (1830), which had some success. This was followed by other stories in the same vein, including: Plick et Plock (1831); Atar Gull (1831); La Salamandre (1832); La Concaratcha (1832). He then wrote a naval history of France, and began to produce quasi-historical novels, one of which was Jean Cavalier (1840). Something of his true talent appeared in Mathilde, ou les Mémoires d'une jeune femme (1841), which was followed by the famous Mystères de Paris (*The Mysteries of Paris*) which appeared in the columns of the Journal des Débats, and which was afterward published in book form in 1843. This was followed by Le Juif Errant (*The Wandering Jew*), which appeared in the Constitutionnel and in book-form in 1845. Both of these works were received with a furor of excitement, not only in France, but in other countries. In 1848 Sue allied himself with the extreme body of Republicans; and in 1850 he was elected to the Legislative Assembly for the Department of the Seine and fulfilled his duties with devotion until he was driven into exile by the *coup d'état* of 1851. Sue then retired to Savoy. His latest works are full of his socialistic ideas. In addition to works already mentioned, Sue published: La Vigil de Koat-Ven (1833); Cécile (1835); Latréaumont (1837); Arthur, journal d'un inconnu (1838); La Marquise de Létorière (1839); Delaytar (1839); Le Morne au Diable (1842); Paula Monti (1842); Thérèse Dunoyer (1842); Martin l'enfant trouvée; ou Mémoires d'un valet de chambre (1847); Les Sept Péchés Capitaux; Le Républicain des campagnes (1848); Le Berger de Kravan (1848-'49); De quoi vous plaignez-vous (1849); Les mystères du peuple (1849-'56); Les enfants de l'amour (1850); Le Bonne aventure (1851); Ferdinand Duplessis (1852); La marquise d'Amalfi (1853); Gilbert et Gilberte (1853); La Famille Jouffroy (1854); Le Fils de Famille (1856); and Les secrets de l'oreiller (1857).

Swift, Jonathan (Dublin, Ireland, Nov. 30, 1667; Oct. 19, 1745). The greatest of all English satirists began life under disadvantages. He was a posthumous child of Jonathan Swift, a member of the King's Inns, Dublin. The son was reared in circumstances of poverty and dependence, the recollection of which embittered his life. Relatives sent him to school in Kilkenny, and he was graduated at Trinity College, Dublin, in 1685-'86; and although he had been about seven years in college, he was more intent on personal satires and political rhymes than on academical honors. Going to England, through his mother's influence he was admitted into the house of Sir William Temple, where he remained until 1694, when he went to Ireland, took orders in the church and obtained a small living. In two years' time he gave this up and returned to Temple, who missed his society and assistance. Temple died in 1698, and Swift returned to Ireland, where he obtained some church livings. In 1712 he became dean of St. Patrick's. Before this, however, he had written his Battle of the Books, a prose mock heroic (1704), and his greater satire, The Tale of a Tub (1704), considered the wittiest and most satirical work of the eighteenth century; also some essays on ecclesiastical subjects and a ridicule of astrology, under the signature of Isaac Bickerstaff, a name that Steele adopted for The Tatler.   Conceiving himself neglected by the Whig ministers, he went over to the Tories, and later identified himself with Irish affairs, feelings, and prejudices.   His Drapier Letters (1724) produced an excitement in Ireland and compelled the Government to abandon the scheme of Wood's copper coinage.   On his last visit to England, in 1726, "the mad parson" published the most popular of his works, *Gulliver's Travels* (1726), or, to quote the title accurately, *Travels into several remote Nations of the World.   In Four Parts.   By Lemuel Gulliver, First a Surgeon and then a Captain of Several Ships*.   Through Pope's help he obtained £200 for the copyright, "the only farthing he ever made by his writings," so he said.   This was a great success, was immediately translated into French, and two plays were founded on it.   It was said that "Gulliver would last as long as the language, because it described the vices of man in all countries," and had "an extraordinary combination of qualities which made it at once a favorite book of children and a summary of bitter scorn for mankind."   He joined Pope, Gay, and Arbuthnot in publishing three volumes of Miscellanies, after which he returned to Ireland.   On his arrival in Dublin he was welcomed with popular rejoicing: bells were rung, bonfires were lighted; the corporation met him and he was taken in triumph to the deanery.   In his last years he became irritable, gloomy, morose, and at last his faculties gave way.   He rallied and wrote some of his best minor pieces, including: The Grand Question Debated; On Poetry, a Rhapsody; The Legion Club; Verses on the Death of Dr. Swift; and The Modest Proposal, in which he proposes to relieve the distress of the Irish by converting their children into food for the rich.   Swift's last three years were passed under the care of keepers.   A mystery involves the history of the two ladies known as Stella and Vanessa.   It is now believed that he was married to the former in 1716 by St. George Ashe, Bishop of Clogher, and he was buried by her side.   The first accurate version of his famous Journal to Stella was published in the edition of Swift's Prose Works in the Bohn Standard Library (vol. 2, 1897). An English critic says: "As a consummate master of ridicule and irony, possessing great powers of wit, invention, illustration, and analogy; possessing also the dramatic faculty that enabled him to assume and portray varieties of character; and as writing a pure, perspicuous English style, unsurpassed for strength and simplicity, Swift must ever be a model in our language and literature. His misanthropy, or degradation of human nature—his Yahoos, Strulbrugs, daring irreverence and indelicacy, are, of course, indefensible. He had a total incapacity, as De Quincey remarks, for 'dealing with the grandeurs of the human spirit, with religion, with poetry, or even with science, when it rose above the mercenary practical.' His business was with the world—with the follies, vices, and absurdities of men."

Tarkington, Newton Booth (Indianapolis, Ind., July 29, 1869). He was graduated at Exeter Academy in 1889, and received his A.M. from Princeton in 1899. He now lives in Paris. His novels are: *The Gentleman from Indiana* (1899); *Monsieur Beaucaire* (1900); The Two Vanrevels (1902); Cherry (1903); In the Arena (1905); The Conquest of Canaan (1905); The Beautiful Lady (1905); and His Own People (1907). Monsieur Beaucaire was dramatized and performed by Richard Mansfield.

Tautphœus, Baroness von (Seaview, County Donegal, Ireland, 1807; Munich, Bavaria, 1893). Her name was Jemima Montgomery, and she was the daughter of James Montgomery, of Seaview and a niece of Sir Henry Conyngham Montgomery, first baronet. In 1838 she married Cajetan Josef Friedrich, Baron von Tautphœus of Marquartstein (1805–1885), chamberlain to the King of Bavaria, and from that time she lived at the Bavarian court. She was at home in all classes of society and was an astute observer of men and manners. Of her most famous novel Dr. Richard Garnett says: "Baroness von Tautphœus is one of the most distinguished members of a highly interesting group of writers of fiction—the Englishmen and Englishwomen who, becoming residents in foreign countries, have devoted their talents to the illustration of foreign manners and have shown themselves entirely at home when abroad. There is no novel in the language to which the epithet 'charming' could be applied with more strict propriety than to her first work, *The Initials* (London, 1850; 6th ed., 1863), with its admirably contrasted pair of German sisters, the almost perfect yet most natural and human character of Hildegarde, the skilful suspense and the happy *dénouement*." Her other novels are: Quits (1857), sprightly in style and true to nature; Cyrilla (1853), founded on the criminal trial of Assenor Zahn; and At Odds (1863).

Taylor, Bayard (Kennett Square, Chester Co., Pa., Jan. 11, 1825; Berlin, Germany, Dec. 19, 1878). He was a descendant of Robert Taylor, who emigrated with William Penn in 1681. His early years were spent on a farm, and he was educated at the High School, Unionville, Pa. In 1842 he was apprenticed to a printer in West Chester, Pa., and he soon began to contribute to the Saturday Evening Post of Philadelphia. He also became connected with the New York Tribune and the United States Gazette, in which his letters from abroad first appeared. These were afterward published as Views Afoot: or, Europe seen with Knapsack and Staff (1846). In 1849 he was sent by the New York Tribune to report on the gold discovery in California, and his observations subsequently appeared as Eldorado: or, Adventures in the Path of Empire. Henceforth Mr. Taylor spent the greater part of his life in travel. He visited Europe again in 1852, and joined Commodore Perry's expedition to Japan; and on his return home he gave many lectures. In 1856 he edited a Cyclopædia of Modern Travel, and he published his experiences and memories of many lands in Northern Travel (1858); Travel in Greece and Rome (1859); At Home and Abroad (2 vols., 1859-'62); Colorado: A Summer Trip (1867); By-ways of Europe (1869); Travels in Arabia (1872); and Egypt and Iceland (1874). His acquaintance with foreign countries qualified him for diplomatic posts; and he was made Secretary of Legation at St. Petersburg in 1862 and Minister to Berlin in 1878. During his active life he found time to write several novels and stories, among which are: Hannah Thurston

(1863) ; *John Godfrey's Fortunes* (1864) ; The Story of Kennett (1866) ; Joseph and His Friends (1870) ; and Beauty and the Beast and Tales of Home (1872). He was, however, more proud of his reputation as a poet; and several volumes attest his industry in this line. These include: Book of Romances, Lyrics, and Songs (1851) ; Poems of the Orient (1854) ; The Poet's Journal (1862) ; Poems (1865) ; The Picture of St. John (1869) ; Ballad of Abraham Lincoln (1869) ; The Masque of the Gods (1872) ; Lars: A Pastoral of Norway (1873) ; The Prophet: a Tragedy (1874) ; Home Pastorals (1876) ; and Prince Deukalion: a Lyrical Drama (1878). His translation of Goethe's Faust has always been admired by scholars for its fidelity and poetic diction. He was selected to write and deliver the National Ode at the opening of the Centennial Exhibition in Philadelphia. His wife, Marie Hansen, the daughter of Professor Peter Hansen of Erfurt, translated some of his novels into German; and, with Horace E. Scudder, compiled the Life and Letters of Bayard Taylor (2 vols., 1884).

Thackeray, Anne Isabella (Mrs. Richmond Ritchie) (London, England, 1838). She is the eldest daughter of William M. Thackeray. Her education was conducted largely in Paris, but she has spent most of her life in Kensington. Her first story, Little Scholars in the London Schools, was published in 1860 in the Cornhill Magazine, of which her father was then the editor. From that time she has been a frequent contributor to English and American magazines, and no small part of her literary activity has been given to editing a complete edition of her father's works. In 1877 she married her cousin, Sir Richmond Ritchie (he was knighted in 1907), and she has a son and a daughter. Her fiction includes: The Story of Elizabeth (1863) ; *The Village on the Cliff* (1865) ; Bluebeard's Keys (1874) ; Miss Angel (1875) ; Miss Williamson's Divagations (1881) ; and Mrs. Dymond (1885).

Thackeray, William Makepeace (Calcutta, India, July 18, 1811; London, England, Dec. 24, 1863). He came of an old Yorkshire family. His grandfather, William Makepeace Thackeray (1749–1813), entered the East Indian service, made a fortune in elephants and other trading speculations, and returned to England. His father, Richmond, became secretary of the Board of Revenue at Calcutta in 1807, and in 1810 married Anne Becher, a reigning beauty of Calcutta. The boy was sent to England and placed under the care of his aunt, Mrs. Ritchie, was sent to a school in Hampshire, to another in Chiswick, and, in 1822–'28, to the Charterhouse. Venables, who broke Thackeray's nose in a fight (a disfigurement that lasted all his life), remembered him as a "pretty, gentle boy," who was popular with a few friends, but who did not distinguish himself in either the school-room, or the play-ground. In 1828 he entered Trinity College, Cambridge, and spent his long vacation in Paris. He inherited from his father, a fortune of £20,000, and traveled throughout Europe with the ambition of becoming an artist; and when his fortune was lost, he turned his attention to literature. He also entered the Middle Temple and tried to find publishers for his caricatures. Thackeray lost money by the failure of an Indian bank, and by gambling. He told Sir Theodore Martin that the story of Deuceau, in the Yellowplush Papers, was based on an experience of his own. Then he went to Paris to qualify himself for art, and copied pictures at the Louvre; and, on his return to London he applied to Dickens to illustrate the Pickwick Papers. After his marriage to the daughter of Col. Shawe at the British Embassy in Paris, Thackeray settled in Great Coram street, London, and engaged in literary work. His most important connection was with Fraser's Magazine, in which appeared the Yellowplush Correspondence in 1838; *Catherine*, by Ikey Solomons, 1839–'40; The History of Samuel Titmarsh and the Great Hoggarty Diamond; *The Luck of Barry Lyndon*, and other sketches. Under the name of Titmarsh he also published The Paris Sketch-Book (1840); The Second Funeral of Napoleon and The Chronicle of the Drum (1841). When Punch was established, in 1841, Thackeray contributed The Legend of Jawbrahim Heraudee (vol. iii.), and Miss Tickletoby's Lectures on English History; and 1843 he became a regular member of the Punch weekly dinner-table. Jeames's Diary appeared in its pages in 1845; The Snobs in England, by One of Themselves (1846); and the burlesques known as Prize Novelists. His clever drawings also frequently appeared. Altogether he contributed three hundred and eighty of these to Punch. "It was a good day for himself, the journal, and the world," said Shirley Brooks, editor of Punch, "when Thackeray joined Punch"; and Thackeray said he owed the good chances that had befallen him to his connection with Punch. From 1846 to 1850 he published an annual Christmas book. In 1847 his reputation was greatly advanced by *Vanity Fair*, published in monthly parts and illustrated by himself, or, as he said, "illuminated with the author's own candles." In 1848 he was called to the bar of Middle Temple, and in that year he published *Pendennis*, in which much of his own life is recorded, and which was interrupted by a long illness. On his recovery he gave a course of lectures on the English Humorists, which he delivered in the United States in 1852, returning to England with £2,500. He then began *The Newcomes* and *Henry Esmond*, and, at Rome, to amuse his children in the Christmas of 1854, he wrote the delightful Rose and the Ring. *The Newcomes* finished, he made a second lecturing tour in the United States and gave his Four Georges. The next novel to appear was *The Virginians* (1857–'59). In 1860 the Cornhill Magazine was founded, and Thackeray was selected as editor. In its pages appeared *Lovel the Widower; The Adventures of Philip; A Shabby Genteel Story;* and Denis Duval. Two books of light and charming essays, chiefly on his travels, appeared as Notes of a Journey from Cornhill to Cairo (1848), and Roundabout Papers, which appeared in the Cornhill Magazine after his return from the United States. A bibliography of Thackeray's works, by Richard Herne Shepherd, appears in Sultan Stork and other stories (1887); and the Biographical edition in thirteen volumes, by his daughter, Mrs. Richmond Ritchie, contains much personal history. "In his delineation of the character and genius of Fielding," says an English writer, "Thackeray has drawn his own. He had the same hatred of meanness, cant, and knavery, the same large sympathy, relish of life, thoughtful humor, keen insight, delicate irony and wit. There was, however, one personal difference: Fielding was utterly careless as to censure of his works, whereas his successor was tremblingly alive to criticism, and was wounded to the quick by the slightest attack. He had suffered much from physical maladies and from domestic calamity; and his earlier works, especially his *Vanity Fair*, were tinged with a degree of cynicism which seemed to countenance the charge of his unfriendly critics that he delighted in representing the baser side of human nature, and was skeptical as to the existence of real virtue in the world. His strength lay in portraying character rather than inventing incidents; and in Becky Sharp, Colonel Newcome, Harry Foker, Laura and Paul de Florac, to say nothing of the picaroon, Barry Lyndon, he has left us a living gallery certainly not surpassed by any modern novelist. In his later writings the dark shades no longer preponderate. The mellowing influence of years and sickness, and calmer as well as more extensive observation of life, had sunk the merciless satirist in the genial humorist and philosophic observer. He had still ample scorn for falsehood and vice, and satire for folly and pretense; but he had also smiles and tears and tenderness and charity that gave a moral beauty and interest to the last decade of his brilliant career as an author."

Theuriet, André (Marly-le-Roi, France, 1833; Bourg-le-Reine, 1907). He studied law in Paris and was admitted to the bar in 1857. In that year he entered the office of the Minister of Finance, and, after holding various offices, became Mayor of Bourg-la-Reine. In 1896 he was elected to the Académie Française. Altogether he wrote about sixty volumes of fiction and a great deal of charming verse, in which the Breton landscape is prominent. His provincial idyls of humble life recall in some respects the work of George Sand. Among his novels are: Mademoiselle Guignon (1874); Le mariage de Gérard (1875); Amour d'automne (1888); Reine des bois (*The Queen of the Woods*, 1891); Claudette (1900); Frida (1900); Le sœur de lait (1902); La Chanoinesse (1893); Fleur de Nice (1896); Sensations de l'enfant, M. Lulu (1902); Histoires galantes et mélancoliques (1903); Les Revenants (1904); and Mon Oncle Flo (1906). His plays include: Jean Marie (1871); La Maison de deux Barbeaux (1885); and Jours d'été (1901). Verses that he contributed in his early years to the Revue de Deux Mondes were published in book-form in 1867;

and Le bleu et le noir, poems of real life, appeared in 1876; and his Souvenirs des vertes saisons (1904) include the two volumes of verse, Années de Printemps and Jours d'été.

Thompson, Daniel Pierce (Charlestown, Mass., Oct. 1, 1795; Montpelier, Vt., April 6, 1868). He was brought up on a farm, was graduated at Middlebury College in 1820, and went to Virginia as a private tutor. While there he studied law and was admitted to the bar. Returning to New England, he settled in Montpelier, where he was register of probate; clerk of the Legislature; Judge of Probate in 1837–'40; and Secretary of State in 1853–'55. From 1849 till 1856 he edited a weekly political paper called The Green Mountain Freeman and wrote for papers, magazines, and political pamphlets. He also compiled the Laws of Vermont (1824–'34). Mr. Thompson made his first appearance in fiction with a satirical novel on the anti-Masonic controversy, entitled The Adventures of Timothy Peacock, Esq.: or, Freemasonry Practically Illustrated. This was published under the pen-name of "Member of the Vermont Bar" (Middlebury, 1835). May Martin: or, The Money-Diggers, a prize tale, appeared in the New England Galaxy in 1835 and was issued in book-form. This was also published in London. *The Green Mountain Boys*, a novel of the Revolutionary period (1840), was also republished in London. His other books were: Locke Amsden: or, The Schoolmaster (1845); Lucy Hosmer: or, The Guardian and the Ghost (1848); The Rangers: or, The Tory's Daughter (1851); Tales of the Green Mountains (1852); Gant Gurley: or, The Trappers of Lake Umbagog (1857); The Doomed Chief: or, Two Hundred Years Ago, a story of King Philip (1860); Centeola, and Other Tales (1864); and an unfinished novel, called The Honest Lawyer: or, The Fair Castaway. He also wrote a History of Montpelier, 1781–1860.

Tolstoy, Lyof (or Leo Nikolajevitch) Count (Yasnaya Polyana, government of Tula, Russia, Aug. 28, 1828). His family, originally from Germany, had lived on this estate for several generations. Young Tolstoy was reared in luxury; and on the death of his father he lived with a rich aunt in Kazan. He entered the University of Kazan, but left before completing his studies, entered the army in 1851, became a captain, and distinguished himself at the siege of Sebastopol. A little of this life satisfied him; and in 1854 he resigned, and, after residing in both Moscow and St. Petersburg and traveling on the Continent, he retired to his country estate of Yasnaya Polyana in 1861. About 1875 he became imbued with mystical religious and philanthropic ideas, adopted the life and habits of the peasantry, formulated a creed based on a communistic interpretation of the Scriptures, organized peasant schools on an original basis, and has promulgated his religious ideas so successfully that a sect called Shalaputui (The Extravagants) has been instituted. He renounced all luxuries and comforts, engaged in manual labor, and transferred all rights in his estates and property to his wife and children. In 1901 he was excommunicated by the Russian synod. Tolstoy's writings fall into three periods: To his first period belong Childhood (1852); Boyhood (1854); Youth (1855); and The Landlord's Morning (1857); The Cossacks (1854); Sevastopol (1855); and other sketches of military life. These contain much autobiographical material. His two great novels, *War and Peace* (1865–'68) and *Anna Karénina* (1873–'76), belong to his second period. To his third belong books that set forth his ideas on religion, art, socialism, and marriage, such as: My Confession (1880); My Religion (1885); *The Kreutzer Sonata* (1888); *Resurrection* (1889); *Master and Man* (1895); A Commentary on the Gospels; Work While Ye have Light; and What is Art? (1898). He has also written three dramas: The Power of Darkness; Fruits of Culture; and The Corpse (1900). Tolstoy's collected works were published in Moscow in fourteen volumes in 1889–'95. An English translation was made of them by Nathan Haskell Dole, in twelve volumes (New York, 1900).

Tourgee, Albion Winegar (Williamsfield, Ohio, May 2, 1838; Bordeaux, France, 1905). He was the son of a farmer of Huguenot blood and was graduated at the University of Rochester in 1862. He served in the National army in the Civil War, was wounded at Bull Run and at Perryville, and

Portrait of Count Lyof Tolstoi

Photogravure after the celebrated painting by F. Repin in the Ermitage Gallery, St. Petersburg, Russia

Portrait of Count Lyof Tolstoi

Photogravure after the celebrated painting by F. Repin in the Eremitage Gallery, St. Petersburg, Russia

was held a prisoner by the Confederates for four months. In 1864 he was admitted to the bar of Ohio. After the war he settled in Greensboro, N. C., as lawyer, farmer, and editor. He prepared the report for the Loyalists' Convention in Philadelphia in 1866, and was a member of the North Carolina constitutional conventions of 1868 and 1875. He was also one of a commission to revise and codify the State laws and was judge of the superior court of the seventh judicial district from 1868 to 1874. In 1876 he was pension agent for North Carolina, and the Ku-Klux party organized several raids for his capture. From 1882 to 1885 he edited Our Continent, a weekly literary paper which he established in Philadelphia. From 1897 till his death he was United States Consul at Bordeaux, France. Judge Tourgee had some success as a lecturer and received the degree of Ph.D. from the University of Copenhagen. In the latter part of his life his home was at Mayville, Chautauqua Co., N. Y. His best known story is *A Fool's Errand by one of the Fools* (1879); but he also published Toinette (1874); Figs and Thistles (1879); Bricks without Straw (1880); John Eax (1882); Hot Plowshares (1883); An Appeal to Cæsar (1884); Black Ice (1887); Button's Inn (1888); Letters to a King (1889); With Gauge and Swallow (1889); Pactolus Prime (1890); Murvale Eastman, Christian Socialist (1890); Out of the Sunset Sea (1892); The Story of a Thousand, and An Outing with the Queen of Hearts (1894); and The Mortgage on the Hip Roof House (1898). He also published the North Carolina Form Book (1869); The North Carolina Code (1878); and Statutory Decisions of the North Carolina Reports (1879). *A Fool's Errand* had an enormous circulation and was used as a political document in the Presidential canvass of 1880.

Trollope, Anthony (London, 1815; Harting, England, 1882). He was the son of Thomas Anthony Trollope, a barrister, and Frances Trollope, a novelist and miscellaneous writer. He was educated at Winchester and Harrow; became connected with the London Post Office; was post-office surveyor in Ireland; inspector of rural deliveries in various English counties; and was sent on postal missions to Egypt and the West Indies.

He visited the United States in 1862, and in 1868 was sent to Washington to negotiate a postal convention, in which he succeeded. In 1871 he retired from the service. During these years he wrote a great number of novels that delighted a large public, novels that present a variety of English types and depict English society and life in a most accurate and enjoyable manner. Altogether he wrote forty-six novels and left one unfinished. He also wrote five volumes of stories. Hawthorne said: "They precisely suit my taste—solid and substantial, written on the strength of beef and through the inspiration of ale, and just as real as if some giant had hewn a great lump out of the earth and put it under a glass case, with all the inhabitants going about their daily business and not suspecting that they were being made a show of. And these books are just as English as a beefsteak. It needs an English residence to make them thoroughly comprehensible; but I still think that human nature would give them success anywhere."

Henry James writes in Partial Portraits: "He never wearied of the pre-established round of English customs—never needed a respite or a change—was content to go on indefinitely watching the life that surrounded him, and holding up his mirror to it. Into this mirror the public, at first especially, grew very fond of looking, for it saw itself reflected in all the most credible and supposable ways, with that curiosity that people feel to know how they look when they are represented, 'just as they are,' by a painter who does not desire to put them into an attitude, to drape them for an effect, to arrange his light and his accessories. This exact and on the whole becoming image, projected upon a surface without a strong intrinsic tone, constitutes mainly the entertainment that Trollope offered his readers. The striking thing to the critic was that his robust and patient mind had no particular bias, his imagination no light of its own. He saw things neither pictorially and grotesquely, like Dickens; nor with that combined disposition to satire and to literary form which gives such 'body,' as they say of wine, to the manner of Thackeray; nor with anything of the philosophic, the transcendental cast—the desire to follow them to their remote relations—which we associate with the name of George Eliot. Trollope had his elements of fancy, of satire, of irony; but these qualities were not very highly developed, and he walked mainly by the light of his good sense, his clear, direct vision of the things that lay nearest, and his great natural kindness. Trollope did not write for posterity; he wrote for the day, the moment; but these are just the writers whom posterity is apt to put into its pocket. So much of the life of his time is reflected in his novels that we must believe a part of the record will be saved; and the best parts of them are so sound and true and genial that readers with an eye to that sort of entertainment will always be sure in a certain proportion to turn to them. Trollope will remain one of the most trustworthy, though not one of the most eloquent, of the writers who have helped the heart of man to know itself."

His first novels were: The Macdermots of Ballycloran (1847); The Kellys and the O'Kellys (1848); and La Vendée (1850); but the first work to attract attention was *The Warden* (1855). This was followed by *Barchester Towers* (1857); The Three Clerks (1858); Doctor Thorne (1858); The Bertrams (1859); Castle Richmond (1860); Tales of All Countries, three series (1861–'63); Framley Parsonage (1861); *Orley Farm* (1862); Rachel Ray (1863); *The Small House at Allington* (1864); *Can You Forgive Her?* (1864–'65); Miss Mackenzie (1865); The Belton Estate (1866); The Claverings (1867); The Last Chronicle of Barset (1867); Nina Balatka (1867); Linda Tressel (1868); Phineas Finn (1869); *He Knew He was Right* (1869); Brown, Jones and Robinson (1870); The Vicar of Bullhampton (1870); An Editor's Tales (1870); Sir Harry Hotspur of Humblethwaite (1871); Ralph the Heir (1871); The Golden Lion of Granpère (1872); The Eustace Diamonds (1873); Phineas Redux (1874); Harry Heathcote of Gangoil (1874); Lady Anna (1874); The Way We Live Now (1875); The Prime Minister (1876); The American Senator (1877); Is He Popenjoy? (1878); John Caldigate (1879); An Eye for an Eye (1879); Cousin Henry (1879); The Duke's Children (1880); Ayala's Angel (1881); Doctor Wortle's School (1881); Frau Frohman and Other Stories (1882); The Fixed Period (1882); Kept in the Dark (1882); Marion Fay (1882); Mr. Scarborough's Family (1883); The Land-leaguers (1883);

and An Old Man's Love (1884). Trollope also wrote several volumes of travel: The West Indies and the Spanish Main (1859); North America (1862); Australia and New Zealand (1874); and South Africa (1878). Biographies of Cæsar (1870), Cicero (1880), Thackeray (1879), and Lord Palmerston (1882), did not add anything to his reputation. An Autobiography was published in 1883.

Trowbridge, John Townsend (Ogden, Monroe Co., N. Y., Sept. 18, 1827). He was educated at common schools and at a classical academy at Lockport, N. Y., and lived on a farm until he was seventeen years old, after which he taught in Illinois and in Lockport. In 1847 he went to New York as a writer for the press, and in the following year he removed to Boston, where he has since been active as a literary worker. In 1870–'73, with Gail Hamilton and Lucy Larcom, he was an editor of Our Young Folks. Mr. Trowbridge has won esteem as a novelist, a poet, and a writer of stories for the young. Many of his scenes are laid in New England, and he is at his best as a writer of "Yankee" dialect and in his portrayal of New England character. His verses, though not voluminous, include some that are very widely known and frequently quoted. Among these may be mentioned The Vagabonds and Darius Green and His Flying-Machine. Dartmouth gave him the honorary degree of M.A. Mr. Trowbridge has married twice—in 1860 Cornelia Warren, of Lowell, Mass., and in 1873 Ada Newton, of Arlington, Mass. Among his published works are: Martin Merrivale (1854); *Neighbor Jackwood* (1857); The Drummer Boy (1863); *Cudjo's Cave* (1863); The Three Scouts (1864); The Vagabonds and Other Poems (1869); Jack Hazard and his Fortunes (1871); A Chance for Himself (1872); Coupon Bonds and Other Stories (1872); Doing his Best (1873); Fast Friends (1874); The Young Surveyor (1875); His Own Master (1877); Tinkham Brothers' Tide Mill (1882); Phil and his Friends (1883); Farnell's Folly (1884); The Little Master (1886); Peter Budstone (1887); A Start in Life (1888); Adventures of David Vane and David Crane (1889); The Kelp Gatherers (1890); The Scarlet Tanager (1891); The Fortunes of Toby Trafford (1892); The Satinwood Box (1894); The Lottery Ticket (1895); The Prize Cup (1896); Two Biddicut Boys (1898); My Own Story (his autobiography, 1903); Poetical Works (1903).

Turgeniev, Ivan Surgeyevich, (Orel, Russia, Nov. 9, 1818; Bougival, near Paris, France, Sept. 3, 1883). He was the son of a wealthy landowner, and was educated at the universities of Moscow and St. Petersburg and later at Berlin, where he went in his twentieth year to study philosophy and the classics. About two years later, owing to disagreement with his family regarding the treatment of serfs, he accepted a government clerkship in the Ministry of the Interior, and he almost immediately began to write and publish verses, which were followed in 1844 by his first novel. In the following year he began to write his Annals of a Sportsman, or Sportsman's Diary (Zapiski Okhotnika), which continued until 1857. These were translated into French, English, and German, and gave him an international reputation. They are generally considered to have contributed largely to the emancipation of the Russian serfs by the Emperor, with whom they were a favorite. Turgeniev freed all his own serfs on his mother's death in 1852. He was exiled to Orel in 1852 on account of some animadversions on the Government, and although he was allowed to return in 1854 he spent most of his life thereafter in France and Germany. His writings, which closely analyze political and social conditions, made him unpopular with both radicals and reactionaries in Russia, though late in life his motives became better understood. Turgeniev originated the term "Nihilist," which he first used and defined in his novel *Fathers and Sons.* As used by him it was applied to one who looks at everything from a critical standpoint, and its extension to anarchistic or socialistic propagandists came later. As variously transliterated, Turgeniev's name is also spelled in Roman characters Turgenieff, Turgeneff, etc. In French it is often written Tourguenieff. Among his published works are: Andrei Kolossoff (1844); Rudin (1855); A Nest of Nobles, sometimes called also A House of Gentlefolk (Dvoryanskoye Gnyezdo, 1858); Helene, afterward called On the Eve (Nakanunye, 1860); *Fathers and Sons* (Ottzy i Dyeti, 1862); *Smoke*

(Dym, 1867); Virgin Soil (Nov., 1876); Spring Floods (Veshniya Vody); Two Friends (Dva Priyatelya); and Klara Milich.

Verga, Giovanni (Catania, Sicily, 1840). His earlier stories, published when he was twenty-five years of age, attracted little attention, but about 1869 the issue of one or two tales of psychological analysis made him widely known among his own countrymen. Later he made Sicilian peasant life his specialty, and his work in this line has gained him international reputation. He is best known through the dramatization of his sketch entitled Rustic Chivalry (Cavalleria Rusticana), which is also the basis of the libretto of Mascagni's well-known opera. Another story, La Lupa, has also been dramatized. Verga's work has been likened to Zola's, and his place as a realistic novelist in Italy is similar to that of the latter in France. Among his published works are: The Story of a Sinner (Storia di una Peccatrice, 1865); The Story of a Black Cap (Storia di una Capinera, 1869); Medda (1874); Eros (1875); Country Life (Vita dei Campi, 1880); *The Malavoglia Family* (I Malavoglia, 1881); Elena's Husband (Il Marito di Elena, 1882); and Maestro Don Gesualdo (1889).

Verne, Jules (Nantes, France, Feb. 8, 1828). After pursuing his education in his native city, he studied law in Paris, but soon devoted himself to literature, writing in 1850 a versified comedy entitled Broken Straws (Les Pailles Rompues), which was performed at the Gymnase, but was only moderately successful. Other plays and operettas met with the same fate, but in the early sixties he began to write pseudo-scientific romances, which gained instant success. They have followed one another rapidly at brief intervals and have been translated into many foreign languages. Several of them have been dramatized, and one, Doctor Ox (Le Docteur Ox, 1874), has been made into an opera libretto. In 1875 he essayed the theater again with an original three-act comedy entitled A Nephew from America (Un Neveu d'Amerique), which was performed in the Cluny Theater. Verne's works, although not written primarily for children, are read largely by young people, and are usually classed in libraries with juvenile fiction.

They contain a somewhat fantastic mixture of scientific fact with imagination, and their merit consists in the narration, the attempts at character-drawing being rarely satisfactory. Verne has received the cross of the Legion of Honor from his Government. Among his published works are: Five Weeks in a Balloon (Cinq Semaines en Ballon, 1863); A Journey to the Centre of the Earth (Voyage au Centre de la Terre, 1864); From the Earth to the Moon (De la Terre à la Lune, 1865); The Wilderness of Ice (Le Désert de glace, 1870); Around the Moon (Autour de la Lune, 1870); *Twenty Thousand Leagues Under the Sea* (Vingt Mille Lieues sous les Mers, 1870); A Floating City (Une Ville Flottant, 1871); The Tour of the World in Eighty Days (Le Tour du Monde en Quatre-vingt Jours, 1873); The Fur Country (Le Pays des Fourrures, 1873); Doctor Ox (1874); Michael Strogoff (1876); Hector Servadac (1877); A Captain at Fifteen (Un Capitaine de Quinze Ans, 1878); Mathias Sandorf (1885); North against South (Nord contre Sud, 1887); Cæsar Cascabel (1890); The Castle in the Carpathians (Le Château des Carpathes, 1892); Wonderful Adventures of Master Antifer (Mérifiques Aventures de Maître Antifer, 1894); The Aerial Village (Le Village Aérieu, 1901), and the Kip Brothers (Les Frères Kip, 1902).

Virgil (Publius Virgilius Maro) (Andes, near Mantua, Cisalpine Gaul, Oct. 15, 70 B.C.; Brundisium, Italy, Sept. 21, 19 B.C.). The spelling Vergil, which seems to have been the original one, is sometimes preferred. His parents were in moderate circumstances, but gave him a good education. From seven to sixteen years of age he studied at Cremona, assuming the toga virilis on the day of Lucretius's death. Then he went to Milan, and afterward to Naples, where he studied medicine and philosophy under the Epicurean Syro and the grammarian Parthenius. The minor poems attributed to him date from this period. About 40 B.C. he was presented to Pollio, Governor of Cisalpine Gaul, at whose request he composed his Bucolics. After the battle of Philippi his estate near Mantua was confiscated for the benefit of the victorious party, but he recovered it at the intercession of Mæcenas and was thenceforward a devoted adherent of Octavius. His Georgics were written at the invitation of the former in accordance with the latter's desire to see the Romans return to their old agricultural pursuits. Later he undertook his greatest poem, the *Æneid*, in which he seconded the efforts of Augustus to re-establish the ancient customs and traditions of Rome and to revivify the old religious feelings. About 37 B.C. he settled in Rome, where he numbered among his intimates the poet Horace. His later years were spent mostly in Campania. Virgil was a great imitator. He borrowed from the Idylls of Theocritus in his Bucolics, not only subjects, but their developments and sometimes whole verses. Homer was his model in the *Æneid*, in which he followed both the Iliad and the Odyssey. He was indebted also to the old Latin poets Nævius, Ennius, and Attius. From all these sources, however, he assimilated what he took so well that it seems his own. He has been called one of the most personal of poets, and his dominating note is perhaps the love and knowledge of nature. There are in existence a great number of Virgilian manuscripts, of which seven date from a period before the fifth century; but all these are incomplete. The first printed edition of his works was issued at Rome in 1469. Virgil's works are as follows: Bucolics or Eclogues (43–37 B.C.); Georgics (37–30 B.C.); the *Æneid* (26–20 B.C.). Among the minor poems attributed to him are the Culex, Dirae, Etna, and Ciris, but authorities differ greatly regarding the authenticity of these and others.

Voltaire, François-Marie Arouet (Paris, France, Nov. 18, 1694; May 30, 1778). Voltaire sprang from the middle class, but his ambitious father placed him, at ten, in the Jesuit College, Louis-le-Grand. Here his precocity of "intelligence and impertinence" attracted much attention. He was early introduced into the Society of the Temple, a circle whose refined Epicurean philosophy sharpened his appetite for the pleasures of the senses and the intellect. He was intended for the law, but he preferred to be a rake and a poet. At twenty-one he was a welcome guest in every distinguished gathering in Paris; at thirty he had access to the court. His irrepressible satire led him into frequent difficulties, and in 1726 he was ordered out of France. The contrast between the liberty of thought

tically that of Unitarianism; her political views are those of an English Liberal. Her published works include: biographical introductions to the first volume of her husband's English Poets (1880–'81); a translation of Amiel's Journal (1885); Miss Bretherton (1886); Robert Elsmere (1888); The History of David Grieve (1892); Marcella (1894); The Story of Bessie Costrell (1895); Sir George Tressady (1896); Helbeck of Bannisdale (1898); Eleanor (1900); *Lady Rose's Daughter* (1902); The Marriage of William Ashe (1905); Fenwick's Career 1906); and The Testing of Diana Mallory (1908). Her play, Agatha, was produced at His Majesty's Theater, London, in 1905. She also has contributed to Smith's Dictionary of Christian Biography (1877–'87), has edited the Haworth Edition of the novels of the Brontë sisters, with introductions (1899–1900), and has done much other miscellaneous literary work.

Warner, Charles Dudley (Plainfield, Mass., Sept. 12, 1829; Hartford, Conn., Oct. 20, 1900). He was graduated at Hamilton College, in 1851, and became a surveyor. After field work on the Missouri frontier he returned to the East and studied law, receiving his degree at the University of Pennsylvania in 1856. From that time until 1860 he practised his profession in Chicago, and in the latter year he entered journalism as assistant editor of the Hartford (Conn.) Press, whose managing editor he became a year later. On the consolidation of the paper with the Hartford Courant in 1867 he became co-editor, and he retained this connection through his life. In 1884 he became also assistant editor of Harper's Magazine, taking charge first of the Editor's Drawer and in 1892 of the Editor's Study department. Besides this, he served as foreign correspondent of several newspapers. Mr. Warner took especial interest in prison reform. His published works, largely collected essays and books of travel, have been admired for their geniality, refined humor, and kindly sympathy. The Spectator, London, said of them: "Banter and paradox, always handled with cleverness and subtlety; an active fancy that sometimes rises into imagination or pathos; irony that is never bitter, and sarcasm that is never savage,—these, and with them what we might call scorn, if scorn were not most ungentle, of all that is uncultured, . . . may be found in Mr. Warner's books." Among his works are: My Summer in a Garden (1870); Saunterings (1872); Backlog Studies (1872); Baddeck, and that Sort of Thing (1874); Mummies and Moslems (reissued as My Winter on the Nile, 1876); In the Levant (1877); Being a Boy (1877); In the Wilderness (1878); Captain John Smith: A Study of his Life and Writings (in the American Worthies series, 1881); Washington Irving (in the American Men of Letters series, 1881); A Roundabout Journey (1883); Their Pilgrimage (1886); On Horseback (1888); Studies in the South and West (1889); A Little Journey in the World (1889); Our Italy (1891); As We Were Saying (1894); and *The Golden House* (1895). With Mark Twain he was the author of The Gilded Age (1873). Besides this he edited the American Men of Letters series and the Library of the World's Best Literature (1896–'97), and wrote many contributions to periodicals that remain uncollected.

Warner, Susan (New York, July 11, 1819; Highland Falls, N. Y., March 17, 1885). Her earlier books were written under the pen-name of Elizabeth Wetherell. She was the daughter of Henry B. Warner, a lawyer of New York. Much of her work was in collaboration with her sister, Anna Bartlett Warner, who also wrote under the pen-name of Amy Lothrop. The sisters were for many years the owners of Constitution Island, in the Hudson, opposite West Point, where they lived together. Both remained unmarried. Miss Warner's novels are didactic and strongly tinged with religious sentiment. Her best known book, *The Wide, Wide World*, has been asserted to be the most widely read novel by any American author, with the exception of Uncle Tom's Cabin. Miss Warner alone is now usually credited with the authorship; but Ellen Montgomery's Book-shelf, which was avowedly collaborated, is said on its title-page to be "by the authors of The Wide Wide World." Miss Warner's work, although always popular, did not maintain the level of its earlier performance. The vogue of her most popular novel is attested by the appearance of such books as Lyrics from the Wide Wide World (1853), containing six songs founded on passages from the novel, the words by W. H. Bellamy and the music by C. W. Glover. The book, as well as other novels by Miss Warner, was translated into many foreign languages. Among the published works credited to Miss Susan Warner alone are: *The Wide, Wide World* (1850); Queechy (1852); The Law and the Testimony (a Biblical anthology, 1853); The Hills of the Shatemuc (1856); The Golden Ladder: Stories illustrative of the Eight Beatitudes (1862); The Old Helmet (1863); Melbourne House (1864); Daisy (1869); What She Could (1870); The House in Town (1871); Opportunities (1871); Trading (1872); The Little Camp on Eagle Hill (1873); Sceptres and Crowns (1874); The Flag of Truce (1875); Wych Hazel (1876); Diana (1877); The Kingdom of Judah (1878); My Desire (1879); The End of a Coil (1880); The Letter of Credit (1882); Nobody (1883); A Red Wall Flower (1884); Daisy Plains (1885); Among those written in collaboration with her sister are: Say and Seal (1860); Sybil and Chrissa (1869); The Gold of Chickaree (1876); Little Nettie (1878); and Carl Krinken (1880).

Warren, Samuel (Denbighshire, Wales, May 23, 1807; London, July 29, 1877). He was a son of a clergyman of the same name, who was the author of several volumes of sermons and other works. The son studied medicine in the University of Edinburgh and law in the Inner Temple, London, was called to the bar in 1837 and became Queen's Counsel in 1851. He was Recorder of Hull from 1854 to 1874, and member of Parliament for Midhurst from February, 1856, serving with a re-election until 1859, when he resigned to accept a mastership in lunacy. He was a Conservative in politics and a strong partisan of Lord Derby, whose policies he supported in his various writings. His books include romances, treatises on law, and political articles. In his History of Europe, Sir Archibald Alison says of his work as a writer of romance: Mr. Warren has taken a lasting place among the imaginative writers of this period of English history. He possesses in a remarkable manner the tenderness of heart and vividness of feeling as well as powers of description, which are essential to the delineation of the pathetic, and which, when existing in the degree in which he enjoys them, fill his pages with scenes which can never be forgotten."

His legal writings were highly commended by Chancellor Kent, but other critics condemned their plan and scope. His published works include: Passages from the Diary of a Late Physician (1831); Popular and Practical Introduction to Law Studies (1835; second enlarged ed., 1845; American introduction and appendix by J. W. Clerke, 1845); Select Extracts from Blackstone's Commentaries, Carefully Adapted to the Use of Schools and Young Persons (with John William Smith, 1837); The Opium Question (1840); *Ten Thousand a Year* (1841); Now and Then (1847); The Moral, Social, and Professional Duties of Attorneys and Solicitors (1848); Letter to the Queen on a Late Court Martial (1850); The Lily and the Bee: an Apologue of the Crystal Palace (1851); The Queen or the Pope: A Letter to S. H. Walpole (1851); Manual of the Parliamentary Law of the United Kingdom (1852); Manual of the Law and Practice of Election Committees (1853); Intellectual and Moral Development of the Present Age (1853); Miscellanies, Critical, Imaginative, and Judicial (1854); Blackstone's Commentaries, Systematically Abridged (1855); and Labor: its Rights, Difficulties, Dignity, and Consolations (1856). His collected writings were issued in five volumes (1854-'55).

Weyman, Stanley John (Ludlow, Shropshire, England, Aug. 7, 1855). He is the second son of the late Thomas Weyman, an English lawyer, and was educated at Shrewsbury and at Christ Church College, Oxford, where he was graduated with a second class in modern history. He then served as classical instructor in the King's School, Chester, and afterward studied law, being called to the bar in 1881, but gave up practice in 1889 to devote himself to literature. His works are nearly all historical romances, especially of certain periods of French history, and have been much admired for their spirit and for the accuracy of their setting. His publications include: The House of the Wolf (1890); The New Rector (1891); The Story of Francis Cludde (1891); *A Gentleman of France* (1893); Under the Red Robe (1894); My Lady Rotha (1894); Memoirs of a Minister of

France (1895); The Red Cockade (1895); The Man in Black (1896); Shrewsbury (1897); The Castle Inn (1898); Sophia (1900); Count Hannibal (1901); In King's Byways (1902); The Long Night (1903); The Abbess of Vlaye (1904); Starvecrow Farm (1905); and Laid up in Lavender (1907). In 1908 Mr. Weyman published a statement that he had determined to write no more books, preferring to stop while at the height of his powers.

Wharton, Edith (New York, 1862). She is the daughter of George Frederic and Lucretia Stevens (Rhinelander) Jones. She was educated at home, and in 1885 married Edward Wharton, of Boston. Her writings consisted at first only of verse, which was admired for its exquisite finish, and of short stories whose analysis of character and motive caused them to be compared to those of Henry James. Afterward she began to write novels, of which she has essayed several different styles. Of her first long story, The Valley of Decision, a study of eighteenth-century Italian life, Prof. Barrett Wendell says in his History of Literature in America, that it is "among the few books which seem better each time you open it. Nothing written in America shows more vivid power of imagination, more firm grasp of subject, more punctilious mastery of style, or more admirably pervasive artistic conscience." Her more recent novels have been studies of contemporary American society, and as such have appealed to a larger circle of readers. Among her published works are: The Greater Inclination (1899); The Touchstone (1900); Crucial Instances (1901); The Valley of Decision (1902); Sanctuary (1903); The Descent of Man and Other Stories (1904); Italian Villas and Their Gardens (1904); Italian Backgrounds (1905); *The House of Mirth* (1905); Madame de Treymes (1907); and The Fruit of the Tree (1907).

Wilde, Oscar Fingall O'Flahertie Wills (Dublin, Ireland, 1856; Paris, France, Nov. 30, 1900). He was the youngest son of Sir William Wilde, eminent as a surgeon, and his wife Jane Francesca (Elgee) Wilde, a writer of verse under the pen-name of Speranza. The son was educated at Trinity College,

Dublin, and Magdalen College, Oxford, where he was the author of the Newdigate prize poem in 1878. On graduation he went to London, where he became chief expositor of the cult of so-called Æstheticism, so keenly satirized by Du Maurier in Punch and by Gilbert in the comic opera of Patience. The character of Bunthorne, in the latter, is by some supposed to be a caricature of Wilde. From 1888 he produced novels, stories, and dramas with great rapidity, and, despite his superficiality and affected sentiment, the astonishing cleverness and felicity of his work and its strikingly epigrammatic style gave him great vogue.

His several light comedies, especially, are replete with bright dialogue and clever situations, although they often fail in dramatic construction. His Salome (1893), written in French for Sara Bernhardt, forms the libretto of Richard Strauss's opera of the same name. The performance of the play was forbidden in London by the censor, and on this account it was said that Wilde threatened to renounce his British allegiance and become a French citizen. He was looked upon as a writer of great promise, but his career became clouded by scandals, and in 1895 he was convicted of an offense against the public morals, for which he underwent imprisonment for two years. One of his strongest poems, the Ballad of Reading Gaol, describes some of his prison experiences. After his release he resided in Paris until his death. His published books are: Poems (1881); The Happy Prince, and Other Tales (1888); Guido Ferranti, a tragedy (1890); Intentions (collected essays, 1891); and *The Picture of Dorian Gray* (1891). A complete edition of his poems was issued (1903) after his death. His plays, all of which were successful on the stage, include: Vera (1882); The Duchess of Padua (1891); Lady Windermere's Fan (1892); A Woman of No Importance (1893); The Ideal Husband (1895); and The Importance of being Earnest (1895).

Wilkins-Freeman, Mary Eleanor (Randolph, Mass., 1862). She was born Mary E. Wilkins and wrote most of her books under her maiden name. She was educated at Mount Holyoke Seminary, South Hadley, Mass., and resided in Massachusetts and Vermont until her marriage on Jan. 1, 1902, to Dr. Charles Manning Freeman, of Metuchen, N. J. In the early eighties her magazine stories of humble New England life began to attract attention, and she was soon regarded as one of the chief expositors of New England character, although she limited herself generally to certain phases of it, portraying especially the narrowness, cheerlessness, and patient dulness of the life on secluded farms and in small villages. Within these limits she is thought by many to have no rival. The portrayal of characters and their immediate environment is her strong point, and her longer tales and novels, in which the construction of a plot has become necessary, are not so highly regarded, although they have always been popular. Since her removal to New Jersey she has laid some of her scenes outside New England, with the result, in one case, that some of the dwellers in a New Jersey town considered themselves aggrieved by what they regarded as too evident portraiture. In this and other instances Mrs. Freeman has always asserted that her portraits are composites. Her published books are: The Adventures of Ann (1886); A Humble Romance (1887); A New England Nun (1891); Young Lucretia (1892); *Jane Field* (1892); Giles Corey (1893); Pembroke (1894); Madelon (1896); Jerome: a Poor Man (1897); Silence and Other Stories (1898); Evelina's Garden (1899); The Love of Parson Lord (1900); The Heart's Highway (1900); The Portion of Labor (1901); Understudies (1901); Six Trees (1903); The Wind in the Rose-Bush (1903); The Givers (1904); Doc Gordon (1906); By the Light of the Soul (1907); and The Jamesons (1908).

Wood, Ellen Price (Mrs. Henry Wood) (Worcester, England, Jan. 17, 1814; Feb. 10, 1887). Her father, Thomas Price, was a manufacturer. In 1836 she married Henry Wood, an English shipping agent residing in Paris. On his death in 1866 she returned to England and devoted herself to literature, which for some years had occupied much of her attention. In December, 1867, she became editor of The Argosy, London, and she was a frequent contributor to several other English magazines. Most of her work has been republished in the United States, and some of her novels were translated into French. Her novel, *East Lynne*, in its dramatized form, gained great vogue and still holds the stage. Her books number thirty or more, but although some have been highly praised, much of her work has been accounted rather feeble and prolix. The Saturday Review said of her: "Mrs. Henry Wood has certain qualities which should have made her one of our best novel-writers. . . . No one lays out the plan of a story better than she does, and even Mr. Wilkie Collins himself . . . is not greater than she is in the cleverness with which she devises her puzzles and fits the parts together. But . . . she is puerile, commonplace, and ineradicably vulgar." Among her published works are: Danesbury House (1860); *East Lynne* (1861); The Channings (1862); Verner's Pride (1863); Lord Oakburn's Daughters (1864); Mildred Arkell (1865); St. Martin's Eve (1866); A Life's Secret (1867); Red Court Farm (1868); Roland Yorke (1869); George Canterbury's Will (1870); Dene Hollow (1871); Within the Maze (1872); The Master of Greylands (1873); Johnny Ludlow (1874); Told in the Twilight (1875); Adam Grainger (1876); Pomeroy Abbey (1878); Court Netherleigh (1881); About Ourselves (1883); Lady Grace and Other Stories (1887). Memorials of her, edited by her son, C. W. Wood, were issued (1895) after her death.

Wyss, Johann Rudolf (Bern, Switzerland, March 13, 1781; Bern, March 31, 1830). He was professor of philosophy and chief librarian in his native city and the author of numerous works in the German language, of which English-speaking readers know chiefly his *Swiss Family Robinson* (Der Schweizerische Robinson, 1813). This, like many other similar books that have not been preserved to posterity, was evidently inspired by DeFoe's Robinson Crusoe. It has been for years a children's classic, and is still loved for its engaging style and ingenuous narrative, despite its impossible plot and preposterous combination of incident and adventure. Among Wyss's other books are: Idyls, Folklore, Legends, and Tales of Switzerland (Idyllen, Volkssagen, Legenden und Erzählungen aus der Schweiz, 1815-'22); A Journey in the Bernese Overland (Reise im Berner oberland, 1808); and Lectures on the Highest Good (Vorlesungen über das hochste Gut, 1811).

Yonge, Charlotte Mary (Otterbourne, Hampshire, England, 1823; March 24, 1901). Her father, W. C. Yonge, was a Hampshire magistrate and landowner. The daughter was educated at home and early came under the influence of John Keble, who held the living of Otterbourne. Throughout her life she lived quietly in her native place, engaged in literary work, which she began to publish shortly after her twentieth year, and which became very voluminous. Allibone's Dictionary records one hundred and eleven titles of her books up to 1888, and she continued active in writing to the end of her life. Besides this, she edited the Magazine for the Young, and for more than thirty years The Monthly Packet, in which many of her tales made their first appearance. Miss Yonge's works are all deeply religious. She was a steadfast adherent of the High Church party in the Church of England, and she fitted out Bishop Selwyn's missionary vessel, The Southern Cross, with the profits of one of her books. The foundation of a missionary college at Auckland, N. Z., was due to the proceeds of another novel. Charles Kingsley was an admirer of Miss Yonge's work and pronounced her Heartease (1854) the "most wholesome and delightful novel" he had ever read. The crusader, Sir Guy Morville, the hero of her best known work, *The Heir of Redclyffe*, was adopted as a model by William Morris, Burne-Jones, and their party at Oxford. Among her published works are: The Abbey Church (1844); Kings of England (1848); Kenneth (1850); Landmarks of History (1853-'57); *The Heir of Redclyffe* (1853); Lances of Lynwood (1855); Daisy Chain (1856); Biographies of Good Women (1862); History of Christian Names (1863); Book of Golden Deeds (1864); The Dove in the Eagle's Nest (1866); Musings on the "Christian Year" [Keble's] (1870); The Caged Lion (1870); A Storehouse of Stories (1871); Pioneers and Founders (Missionary biographies, 1871); Little Lucy's Wonderful Globe (1871); Life of Bishop Patteson (1873); My Young Alcides (1875); The Three Brides (1876); Story of the Christians and Moors of Spain (1878); Magnum Bonum: or, Mother Carey's Brood (1879); Gold Dust; Counsels for the Sanctification (1880); Love and Life (1880); Lads and Lassies of Langley (1881); Aunt Charlotte's Evenings at Home with the Poets

(1881); How to Teach the New Testament (1881); Langley Little Ones (1882); Sowing and Sewing: a Sexagesima Story (1882); Stray Pearls: Memoirs of Margaret de Ribaumont (1883); The Armourer's Prentices (1884); The Two Sides of the House (1885); A Modern Telemachus (1886); Cameos from English History (1887); Life of Hannah More (in the Eminent Women series, 1888); Nurse's Memories '(1888); Life of the Prince Consort (1889); and Forget Me Not (1900). An illustrated edition of her best novels was issued in thirty-five volumes (1888–'89). Her life has been written by Christabel Coleridge (1903).

Zangwill, Israel (London, England, 1864). His father, M. Zangwill, a Hebrew immigrant, came to England in 1848. The son was self-educated in early life except for attendance at the Jews' Free School, Spitalfields, in the East End of London. Later he took his bachelor's degree with honors at the University of London. He then became a teacher, journalist, and lecturer, in which last-mentioned capacity he has traveled in Ireland, Holland, Palestine, and the United States. For some time he was the editor of Ariel. Zangwill has achieved success as a writer of novels, essays, verses, and plays. He is active as an advocate of Zionism and is president of the International Jewish Territorial Association. His work bears particularly on various aspects of Jewish life, to the humor and pathos of which he is equally sensitive. Mr. Zangwill married, in 1903, Edith, daughter of Prof. William E. Ayrton, the well-known English electrician. Zangwill's plays are as follows: Six Persons, produced at the Haymarket, London, in 1892; Children of the Ghetto, his own dramatization of his novel of the same name, produced at the Adelphi, London, and the Herald Square, New York, 1899; The Moment of Death, at Wallack's, New York, 1900; The Revolted Daughter, a comedy, 1901; Merely Mary Ann, 1903; The Serio-Comic Governess, 1904; Jinny the Carrier, 1905; and Nurse Marjorie, 1906. Among his published books are: The Premier and the Painter (1888); The Bachelors' Club (1891); The Big Bow Mystery (1892); The Old Maids Club (1892); *Children of the Ghetto* (1892); Merely Mary Ann (1893); Ghetto Tragedies (1893);

The King of Schnorrers (1894); The Master (1895); Without Prejudice, essays contributed to the Pall Mall Gazette (1896); Dreamers of the Ghetto (1898); They that Walk in Darkness (1899); The Mantle of Elijah (1900); The Grey Wig (1903); Blind Children (verses, 1903); and Ghetto Comedies (1907).

Zola, Émile (Paris, France, April 2, 1840; Sept. 2, 1902). His father was an Italian engineer of partial Greek descent; his mother was French. The son was educated at the Lycée St. Louis in Paris, but failed to get his degree, and in 1862, after living for some time in poverty, he became a clerk in the publishing firm of Hachette et Cie., at the same time entering journalism and beginning to write stories, the first of which were published by himself in book form two years later. He then undertook a series of works depicting the fortunes of a French family under the Second Empire. These attracted little attention until the appearance of the seventh, L'Assommoir, a picture of life among the working class, which attained instant success. From that time (1878) until his death Zola was one of the foremost literary figures of Paris. His work, which his disciples call "naturalism," is boldly realistic, often to the point of indecency. It is uneven, sometimes very powerful, but also at times nauseating and tedious. In 1898 Zola entered the lists as a champion of Capt. Alfred Dreyfus, whom he regarded as unjustly punished for betrayal of French military secrets to Germany. He denounced the prosecutors of Dreyfus as the real criminals, in a celebrated letter to President Faure, containing many times the words "J'accuse" (I accuse). Zola was convicted of libeling the military authorities, and an appeal resulted in a second conviction; but he escaped to England, where he remained until 1899, when amnesty was granted to all those connected with the Dreyfus case. For his action Zola was acclaimed by his supporters as a noble defender of human rights. Three years later he was found dead in his bed, where he had been suffocated by gas from a defective flue. He received a public funeral, and in 1908 his body was reinterred in the Panthéon, with much civic and military ceremony. His books include: *Claude's Confessions* (La Confession de Claude, 1865); *Thérèse Raquin* (1867); the twenty novels of the Rougeon-Macquart series (1871–'93), including: *The Abbé Mouret's Transgressions* (La faute de l'Abbé Mouret, 1875); *Drink* (L'Assommoir, 1877); *A Page of Love* (Une page d'amour, 1878); *Nana* (1880); Pot-Bouille (1882); *Germinal* (1885); *The Earth* (La Terre, 1887); The Dream (Le rêve, 1888); The Human Beast (La bête humaine, 1890); Money (L'Argent, 1891); *The Downfall* (La débâcle, 1892); and Doctor Pascal (1893); a "trilogy of three cities," including Lourdes (1894), Rome (1896), and Paris (1898), and what he called his "four gospels," including *Fruitfulness* (Fécondité, 1899), *Labor* (Travail, 1900), Truth (Verité, 1902), and Justice, unfinished at his death.